BEGINNING RUSSIAN

Volume I

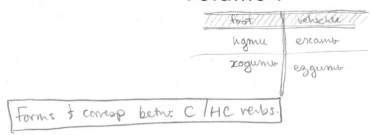

foot *vehicle*
идти *ехать*
ходить *ездить*

forms & corresp betw: C/HC verbs.

by

Richard L. Leed
Cornell University

Alexander D. Nakhimovsky
Cornell University

Alice S. Nakhimovsky
Colgate University

Monday·
Final 12/14 7PM Goldwin-Smith 156 (Ball)

1981

Slavica Publishers, Inc.

For a list of some other books from Slavica, see the last page of this book. For a complete catalog, with prices and ordering information, write to:
Slavica Publishers, Inc.
P.O. Box 14388
Columbus, Ohio 43214

ISBN: 0-89357-077-X.

Printed in the United States of America.

НАЧАЛЬНЫЙ КУРС РУССКОГО ЯЗЫКА

или

НЕОБЫЧАЙНЫЕ ПРИКЛЮЧЕНИЯ ЗЮЗИ
В МОСКВЕ И ДРУГИХ МЕСТАХ

а также Подлинная и Душераздирающая История Любви
Двойного Агента Семёна Сергеевича
и Официантки Кати

записанная, дополненная и прокомментированная
Ричардом Лидом, Александром Нахимовским и Алисой Нахимовской

THE BEGINNING RUSSIAN TEXTBOOK

or

THE EXTRAORDINARY ADVENTURES OF ZYUZYA
IN MOSCOW AND OTHER PLACES

Together with the True and Heart-Breaking Love Story of
Semyon Sergeevich, the Double Agent
and Katya, the Waitress

recorded, expanded, and commented upon by
Richard L. Leed and A. D. Nakhimovsky, Cornell University
and Alice Stone Nakhimovsky, Colgate University

Preface to the Preliminary Edition

    We hope that this edition is reasonably
free of errors. It is based on a prepublication
draft that was tested in the classroom and was
revised without retyping the whole thing so that
misprints wouldn't creep in. We ask the reader's
indulgence for any typographical inelegance that
has resulted from this procedure.

    We also ask the users of this book to do us
the favor of sending us criticisms of the book
so that the next edition will be as good as
possible. Please write to Slavica Publishers or
to R. L. Leed, Department of Modern Languages
and Linguistics, Morrill Hall, Cornell University,
Ithaca, New York 14853.

                        The Authors

```
┌─────────────────────────────────────────────────────┐
│       Each Lesson consists of the following sections: │
│                                                       │
│       TEXT                                            │
│           Vocabulary                                  │
│           Comments                                    │
│       DIALOGS FOR MEMORIZATION                        │
│           Translation                                 │
│           Active Word List                            │
│           Comments                                    │
│       ANALYSIS with PRACTICES                         │
│       EXERCISES                                       │
└─────────────────────────────────────────────────────┘
```

INTRODUCTION

For a long time, we have been aware of the need for a beginning Russian textbook that would provide an engaging introduction to colloquial speech at the same time as it prepared students to deal with unabridged prose of reasonable complexity. Our experience with *Advanced Russian* has led us to believe that some of the principles at work in that book—colloquial texts and drills, serious discussion of grammar, mature social and cultural commentary—could be successfully applied to a first-year text.

The Beginning Russian Book, or the *Extraordinary Adventures of Zyuzya in Moscow and other places* is designed as an all-skills language program that can be covered in two or three semesters of a college course or in two years of a high school course. Used with cassettes (available from the Cornell University Language Lab) it would be appropriate for self-instruction. Combined with *Advanced Russian* and an intermediate book now in preparation, it forms the starting point of a three or four year sequence.

The *Beginning Russian Book* is in two volumes, each consisting of ten complete lessons plus appendices, glossaries, and indices. Volume II has four additional reading lessons which bring the narrative of the Texts to a close. The lessons are identical in structure, although the relative length of the component parts changes as the book progresses. Each lesson has the following structure:

Text
>   Comments to the text
Dialogs for memorization
>   Comments to the dialogs
Grammatical analysis
Exercises

One of the distinctive features of this book is the virtually complete separation of *passive* from *active* vocabulary. The passive vocabulary is presented in the *Texts*, the active vocabulary in the *Dialogs*. The Texts are designed for *Russian-to-English* translation and for comprehension, while the Dialogs are designed to be memorized, used in exercises, and ultimately to provide the bases for *conversation in Russian*. The distinction between passive and active is maintained in the supplementary sections at the end of the book: the Passive Vocabulary *Glossary* contains the words from the Texts with their English equivalents, while the Active Word *Index* contains the words from the Dialogs, along with their irregular forms and their locations in the book, but with no English equivalents. There is, of course, some overlap in the vocabulary of the Texts with that of the Dialogs, especially in the early lessons; it is helpful to the beginner to see and hear a word before learning to use it actively. But in the second volume of *Beginning Russian* any overlap is purely accidental —the story in the Texts takes off on its own.

Active use of Russian is developed in the Exercises; consequently, the exercises never require the student to use vocabulary items that have occurred only in the Texts. The Exercises are based on the Active Word Lists, not on the Passive Vocabulary Glossaries.

Below we comment on each part of the textbook.

TEXTS

The texts form a continuous narrative which eventually involves the White House as well as the Moscow offices of the KGB. Some satire aimed at both was unavoidable, though we hope we left room for more innocent pleasures. The story starts out very simply with the arrival of Zyuzya on earth. It gradually becomes more involved both linguistically and narratively, and beginning at about Lesson 14 it employs almost the full range of Russian grammar. Except for the fact that it starts simply and only gradually increases in sophistication, the story was not contrived for the presentation of specific grammatical detail. Our first impulse in writing the story was to make it independently interesting and valuable as an introduction to—and the first sample of—non-textbook Russian. The story is divided into twenty four units, which cover the twenty full lessons of the course plus the four reading lessons at the conclusion of Volume II.

Each Text is followed by a Vocabulary which contains the glosses of all words not occurring in previous Texts or Dialogs. These vocabularies match the Passive Vocabulary Glossary at the back of the book.

COMMENTS TO THE TEXTS

Problems in reading Russian are taken up in the Comments to the Text, which also provide a convenient vehicle for introducing cultural information.

DIALOGS

The Dialogs for memorization introduce the Active Vocabulary of the course. They have three functions: to illustrate the grammatical phenomena discussed in the Analyses, to serve as a basis for exercises, and to provide material for conversation in class. Beginning with Lesson 6, the dialogs of each lesson revolve around one or more specific lexico-situational topics.

The Dialogs of early lessons are, naturally, quite simple, but at no point is simplicity mistaken for lack of idiomaticity. They are designed to be as idiomatic as possible, and we have tried to avoid the kind of simplification that later has to be corrected, rather than expanded and built on. This principle determined our recordings, too: each dialog has been recorded twice, first slowly and with pauses for repetition, then in a normal, even fast tempo, with all the ellipses and pronunciational short-cuts that native speakers are likely to employ.

The dialogs of each lesson are followed by a translation and an Active Word List. This list contains all words not occurring in previous dialogs. These words are arranged by parts of speech and the necessary inflected forms are provided. These lists match up with the Active Word Index at the back of the book.

COMMENTS TO THE DIALOGS

The Comments to the Dialogs serve basically the same function as the Comments to the Texts, except that the Comments to the Texts facilitate understanding, while the Comments to the Dialogs take up and expand on the details of grammar and usage that eventually end up in the student's active repetoire. Some of the comments to the dialogs again treat cultural information.

ANALYSES

These grammatical explanations are rather longer than in most pedagogical grammars. It was difficult for us to keep them brief because some of the complexities we introduce early, (e.g., verbs of motion) require lengthy explanation in any kind of grammar. Much of the space in the Analysis section is taken up by illustrative material, some of which is arranged in the format of exercises which we call Practices. These practices can be used for self-testing on the part of the student or for classwork; many of them have answers provided on the page, and all of them have answers provided on the cassettes.

We have presented the main features of Russian grammar in Lessons 1-8. All of the noun and verb endings, as well as the notion of verb aspect, are introduced as fast as possible, so that the learner has a balanced overview of the language. After Lesson 8, which is a review lesson, these fundamentals receive more detailed attention.

Whenever possible, sets of lexical and grammatical features are presented in such a way as to show how they contrast with each other. For example, instead of introducing the Accusative case in isolation, we contrast it with the Nominative and Prepositional. In some instances we have introduced the tricky member of a contrasting set before the seemingly simpler one, because students are known to err or misuse them. Thus, зачем is introduced before почему , а before и , round-trip aspectual meaning before on-going meaning, etc.

EXERCISES

The exercises treat material from the grammatical analysis in the framework of the dialogs for memorization. (Since the Texts are designed for developing passive vocabulary, none of the words that occur exclusively in Texts are used in the Exercises.) There are three basic groups of exercises. The first group pairs students in a brief conversational exchange, with grammatical material tested by blanks in the conversation. The language of these exercises, and the situations they represent, have been kept as natural as possible. It is hoped that through repetition they will function as additional dialogs in the sense that they provide memorized frames for common linguistic situations. We have tried as often as we could to provide exercises that involve a genuine exchange of information. Often, particularly in the early lessons, this involves bringing real objects into the classroom and working with them. Other exercises of this sort are headed "Answer factually" and make use of general knowledge. The aim of these exercises is to overcome the hypothetical nature of language learning by providing an obvious "right" answer to be conveyed. They serve as a bridge between strictly language drill on the one hand, and real communication on the other.

A second set of exercises is more concerned with the mastery of lexical material. Each lesson has fluency drills which present short English sentences for translation into Russian. The sentences are based on the dialogs and they are intentionally repetitious and interconnected. The purpose is not for a student to construct a translation, but to provide one as quickly and effortlessly as possible. Beginning in Lesson 6, where the dialogs start to reflect one or more lexical topics, there are more and more exercises in guided conversation. These exercises make use of the dialogs by providing a dramatic situation for acting out. Most of the conversation drills are preceeded by fluency drills which rehearse the types of sentences that will arise in conversation.

Our third group of exercises falls into the traditional category of transformation drills, substitution drills, and fill-in-the-blanks. These are suitable for practice in writing.

Exercises which are directly related to a particular Dialog and/or a particular section of the Analysis are cross-referenced accordingly.

USING THE BOOK

Volume I of *Beginning Russian* is designed to fill the equivalent of one semester of a semi-intensive college course having 7 class hours per week. A less intensive course may conveniently get through the review Lesson (Lesson 8).

Detailed suggestions on how to use the book in the classroom can be found in the *Teacher's Manual*. This Manual is available from Slavica Publishers free of charge to users. It contains various teaching aids, including a set of writing practices for teaching Russian script. A large portion of the Manual is devoted to word lists that were generated from a computer data base containing all of the words in the Texts and Dialogs, along with their locations, frequencies, glosses, inflected forms, and semantico-grammatical categories (animate nouns, place nouns, transitive verbs, etc.). These lists are cumulative, i.e., they contain words from Lessons 1-2, 1-3, 1-4, etc. There are three sets of cumulative lists: Dialog words listed by category, Dialog words listed alphabetically, and Text words listed alphabetically. The Manual also contains a list of major grammatical topics and suggestions for pacing, scheduling, and assignments. The Manual is not copyrighted, so that the user can reproduce any of the lists or practices for classroom use.

ACKNOWLEDGMENTS

We are very grateful to our colleagues and students who have read the preliminary versions of the book and provided criticisms and suggestions. Special thanks go to our colleagues at Cornell: Leonard Babby, Nils Bjervig, Julia Bosky, Wayles Browne, Charlene Castellano, Gerald Greenberg, Alexander Kraft, Kevin Moss, and Peter Zimmerman. Michael Nicholson of the University of Lancaster, England, visiting the past two years at Colgate, has been extraordinarily conscientious in hunting down errata and making the book easier to teach. Genevra Gerhard provided us with her comments, and Nina Loseff of Dartmouth, who left a significant imprint on our Advanced Russian, was of great help with the Beginning Russian as well.

The pre-publication version of Beginning Russian has been used in three courses at Cornell, as well as at Colgate University and Eisenhower College. The teachers and teaching assistants who were running those courses have made an important contribution to the book: Kevin Moss, Peter Zimmerman, and Charlene Castellano of Cornell, Professor Michael Nicholson of Colgate, and Professor Mark Green of Eisenhower College. Our special thanks go to Alexander Kraft of Cornell, a superb language teacher whose many objections and suggestions have brought changes to every lesson in the book. We have also had the benefit of consultation with colleagues in applied linguistics, particularly Professor Eleanor Jorden of the Cornell FALCON Program in Japanese, and Professor James Noblitt.

As mentioned in the Introduction, our project involved extensive use of the computer, and our deepest gratitude goes to the people who made it work: Renée van Bramer, the typist and computer operator, who developed the unique ability to diagnose and correct all the quirks in the machine's idiosyncratic behavior; Peter Siegel, the programmer, who has devised, written, and elaborated our entire software package; and David Walters of the Cornell Phonetic Lab, who did a lot of tinkering with our hardware before it could print legible Russian. Renée van Bramer, in addition to her other duties, typed large portions of the book on the typewriter. Mary Musgrave battled time to produce the camera-ready copy, which Tatyana Korelskaya was kind enough to proofread. Most of the photographs in the book were taken by Professor Richard Sylvester of Colgate; they were expertly printed by Helen Kelley. For the remaining photographs we are indebted to G. Prikhod'ko, Konstantin Kuzminsky, and V. Paperno. Finally, we are grateful to the Department of Modern Languages and Linguistics at Cornell, its Phonetics Lab, and the Cornell Committee on Soviet Studies for their financial help.

Moscow park in late fall

УРÓК ПÉРВЫЙ

ТÉКСТ А : КТÓ ЗДÉСЬ?

In a first-year textbook of Russian it is always nice to start off with somebody who does not speak that language. We were lucky: Zyuzya fell down from the sky and right into the apartment of our main characters, Ivan Petrovich Sidorov and his daughter, Lena. Zyuzya looked funny, and Lena was surprised.

Лéна: Óй![1] Ты́ ктó? Кáк тебя́[2] зовýт?

Зю́зя: ???

Лéна: *(pointing at herself)* Лéна! Меня́ зовýт Лéна. *(pointing at Zyuzya)* Кáк тебя́ зовýт?

Зю́зя: *(getting the idea quickly because Zyuzya is very smart)* Зю́зя! Меня́ зовýт Зю́зя! Кáк тебя́ зовýт?

Лéна: *(laughing)* Лéна! Меня́ зовýт Лéна! А тебя́?

Зю́зя: ???

Лéна: *(pointing at herself)* Меня́ зовýт Лéна, *(pointing at Zyuzya)* а тебя́?

Зю́зя: *(getting the idea)* Меня́ зовýт Зю́зя, а тебя́?

Лéна: Меня́ зовýт Лéна, а тебя́?

Зю́зя: Меня́ зовýт Зю́зя, а тебя́?

Лéна: Меня́ зовýт Лéна, а тебя́?

They are interrupted by Ivan Petrovich,[3] who suddenly enters the room.

Ивáн Петрóвич: *(surprised, asks Lena)*
Óй,[1] ктó э́то? Кáк егó[4] зовýт?

Лéна: Э́то не óн, а онá.

Ивáн Петрóвич: Кáк её зовýт?

Лéна: *(feigning ignorance)* Я́ не знáю. Спроси́ её, кáк её зовýт.

Ивáн Петрóвич: *(to Zyuzya)* Кáк тебя́ зовýт?

Зю́зя: Меня́ зовýт Зю́зя, а тебя́?

Лéна: *(correcting Zyuzya)* А вáс?[5]

Зю́зя: *(getting the idea)* Кáк вáс зовýт?

Ивáн Петрóвич: Меня́ зовýт Ивáн Петрóвич, а тебя́?

Зю́зя: Меня́ зовýт Зю́зя, а вáс?

Ивáн Петрóвич: Меня́ зовýт Ивáн Петрóвич, а тебя́?

Зюзя: Меня зовут Зюзя, а вас?

Лена: (laughing) Хорошо! (calling her mother) Мама!

Lena's mother comes running from the living room.

Лена: Мама! Это Зюзя. Зюзя, это моя мама, Нина
Степановна.

Нина Степановна (extending her hand to Zyuzya)
Здравствуйте,[6] очень приятно.

Лена: Зюзя, ты молодец! Я буду тебя учить говорить,
читать и писать по-русски.

Vocabulary

первый first

кто who

здесь here
     Кто здесь? Who's here?

ты you (familiar form, Nom-
     inative case)
     Ты кто? Who are you?

как how

тебя you (familiar form,
     Accusative case)

зовут they call
     Как тебя зовут? What's
     your name? (Literally,
     'How do they call you?')

меня me (Accusative case)

а and; but
     А тебя? And you?
     Это не он, а она.
     That's not (a) he, but (a)
     she.

это this, that
     Кто это? Who's this?,
     Who's that?

его him (Accusative case)

он he (Nominative case)

она she (Nominative case)

её her (Accusative case)

я I (Nominative case)

не not

знаю I know

спроси ask

вас you (Accusative case)

хорошо fine, good

мама mom, mother

моя my (feminine)

здравствуйте hello

очень very

приятно pleasant
     Очень приятно. Pleased to
     meet you.

молодец
     Ты молодец! You're great!
     Молодец! Good for you! Nice
     going!

буду I will

учить (to) teach

говорить (to) speak

читать (to) read

и and

писать (to) write

по-русски (in) Russian

COMMENTS

1. Exclamation ой

This exclamation expresses a painful surprise; if the pain
is physical, it corresponds to 'ouch.' The pronunciation
varies according to the sex of the speaker: women generally
pronounce it as the spelling indicates, while men often say
it with a gasping inhalation of breath, as though spelled 'a'
rather than ой. (Listen to the recording of the male voice.)

2. Nominative case vs. Accusative case: ты vs. тебя

The difference between the English forms *he* and *him* (*I* and *me*,
they and *them*, etc.) is said to be a difference in *case*
forms; *he*, *I*, *they*, etc. are said to be in the *Nominative*
case, while *him*, *me*, *them* are said to be in the *Accusative*
case. The same is true for Russian pronouns. Russian differs
from English in that not only Russian pronouns but also
Russian nouns have case forms.

Differences in case forms correspond to differences in the
röle of the word in the sentence. For example, Nominative
plays the role of *subject* (*I* saw John), while Accusative
plays the role of *direct object* (John saw *me*).

The Nominative and Accusative pronouns in this lesson are,
respectively,

я	меня	I	
ты	тебя	you⎫	
вы	вас	you⎭	see Comment 4.
он	его	he	
она	её	she	

3. Russian names

The father is referred to here by his first and middle names,
Иван Петрович. This is the polite form of address in Russian, corresponding to Mr./Mrs./Miss/Ms. If you met a man
named Ivan Petrovich Sidorov, you would address him as Ivan
Petrovich, not as Mr. Sidorov. Russian-speaking foreigners
adhere to this convention when speaking to Russians, but
the convention is not ordinarily applied to foreign names,
i.e., Samuel Peter Smith is Samuel Smith, not Samuel
Petrovich.

The middle name is called the *patronymic* because it is based
on the father's first name; we know from the patronymic
Петрович that the bearer's father's first name is Пётр,
'Peter.' Similarly, a woman whose name is Нина Степановна
Сидорова has a father whose first name is Степан
'Stephen,' because her patronymic is based on that name.

In the classroom situation, where students soon get to know
each other rather well, nicknames are appropriate. The
teacher, however, is conventionally addressed by name and
patronymic as described above.

Listed below are some common Russian nicknames. The full
names from which they are derived are in parentheses.

Look over the list and select a "stage name" for yourself for
acting out roles in subsequent lessons. English equivalents
or near-equivalents are given for most of the names, but you
don't have to choose a name equivalent to your own English
name if you don't want to. You can use your English name if
it ends in the vowel -a, but not if it ends in any other
vowel or if it ends in a consonant. (The reason for this
will become clear when you begin learning the Accusative
case.)

Women's names
Áня (Áнна) Ann(a)
Вáря (Варвáра) Barbara
Вéра Vera
Кáтя (Екатерúна) Kathy
Лéна (Елéна) Ellen, Helen
Зóя Zoya
Úра (Ирúна) Irene
Кúра Kira
Лúда (Лúдия) Lidia
Мáша (Марúя) Mary
Нáдя (Надéжда) Hope
Нúна Nina
Óля (Óльга) Olga
Сóня (Сóфья) Sophie
Тамáра Tamara
Тáня (Татьяна) Tanya
Натáша (Натáлья) Natalie

Men's names
Сáша (Алексáндр) Alex
Алёша (Алексéй) Alex
Андрюша (Андрéй) Andy
Бóря (Борúс) Boris
Дúма (Вадúм) Vadim
Вáся (Василий) Basil
Волóдя (Владúмир) Vladimir
Дáня (Даниúл) Dan, Daniel
Дúма (Дмúтрий) Dima
Жéня (Евгéний) Gene
Вáня (Ивáн) John
Óся (Иóсиф) Joe
Мúша (Михаúл) Mike
Кóля (Николáй) Nick
Пéтя (Пётр) Pete
Серёжа (Сергéй) Seryozha
Юра Юрий George
Яша Яков Jake

4. Spelling Exception: егó

The letter г usually represents the sound /g/ as in *get*,
e.g., кнúга /knúga/. However, in the word егó it is
pronounouced /v/: /yivó/, as in the sentence Как егó
зовýт? 'What's his name?' (Lit., 'How do they call him?').
Later, when you learn the Genitive/Accusative case forms,
you will learn that г has this exceptional pronunciation
quite regularly - in *all* Genitive/Accusative endings, and
nowhere else.

5. Formal and informal styles

Zyuza has made a serious blunder in using the informal pronoun тебя in talking to someone of greater age and status. Russian is pretty much like other European languages in having two sets of pronouns and verb forms for two styles of address (French *vous/tu*, Spanish *Usted/tu*, German *Sie/du*), although details in usage vary from language to language.

Formal	*Informal*	
вы	ты	you (Nominative case)
вас	тебя	you (Accusative case)
Здравствуйте!	Здравствуй!	Hello!/Hi!
Спросите его.	Спроси его.	Ask him.

Normally you would use the formal forms and name + patronymic in addressing your teacher (Здравствуйте, Пётр Петрович) and the informal forms and nicknames in addressing each other (Здравствуй, Петя). Your teacher, in addressing you. is likely to use the formal pronouns and verbs, but with nicknames rather than the formal name + patronymic (Здравствуйте, Петя).

Read through the text and identify the formal vs. informal styles as used by the characters. You will note that Zyuza and Lena are equals, that Ivan Petrovich and his wife have different personalities, that family membership overrides differences in age and status (Lena and her father), etc.

6. Spelling exception: здравствуйте

Russian words, as they appear in their written form, sometimes have long clusters of consonants which, when spoken, are simplified into shorter clusters. This is the case with здравствуйте, in which the fifth letter (в) is not pronounced: /zdrástvuyţi/. This is small consolation for the beginner, however, since there are still a lot of unfamiliar groupings of consonants in Russian, like книга /kņíga/ 'book,' Псков /pskóf/ 'Pskov,' etc., and it is difficult to resist the temptation to stick in a vowel between them. However strong, the temptation should be resisted.

The word здравствуйте is sometimes shortened even further; you will hear it with the other в omitted, too: /zdrástuyţi/, or even /zdrásţi/.

ТЕ́КСТ Б : ЛЕ́НА У́ЧИТ ЗЮ́ЗЮ[1] ГОВОРИ́ТЬ ПО-РУ́ССКИ

Immediately after getting acquainted, Lena and Zyuzya proceed to Lena's room. Lena shows Zyuzya various objects.

Ле́на: Э́то ру́чка.[2] Повтори́, Зю́зя, — "ру́чка."

Зю́зя: Ру́чка.

Ле́на: Молоде́ц! А э́то — стака́н.

Зю́зя: Стака́н.

Ле́на: Хорошо́.

Now Lena places the glass at the far end of the table and puts the pen and letter near where she is standing.

Ле́на: Где́ стака́н?

Зю́зя: ???

Ле́на: Стака́н та́м, а ру́чка зде́сь. (*pointing*) Понима́ешь?

Зю́зя: Да́, понима́ю. Стака́н та́м, а ру́чка зде́сь.

Ле́на: А письмо́?

Зю́зя: Письмо́ то́же зде́сь.

Ле́на: (*pointing to a newspaper across the table*)
Э́то[3] газе́та. Где́ газе́та?

Зю́зя: Газе́та та́м.

Ле́на: О́чень хорошо́.

Lena and Zyuza continue their lesson. Nina Sergeyevna goes to the kitchen to cook a meal for their guest. Ivan Petrovich goes to the telephone to inform his superiors that a tentacled creature has turned up in his apartment.

Vocabulary

у́чит teaches	понима́ешь you understand
ру́чка pen	(informal)
повтори́ repeat	да́ yes
стака́н (drinking) glass	понима́ю I understand
где́ where	письмо́ letter
та́м there	то́же also
	газе́та newspaper

COMMENTS

1. Accusative case

The form Зюзю is the Accusative case form of Зюзя. (See Text A, Comment 2.)

2. am, is, are

There is no verb in Russian corresponding to 'am, is, are.'

Я студе́нт.	I (am) a student.
Он студе́нт.	He (is) a student.
Кто́ здесь?	Who ('s) here?
Они́ здесь.	They (are) here.
Э́то ру́чка.	This (is) a pen.
Э́то стака́н.	This (is) a glass.
Кто́ э́то?	What (is) this?
Э́то моя́ ма́ма.	This (is) my mother (Mom).

When there are two nouns, a dash is often used in printed texts:

Мой па́па — генера́л.   My dad is a general.

3. э́то = this, that

In English you have to distinguish between things near at hand vs. things further away by using either *this* or *that*. In Russian you don't; э́то can be translated as either 'this' or 'that.'

Э́то газе́та.   This is a newspaper.
                        OR: That is a newspaper.

DIALOGS FOR MEMORIZATION

Listen to these dialogs and repeat them over and over at normal (fast) speed until you know them by heart and don't have to think or hesitate when you say them. Learn them the way an actor learns roles, using the right intonation and, where appropriate, proper gestures.

W 1a. Formal style — Здра́вствуйте! Ка́к ва́с зову́т?
— Меня́ зову́т Ива́н Петро́вич. А ва́с?
- Меня́ зову́т Ни́на Степа́новна.

W 1b. Informal style- Здра́вствуй! Ка́к тебя́ зову́т?
— Меня́ зову́т Ва́ня. А тебя́?

R 2. — Ка́к сказа́ть по-ру́сски Pete?
— Pete по-ру́сски — Пе́тя. Понима́ете?
— Не́т, не понима́ю. Повтори́те, пожа́луйста.

R 3. — Э́то кни́га?
— Да́, э́то кни́га.
— А что́[1] э́то?[2] Э́то ру́чка?
— Не́т, э́то не ру́чка, а каранда́ш.

R 4. — Где́ газе́та?
— Газе́та зде́сь.
— А письмо́?
— Письмо́ та́м.

F 5. Classroom — Откро́йте, пожа́луйста, кни́гу.
Expressions — Кака́я э́то бу́ква?
— Чита́йте, пожа́луйста.
— Не та́к.
— Та́к лу́чше.
— О́чень хорошо́.
— До свида́ния.

Translation

Look at the English and test yourself by trying to say the Russian as smoothly as possible without looking at the Russian version.

1a. Hello! What's your name? (Lit., 'How do they call you?')
My name's Ivan Petrovich. And yours? (Lit., 'And you?')
My name's Nina Stepanovna.
1b. Hi! What's your name?
My name's Vanya. And yours?

2. How do you say "Pete" in Russian?
"Pete" in Russian is Petya. Do you understand?
No, I don't understand. Repeat, please.

3. Is that a book?
Yes, that is a book.
And what's that? Is that a pen?

No, that's not a pen, but (rather) a pencil.

4. Where's the newspaper?
   The newspaper is here.
   And the letter?
   The letter is there.

5. Open the book, please.
   What letter is this?
   Read, please.
   That's wrong. (Lit., 'Not thus/so.')
   That's better. (Lit., 'Thus/so better.')
   Very good.
   Goodbye.

ACTIVE WORD LIST

You will need the words on the Active Word List and in the Dialogs for use in grammatical exercises, in conversation exercises, and in written homework. They should be memorized thoroughly. Active Word Lists contain all the new words that occur in the Dialogs, plus a few additional items marked "*".

Nouns ending in -a

ру́чка	pen
газе́та	newspaper
кни́га	book
бума́га *	paper
бу́ква	letter (of the alphabet)

Nouns ending in -o

вино́ *	wine
письмо́	letter
яйцо́ *	egg
кольцо́ *	ring

Nouns with no vowel ending

стака́н *	(drinking) glass
конве́рт *	envelope
ме́л *	chalk
каранда́ш	pencil

Pronouns

я́ *	I *(Nominative case)*
меня́	me *(Accusative case)*
вы́ *	you *(Nom., Formal)*
ва́с	you *(Acc., Formal)*
ты́ *	you *(Nom., Informal)*
тебя́	you *(Acc., Informal)*
что́[1]	what
э́то	this, that

Adverbs

где́	where
зде́сь	here
та́м	there
ка́к	how
та́к	thus, so
хорошо́	fine, good, well
лу́чше	better
о́чень	very
по-ру́сски	in Russian

Misc.

до свида́ния	goodbye

pronounced as one word, as though spelled "дасвида́ния"

зову́т	(they) call
сказа́ть	(to) say
понима́ете	(you) understand (*Formal*)
понима́ешь *	(you) understand (*Informal*)
понима́ю	(I) understand
Повтори́те!	Repeat! (*Imperative*)
Откро́йте!	Open! (*Imperative*)
Чита́йте!	Read! (*Imperative*)
кака́я	which, what
Здра́вствуйте.	Hello. (*Formal*)
Здра́вствуй.	Hi. (*Informal*)
пожа́луйста	please
не́т	no
да́	yes
не	not
а	and, but

COMMENTS

1. Spelling exception: что

The usual pronunciation for the letter ч is *ch* as in *church*, e.g., чита́ть '(to) read.' However, the word что is pronounced with the sound *sh* as in *ship*, as though spelled што.

2. Word order and intonation: Что́ э́то?

The usual way to say *What's that?* or *What's this?* is with stress and high pitch on Что, after which the pitch falls:

что́ э_{то}?

After the word а 'and' you can say it either of the following ways, with stress on э́то:

А что э_{то}?   А э_{то} что?

For further information on the pitch of the voice, see Analysis 3.1.

ANALYSIS

1. Declension classes of nouns

There are four declension classes of Russian nouns, three of
which are represented in this lesson. We'll take up the
fourth one later.

The term *declension class* refers to the *endings* that come
after the noun *stem*. If a noun has the ending -a (like
кни́га, бума́га, газе́та, ру́чка, бу́ква, Ле́на, Са́ша,
Ми́ша, etc.) it belongs to the a-class. The part of the
word that preceeds the vowel ending is called the stem; thus:

stem	*ending*	
книг	-a	book
бумаг	-a	paper
газет	-a	newspaper
ручк	-a	pen
букв	-a	letter (of the alphabet)
Лен	-a	Lena
Саш	-a	Sasha
Миш	-a	Mike

If the ending on a noun is -o, the noun belongs to the o-
class. You have met the following o-class nouns:

stem	*ending*
вин	-o
письм	-o
яйц	-o
кольц	-o

If there is no vowel ending on the noun, it belongs to the
zero-class. We are going to use the symbol -# to refer to
the zero ending. Here are some examples:

stem	*ending*	
стакан	-#	(drinking) glass
конверт	-#	envelope
мел	-#	chalk
карандаш	-#	pencil

2. The Cyrillic alphabet

The Russian alphabet is often referred to as the *Cyrillic*
alphabet; it was allegedly devised in the ninth century by
two missionaries, Cyril and Methodius, who were later canon-
ized as saints in the Orthodox Church. (There is a scholarly
dispute about whether they devised this alphabet or another
one, no longer used; in any case, they deserve the credit
for providing the Slavs with a writing system.)

We list the letters of the alphabet here for reference purposes, *not* for the purpose of teaching pronunciation.

Upper Case	Lower Case	Approximate sound	Upper Case	Lower Case	Approximate sound
А	а	a as in *father*	Т	т	t as in *stand*
Б	б	b	У	у	u as in *flute*
В	в	v	Ф	ф	f
Г	г	g as in *get*	Х	х	No comparable
Д	д	d			English sound.
Е	е	e as in *yet*			Like ch in Ger-
Ё	ё	o as in *York*			man ach, but
Ж	ж	z as in *seizure*			not as rough
З	з	z as in *zoom*			sounding.
И	и	i as in *machine*	Ц	ц	ts as in *bolts*
Й	й	y as in *yet*	Ч	ч	ch as in *chin*
		or *boy*	Ш	ш	sh as in *shin*
К	к	k	Щ	щ	shch as in
Л	л	l			*Danish ship*
М	м	m	Ъ	ъ	Represents no
Н	н	n			sound (See
					Lesson 5.4)
О	о	o as in *story*	Ы	ы	i as in *bit*
П	п	p		Ь	Represents no
Р	р	dd as in *ladder*			sound; (See 4.1
					below)
			Э	э	e as in *bet*
			Ю	ю	u as in *yule*
С	с	s as in *silly*	Я	я	a as in *yacht*

```
+-----------------------------------------------+
|                  PRACTICE 1                    |
+-----------------------------------------------+
| Listen to the pronunciation of the names      |
| of the letters of the Cyrillic alphabet       |
| and imitate.                                   |
+-----------------------------------------------+
```

3. Pronunciation

In general, you learn to pronounce foreign sounds by listen-
ing, imitating, being corrected, and practicing — not by
reading descriptions of how to make sounds. The descriptions
we give below may help you to learn Russian pronunciation,
but your ear will be more helpful than your eye.

3.1 Intonation

The musical rise and fall of the voice conveys information
as well as emotion. The information conveyed is of the type

"statement" vs. "question." The emotional content of intonation is very firmly ingrained — we learn it very early in
life for our native language — and it is important for the
language learner to make every effort to rid him or herself
of emotional reactions to foreign intonation contours which,
in the foreign language, are quite devoid of emotional
content.

All three contours described below are emotionally neutral
in Russian, but sound emotionally loaded to the English ear.
If you master these tunes, you will be conveying the proper
information. If you do not master them, and if you substitute English tunes, you will either be conveying the wrong
information or you will be expressing emotion when none is
intended.

Statement Contour

            га   ᶰéʷsₚₐₚₑᵣ.
э́то   This
            зе́та.   is a

The most heavily stressed syllable of the sentence, зе, has
low pitch. The preceding unstressed syllable га has higher
pitch. Compare the English sentence, where the most heavily
stressed syllable has the *highest* pitch. If you were to use
this English contour on the Russian sentence, it would mean
'This is a *newspaper* (you fool, not a *magazine*)!' or it would
convey some sort of emphasis or excitement. The Russian
statement contour occurs in English, too, but with the meaning 'boredom,' or something of the sort, as in:

            don't
    I
            cáre.

Question-word Contour

Question words are words like *who, what, where, which,* etc.
In Russian, many of them begin with к or г, e.g., как 'how,'
где 'where.' There are two ways to intone a question-word
question:

1) Где газе́   Where's the ᶰéʷsₚₐₚₑᵣ?
            та?

2) Где́   (same meaning)
        газета?

The first variant sounds pretty much like English, but the
second variant sounds rude to the English ear; if you used
this contour in English, it would sound very insistent:

    Whére's
            the newsₚₐₚₑᵣ?

Yes-no Contour

This contour is perhaps the most important one and the one most difficult to master or to perceive. It is used in questions that elicit either 'yes' or 'no' as an answer.

$$\text{это } _{\text{га}}{}^{{}_{3}\acute{e}}{}_{\text{та?}}$$ Is this a $n\hat{e}wsp^{ap}\!\!^{er?}$

Three points:

(1) The pitch on the most heavily stressed syllable is very high, higher than the top of the neutral (American) English range. The pitch range of American English is very narrow (unlike British English) and in American English, extra-high pitch always conveys emotion. This Russian contour is strictly informational, not emotional, despite its high pitch.

(2) The pitch is not only high, it has a *rising* contour. If you don't sing this lilting rise, the sentence will sound like an exclamation, rather than a question.

(3) The syllables after the stress fall. Compare English, where the syllables after the *news* rise.

The Russian contour has its conterpart in English, but with a totally different meaning, i.e., 'jocular disbelief.'

This is $_{a}n\hat{e}w^{s}p_{a}p_{e}{}_{r?!}$ (You must be kidding!)

Yes-no Contour: Special case

If the sentence ends in a stressed syllable and there are no subsequent unstressed syllables, then there is no fall in pitch:

$$\text{это }_{\text{ста}}{}^{\text{кáн?}}$$ Is this a $g^{l\acute{a}ss?}$

This variant is unlike English because of the sharply higher pitch rather than a smooth rise.

Do not use the above Contour with questions beginning with a, 'and'. The correct contour for a-questions is :

$A_{в}\hat{a}^{c?}$ And y^{o}u?

This type of question has a gentle rise and doesn't go so high.

PRACTICE 2

Listen and imitate the three contours.

1. Statement contour.

   Э́то газе́та.
   Э́то стака́н.
   Это бума́га.

2. Question-word contour.

   Гдé газе́та?
   Ка́к ва́с зову́т?
   Гдé стака́н?

3.(a) Yes-no contour.

   Э́то газе́та?
   Э́то бума́га?

3.(b) Yes-no contour, final syllable stressed.

   Э́то стака́н?
   Э́то вино́?
   Э́то каранда́ш?

3.2 Palatalization

One of the most striking features of Russian pronunciation is a phenomenon called *palatalization*.

The term palatalization is used in phonetics to refer to tongue position against or close to the palate (the roof of the mouth), as in the first sound of English *yes*. The closest we can come to a palatalized consonant in English is the /p/ in *pure*, which we might spell 'pyoor,' as against the plain /p/ of 'poor;' or the /t/ in some people's pronunciation of *tune*, 'tyoon,' as against the plain /t/ in 'too;' or in the children's mocking cry *nyah nyah nyah*. To the Russian ear, however, these   English sounds are not palatalized consonants at all;   rather, they are the consonants /p t n/ *followed by* the y-sound.   In Russian, palatalization is made *simultaneously* with the consonants.   To produce a palatalized consonant at the beginning of a word, put your tongue in the position of the /y/ in English 'yes' *before you start talking;*   then pronounce the consonant.

What is striking about Russian is not just the fact that it has palatalized   consonants, but that most of the consonants of Russian come in two varieties, plain **and** palatalized, e.g., there are two /n/-sounds in Russian, one plain, the other palatalized.   In the following examples we will write Russian sounds with English letters, using a hook under the consonants to indicate palatalization.

```
┌─────────────────────────────────────────────┐
│                 PRACTICE 3                    │
├─────────────────────────────────────────────┤
│  Listen and imitate.                          │
│                                               │
│     pa ta ba da sa ma na la ra                │
│     p̣a ța ḅa ḍa șa m̦a ṇa ḻa ŗa                │
│                                               │
│     po to bo do so mo no lo ro                │
│     p̣o țo ḅo ḍo șo m̦o ṇo ḻo ŗo                │
│                                               │
└─────────────────────────────────────────────┘
```

If you pronounce the y-sound simultaneously with the consonant, you should hear a nice, crisp, quick transition from
the consonant to the following vowel, and it should take no
more time to utter the syllable /ṇa/ than it does to utter
/na/, with a plain consonant. If you drawl it out, however,
and say /ṇya/ instead of /ṇa/, you will not only have a
foreign accent, you will be misunderstood: there are pairs
of words in Russian that differ in sound and meaning only by
virtue of the contrast between palatalization (simultaneous
with the consonant) and the y-sound (following the consonant). For example:

　　　　/paḻót/　　flight　　　/șésț/　　sit down

　　　　/paḻyót/　will pour　　/șyésț/　eat

4. The Cyrillic writing system

4.1 Cyrillic palatal indicators

The Cyrillic alphabet contains a special symbol to indicate
the palatalization of the preceding consonant. This symbol,
ь , is called мягкий знак /m̦axḳiy znak/ (Literally, 'soft
sign').

Examples:

At the end of a word:

здéсь	/zḍéș/	here
цáрь	/tsáŗ/	czar
читáть	/chitáț/	(to) read

Before another consonant:

письмó	/p̣ișmó/	letter

PRACTICE 4

Here are some pairs of words which differ only by virtue of the plain vs. palatalized consonant distinction. Listen to the pronunciation and observe the palatal indicator letter ь.

ма́т	checkmate	сто́л	table
ма́ть	mother	сто́ль	so
ве́с	weight	по́лка	shelf
ве́сь	all, entire	по́лька	Polish woman, Polish dance

When a vowel sound follows a platalized consonant, the symbol ь is not used. Instead, a special series of vowel letters, called palatal indicators, is used. For the vowel letter a, for example, there is a matching letter я, which represents not only the vowel sound /a/, but also the fact that the preceding consonant is palatalized.

PRACTICE 5

Here are the syllables we listed in Section 3 Practice 3, on pronunciation, printed here in Cyrillic. Listen again to the pronunciation and note the use of the plain indicator a vs. the palatal indicator я for the vowel sound /a/.

plain consonant		palatalized consonant	
па	/pa/	пя	/p̢a/
та	/ta/	тя	/t̢a/
ба	/ba/	бя	/b̢a/
да	/da/	дя	/d̢a/
са	/sa/	ся	/s̢a/
ма	/ma/	мя	/m̢a/
на	/na/	ня	/n̢a/
ла	/la/	ля	/l̢a/
ра	/ra/	ря	/r̢a/

This system of plain vs. palatal indicators applies to all five vowels of Russian. There are five vowel *sounds* in Russian, but ten vowel *letters* in the Cyrillic writing system.

Five vowel letters indicate preceding consonant plainness,
and the other matching five represent preceding consonant
palatalization.

The whole system looks like this:

Vowel sound (stressed vowels)	Plain Indicators	Palatal Indicators
/í/	ы́	и́
/é/	э́	é
/á/	á	я́
/ó/	ó	ё
/ú/	у́	ю́

The two dots over the letter ё serve two functions: (1) they
distinguish the sound /ó/ from the sound /é/ (written é), and
(2) they act as a stress mark. Thus, the syllable ТЁ   is
pronounced /țó/ and the syllable ТЕ́ is pronounced /țé/.

PRACTICE 6

*Listen to the pronunciation, imitate, and observe the use of
plain vs. palatal indicators:*

plain consonant		palatalized consonant		plain consonant		palatalized consonant	
пы	/pi/	пи	/p̦i/	по	/po/	пё	/p̦o/
ты	/ti/	ти	/ți/	то	/to/	тё	/țo/
вы	/ví/	ви	/y̦i/	во	/vo/	вё	/yo/
лы	/li/	ли	/ḻi/	ло	/lo/	лё	/ḻo/
пэ	/pe/	пе	/p̦e/	пу	/pu/	пю	/p̦u/
тэ	/te/	те	/țe/	ву	/vu/	вю	/yu/
вэ	/ve/	ве	/y̦e/	лу	/lu/	лю	/ḻu/
				ру	/ru/	рю	/ṟu/

It is important to note the grammatical consequences of this
writing system. In Section 1 we discussed the declensional
classes of Russian nouns and said that there is a class of
nouns ending in -а (книга, Нина, газета, ручка, etc.);
to which class do nouns like Аня, Ваня, Петя, etc. belong?
They belong to the same class as книга, Нина, газета and
ручка, because they have the same vowel ending /-a/. Since
their *stems* end in a palatalized consonant, the last letter is
-я rather than -а. The Cyrillic writing system, which is
otherwise a very effective and reasonable system, conceals this
identity of endings by using two different letters for the
same ending. The grammatical equivalence of the Cyrillic
endings -а and -я emerges more clearly when the stems and endings are written with English letters, using a hook to represent palatalization:

plain stem final consonant:	*stem + ending:*	
кни́га	kņíg-a	book
Ни́на	ņín-a	Nina
газе́та	gaẓét-a	newspaper
ру́чка	**ruch**k-a	pen

palatalized stem final consonant:

А́ня	áņ-a	Annie
Ва́ня	váņ-a	Johnny
Пе́тя	ṗéț-a	Pete
ды́ня	díņ-a	melon

Thus, all of these nouns belong to the a-class. From the
point of view of *grammatical endings,* the letters а and я
can be said to be *equivalent*. The same can be said for the
other matching pairs, ы/и, у/ю, etc.

There are a few consonants which do not have plain and palatalized partners (ц ш ж щ ч й). These consonants, and the
spelling of vowel letters after them, will be discussed in
Lesson 3.

⊩ 4.2 Reading Cyrillic vowels in unstressed position

The vowel letters in the chart in the preceding section were
given their values in stressed position. In unstressed position, и,е, and я all sound the same — like a very short и
/i/ (there are exceptions to this) and the letters а and о
both sound the same — like a /a/. This /a/-sound is like the
a in *father* right before the stress (e.g. стака́н) and like
the *a* in *sofa* in other undtressed positions (e.g. ру́чка).

Thus, the first syllable of each of the following words has the same vowel sound:

приятно	/pri yátna/	pleasant
тебя	/ṭi ḅá/	you
яйцо́	/yi ytsó/	egg

Similarly, the first syllable of each of the following words has the same vowel sound:

| зову́т | /za vút/ | they call |
| Ната́ша | /natásha/ | Natasha |

| хорошо́ | /kharashó/ | good |
| каранда́ш | /karandásh/ | pencil |

The last vowel of the following words sounds the same:

| э́то | /éta/ | this |
| ру́чка | /rúchka/ | pen |

Summary chart:

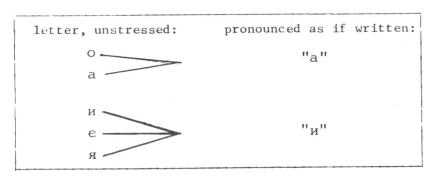

It's easy to read Cyrillic aloud from the printed page (if stress is marked), but it's hard to write unstressed vowels correctly from dictation if you don't know Russian well.

```
┌─────────────────────────────────────────────┐
│                PRACTICE 7                     │
├─────────────────────────────────────────────┤
```

Here are further examples of unstressed vo-wels. Listen and imitate.

онá *is pronounced as though written* "анá"

прия́тно	"	"прия́тна"
молодéц	"	"маладéц"
óчень	"	"óчинь"
говори́ть	"	"гавари́ть"
по-рýсски	"	"па-рýсски"
спроси́	"	"спраси́"
конвéрт	"	"канвéрт"
кольцó	"	"кальцó"

```
┌─────────────────────────────────────────────┐
│                PRACTICE 8                     │
├─────────────────────────────────────────────┤
```

Here are examples of words with plain and palatalized consonants, as well as unstressed vowels. Read them aloud and check your pronunciation.

онá	меня́	письмó
Ни́на	А́ня	здéсь
кни́га	тебя́	кольцó

F 5. Verb forms.

If a verb form ends in −ю , it means that the subject is
Я 'I'; if in −шь, ты 'you' (informal); if in −те, вы
'you' (formal).

Pronoun	*Ending*	*Example*	
я	−ю (or −у)	я понимáю	'I understand'
ты	−шь	ты понимáешь	'you understand'
вы	−те	вы понимáете	'you understand'

If the context makes it clear who the subject is, you don't
have to use the pronoun:

Ты́ понима́ешь?   Do you understand?

–Да́, понима́ю.   –Yes, (I) understand.

Imperative forms of verbs are used to give commands. The
formal style requires the addition of –те , e.g.,

Informal	*Formal*	
Повтори́!	Повтори́те!	Repeat!
Чита́й!	Чита́йте!	Read!
Откро́й!	Откро́йте!	Open!

УПРАЖНЕНИЯ

Conversation Exercises

These exercises consist of very short conversations between two or three people. The roles are indicated by the letters П and С (П for Преподаватель /pṛipadaváṭiḷ/ *teacher* and С for Студéнt /stuḍént/ *student*). After you practice a conversation often enough so it goes smoothly, the teacher's role can often be taken over by a student; when this happens, i.e., when the conversation is between two students, the appropriate form of address would usually be in the informal style (ты, тебя́, здра́вствуй, etc.) rather than the formal style required in a conversation between student and teacher; however, this switch will not always be indicated in the exercise models. You should get used to making the switch automatically, without being told.

1. *Give your first and last name when the teacher asks for it.*

   П: Ка́к ва́с зову́т?

   С: (first and last name)

2. *Answer the same question with a full sentence.*

   П: Ка́к ва́с зову́т?

   С: Меня́ зову́т (first and last name).

3. *Pronunciation.*

   The vowel written with the letter у *as in* зову́т *is much shorter and less drawled out than the* oo *in English* boot. *Imitate these words:*

зову́т	they call
бу́ква	letter
су́п	soup
луна́	moon

4. *Answer the same question and ask it back; see Text Comment 2 for information on Russian names.*

   П: Ка́к ва́с зову́т?

   С: Меня́ зову́т _____. А ва́с?

   П: Меня́ зову́т _____.

5. *Pronounce the names of these twelve objects in the sentence 'This is a _____.' They are listed here according to their declension class; see Analysis 1. Imitate the intonation of the sentence as best you can (see Analysis 3.1).*

П: Повторите, пожалуйста: э́то ру́чка.

С: Э́то ру́чка.

Substitute:

газе́та	конве́рт	письмо́
кни́га	стака́н	кольцо́
бума́га	ме́л	вино́
ру́чка	каранда́ш	яйцо́

6. *Pronunciation.*

The letter р *represents a sound similar to the one in the middle of the English words* latter, ladder, Betty, gotta, *etc. Imitate these syllables:*

га́ра *(like* gotta*)*

ка́ра *(like* cotter*)*

каранда́ш

Э́то каранда́ш.

This sound is more difficult to pronounce when it is at the beginning of a word, because there is no similar sound in English in this position. Imitate:

ка́ру

кару́чка

  ру́чка

Э́то ру́чка.

7. *As the teacher holds up an object and asks the question, answer in the affirmative. The teacher's question will have the rise-fall melody of the Yes-no intonation contour (Analysis 3.1); your answer should have the low melody of the statement contour, as in Exercise 5.*

П: Э́то ру́чка?

С: Да́, э́то ру́чка.

Substitute the items listed in Exercise 5.

8. *Answer in the affirmative, as above; then identify the second object.*

   П: Э́то ру́чка?

   С: Да́, э́то ру́чка.

   П: А э́то?

   С: Э́то каранда́ш.

Substitute the items listed in Exercise 5.

9. *Locate the objects as to whether they are near you (здесь 'here') or farther away from you (та́м 'there'). Use the statement contour in your answer.*

   П: Где́ газе́та?

   С: Газе́та здесь.

   П: А ру́чка?

   С: Ру́чка та́м.
      Ру́чка то́же здесь.

Substitute various items.

10. *Pronunciation.*

The vowel written with the letter e *generally sounds like the vowel in English* bet; *however, when it is followed by a palatalized consonant, as in* здесь *(see Analysis 3.2), it sounds more like the vowel in English* bait. *Listen, compare, and imitate:*

газе́та	здесь
ме́л	здесь
конве́рт	здесь
где́	здесь

11. *Pronunciation.*

The sounds represented by the letters п, т, к *do not have the puff of breath after them as their English counterparts do. In English there is no puff of breath when an* s *preceeds (compare* spin - *no puff -* vs. pin), *and therefore the column of syllables on the left, below, should be easy to pronounce. Try to make the consonants in the right-hand column sound the same way (they may sound like* b d g *to you, rather than* p t k).

спа	па
ста	та
ска	ка
стака́н	там

12. *Identify the objects when asked 'What is this?'*

П: Чтó э́то?

С: Э́то _____ .

П: Хорошó. 'Good.'

13. *Pronunciation.*

Stressed ó, like the vowel represented by the letter у (as in рýчка) is much more clipped and less drawled out than the English vowel in story. The lips should be rounded, puckered out, and fairly wide apart. Imitate:

чтó	письмó	егó
винó	яйцó	её
кольцó	хорошó	

14. *Repeat Exercise 12, but a student (М for Мáша) rather than the teacher will ask the question, and another student (С for Сáша) will answer.*

П: Мáша, спросúте егó, чтó э́то *(pointing to the glass)*.

М: Сáша, чтó э́то?

С: Э́то стакáн.

М: Хорошó.

15. *Read Text Comment 3 and choose a nickname for yourself.*

П: Здрáвствуйте! Кáк вáс зовýт?

С: Меня́ зовýт *(nickname)*. А вáс?

П: Меня́ зовýт *(name and patronymic)*.

Continue around the class.

16. *One student asks another his/her name. Use the informal terms* здрáвствуй *and* тебя́ *(Text Comment 5).*

П: Мáша, спросúте егó, кáк егó зовýт *(pointing to Сáша)*.

М: Здрáвствуй! Кáк тебя́ зовýт?

С: Меня́ зовýт Сáша. А тебя́?

М: Меня́ зовýт Мáша.

Substitute various members of the class.

W 17. *Pronunciation.*

*Read Analysis 3.1 and practice the yes-no intonation contour.
As you do this exercise, observe the melody of the teacher's
question.*

П: Вáс зовýт Лéна? *(The wrong name.)*

М: Нéт, меня́ зовýт не Лéна, а Мáша.

Substitute various members of the class.

W 18. *This exercise is the same as the above, except that the student rather than the teacher uses the yes-no contour. Use the
informal terms of address.*

Мáша: Тебя́ зовýт Пéтя? *(Wrong name)*

Сáша: Нéт, меня́ зовýт не Пéтя, а Сáша.

W 19. *Answer as in the model.*

П: Сáша, э́то стакáн?

С: Нéт, э́то не стакáн, а рýчка.

П: Сáша, вы́ молодéц!

Substitute the usual items.

W 20. *Pronunciation.*

The vowel sound represented by the letter ы *is made with the
tongue in the back of the mouth, like the* oo *in* tool, *but
without rounding the lips. Avoid making a drawling dipthong
as in* Louie. *Imitate.*

ТЫ	ДЫ
ВЫ	МЫ

W 21. *Switch to* ты; *use the yes-no intonation contour.*

Мáша: Сáша, э́то стакáн?

Сáша: Нéт, э́то не стакáн, а рýчка.

Мáша: Сáша, ты молодéц!

W 22. *Cyrillic letter names.*

*Imitate the pronunciation of the names of these Cyrillic
letters as you hear them from the recordings or your teacher.*

П: Э́то бýква о.
   Повторúте, пожáлуйста: о.

С: О.

Substitute:

letter:	а	п	т	к	б	д	г	л	р	м	ш
name:	а	пэ	тэ	ка	бэ	дэ	гэ	эл	эр	эм	ша

23. Identify the letter as the teacher points.

П: Кака́я э́то бу́ква?

С: Э́то — бу́ква *(name)*.

R *24. Reading practice.*

Read these words and syllables aloud.

П: Са́ша, чита́йте, пожа́луйста.

С: *(reads)*

П: Хорошо́. Ма́ша, чита́йте да́льше. *('Read further')*

М: *(reads)*

па	та	ка	по	то	ко	как
ба	да	га	бо	до	го	так

ма́ма	mamma	бо́мба	bomb
то́м	tome	ка́к	how
а́кт	act	ма́т	checkmate

R 25. *As in Exercise 24.*

а да́	апа́	ала́	ага́	ара́	аша́
адо́	апо́	ало́	аго́	аро́	ашо́

ма́ма	mamma	да́ма	lady
да́та	date	па́па	papa
то́м	tome	паке́т	package
по́рт	port	а́кт	act
па́кт	pact	ла́ма	llama
ла́мпа	lamp	тала́нт	talent
ба́л	ball (party)	балко́н	balcony
ма́рка	stamp	до́ллар	dollar
дра́ма	drama	па́рк	park
ка́рта	map	шта́т	state
шко́ла	school		

F 26. *Pronunciation.*

Unstressed a *and* o *sound the same.*

(1) *If they occur in the syllable immediately preceding the stressed syllable, they sound like the* a *in* father. *Imitate:*

онá	she	по-рýсски	in Russian
моя́	my	балкóн	balcony
пакéт	package	кольцó	
зовýт	they call	спросúте	

(2) *If, on the other hand, they occur unstressed at the end of a word, they sound like the* a *in* sofa.

э́то	this, that
кáрта	map
дрáма	drama

(3) *In most other positions they sound like the* a *in* sofa, *e.g. the first syllable of* хорошо. *Thus, the first syllable of this word has the* a *of* sofa *and the second syllable has the* a *of* father. *Imitate:*

хорошó	good
молодéц	good for you
повторúте	repeat
говорúть	to speak
карандáш	pencil

☞ 27. *Pronunciation.*

*Listen to the melody of these questions and responses.   The
questions have the yes-no Intonation Contour; the responses
have the Statement Contour.   See Analysis 3.1.   Practice
both the questions and the responses.*

Э́то ру́чка?   —Да, э́то ру́чка.

Э́то каранда́ш?   —Да, э́то каранда́ш.

Э́то Ле́на?   Вас зову́т Ми́ша?
Э́то Зю́зя?   Её зову́т Зю́зя?
Э́то вино́?   Его́ зову́т Ва́ня?
Э́то кни́га?   Тебя́ зову́т А́ня?
Э́то она́?   Э́то ты?
Э́то вы?   Э́то он?
                                  Э́то Са́ша?

**The Pravda Publishing House (издательство Правда)
with the editorial offices of three newspapers**

УРО́К ВТОРО́Й

ТЕ́КСТ: ПЕРЕДА́ЙТЕ, ПОЖА́ЛУЙСТА, ИКРУ́.

1. Lena and Zyuzya are still studying Russian.

Зю́зя: Дава́й де́лать на́ши упражне́ния. *(She hands Lena a batch of pictures)* Спроси́ меня́, кто́ э́то.

Ле́на: Кто́ э́то?

Зю́зя: Э́то Пётр Пе́рвый, ру́сский ца́рь.

Ле́на: А э́то?

Зю́зя: Э́то Джо́рдж Ва́шингто́н, пе́рвый америка́нский президе́нт.

Ле́на: А э́то?

Зю́зя: Э́то Валенти́на Терешко́ва, пе́рвая же́нщина-космона́вт.

Ле́на: Хорошо́, Зю́зя, молоде́ц. Что́ э́то?

Зю́зя: Э́то америка́нский фла́г.

Ле́на: А э́то?

Зю́зя: Э́то англи́йский фла́г.

Ле́на: О́чень хорошо́. А э́то како́й фла́г?

Зю́зя: Э́то...э́то, ка́жется, алба́нский фла́г.

Ле́на: Не́т, Зю́зя, э́то не алба́нский, а болга́рский фла́г.

2. They are interrupted by the doorbell. It turns out that Ivan Petrovich has invited two guests to breakfast. He brings them to Lena's room to meet Zyuzya.

Ива́н Петро́вич: Зю́зя, э́то Шу́ра и[1] Ю́ра, мои́ молоды́е колле́ги. Мы́ рабо́таем вме́сте. *(To Shura and Yura)* Э́то Зю́зя. А э́то моя́ до́чка Ле́на.

Зю́зя: Здра́вствуйте. О́чень прия́тно.

Шу́ра и Ю́ра (хо́ром): О́чень прия́тно.

Ле́на: Сади́тесь, пожа́луйста.[2]

(Все́[3] садя́тся. Па́уза.)

Зю́зя: *(showing a picture to the guests in an attempt to entertain them)* Кто́ э́то?

Шу́ра: Я́ не зна́ю.

Зю́зя: А э́то?

Ю́ра: Я́ не зна́ю.

Зю́зя: А кто́ э́то?

Шу́ра и Ю́ра (хо́ром): Мы́ не зна́ем.

Зю́зя: *(to Lena)* Они́ ничего́[4] не[5] зна́ют! *(To the guests)* Где́ вы рабо́таете?

Ю́ра: Мы́ рабо́таем в секре́тном институ́те. Приходи́те сего́дня[4] в на́ш институ́т.[6] Ива́н Петро́вич зна́ет, где́ э́то.

Зю́зя: Спаси́бо, с удово́льствием. *(To Ivan Petrovich)* А где́ Ни́на Степа́новна? Она́ до́ма?

Иван Петрович: Да, Лена, где мама?
Лена: Мама дома. Завтрак, наверно, уже на столе.[6]

3. *Indeed, the door opens and Nina Sergeyevna invites everybody to the dining room.*

      (Всё садятся.)

Зюзя: Где мой нож?
Лена: Вот[7] твой нож, справа.
Зюзя: А где моя вилка?
Лена: Вилка здесь, слева.
Зюзя: А моя ложка?
Лена: А ложка напротив.
Иван Петрович: А где вино?
Нина Степановна: Всё в порядке, Ваня. Вино на столе.
Иван Петрович: А, вот оно!
Нина Степановна: Зюзя, передайте, пожалуйста, икру.
Зюзя: Вот, пожалуйста.[8]
Нина Степановна: Спасибо, Зюзя.
Иван Петрович: *(lifting his glass)* Ваше здоровье.
Всё (хором): Ваше здоровье.

Vocabulary

    Nouns and adjectives will henceforth be listed in their Nominative case forms (dictionary forms), either singular or plural, regardless of the form the words have in the text.

второй second
передайте pass
икра caviar
давай let's
делать (to) do
наш our
упражнения exercises
первый first
русский Russian
царь tsar
американский American
президент president
женщина woman
космонавт cosmonaut
флаг flag
английский English
кажется it seems
    Это, кажется,
    албанский флаг. I think
    that's the Albanian flag.
албанский Albanian
болгарский Bulgarian
молодые young
коллеги colleagues

мы we
работаем (we) work
вместе together
дочка daughter
хор chorus
  хором in chorus
садитесь sit down
всё everybody
садятся (they) sit down
пауза pause
знаю (I) know
знаем (we) know
ничего nothing
они they
знают (they) know
знаете (you) know
работаете (you) work
секретный secret
в in; to
институт institute
приходите come
сегодня today
знает (he, she) knows

с with
удово́льствие pleasure
  с удово́льствием I'd be
  glad to (Lit., 'with pleasure').
до́ма at home
за́втрак breakfast
наве́рно probably
уже́ already
на on
сто́л table
тво́й your (informal)
но́ж knife
спра́ва on the right
ви́лка fork

сле́ва on the left
ло́жка spoon
напро́тив opposite, across the
  way, over there
поря́док order
  Всё в поря́дке. Everything's
  OK.
во́т here
оно́ it
спаси́бо thanks
ва́ш your (formal)
здоро́вье health (neuter)
  Ва́ше здоро́вье! Cheers!
  Here's to you!

COMMENTS

1. и vs. а

The basic meaning of the word и is 'addition, also'.

Э́то Шу́ра и Ю́ра.   This is Shura and (also) Yura.

You have alreadly learned that the word а can be translated
'and', e.g.

Меня́ зову́т Пе́тя. А тебя́? My name's Pete. *And* yours?

Notice that it doesn't make any sense to substitute the word
also for *and* in this sentence, i.e., you can't say 'My name's
Pete. Also yours?' The same thing is true for Russian: you
can't substitute и for а in the above sentence. If, on the
other hand, you are making a list of things, simply adding
things together, you can indeed use *also*, e.g. 'I want eggs,
cheese and *also* butter. It is in this situation that you
have to use и rather than а in Russian:

Он предста́вил Шу́ру,   He introduced Shura, Yura
  Ю́ру, и Ми́шу.   and (also) Misha.
Я чита́ла и писа́ла.   I read and (also) wrote.
Зю́зя, э́то Шу́ра и Ю́ра. Zyuzya, this is Shura and
                       (also) Yura.

Ле́на у́чит Зю́зю говори́ть, Lena teaches Zyuzya to speak,
  чита́ть и писа́ть   read, and (also) write in
  по-ру́сски.   Russian.

Compare:

Шу́ра и Ю́ра зде́сь.   Shura and (also) Yura are
                 here.

Шу́ра зде́сь, а Ю́ра та́м. Shura is here, and (but) Yura
                 is there.

Sometimes, as in the last example above, the word а can be
translated as either 'and' or 'but'. Sometimes the translation 'and' is impossible, e.g.,

Это не о́н, а она́.   That's not (a) he, *but rather*
                               (a) she.
Это не Шу́ра, а Ю́ра.   That's not Shura, but (rather)
                               Yura.

2. Spelling exception: пожа́луйста.

Pronounce as though spelled "пажа́лста", with the letters
-уй- left unpronounced.

3. всé vs. всё

These words mean 'all'. Всé is plural and means 'all' in
the sense of 'everybody'; всё is neuter, singular and means
'all' in the sense of 'everything'.

Всé садя́тся.   Everybody sits down.
Всé говори́ли по-ру́сски.   Everybody spoke Russian.
Всё хорошо́.   Everything's OK (fine).
Всё в поря́дке.   Everything's OK (in order).
Всё бы́ло о́чень прия́тно.   Everything was very pleasant.
Всё на столе́.   Everything is on the table.

Compare:

Всé здéсь.   Everybody's here.
Всё здéсь.   Everything's here.

4. Spelling exception: ничего́, сего́дня.

Pronounce as though spelled "ничиво́" and "сиво́дня", with
the letter г pronounced /v/. See Lesson 1, Text A, Comment
4.

5. Double Negatives.

This sentence means 'They don't know anything' or 'They
know nothing', literally 'They don't know nothing'. English
forbids double negatives; Russian requires them.

6. The prepositions в and на.

The meaning of these prepositions depends on the form of the
noun that follows.

The preposition в followed by a noun in the Prepositional
case form (в институ́те) means '(located) in, at'; if it
is followed by a noun in the Accusative form (в институ́т)
it means '(motion) to, into'.

Мы́ рабо́таем в институ́те.   We work *in* an institute.
Приходи́те в на́ш институ́т.   Come *to* our institute.

The preposition на works the same way:

на столе́(Prepositional)	'(located) on the table'
на сто́л (Accusative)	'(motion) onto the table'

Всё на столе́.	Everything's on the table.
Она́ положи́ла всё на сто́л.	She put everything on(to) the table.

The contrast between Prepositional and Accusative will be discussed in greater detail in Lesson 3.

The word институ́т has two meanings: (1) institute of technology, where students study, and (2) a think tank, where research workers devise plans and apparatus for the government. It has only the latter meaning when used with the adjective секре́тный.

7. во́т VS. зде́сь.

The word во́т is used for pointing out things. It is translated as 'Here (it is)' 'There (it is)', like French *voici* or *voilà*. It means something like the obsolete English words *behold!*, *lo!*

Compare:

Во́т вино́.	Here's/There's the wine. (Behold!)
Вино́ зде́сь.	The wine is here. (It is located here.)

When you hand something to somebody you can say both во́т and пожа́луйста (see also Comment 8):

Са́ша: Переда́й, пожа́луйста, икру́.	Pass the caviar, please.
Ма́ша: Пожа́луйста.	Here you are.
OR: Пожа́луйста, во́т икра́.	
OR: Во́т, пожа́луйста.	

The word зде́сь cannot be used in this situation; it means 'located in this place' and is a response to где́ "where?", like French *ici*.

Са́ша: Где́ икра́?	Where's the caviar?
Ма́ша: Икра́ зде́сь.	The caviar is here.
OR: Во́т икра́.	Here's/There's the caviar. (handing it or pointing to it).
OR: Икра́ во́т зде́сь.	The caviar's right here.

8. When to use пожа́луйста.

   This word is used in three situations:

   (a) in making polite requests, like English *please*;
   (b) in acceding to another's wish, in positive response to re-
       quests like 'Hand me the screwdriver', 'Close the door',
       etc. English uses various phrases like *sure, be glad to,
       here you are*, etc.
   (c) in response to спаси́бо 'thanks', like English *You're
       welcome*.

   Са́ша: Переда́йте, пожа́луйста,   Pass the caviar,
         икру́.   *please.*   (a)
   Ма́ша: Пожа́луйста.   *Sure*/Here you are.   (b)
   Са́ша: Спаси́бо.   Thanks.
   Ма́ша: Пожа́луйста.   *You're welcome.*   (c)

   You may be surprised that, although it's breakfast time, our
   family eats caviar and drinks wine. Russians eat anything
   for breakfast, and some people even have a regular three-
   course meal. Naturally, Ivan Petrovich, who is a mere guard
   at the secret institute, doesn't normally eat caviar for breakfast. Presumably the two young officers stopped off at the
   government store along the way in order to be able to welcome
   Zyuzya with truly Russian hospitality.

- Переда́йте, пожа́луйста, икру́.
- Пожа́луйста. Почему вилки справа?

DIALOGS FOR MEMORIZATION

F 1. Преподаватель: Máша, ктó э́то?
     Máша: Э́то Cáша.
     Преподаватель: Предста́вьте меня́, пожа́луйста.
     Máша: Cáша, э́то мóй преподава́тель,
                    (name and patronymic)

     Преподаватель: О́чень прия́тно.
     Cáша: О́чень прия́тно.
     Преподаватель: Ната́ша, ктó предста́вил Cáшу?   (m)
     Ната́ша: Cáшу предста́вила Máша.   (f)

T 2. Преподаватель: Máша, гдé икра́?
W   Máша: Икра́ на столе́.
     Преподаватель: Попроси́те у негó икру́. (Pointing to   request — of him.
                    Sasha.)
     Máша: Cáша, переда́й,   пожа́луйста, икру́.
     Cáша: Вóт, пожа́луйста. (Passing it to her.)
     Máша: Спаси́бо.
     Cáша: Пожа́луйста.
     Máша: Переда́й и винó тóже.[1]
     Cáша: Вóт онó.
     Преподаватель: Ната́ша, ктó переда́л икру́?
     Ната́ша: Икру́ переда́л Cáша.

F 3. Преподаватель: Ктó учи́л Зю́зю чита́ть и писа́ть
                    по-ру́сски?
     Cáша: Зю́зю учи́ла Лéна.
     Преподаватель: А ктó учи́л Лéну?
     Cáша: Лéну учи́ли пáпа и мáма.
     Преподаватель: А ктó учи́л вáс?
     Cáша: Меня́ учи́л преподава́тель в университéте.

M 4. *Useful Expressions:*
     Повтори́те хóром.
     Всé вмéсте.
     Ещё рáз.[2]
     Да́льше.
     Э́то вторóй урóк.
     Спроси́те[3] егó, кáк егó зову́т.
     Спроси́те её, кáк её зову́т.
     Попроси́те[3] у негó икру́.
     Попроси́те у неё икру́.

Translation

1. Teacher: Masha, who's that?
   Masha: That's Sasha;
   Teacher: Introduce me, please.
   Masha: Sasha, this is my teacher, (name).
   Teacher: Pleased to meet you.
   Masha: Pleased to meet you.
   Teacher: Natasha, who introduced Sasha?
   Natasha: Sasha was introduced by Masha. (=Masha introduced Sasha.)

2. Teacher: Masha, where's the caviar?
   Masha: The caviar is on the table.
   Teacher: Ask him for the caviar. (Lit. 'Request of him the caviar.')
   Masha: Sasha, pass the caviar, please.
   Sasha: Here you are.
   Masha: Thanks.
   Sasha: You're welcome.
   Masha: Pass the wine, too.
   Sasha: Here it is.
   Teacher: Natasha, who passed the caviar?
   Natasha: Sasha passed the caviar.

3. Teacher: Who taught Zyuzya to read and write in Russian?
   Sasha: Zyuzya was taught by Lena. (=Léna taught Zyuzya.)
   Teacher: And who taught Lena?
   Sasha: Lena was taught by (her) dad and mom.
   Teacher: And who taught you?
   Sasha: I was taught by (my) teacher at the university.

4. *Useful   expressions*
   Repeat in chorus.
   All together.
   Again. Once more.
   Keep going. Continue.
     (Lit. 'further'.)
   This is the second lesson.

   Ask him what his name is.
   Ask her what her name is.
   Ask him for the caviar.
   Ask her for the caviar.

ACTIVE WORD LIST

#-nouns (Masculine)

преподава́тель	teacher (male)
университе́т	university
в университе́те	at the university
сто́л	table
на столе́	on the table
слова́рь *	dictionary
ка́мень *	stone
фла́г ^{2} *	flag
но́ж^2 *	knife
уро́к	lesson
хо́р	chorus
хо́ром	in chorus
ра́з	time, occurrence

a-nouns (Feminine)

икра́	caviar
ды́ня*	melon
ви́лка *	fork
ло́жка *	spoon
па́па	father, dad
ма́ма	mother, mom
преподава́тельница *	teacher (female)

Imperatives

попроси́(те)	request, ask for
Попроси́ у него́ X.	Ask him for X. (Lit., Ask of him X.)
Попроси́ у неё X.	Ask her for X. (Lit., Ask of her X.)
спроси́(те)	inquire, ask
переда́й(те)	pass, hand
предста́вь(те)	introduce
возьми́(те) *	take

Past tense

переда́л, передала́	passed, handed
взя́л, взяла́ *	took
учи́л(а)	taught
предста́вил(а)	introduced
чита́л(а) *	read
ви́дел(а) *	saw

Infinitives

чита́ть	(to) read
писа́ть	(to) write
говори́ть *	(to) speak

Misc.

в	in, at
на	on
вóт	here (it is), there (it is)
спасúбо	thanks
и...тóже	too
и	and
ктó	who
онó	it (Nominative)
óн *	it, he (Nominative)
онá *	it, she (Nominative)
егó	it, him (Accusative)
её	it, her (Accusative)
всé	everybody, all
слéва *	on the left
спрáва *	on the right
напрóтив[2] *	opposite, across the way
пéрвый *	first
вторóй	second
мóй	my
прийтно	pleasant
вмéсте	together
ещё	still
дáльше	further
знáю *	(I) know
знáете *	(you) know

COMMENTS

1. too, also

There are two ways of expressing 'too, also' in Russian:
(1)   X тóже...
(2)   ...и X (тóже)

Examples:

(1)   Сáша рабóтает в инститýте. Пáша тóже тáм
      рабóтает. Sasha works at the institute. Pasha works
      there too.

(2)   Сáша рабóтает в инститýте. Он рабóтает и
      в университéте (тóже). Sasha works at the insti-
      tute. He works at the university too.

In (2) the word тóже is optional; 'also' is expressed by и.
(See Text Comment 1.) The rule of thumb for using тоже vs.
и is:

(1) If you change something at the beginning of the sentence
(Сáша ⟶ Пáша), use тóже alone, with heavy stress;
(2) If you change something at the end of the sentence (i.e.,
the "punch line:" в инститýте ⟶ в университéте), use
и, with or without тóже at the end.

Further examples:

(1)   Мáша передалá винó.

      Сáша тóже передáл винó.   Sasha too/also passed the
                                           wine.
(2)   Передáйте, пожáлуйста, икрý.

      Передáйте и винó (тóже). Pass the wine too.

2. Pronunciation: word-final devoicing and assimilation

Many consonants come in voiced-voiceless pairs. When you produce a *voiced* consonant, the vocal cords are buzzing. Thus, *z*
and *s* are voiced and voiceless partners, respectively.

Similarly,

voiced:	б д г в з ж
voiceless:	п т к ф с ш

At the end of a phrase, i.e., when you pause, read the voiced
letters as voiceless.

Read:	*as though spelled:*	
флáг	"флáк"	flag
нóж	"нóш "	knife
рáз	"рáс "	time
напрóтив	"напрóтиф"	over there
предстáвь	"притстáфь"	introduce

(The rule doesn't apply to р л м н because they have no
voiceless partners.)

The same alternation takes place within a word: in a cluster
of consonants it is the voicing of the last consonant that de-
termines the voicing of the preceding ones. This is like English *raspberry*, in which the voiced *b* causes the letter *s* to
be pronounced like *z* (voicing), or like *extra*, in which the
voiceless *t* causes the letter *x* to be pronounced like *ks* (devoicing) rather than *gz* (exam). This phenomenon is called
assimilation.

Examples:

предстáвьте	=	"притстáфьте "	introduce
лóжка	=	"лóшка "	spoon

Although в *gets* devoiced (предстáвьте ="притстáфьти"), it
does not *cause* assimilation; буква, for example, is pronounced
as it is spelled (the в does *not* cause the letter к to be
pronounced г).

In fast speech, voicing assimilation takes place between words,
e.g.,

Кáк вáс зовýт? = "ваззавýт "(with сз pronounced "зз")

3. Спросúте егó vs. попросúте у негó

Note that there are two different expressions corresponding
to English *ask:*

(a) спросúте егó/её   ask him/her (inquire)
(b) попросúте у негó/у неё   ask him/her *for* (request)

(a) Спросú егó, гдé винó.   Ask him where the wine is
                                (inquire).

(b) Попросú у негó винó.   Ask him *for* the wine
                                (request).

ANALYSIS

M 1. Palatalization and noun endings: Review

In Lesson 1 it was pointed out that the symbol ь (мя́гкий
зна́к) has no sound of its own; it is used to indicate palatalization of the preceding consonant, as in ца́рь /tsár̦/
'czar.' The grammatical consequences of this are that a noun
spelled with ь at the end has the same grammatical *ending* as
a noun spelled without ь. The noun ца́рь belongs to the
same declension class as the noun стака́н and it has the
same ending, namely -# (zero). Here are some more examples:

Cyrillic:	*stem + ending:*	
ца́рь	tsár̦-#	czar
преподава́тель	pr̦ipadaváțil̦-#	teacher
ка́мень	kám̦in̦-#	stone
слова́рь	slavár̦-#	dictionary

Here are some more examples illustrating the fact that Cyrillic -a and -я represent the same grammatical ending (Lesson 1, Analysis 4.1), with я indicating palatalization of
the consonant of the *stem*:

дь́ня	dín̦-a	melon
А́ня	án̦-a	Annie

M 2. Cyrillic й

The letter й stands for the consonant sound /y/ as in *yes,
boy*.

Examples:

мо́й	/móy/	my (masculine)
тво́й	/tvóy/	your (informal, masculine)

пе́рвый	/p̦érviy/	first
переда́йте	/p̦ir̦idáyți/	pass

If you examine all of the occurrences of й in the above list,
you will notice that it occurs only when no vowel follows it,
i.e., it occurs only at the end of a word or before another
consonant. The reason for this is that the Cyrillic writing
system has two different ways of representing the sound /y/:

(1) й when no vowel follows (e.g., мо́й /móy/)
(2) palatal indicator when a vowel follows (e.g., моя́ /mayá/).

Thus, the palatal indicators и е я ё ю serve two functions: they indicate either:

(1) palatalization of the preceding consonant (See Lesson 1, Analysis 4.1, e.g., тя = /ṭa/), or

(2) the sound /y/ (e.g., моя́ = /mayá/).

This system of writing the sound /y/ with palatal indicators is very economical, because it saves space on the page: instead of using four letters to write /mayá/, you need only three. In other words, instead of writing мойа́ for /mayá/, Cyrillic writes моя́. However, there's a price paid for this economy: the division between stem and ending is obscured. Compare the masculine, feminine, and neuter gender forms of the word for 'my' (more will be said about gender in the next section):

    мо́й

    моя́

    моё

If one looks only at the spelling of this word, one might come to the erroneous conclusion that the *stem* of this word is мо- and that the three *endings* are -й, -я, -ё. The fact is, however, that the endings of this word are really the same ones you have already learned for nouns, namely, -# (zero), -a, and -o, as in стака́н, икра́, and вино́.

spelled:	*pronounced:*	*stem + ending:*
мо́й	"мо́й"	мо́у-#
моя́	"майа́"	may-á
моё	"майо́"	may-ó

In sum, if you understand the two tricks of Cyrillic, palatalization (Lesson 1) and writing the sound /y/, Russian grammar is enormously simplified; endings are simpler than a superficial glance at Cyrillic would lead you to believe.

Here are some further examples of the use of the palatal indicators и, е, я, ё, ю:

(1) To indicate palatalization of the preceding consonant:

не́т	/ṇét/	no
газе́та	/gaẓéta/	newspaper
меня́	/miṇá/	me
Зю́зя	/ẓúza/	Zyuzya
спроси́	/spraṣí/	ask

всё	/fşé/	everybody
всё	/fşó/	everything
напро́тив	/napróţif/	over there

(2) To indicate the sound /y/:

прия́тно	/pŗiyátna/	pleasant
кака́я	/kakáya/	which, what (feminine)
како́е	/kakóya/	which, what (neuter)
яйцо́	/yiytsó/	egg
упражне́ния	/uprazhņéņiya/	exercises
рабо́таем	/rabótayim/	(we) work
зна́ю	/znáyu/	(I) know
зна́ете	/znáyiţi/	(you) know
зна́ют	/znáyut/	(they) know

Now compare plain indicators with palatal indicators at the beginning of a word: the plain indicators, of course, represent vowels alone (with no /y/ sound), while the palatal indicators represent the vowel preceded by the /y/ sound.

э vs. е <	э́то	/éta/	this, that
	ест	/yest/	he eats
а vs. я <	а	/a/	and
	я	/ya/	I
о vs. ё <	о́н	/on/	he
	ёж	/yosh/	hedgehog
у vs. ю <	у́чит	/úchit/	teaches
	Ю́ра	/yúra/	Yura

EXCEPTION:
At the beginning of a word the palatal indicator и stands for /i/, not /yi/. (Its plain partner ы never occurs at the beginning of a word.)

(ы) и	и	/i/	and, also
	Ива́н	/iván/	Ivan
	икра́	/ikrá/	caviar
	институ́т	/inşţitút/	institute

NOTE ON PRONUNCIATION:

In list (2), above, note that the last vowel of кака́я and како́е is /a/. This is the end-of-the-word exception to the unstressed vowel rule stated in Lesson 1.4.2. The letters я and е sound like the unstressed *a* in *sofa* in the endings of nouns and adjectives. See also the note in section 3.2, below, on the identical pronunciation of ва́ша and ва́ше.

3. Gender

3.1 Nouns and pronouns.

The gender of a noun controls the choice of a pronoun used to refer back to it.

masculine Где Саша? -Вот он!	Where's Sasha? There *he* is!
vs. feminine Где Маша? -Вот она!	Where's Masha? There *she* is!

A Russian noun will be one of three genders — masculine, feminine or neuter. The corresponding pronoun forms are:

он	he, it	(referring to a masculine noun)
она	she, it	(referring to a feminine noun)
оно	it	(referring to a neuter noun)

Где стакан?	— Вот он!	Where's the glass? There it is!
Где ручка?	— Вот она!	Where's the pen? There it is!
Где вино?	— Вот оно!	Where's the wine? There it is!

The above examples illustrate the following facts:

(1) The endings of the pronouns are the same as the noun endings of the three declension classes:

-# (masculine)	стакан-#	он-#
-а (feminine)	ручк-а	он-а
-о (neuter)	вин-о	он-о

(2) Nouns of the #-class are masculine; nouns of the o-class are neuter, and, with certain exceptions, nouns of the a-class are feminine.

The main exception is men's nicknames like Саша, Миша, Ваня Юра, etc. They belong to the a-declension class, but they are of the masculine gender, as illustrated in the first example in this section, above.

There are a few a-declension nouns which can be either masculine *or* feminine, depending on the sex of its referent, e.g., коллега:

Она моя коллега.	She's my colleague.
Он мой коллега.	He's my colleague.

PRACTICE 1

Answer the following questions with the sentence "Here he/she/ it is,' e.g. Где миша? — Вот он!

Где кольцо?	Где словарь?	Где икра?	Где Зюзя?
Где письмо?	Где карандаш?	Где Аня?	Где флаг?
Где бумага?	Где конверт?	Где Маша?	Где Саша?
Где папа?	Где мама?	Где мел?	Где яйцо?
Где камень?	Где нож?		

3.2 Nouns and Adjectives

The gender of a noun also controls the form of the adjective
that modifies it. Thus, adjectives are said to *agree with*
nouns:

masculine:	Э́то мо́й стака́н.	That's my glass.
vs. feminine:	Э́то моя́ ру́чка.	That's my pen.
vs. neuter:	Э́то моё кольцо́.	That's my ring.

There are two kinds of adjectives in Russian: *special* adjectives and *ordinary* adjectives.

The words for *my* and *your* are special adjectives:

	my	*my (informal)*	*your (formal)*
masc.	мо́й	тво́й	ва́ш
fem.	моя́	твоя́	ва́ша
neut.	моё	твоё	ва́ше

Their endings are identical to the endings of the three noun
classes: -#, -a, -o (spelled with the letters а/я, о/е—
see Lesson 1.4.1).

Э́то ва́ш стака́н.   That's your glass.
Э́то ва́ша ру́чка.   That's your pen.
Э́то ва́ше кольцо́.   That's your ring.

> Note on pronunciation: the forms ва́ша and
> ва́ше do not differ in pronunciation.

Ordinary adjectives — the overwhelming majority of adjectives
— have the following endings, similar, though not identical,
to noun endings:

	what, which	
masc.	како́й	
fem.	кака́я	/а́ча/
neut.	како́е	/о́уа/

Similarly, второ́й/втора́я/второ́е, *second*.

If the adjective has stress on the stem rather than on the
ending, the masculine form is -ый rather than -о́й.

	first
masc.	пе́рвый
fem.	пе́рвая
neut.	пе́рвое

> Note on pronunciation: пе́рвая and пе́рвое
> do not differ in pronunciation, as their
> endings are not stressed. See the note
> on pronunciation at the end of section 2,
> above.

Examples:

Где́ стака́н?	Како́й стака́н?	Which glass?
Где́ ру́чка?	Кака́я ру́чка?	Which pen?
Где́ письмо́?	Како́е письмо́?	Which letter?
Где́ Ми́ша?	Како́й Ми́ша?	Which Mike?
Где́ Ма́ша?	Кака́я Ма́ша?	Which Masha?
Како́й преподава́тель?		Which teacher?
Второ́й преподава́тель.		The second teacher.
Пе́рвый преподава́тель.		The first teacher.
Втора́я преподава́тельница.		The second (woman) teacher.
Пе́рвая преподава́тельница.		The first (woman) teacher.

PRACTICE 2

Read these sentences aloud. Translate. Say whether the nouns is masculine, feminine, or neuter.

(H)
[MAYA]

Како́й э́то уро́к?
Э́то пе́рвый уро́к.
Э́то второ́й уро́к.
Э́то моя́ икра́.
Э́то моя́ колле́га.   f
Э́то мо́й колле́га.   m
Э́то ва́ш па́па?
Э́то ва́ша ды́ня.
Моё вино́ на столе́.
Э́то ва́ше вино́?
Спроси́те Са́шу, где́ мо́й стака́н.
Э́то како́й фла́г?
Э́то моя́ газе́та.
Э́то мо́й слова́рь.
Како́й э́то университе́т?

---

4. Past tense

The past tense endings are identical to the endings you have already learned for nouns, pronouns, and special adjectives (the ваш type): -#, -a, -o, plus the plural -и:

я (masc)	ты (masc)	он предста́вил :	I, you, he introduced
я (fem)	ты (fem)	она предста́вила:	I, you, she introduced
		оно предста́вило:	it introduced
мы	вы	они предста́вили:	we, you, they introduced

As you can see, the past tense agrees with the gender (or sex) of the subject, except for вы, which always takes a plural verb ending, even if you're speaking to only one person. Examples:

Вы́ предста́вили Са́шу?	Did you introduce Sasha?
Ты́ предста́вил Са́шу?	Did you (male) introduce Sasha?
Ты́ предста́вила Са́шу?	Did you (female) introduce Sasha?
Я́ предста́вил Са́шу.	I (male) introduced Sasha.
Я́ предста́вила Са́шу.	I (female) introduced Sasha.
О́н предста́вил Са́шу.	He introduced Sasha.
Она́ предста́вила Са́шу.	She introduced Sasha.
Они́ предста́вили Са́шу.	They introduced Sasha.
Ма́ша предста́вила Са́шу.	Masha introduced Sasha.
Са́ша предста́вил Ма́шу.	Sasha introduced Masha.

Notice the last example: the verb is masculine because
Sasha is of the masculine *gender* (don't be deceived by the
fact that Sasha is of the a-declension class). Past tense
verbs, in other words, work just like adjectives.

	Adjective	*Noun*	*Verb*
feminine	Ва́ша	ма́ма	предста́вила Ма́шу.
masculine	Ва́ш	па́па	предста́вил Ма́шу.
	Ва́ш	преподава́тель	предста́вил Ма́шу.

Watch out for the plural form of the past tense; it is always spelled with the palatal indicator и, which means
that the preceding consonant is palatalized /l̩/, whereas
the other three forms have plain /l/. Both of these sounds,
/l/ and /l̩/, are very difficult for English speakers to
learn. (See exercise 17).

Stems

Russian and English both exhibit some radical changes in the
form of the stem as you go from one tense to another. In
English, for example, the stem changes as you go from *take*
to *took*. In Russian we find a similar change in the verb
'take.' Its imperative form is возьми́, while its past
form is взя́л. Don't worry about these changes for now;
we'll take them up later. As in English, most verbs do *not*
undergo such radical changes.

The suffix -л-

In the past tense (предста́вил) it is the -л- that renders
the meaning "past." Here are other examples of past tense
verb forms; note that all contain the suffix -л-. Watch
out for shifts in the stress, as in the first two examples.

взя́л	взяла́	взя́ло	взя́ли	took
переда́л	передала́	переда́ло	переда́ли	passed
чита́л	чита́ла	чита́ло	чита́ли	read, was reading
писа́л	писа́ла	писа́ло	писа́ли	wrote, was writing
ви́дел	ви́дела	ви́дело	ви́дели	saw

⌐5. Nominative vs. Accusative case

5.1. The forms and functions of the Accusative

Nouns, along with the adjectives that modify them, change their endings according to their function in the sentence. Compare:

(1) Кни́га зде́сь.   The book is here.
(2) Переда́й кни́гу.   Pass (me) the book.

In sentence (1), кни́га is the subject of the sentence, as indicated by its Nominative case ending -a. In (2), кни́гу is the direct object of the sentence, as indicated by its Accusative case ending -y.

Now observe that the modifying adjective changes its form to agree with the noun:

Моя́ кни́га зде́сь.   My book is here.
Переда́й мою́ кни́гу. Pass (me) my book.

Similarly,

Где́ кни́га? —Кака́я кни́га?   What book? (Nom.)
Переда́й кни́гу! —Каку́ю кни́гу? What book? (Acc.)

In our discussion of Cyrillic we pointed out that the members of matching pairs of plain and palatal indicators are grammatically equivalent, e.g., a = я, у = ю, etc. Thus, if we substitute a noun whose stem ends in a palatalized consonant (дъ́ня /dín̦-a/) for the word кни́га /kn̦íg-a/ in the above examples, we get the Accusative дъ́ню, with -ю instead of -y.

Моя́ дъ́ня здесь.   My melon is here.
Переда́й дъ́ню! —Каку́ю дъ́ню? Pass the melon. —Which melon?

RULE: The Accusative ending for a-declension nouns is -y.

Spelling: If the Nominative ends in -я the Accusative will end in -ю rather than -y. E.g., дъ́ня, дъ́ню.

Further examples:

Переда́йте, пожа́луйста, икру́.   Pass the caviar, please.
                  газе́ту.   newspaper
                  ру́чку.   pen
                  дъ́ню.   melon
Спроси́те, пожа́луйста, Ми́шу.   Ask Mĭsha, please.
                  Ма́шу.   Masha
                  ма́му.   Mom
                  А́ню.   Annie
Предста́вьте Ма́шу.   Introduce Masha.
          С̧а́шу.   Sasha.
          А́ню.   Annie

The other noun classes, -# declension (стакáн) and о-declension (винó), make no distinction between Nominative and Accusative, provided that the noun refers to an inanimate object (like стакáн), as opposed to an animate being (like преподавáтель). We shall take up animate Accusatives in a later Lesson, so avoid them for the time being. Thus, the noun стакáн, along with its modifying adjectives, has the same form when subject of the sentence as it does when it is the direct object:

Nom.	Стакáн здéсь.	The glass is here
Acc.	Передáй стакáн.	Pass the glass.

Nom.	Мóй стакáн здéсь.	My glass is here.
Acc.	Передáй мóй стакáн.	Pass my glass.

Nom.	Гдé стакáн?	Where's the glass?
	—Какóй стакáн?	—What glass?
Acc.	Передáй стакáн!	Pass the glass!
	—Какóй стакáн?	—What glass?

Nom.	Гдé винó?	Where's the wine?
	—Какóе винó?	—What wine?
Acc.	Передáй винó!	Pass the wine!
	—Какóе винó?	—What wine?

Further examples of Accusative forms:

Передáйте, пожáлуйста, письмó.	Pass the letter, please.
Передáйте, пожáлуйста, кáмень.	Pass the stone, please.
Возьмúте кнúгу.	Take the book.
Возьмúте нóж.	Take the knife.
Попросúте у неё карандáш.	Ask her for the pencil.
Попросúте у неё письмó.	Ask her for the letter.
Попросúте у неё дьíню.	Ask her for the melon.
Попросúте у неё вúлку.	Ask her for the fork.

The feminine Accusative forms of special adjectives (the ваш type) are identical to noun endings:

Nom.	Acc.	
вáша/моя́ дьíня	вáшу/мою́ дьíню	your/my melon
вáша/моя́ кнúга	вáшу/мою́ кнúгу	your/my book

Ordinary adjectives (the какóй type) double the vowel, i.e., - ую instead of - у.

какáя дьíня	какýю дьíню	which melon
пéрвая дьíня	пéрвую дьíню	the first melon
вторáя кнúга	вторýю кнúгу	the second book

You have met the Accusative forms of the personal pronouns in the sentence, Как вас зовут? (literally, 'How [do they] call *you?*)

Nom.	*Acc.*	
я	меня	me
ты	тебя	you
он		
оно }	его	him, it (masc. and neut.)
она	её	her, it (fem.)
вы	вас	you

Note that there is no distinction between masculine and neuter: both are его.

Вы передали стакан? (masc.)	Did you pass the glass?
—Да, я его передала.	Yes, I passed it.
Вы передали вино? (neut.)	Did you pass the wine?
—Да, я его передала.	Yes, I passed it.
BUT:	
Вы передали икру? (fem.)	Did you pass the caviar?
—Да, я её передала.	Yes, I passed it.

Further examples of Accusative pronouns:

Как тебя зовут?	What is your name? (Familiar)
Как вас зовут?	What is your name? (Formal)
Меня зовут Миша.	My name is Misha.
Её зовут Нина.	Her name is Nina.
Его зовут Юра.	His name is Yura.

PRACTICE 3

Transform the questions 'Where is the X?' into imperative sentences meaning 'Pass the X, please.' The questions have Nominative case forms; your imperative sentence has Accusative.

Model: Где икра?
        →   Передайте, пожалуйста, икру.

Где вино?	Где моё вино?
Где ручка?	Где моя ручка?
Где стакан?	Где мой стакан?
Где камень?	Где мой карандаш?
Где дыня?	Где мой словарь?
Где ложка?	Где моё письмо?
Где вилка?	Где мой нож?
Где кольцо?	Где моя книга?

```
┌─────────────────────────────────────────┐
│                PRACTICE 4                 │
├─────────────────────────────────────────┤
│ Repeat Practice 3, but use a pronoun      │
│ instead of the noun, e.g.                 │
│        Где́ мое́ вино́?                     │
│   →  Переда́йте его́, пожа́луйста.         │
└─────────────────────────────────────────┘
```

5.2 Case and Word Order

If you take the sentence Переда́й икру́ 'Pass the caviar'
and ask yourself why the Russian language bothers to mark
the direct object with the Accusative ending -y, the answer
may well be that there is no good reason for it — it's so
much useless baggage; after all, there's no other word in
the sentence that could be the direct object, so why bother
with case endings? However, observe the following dialog:

(1) Кто́ предста́вил Ма́шу?
(2) Ма́шу предста́вил Са́ша.

If you translate (2) word-for-word into English, it seems to
mean 'Masha introduced Sasha,' but this is wrong. Since
Ма́шу is marked with the Accusative ending -y, she must be
the direct object; since Са́ша is marked with the Nominative ending -a, he must be the subject. The sentence must
mean, therefore, "Sasha introduced Masha,' or, using the
English passive, 'Masha was introduced by Sasha.' In short,
Russian *case endings* are not useless baggage; case endings
tell you who does what to whom. In English, on the other
hand, it is *word order* that tells you who does what to whom.

In the English sentence 'Jake introduced Mike' you know who
introduced whom because the word Jake preceeds the verb
(hence is the subject) and the word Mike follows the verb
(hence is the object). If you reverse the word order, the
meaning changes: 'Mike introduced Jake.'

In Russian, if you reverse the word order, the basic meaning
does *not* change. In both of the following sentences it is
Jake who introduced Mike.

Я́ша предста́вил Ми́шу.
Ми́шу предста́вил Я́ша.   > Jake introduced Mike.

If you want to change the meaning and have Mike rather than
Jake do the introducing, you switch the *endings* on the nouns:

Я́шу предста́вил Ми́ша.
Ми́ша предста́вил Я́шу.   > Mike introduced Jake.

PRACTICE 5

Examine the following sentences and identify who is performing the action (i.e., which word is the Nominative subject) and to whom it is being done (i.e., which word is the Accusative direct object). Translate.

Са́ша предста́вил Ма́шу.
Ната́шу предста́вил Я́ша.
Па́шу предста́вила А́ня.
Ва́ня предста́вил Я́шу.

А́ню предста́вила Ма́ша.
Ма́шу предста́вил Па́ша.
Ната́ша предста́вила А́ню.
О́н её предста́вил.

---

6. Word Order

If word order, as we've seen above, is not significant in indicating subject vs. direct object in Russian, what *is* its function? Are there any rules for word order, or are you free to arrange words in the sentence in any order you choose?

The function of word order is to highlight the main part of your message and the general rule for this is to save the punch line till last. Our first example will be taken from the subject/direct object illustrations in the preceding section.

When you answer a question, your answer may be a short, one or two-word utterance or it may be a full sentence. For example,

Who introduced Masha?   —*Sasha.*
                OR: —*Sasha* introduced Masha.

The full sentence consists of (1) the *short answer* (Sasha), followed by (2) a *repetition* of the words in the question (...introduced Masha.) The "punch line" of this sentence, the part you want to highlight in your answer, is *Sasha* (we use the symbol ◜ to indicate main sentence stress — the most prominent syllable in the sentence).

> Who introduced Masha?   (1) —*Sásha*.
>   OR: (1 + 2) —*Sásha* introduced Masha.

Turning now to Russian, we see that the order of these elements in the full answer is reversed; instead of 1 + 2 in the full sentence, you use the order 2 + 1:

> Кто́ предста́вил Ма́шу?   (1) —Са́ша.
>   (2 + 1) —Ма́шу предста́вил Са́ша.

Notice that the punch line, the word with the main sentence stress, comes at the end of the sentence.

Further examples:

Кто́ взя́л кни́гу?   Who took the book?
short: —Ната́ша.   Natasha.
full: —Кни́гу взяла́ Ната́ша.   Natásha took the book.

Где́ Пе́тя?   Where's Pete?
short: —Та́м.   There.
full: —Пе́тя та́м.   Pete's thére.

Кто́ та́м?   Who's there?
short: —Пе́тя.   Pete.
full: —Та́м Пе́тя.   Péte's there.

Ка́к ва́с зову́т?   What's your name?
   —Меня́ зову́т Пе́тя.   My name is Péte.

Кто́ переда́л икру́?   Who passed the caviar?
   —Икру́ переда́л Са́ша.   Sásha passed the caviar.

Кто́ взя́л мою́ кни́гу?   Who took my book?
   —Ва́шу кни́гу взяла́   Natásha took (your) book.
        Ната́ша.

Кто́ попроси́л ды́ню?   Who asked for the melon?
   —Ды́ню попроси́ла Ма́ша.   Másha asked for the melon.

Кто́ учи́л Зю́зю писа́ть   Who taught Zyuzya to write
        по-ру́сски?   Russian?
   —Зю́зю учи́ла Ле́на.   Léna taught Zyuzya.

А кто́ учи́л ва́с?   And who taught you?
   —Меня́ учи́л па́па.   Pápa taught me.

W **7. Vowel Quality. Vowels next to palatalized consonants: /i/**

The quality of vowels is colored by neighboring consonants.
A particular vowel will sound one way after a plain consonant, and another way after a palatalized consonant.   An example of this is the Russian vowel we are transcribing as
/i/:   in the words спроси́ /spraşí/ 'ask,' or говори́ть
/gavaŗít/ 'to speak,' it sounds like the *i* in *machine*, but
in the words вы /vi/ 'you,' and ты /ti/ 'you,' it sounds
like no vowel in English. (The closest we come to it is the
i in *pit.)*

The /i/-variant after plain consonants (as in вы, ты) was
introduced in Lesson 1, Exercise 20.   It is made
with the tongue in the back of the mouth, like the *oo* in
English *tool,* but without rounding the lips. Practice in
front of the mirror by saying *too,* spreading your lips into
a smile before you start saying the word. If you can't control your facial muscles, put a finger in each corner of your
mouth to spread your lips. The result should sound something
like ты. Be sure to avoid rounding your lips; if you do
round them, you'll be making a dipthong, as in *Louie,* which
is quite wrong.

We will take up variants of other vowels in subsequent
lessons.

PRACTICE 6			
Imitate:			
МЫ	ДЫ	НЫ	СЫ
МИ	ДИ	НИ	СИ
МЫ	НЫ	БЫ	ВЫ
МИ	НИ	БИ	ВИ
алы́	лы	ары́	ры
али́	ли	ари́	ри

8. The rhythm of Russian speech

Stress

Long English words have two stresses, e.g. *cònstitútion*. Russian words also have two stresses, but with this difference: secondary stress always occurs *immediately before* the main stress, e.g., хорòшó. If there is no syllable before the main stress, then there is no secondary stress, e.g., здрáвствуйте.

English has a kind of bouncing *là-di-dá* rhythm, while Russian has more of a *crescendo-decrescendo* rhythm.

In addition to stress, there are two other factors which contribute to this *crescendo* effect: vowel quality and intonation.

Vowel quality

Vowels are more severely reduced in unstressed position than in pre-stressed position. They are extremely short and they differ in quality. The first two vowels in хорошо sound different: the first syllable has the sound [ə] as in _about_, _sofa_, while the second syllable has the sound [a] as in _father_:

$$\text{хорошó} = \text{[khəràshó]}$$

Thus, the opening of the mouth becomes progressively wider, the sound becomes louder, and the effect is that of a *crescendo*.

Intonation

The *crescendo* effect is enhanced by high pitch on the pre-stressed syllable in normal sentence intonation.

Compare the rhythm of the following English and Russian words and expressions. The first syllable of each Russian word contains the sound [ə].

УПРАЖНЕНИЯ

1. Review.

Say these sentences, using the informal imperative of the words in parentheses.

(1) (Open), пожалуйста, книгу.
(2) (Read), пожалуйста.
(3) (Repeat), пожалуйста.

Say them again, using the formal imperative.

2. Review.

Say these sentences, using the proper form of the verb "understand." Use the correct intonation contour on the verb.

(1) Вы _____ ?
(2) Нет, я не _____ .
(3) Ты _____ по-русски?
(4) Да, я _____ по-русски.

3. Переведи́те на ру́сский язы́к. (Translate into Russian.)

(a) Hello! What's you name (informal)? What's my name? My name is Ványa. And yours? My name is Natásha. And yours? My name is Ólya. And yours?

(b) How do you say 'wine' in Russian? 'Wine' in Russian is вино́. Where's the wine? The wine is here. How do you say 'newspaper' in Russian? 'Newspaper' in Russian is газе́та. Do you understand? Yes, I understand. No, I don't understand. Repeat, please.

(c) Is this a glass? No, it's not a glass, it's an egg. Is this a pencil? No, it's not a pencil, it's chalk. I don't understand. Repeat, please. This is a pencil. The pencil is here. And the chalk? The chalk is there. Very good. Goodbye.

4. Conversation topic.

Two students have a conversation based on the preceding exercise: (a) they get each others names, then (b) the first student asks how to say things in Russian, then (c) the second student gives the first one a quiz.

5. Reading Exercise. Cyrillic letters: ю у и н з в с.

П: Какáя э́то бýква?
С: Это — бýква ю.

Читáйте:

(а)

нóс	nose	лимóн	lemon	мúнус	minus
банáн	banana	машúна	machine	минýта	minute
бáнк	bank	пикнúк	picnic	лунá	moon
тóн	tone	капитáн	captain	инструмéнт	instrument
плáн	plan	пúнг-пóнг	pingpong	институ́т	institute
клúмат	climate	гитáра	guitar	диплóм	diploma

(б)

зóна	zone	сóда	soda	аспирúн	aspirin
рóза	rose	спóрт	sport	вúски	whisky
газéта	newspaper	сигáра	cigar	таксú	taxi
вáза	vase	сигарéта	cigarette	сýп	soup
бáза	base	Мáрс	Mars	áтлас	atlas
винó	wine	Кáрл Мáркс	Karl Marx	спýтник	sputnik

(в)

плюс	plus	юрúст	lawyer	Югослáвия	Yugoslavia

(г)

Аню	Annie	Пéтю	Pete	Кóлю	Kolya
Анну	Ann	газéту	newspaper	Аллу	Alla

6. Nationalities

(a) Answer 'Yes, it is,' as in the model, by repeating the
     adjective. Use the statement contour.

П: Это америкáнский флáг?

С: Дá, америкáнский.   немéцкий   (German)
   совéтский   пóльский
                              израúльский
   францýзский   егúпетский
   канáдский   албáнский
   мексикáнский   болгáрский
   испáнский

(б) Give the correct answer.

П: Какóй э́то флáг?

С: Это америкáнский флáг.

W 7. Pronunciation Exercise: й vs. и

Singular: мóй   твóй   трамвáй   буржýй
Plural: мои́   твои́   трамвáи   буржýи

T 8. Reading Exercise: Cyrillic letters: ч ж ц ф ь

(а) пóчта   post office
    читáть   (to) read
    журнáл   journal
    журналúст   journalist
    журналúстика   journalism

    цúрк   circus
    лéкция   lecture
    стáнция   station
    цéнтр   downtown

    лúфт   elevator
    фúзика   physics
    шáрф   scarf
    фáбрика   factory
    фамúлия   family name
    фрáза   sentence

(б) пóлька   polka   пóлка   shelf
    фúльм   film   хóлм   hill
    вóльт   volt   бóлт   bolt
    Óльга   Olga   Вóлга   Volga
    бинóкль   binoculars цúкл   cycle
    вéсь   all   вéс   weight
    цáрь   czar   шáр   globe

T 9. Всé vs. всё (Text Comment 3)

Answer the questions as in the model, using either всé
'everybody' or всё 'everything', as appropriate.

П: Чтó вы понимáете?
С: Я всё понимáю.

П: Ктó здéсь?
С: Всé здéсь.

П: Чтó здéсь?
С: Всё здéсь.

Чтó на столé?
Ктó в институ́те?
Ктó передáл икрý?
Чтó вы знáете?
Ктó читáл кнúгу?
Чтó вы понимáете?

T 10. Reading Exercise. Cyrillic Letters: я э щ х

    хи́мия   chemistry
    исто́рия   history
    э́то   this/that
    бо́рщ   borsch
    хо́р   chorus

W 11. Introductions. Dialog 1. Analysis 5.

   (a) П: Ма́ша, кто́ э́то?
        М: Это Са́ша.
        П: Представьте меня́, пожа́луйста.
        М: Са́ша, э́то мо́й преподава́тель, (first name and
           patronymic). (To the teacher): Э́то Са́ша.
        П: О́чень прия́тно.
        С: О́чень прия́тно.

   Switch to ты:

        П: Ма́ша, спроси́те Са́шу, кто́ э́то. (Pointing to
           Natasha.)
        М: Са́ша, кто́ э́то?
        С: Э́то Ната́ша.
        М: Предста́вь меня́, пожа́луйста.
        С: Ма́ша, э́то Ната́ша.
        М: О́чень прия́тно.
        Н: О́чень прия́тно.

Continue until everybody in the class is introduced.

   (б) Repeat (a), and add the following question. Observe
      the proper word order and note the Accusative case
      (Analysis 5).

        П: А́ня, кто́ предста́вил Са́шу?
        А: Са́шу предста́вила Ма́ша.

W 12. Reply as in the model, first affirmatively, then negatively,
    using names of people in the class. Observe the word order:
    the pronoun его́/её in the second answer comes *after* the
    word я.

        П: Вы зна́ете Са́шу?
        С: Да́, Са́шу я хорошо́ зна́ю.
        П: А Пе́тю?
        С: Не́т, я его́ не зна́ю.

W 13. Pronunciation Exercise: Variants of /i/.

Imitate. Then read each row.

вы́	ви́	выви́	вы ви́дели	Вы ви́дели ви́лку?
мы́	ми́	мыви́	мы ви́дели	Мы ви́дели ви́лку.
ты́	ти́	тыви́	ты ви́дела	Ты ви́дела ви́лку?

ди́	ды́	Сади́тесь, молоды́е колле́ги!
си́	ды́	Спаси́бо, молоды́е колле́ги!

W 14. Reply in the affirmative with a short answer, as in the model (See Analysis 4). Men: use the past form –л. Women: use the past form –ла. All you have to do in giving the short answers is to repeat the verb. This corresponds to English 'I did.' Use the statement contour.

П: Ма́ша, вы предста́вили ма́му?
М: Да́, предста́вила.
П: Са́ша, вы предста́вили ма́му?
С: Да́, предста́вил.

Вы учи́ли Зю́зю чита́ть по-ру́сски?
          говори́ть
          писа́ть

Вы переда́ли икру́?
          стака́н?

Вы чита́ли кни́гу?
          письмо́?
          слова́рь?
          уро́к?

Вы взя́ли икру́?
          ды́ню?
          слова́рь?

Вы ви́дели мою́ кни́гу?
          моё кольцо́?
          мо́й но́ж?
          мо́й италья́нский фла́г?
          мо́й англо-ру́сский слова́рь?
          мою́ болга́рскую кни́гу?
          моё вино́?

Вы попроси́ли у него́ вино́?
          у неё ды́ню?

W 15. Reply in the affirmative with a full answer, using the pro-
       per Accusative pronoun его́, её. Men: use past form –л.
       Women: use past form – ла. (Analysis 5)

       Model:
           П: Ма́ша, вы предста́вили па́пу?
           М: Да́, я его́ предста́вила.
           П: Ма́ша, вы предста́вили ма́му?
           М: Да, я́ её предста́вила.

           П: Са́ша, вы предста́вили па́пу?
           С: Да́, я его́ предста́вил.
           П: Са́ша, вы предста́вили ма́му?
           С: Да́, я её предста́вил.

       Continue, using sentences from the preceding exercise.

W 16.   Pronoun practice.   Analysis 5.

       Take an object from the table and present it to somebody,
       saying, 'Here's an X, take (*it*).' Use informal возьми́
       'take' if you present it to a fellow student, but formal
       возьми́те if you present it to the teacher.

       Before you start the exercise, read these sentences aloud
       until you can say them smoothly.

           1. Во́т икра́, возьми́те.
           2. Во́т стака́н, возьми́те.
           3. Во́т яйцо́, возьми́те.
           4. Во́т письмо́, возьми́те.
           5. Во́т ка́мень, возьми́те.
           6. ...

       Now expand as follows, using the appropriate pronoun
       (его́ or её):

           П: Кто́ взя́л икру́?
           С: Её   взяла́ Ма́ша.

F 17. Gender (Analysis 3 , 5; Dialog 2)

   (а) П: Máша, гдé дыня?
       М: Вóт онá.

   Substitute: стакáн, кнúга, бумáга, кольцó, рýчка,
               мéл, газéта, конвéрт, икрá, винó, нóж,
               флáг, яйцó, словáрь, письмó, камéнь,
               вúлка, лóжка.

   (б) Expand:

       П: Máша, гдé дыня?
       М: Вóт онá, слéва/спрáва/напрóтив.
       П: Передáйте, пожáлуйста, дыню.
       М: Вóт, пожáлуйста.

   Substitute: as above.

   (в) Repeat, and add the following. Observe the proper word
       order (Analysis 5.2).

       П: Сáша, ктó передáл дыню?
       С: Дыню передалá Máша.

       (If C. is wrong, add: Нéт, э́то не тáк. Дыню
       передалá не Máша, а Натáша.)

F 18. Informal Style

    П: Сáша, попросúте у неё дыню. (Pointing to Masha.)
    С: Máша, передáй, пожáлуйста, дыню.
    М: Вóт, пожáлуйста.
    С: Спасúбо.
    М: Пожáлуйста.
    П: Попросúте у неё и кнúгу тóже.
    С: Передáй, пожáлуйста, и кнúгу тóже.
    М: Вóт, пожáлуйста.
    П: Бóря, ктó попросúл кнúгу?
    Б: Кнúгу попросúл Сáша.
    П: Натáша, ктó передáл кнúгу?
    Н: Кнúгу передалá Máша.

₽19. Dialog 3, Analysis 4,5.

Say these sentences with the proper past tense form of the verb in parentheses.

1. Лéна (passed) икрý.
2. Пéтя (passed) стакáн.
3. Вáня (took) газéту.
4. Мáша (took) нóж.
5. Мáшу (introduced) Вáня.
6. Мáша (introduced) Вáню.
7. Мáша (taught) Лéну читáть по-рýсски.
8. Лéну (taught) Мáша.
9. Мáша (read) по-рýсски.
10. Пéтя (read) газéту.
11. Пéтя (saw) газéту.
12. Ктó (read) газéту?
13. Газéту (read) Мáша.

F20. Verbs (Dialog 3)

П: Сáша, спросúте Мáшу, ктó учúл её говорúть по-рýсски.
С: Мáша, ктó учúл тебя́ говорúть по-рýсски?
М: Меня́ учúл(а)   (name of a classmate).
С: А ктó егó/её учúл?
М: Егó/её учúл преподавáтель в университéте.
П: Натáша, спросúте Бóрю, ктó учúл егó читáть по-рýсски.

Substitute:

— ктó учúл егó писáть по-рýсски.
— ктó учúл егó писáть по-англúйски.
— ктó учúл егó читáть по-англúйски.
— ктó учúл егó говорúть по-англúйски.

— ктó учúл егó говорúть по-францýзски.
— ктó учúл егó говорúть по-испáнски.

21. Ктó гдé?

П: Сáша, гдé Мáша?
С: Вóт онá, слéва/спрáва/напрóтив.
П: А гдé (names of the other members of the class)?

M R 22. Pronunciation Exercises

   (a) /t d n/

These three consonants are pronounced with the tongue
against the teeth, like the *th* in English *thin, then*.

там	ты	то	ту
да	ды́ня	до	ду
на		но	ну

When you find *t* between vowels, don't say it like the *tt*
in *Betty*.

э́то	газе́та	сигаре́та	напро́тив
э́ту	газе́ту	сигаре́ту	преподава́тель

   (б) Palatalized vs. plain: -ть vs. -т.

Be sure to make ть different from ц and ч.

мат	мац	ты	та	то	ту
мать	мач	ти	тя	тё	тю
мят	мяч				
рот	роц				
роть	роч				

   (в) Palatalized vs. plain: -ль vs. -л.

мал	жал	стол	по́лка	Во́лга
маль	жаль	столь	по́лька	О́льга

лы	ла	ло	лук
ли	ля	лё	люк

plain:	предста́вила	чита́ла	учи́лась	де́лала
pala- talized:	предста́вили	чита́ли	учи́лись	де́лали

R 23. Write и or a in the blank as appropriate to the context,
and supply the proper English translation (See Dialog
Comment 1).

a - contrast

Меня́ зову́т Ми́ша. _____ тебя́?

Во́ва рабо́тает в институ́те _____ в университе́те.

Переда́йте, пожа́луйста, икру́ _____ вино́.

Э́то не ви́лка, _____ нож.

Са́ша, э́то Ми́ша _____ Ма́ша.

Его́ зову́т не Ми́ша, _____ Ва́ня.

Они́ чита́ли _____ говори́ли по-ру́сски.

Во́ва рабо́тает в институ́те, _a_ Бо́ря в университе́те.

_a_ где́ вы рабо́таете?

Ле́на учи́ла её чита́ть, говори́ть, _____ писа́ть
по-ру́сски.

R 24. Write the words попросите у него 'request of him, ask him for' or спросите его 'inquire, ask him' as required by the context (See Dialog Comment 3). Write in cursive script: попросите у него/спросите его.

_____*Спросите его*_____, как его зовут.

_____*попросите у Него*_____ вино, пожалуйста.

Маша, _____*спросите его*_____ где он работает.

Саша, _____*спросите его*_____ кто это.

Маша, _____*попросите у Него*_____ мой стакан.

Саша, _____*спросите его*_____ что стоит на столе.

Маша, _____*попросите у него*_____ икру, дыню, и вино.

_____*спросите его*_____ как это по-русски.

M 25. Gender (Analysis 3, Dialog 4).

П: Саша, спросите Машу, где стакан.
С: Маша, где стакан?
М: Какой стакан?
С: Мой стакан.
М: Я не знаю, где твой стакан.

Substitute:

словарь	дыня	паспорт
книга	телевизор	ваза
письмо	грейпфрут	револьвер
телефон	гитара	кольцо

Ⓜ 26. Переведи́те на ру́сский язы́к:

(1) Nadya, who's this? It's Volódya. Introduce me please.
Lěnya, this is Volodya. Pleased to meet you, Volódya.
Who introduced Volódya? Volódya was introduced by
Nádya.

(2) Where's the caviar? Here it is, on the table. Where's
the wine? Here it is, on the table. Pass the caviar.
Pass the wine, too. Where's my glass? Here it is. It's
my first glass. No, that's your second glass. Where's
a spoon? Here it is. Thanks. Who taught you to
speak Russian? My mother taught me. Who taught you?
My teacher at the university taught me. Lena taught
me. Who taught Lena to read and write? I taught Lena.
Do you understand? No, I don't understand.

(3) What's your name? My name is Petya, and yours? My
name's Misha. Nice to meet you. Ask him what his name
is. Ask her what her name is. Ask him for a spoon.
Ask him for the wine. Ask him for the dictionary. Who
taught you to read?

Ⓜ 27. Conversation topic.

Three students, A, B, and C, hold a conversation. Student A
introduces B to C. B asks C where things are and wants C to
pass things. A constantly interrupts with irrelevant questions, like who taught whom to speak Russian, who passed
what, how to say things in Russian, etc.

УРОК ТРЕТИЙ

(T) ТЕКСТ А: В СЕКРЕТНОМ ИНСТИТУТЕ.

After a tour of the institute, Zyuzya meets the director.

Директор: Здравствуйте, Зюзя, рад[1] вас видеть. Мне[2] о вас много говорил товарищ[3] Сидоров.

Зюзя: Кто это Сидоров?

Д: Ваш друг, Иван Петрович. Что вы уже видели в институте?

З: Я видела лаборатории, аудитории, кабинеты.

Д: Что вы думаете о нашем институте?

З: Я мало о нём знаю.[4]

Д: Хотите работать в нашем институте?

З: С удовольствием. Что вы делаете?

Д: Это секрет. Мы делаем ракеты.

З: Какую работу я буду делать в вашем институте?

Д: Вы будете рассказывать о вашей планете, где она, кто там живёт, что вы там делаете. Как вы прилетели на нашу планету?

З: Это секрет. Я прилетела на ракете.

Д: Где она?

З: Она улетела[5] обратно на мою планету. На моей планете только одна ракета.

Д: Ваша ракета прилетит ещё раз на нашу планету?

З: Не знаю. Думаю, что нет.   *Set expression*

Д: Что вы знаете о нашей планете?

З: Хорошая планета, большая.

Д: Ваша планета маленькая?

З: Да, моя планета очень маленькая.

Д: Поэтому вы прилетели на нашу планету?

З: Нет, я прилетела на вашу планету, потому что я много думала о ней и я часто видела её во сне.

(R) ТЕКСТ Б: В БЕЛОМ ДОМЕ.

В это время в Вашингтоне, в Белом доме, директор ЦРУ[6] делает доклад в кабинете президента.[7]

Директор: Господин[8] президент, сегодня утром неизвестная ракета прилетела на нашу планету. Мы не знаем, откуда она прилетела и кто на ней прилетел. Мы только знаем, что ракета прилетела издалека. Наш спутник АСК-3 сфотографировал ракету, когда она влетела[5] в атмосферу. Эту ракету сделали[9] не[4] на нашей планете. На нашей планете никто не умеет делать такие ракеты. Ракета села в Москве, была в Москве один час и улетела.

Президент: Очень интересно. ТАСС, конечно, ничего не передавало?

Д: Ничего.

П: Хм...Мы непременно должны узнать, кто прилетел на этой ракете.

Д: Наши агенты в Москве уже знают об[10] этой ракете, господин Президент.

Vocabulary

третий third

секретный secret

директор director

рад glad

видеть (to) see

мне (to) me

о, об about

говорил spoke, talked

товарищ comrade

друг friend

уже by now

лаборатории laboratories (pl. of лаборатория)

аудитории classrooms, lecture halls (pl. of аудитория)

кабинеты offices (pl. of кабинет)

думаете (you) think

мало not much, little

нём it (Prepositional case, masc. and neut.)

хотите (do you) want

работать (to) work

делаете (you) do; make

секрет secret

делаем (we) do; make

ракеты rocket ships (pl. of ракета)

работа work

буду (I) will

делать (to) do

будете (you) will

рассказывать (to) narrate, tell stories, tell about

планета planet

живёт (he, she) lives

как how

прилетели (you) arrived (flying), flew in

улетела flew away

обратно back

только only

одна one

прилетит will come (by air)

думаю (I) think

хороший good

большой big, large

маленький little, small

поэтому therefore, that's why

потому что because

много many

думала thought

ней it (Prepositional case, feminine)

часто often

во (=в) in

сне sleep (Prepositional case of сон)
   видеть X во сне dream about X (Lit., see X in (one's) sleep)

белый white

дом house

время time (Irregular noun: neuter)

Вашингтон Washington

ЦРУ CIA (pronounced: /tsè-èr-rú/ or /tserú/)

доклад report

господин Mr.

утром in the morning
   сегодня утром this morning (Lit., 'today in the morning')

неизвестный unknown

откуда whence, from where, where from

издалека from afar, from a (great) distance

спутник satellite

сфотографировал photographed

когда́   when
влете́л   flew into, entered
  (by air)
атмосфе́ра   atmosphere
сде́лали   (they) made, was
  made
никто́   nobody
уме́ет   knows how (to)
тако́й, pl. таки́е   such (a),
  that kind of
се́ла   (she, it) landed
Москва́   Moscow
была́   (she, it) was
оди́н   one

ча́с   hour
интере́сно   interesting
ТАСС   Tass (the Soviet news
  agency)
коне́чно   of course
передава́ло   transmitted,
  broadcast
хм   (pronounced in various ways,
  like English hn, huh, hmm)
непреме́нно   without fail,
  certainly
должны́   (we) must
узна́ть   (to) find out, learn
аге́нт   agent

COMMENTS

1. ра́д

   This is the masculine form.

Я ра́д.	I'm glad (man speaking).
Он ра́д.	He's glad.

   The feminine form is ра́да.

Я ра́да тебя́ ви́деть.	I'm glad to see you (woman speaking).
Она́ ра́да.	She's glad.

2. Dative case

   Мне́ is the Dátive case form of Я, to be discussed in Lesson 5;
   'Comrade Sidorov told *me* a lot about you,' 'He spoke *to me*
   about you.'

3. това́рищ

   This word is used in official forms of address:

   това́рищ дире́ктор

   It can also be used with last names:

   това́рищ Си́доров

   Compare:

   господи́н президе́нт (Те́кст Б, Comment 8)

4. Negation: English vs. Russian

   This sentence can be literally translated 'I know little
   about it'. A more everyday translation would be 'I don't
   know much about it'. Note that Russian does not negate the
   verb in sentences like this.

Similarly (later on in the text):

Ду́маю, что нет.   I don't think so. (Lit., 'I
                                    think [that] not.')

Here again, English (illogically) negates the verb; Russian
rarely does. Compare French: Je pense que non. (NOT: Je ne
pense pas.)

Still further on in the text is this sentence:

Э́ту раке́ту сде́лали не   This rocket wasn't made on
   на на́шей плане́те.   our planet. (Lit., '[They]
                                    made this rocket not on
                                    our planet.')

Again, English negates the verb (despite the fact that the
rocket was indeed manufactured somewhere), while Russian negates the phrase на на́шей плане́те.

5. Prefixes

Compare the words прилете́ла 'flew in, arrived by air' and
улете́ла 'flew away'. They both mean 'flew', but they differ by virtue of the prefixes при- vs. у-. The most common meanings of these prefixes are: при- 'here' (in the sense
of *arrive*) and у- 'away'. English makes use of post-verbal
particles (flew away, flew up, flew off, flew out, flew in,
flew around, etc.), while Russian renders the same kinds of
meanings with prefixes.

Later in the text the word влете́ла 'flew in, entered (by
air)' occurs. Note the similarity between the meaning of
the prefix в- 'in' and the preposition в 'in'.

6. CIA

Since all English speakers know what the CIA is, and all Russian speakers know what the ЦРУ is, there's no need to know
what the letters stand for — but here it is anyway:
Центра́льное Разве́дывательное Управле́ние.

7. Genitive case

The form президе́нта 'of the President' is the Genitive of
президе́нт.

8. господи́н

This is a prerevolutionary form of address. It is used in
two situations: (a) among emigrés and (b) in the Soviet Union as an official form of address to people representing
capitalist countries. The feminine form is госпожа́.

9. Passive

There is no regular passive form in Russian. Instead of a
special passive form to say 'This rocket *was made* in Moscow',
Russian uses a plural form with the literal meaning '(*They*)
made this rocket in Moscow':

Э́ту раке́ту сде́лали в   This rocket was made in
  Москве́.   Moscow.

The plural verb form сде́лали is *not* accompanied by the
plural pronoun они́.

Similarly:

Зю́зю учи́ли лета́ть.   Zyuzya was taught to fly.

10. о, об

This preposition has two forms: о before words beginning
with a consonant, об before a vowel.

DIALOGS FOR MEMORIZATION

ᴡ 1. Предло́жный паде́ж

   С: Господи́н профе́ссор, расскажи́те, пожа́луйста, о
      предло́жном падеже́.
   П: В конце́ семе́стра[1] о ка́ждом плохо́м студе́нте и о
      ка́ждой плохо́й студе́нтке[2] напи́шут во все́х
      больши́х газе́тах.[3]

ꜰ 2. Где́ ру́чка?

  (а) П: Где́ ру́чка?
      М: Ру́чка у меня́ в пра́вой руке́.
      П: Положи́те[4] её на сто́л.
      М: На како́й сто́л?
      П: На большо́й.

  (б) П: Где́ ру́чка? (*Having given Masha a pen.*)
      С: Ру́чка лежи́т на столе́.
      П: На како́м столе́?
      С: На большо́м.
      П: Кто́ положи́л ру́чку на сто́л?
      С: Ру́чку на сто́л положи́ла Ма́ша.
      П: Чья́ э́то ру́чка?
      С: Э́то ма́шина ру́чка.

  (в) П: Куда́ вы положи́ли ру́чку?
      М: Я положи́ла её на сто́л.

Ⅿ 3. Зачём?

    (а)М: О чём ты говорил?
       С: Об икре́.
       М: Зачём тебе́ икра́?
       С: Что́бы е́сть.

    (б)М: О ко́м ты говорил?
       С: О сестре́.[5]
       М: Зачём говори́ть о сестре́?
       С: Про́сто та́к.

4. Где́ ты была́?

    П: Са́ша, спроси́те Ма́шу, где́ она́ была́ вчера́, в
       рестора́не и́ли в теа́тре?
    С: Где́ ты была́ вчера́, в рестора́не?
    М: Да, я ходи́ла[6] в рестора́н.
    С: Ка́к та́м бы́ло?
    М: Та́м бы́ло хорошо́.
    С: Что́ ты та́м де́лала?
    М: Я е́ла икру́.

5. Бе́лый до́м

    П: В како́м го́роде нахо́дится Бе́лый до́м?
    С: В Вашингто́не.
    П: Э́то в како́й стране́?
    С: В Аме́рике.

Translation

1. *The prepositional case*

    S: Professor, sir, please tell us about the prepositional
       case.
    T: At the end of the semester they will write about every
       poor student (male and female) in all the big newspapers.

2. *Where's the pen?*

    (a) T: Where's the pen?
        M: The pen's in my right hand. (Lit., 'The pen [is] by
           me in [the] right hand.')
        T: Put it on the table.
        M: On which table?
        T: On the big one.

    (b) T: Where's the pen?
        S: The pen is lying on the table.
        T: On which table?
        S: On the big one.
        T: Who put the pen on the table?
        S: The pen was put on the table by Másha. (OR: Másha
           put the pen on the table.)
        T: Whose pen is this?

     S: It's Masha's pen.

  (c) T: Where did you put the pen?
      M: I put the pen on the table.

3. *What for?*

  (a) M: What were you talking about?
      S: About caviar.
      M: What do you want (need) caviar for? (Lit., Why for you
         [Dative case] caviar?)
      S: To eat.

  (b) M: Who were you talking about?
      S: About [my] sister.
      M: Why talk about [your] sister?
      S: Just because. (Lit., 'Simply thus.')

4. *Where were you?*

  T: Sasha, ask Masha where she was yesterday, at the res-
     taurant or at the theater?
  S: Where were you yesterday? At the restaurant?
  M: Yes, I went to the restaurant.
  S: How was it there?
  M: It was nice there.
  S: What did you do there?
  M: I ate caviar.

5. *The White House.*

  T: In what city is the White House located?
  S: In Washington.
  T: That's in what country?
  S: In America.

ACTIVE WORD LIST

Places to go (Dialog 4).

театр	theater
ресторáн	restaurant
библиотéка	library
секрéтный институ́т	secret institute
домóй	home
кинó[7]	movies, movie theater
университéт	university

Things to do.

смотрéла пьéсу	saw a play (Lit., watched)
пилá винó	drank wine
читáла {газéту / кни́гу	read the paper / a book
дéлала {бóмбу / ракéту	made a bomb / rocket

писа́ла письмо́	wrote a letter
ничего́ не де́лала	did nothing
смотре́ла фильм	saw/watched a movie
писа́л упражне́ния	wrote exercises (plural of упражне́ние)
говори́ла по-ру́сски	spoke Russian

Other Nouns, masc.

Вашингто́н	Washington
паде́ж	case
господи́н	Mr., sir
профе́ссор	professor
коне́ц	end
семе́стр	semester
студе́нт	undergrad (masc.)
бра́т *	brother
го́род	city
до́м	house, home, building

Other Nouns, fem.

Аме́рика	America
студе́нтка	undergrad (fem.)
рука́	hand, arm
сестра́	sister
страна́	country

Verbs

расскажи́те	tell (imperative)
положи́те	put, lay (imperative)
напи́шут	(they) will write
лежи́т	(it) is lying
нахо́дится	(it) is located
е́сть	(to) eat
е́ла	ate
положи́ла	put, lay
говори́ть	(to) speak, talk
говори́ла	spoke, talked
бы́л, была́, бы́ло	was, were
ходи́ла	went (on foot)
де́лала	did; made

Adjectives

предло́жный   prepositional
вини́тельный *   accusative
ка́ждый   each, every
плохо́й   poor, bad
чей, чья, чьё   whose?
тре́тий, тре́тья, тре́тье *   third
ма́шин   Masha's
пра́вый   right
ле́вый *   left
большо́й   big, large
ма́ленький *   little, small
бе́лый   white
чёрный *   black

Miscellaneous

заче́м   what for
что́бы   in order to, to
тебе́   for/to you (Dative case)
в, во   in, at; to
о, об   about, concerning
у (У меня́ в руке́)   by (in my hand = Lit., 'by me in
                                       the hand')

чём   (Prepositional case of что)
ком   (Prepositional case of кто)
про́сто   simply
вчера́   yesterday
домо́й   home(ward)
куда́   where, whither (*motion*, as
                                       against где "where' *location*)

и́ли   or
ничего́   nothing

COMMENTS

1. Genitive case.

   The form семе́стра '*of* the semester' is the Genitive of
   семе́стр. Cf. кабине́т президе́нта 'the office *of* the
   president' in Text Comment 7.

   Incidentally, the form of address used in this facetious
   dialog, господин профессор, is as stuffy as the English
   translation indicates. In actual practice you would use the
   normal polite form: first name and patronymic.

2. студе́нтка, студе́нт

These words do not mean 'student' in general, but only 'student' in the sense of *undergrad*, i.e., they do not include elementary and secondary pupils (учени́к, учени́ца) or grad students (аспира́нты).

3. Prepositional plural

The forms все́х больши́х газе́тах are Prepositional plural, the endings for which will not be discussed until Lesson 6. Note the variant во (=в 'in') which occurs before certain consonant clusters.

4. Положи́ть

The verb положи́ть means 'to lay, to put in a lying position'. Don't use it with nouns like вино́ or стака́н, because they are put in a standing positon, for which there is a different verb.

5. Possessives with family words

The translation of this sentence is 'About *my* sister'. The Russian version lacks the word for 'my', it being understood that it is the subject's sister. Avoid the use of possessives with family words (brother, sister, father, etc.) and with parts of the body (arm, leg, etc.) unless the situation requires that you be specific.

6. ходи́ла: 'on foot'

This verb means 'went *on foot*', so don't try to use it to go to distant places where a vehicle would be required.

7. кино́ : indeclinable nouns

Words which Russian has borrowed from other languages and which end in a vowel other than –a are usually indeclinable, i.e. they have no case endings. Compare:

	Russian words	*Borrowed words*	
Accusative	в теа́тр	в кино́	'to'
Prepositional	в теа́тре	в кино́	'at'

ANALYSIS

1. Cyrillic vowel letters after non-paired consonants.

Russian consonants come in two varieties, plain and palatalized (Lesson 1, Analysis 3.2). This distinction is marked
by the subsequent vowel letter; plain indicators ы э а о у
vs. palatal indicators и е я ё ю (Lesson 1, Analysis 4.1).
Thus, ты = /ti/ and ти = /ţi/. This system works for all
Russian consonants except six. These six do not come in
plain vs. palatalized pairs; therefore, they are called *non-
paired* consonants. One of the six is й, which was discussed
in Lesson 2, Analysis 2. The remaining five are:

>   (a) ч щ
>
>   (b) ш ж ц

Group (a) is *always* pronounced in the palatal fashion, with
the broad flat blade of the tongue front in the mouth, close
to the palate.

Group (b) is *always* pronounced in the plain fashion, with the
tongue retracted.

By "always" we mean "no matter what vowel letter follows."
For example, ш is always followed by the letter и, which is,
for paired consonants, a palatal indicator; nevertheless, the
sequence ши is pronounced as though spelled "шы", because ш is
always pronounced in the plain fashion. Conversely, the
sequence ча is pronounced as though spelled "чя", because
ч is *always* pronounced in the palatal fashion.

In sum: for purposes of reading Russian aloud from
the printed page, you can ignore the vowel letter distinction
"plain vs. palatal indicator" after these consonants.

1.1 Spelling rules: ч щ ш ж ц.

In the previous section we gave the rule on how to *pronounce*
non-paired consonants; here we give the two rules needed for
writing vowel letters after non-paired consonants in noun
and adjective endings.

Noun and adjective endings begin with vowel; in these examples stems are separated from endings with a hyphen:

masc.	пе́рв-ый уро́к	the first lesson
fem.	чёрн-ая икр-а́	black caviar
neut.	бе́л-ое вин-о́	white wine
plural	бе́л-ые конве́рт-ы	white envelopes

Normally, you use plain indicators when you write endings.
If the stem ends in a palatalized paired consonant, then of
course you must rewrite these plain indicators as palatal
indicators, as stated in Lesson 1:4.1 and Lesson 2:1, e.g.,

$$а → я \qquad икр-а → дын-я$$
$$ /ikr-a/ \quad /diṇ-a/$$

The rule for writing noun and adjective endings after non-
paired consonants is that you write the same vowel you would
after plain stems except for:

(1) ы → и		after ч щ/ш ж
(2) о → е	unstressed	after ч щ/ш ж *and* ц

Examples:
> *Rule (1)*
>> -ый → -ий   (masc. adj.)
>> бе́л-ый → хоро́ш-ий

This rule applies to many plural forms, which you will be
meeting soon:
>> -ые → -ие   (plural adj.)
>> бе́л-ые → хоро́ш-ие

>> -ы → -и   (plural nouns, masc. and fem.)
>> конве́рт-ы → нож-и́

> *Rule (2)*
>> -ое → -ее
>> бе́л-ое → хоро́шее

>> -ом → -ем
>> о плох-о́м студе́нте → о хоро́ш-ем студе́нте
>> на как-о́м столе́ → на хоро́ш-ем столе́

>> -ой → -ей
>> о плох-о́й студе́нтке → о хоро́ш-ей сту-
>>   де́нтке

Rule (2) depends on stress; if the ending is stressed, the
rule doesn't apply, e.g., the stems for 'big' and 'good'
both end in -ш-, but the rule applies only to the endings
of 'good' because they are unstressed:

>> -ом → -ем
>> на как-о́м столе́ → на хоро́ш-ем столе́
>> об э́т-ом студе́нте → о хоро́ш-ем студе́нте

> BUT: -ом = -о́м
>>   на больш-о́м столе́

Similarly, -ой → -ей
>> об э́т-ой дын́е → о хоро́ш-ей ды́не
>>   о больш-о́й ды́не

> BUT: -ой = -о́й

PRACTICE 1

Listed below are the feminine forms of some adjectives. Write the masculine, and neuter endings according to the rules stated above.

fem.   *masc.*   *neut.*

Example:
бéлая *white*   -ый   -ое

горя́чая *hot*
чёрная *black*

хорóшая *good*
секрéтная *secret*
мла́дшая *junior*

1.2 Pronunciation hints on non-paired consonants.

In the preceding section we made some remarks about the tongue position in producing these consonants. Such remarks aren't universally helpful, because most people don't have conscious control over tongue movements in speech sounds — the tongue moves automatically when you speak your native language. Most people, however, have the ability to recognize high vs. low pitch, as with musical tones, and this ability may be helpful in learning to recognize and produce non-paired consonants correctly.

Plain non-paired consonants (ш ж ц) have low pitch, lower than their English counterparts. Palatal non-paired consonants (ч щ) have high pitch, higher than their English counterparts.

To make a low pitched *plain* ш, say /r/ as in *root*; keep your tongue in that position and say /sh/ as in *shoot*. (Note that your lips will be rounded for English /r/ and Russian /sh/.) The same goes for ж, the voiced counterpart of ш.

The *palatal* щ is not only high pitched, it is a long consonant in most people's pronunciation.

1.3 Spelling rules: к г х

These three consonants are called *velar* consonants.

Rule (1) applies to velar consonants: ы → и.   [Rule (2) does not.]

Examples:

бе́л-ый → ма́леньк-ий	(Nom. Sing. masc.)
бе́л-ые → ма́леньк-ие	(Plural adj.)
бу́кв-ы → ру́чк-и	(Plural, fem. nouns)

Spelling rules (1) and (2), which have to do only with non-paired consonants and velars, should be kept distinct from the rule which says that the Nominative Singular masculine ending is −ой when stressed (Lesson 2: 3.2), because this latter rule applies to *all* ordinary adjectives, no matter what their stem-final consonant is.   Thus:

Dictionary forms

	unstressed endings	*stressed endings*
plain	бе́лый	второ́й
	ка́ждый	
	ле́вый	
	чёрный	
non-paired	хоро́ший	большо́й
velar	ма́ленький	како́й
	ру́сский	плохо́й

PRACTICE 2

Do as you did in Practice 1. This list includes stem final velars as well as paired and non-paired consonants and stressed endings.

fem.		m.	n.	pl.
бе́лая		-ый	-ое	-ые

ру́сская	*Russian*
кра́сная	*red*
мужска́я	*masculine*
же́нская	*feminine*
пе́рвая	*first*
друга́я	*other*
чужа́я	*another's*
англи́йская	*English*
втора́я	*second*
плоха́я	*bad*
больша́я	*big*
ка́ждая	*each*
болга́рская	*Bulgarian*
ни́щая	*poverty-stricken*
ма́ленькая	*little*
молода́я	*young*

⊤ 2. More on the sound /y/.

2.1 The pronunciation of й.

At the end of a word the sound /y/ has a lot more friction noise than it does elsewhere. For example, the word мой sounds almost as though spelled мойх, though the friction noise is not as great as for the consonant x: Compare final vs. non-final position in the following examples:

мо́й /móy/ 'my' (masc.) vs. моя́ /mayá/ 'my' (fem.)

музе́й /muẓéy/ 'museum' vs. война́ /vayná/ 'war'

переда́й /p̦iṛidáy/ 'pass' vs. переда́йте /p̦iṛidáyṭi/ 'pass'

2.2 Palatal indicators in word-initial position: и.

It was stated in Lesson 2.2 that the palatal indicators
(и е я ё ю) stand for the sound /y/ when no consonant
precedes, e.g. моя́ /mayá/, я́ /yá/. It was also stated that
word-initial position is a special case, because и stands
only for the vowel /i/, not for /yi/, e.g., институ́т
/insţitút/.

In fast speech this initial и will sound like ы if the preceding word ends in a plain consonant:

он и Са́ша   = "о́ныса́ша"   he and Sasha

в институ́те = "вынinstitу́ти"   at the institute

от Ива́на   = "атыва́на"   from Ivan

2.3 Мя́гкий зна́к (ь) before vowel letters.

Recall that palatal indicators are used to represent the
sound /y/ (as in *yes*; see Lesson 2.2), e.g.,

есть /yéşţ/   as though spelled   "йэ́сть"

я /ya/   as though spelled   "йа"

ёж /yósh/   as though spelled   "йо́ш"

Ю́ра /yúra/   as though spelled   "йу́ра"

Now observe the first three letters in Нью-Йо́рк. The letter ю cannot represent the palatalization of the immediately
preceding consonant, because no consonant immediately precedes it — the letter ь precedes; therefore, the letter ю is
pronounced as though spelled йу, just as in Ю́ра. The

whole sequence нью is pronounced as though spelled нйу and
it sounds different from the sequence ню.   In transcription, the two sequences look like this:

> нью = /n̦yu/

vs. ню = /n̦u/

This distinction is difficult for English speakers to perceive and to reproduce.   Recall the discussion of palatalization in Lesson 1.3.2, where it was pointed out that palatalization is a /y/-like sound made *simultaneously* with the
consonant, and that palatalization is distinct from a *sub-*
sequent /y/-sound.   We repeat the pair of examples used
there:

> польёт 'it will pour', as though spelled "палйóт", and
pronounced /pal̦yót/

vs. полёт   'flight', pronounced /pal̦ót/

The word польёт contains six sounds and it takes longer to
say than полёт, which contains five sounds.

Compare:

> семья́ 'family' /șim̦yá/ as though spelled "семйá"

> сломя́ 'breaking' /slam̦á/

> чья́ 'whose' /chyá/ as though spelled "чйá"

> ча́сто 'often' /chásta/

Similarly,

> итальянский 'Italian' /ital̦ánsk̦iy/

> тре́тья   'third' /țŗéţya/

> пье́са 'play' /p̦yésa/

(Incidentally, the second word of Нью-Йо́рк is a spelling
exception typical of foreign words in Russian; you'd expect
it to be spelled Ёрк.)

W **3. Adjectives**

In Lesson 2.3 it was pointed out that there are two types
of adjectives in Russian, *ordinary* adjectives of the како́й
type and *special* adjectives of the мо́й type.

3.1 Ordinary Adjectives

In this lesson you have had a number of new ordinary adjectives.   They present no problems except for the application
of the non-paired and velar spelling rules; remember, however, that the masc. form is -о́й when stressed, rather than
-ый/-ий.   We add here молодо́й 'young' and хоро́ший

'good' — note that the stress is different from the adverb хорошо́ 'well, fine'.

non-paired: большо́й, хоро́ший

velar: плохо́й, ма́ленький

other: предло́жный, вини́тельный, ка́ждый, пра́вый, ле́вый, бе́лый, чёрный, молодо́й

The spellings of the Nom./Acc. endings are all like бе́лый except as noted:

Nom. masc. бе́лый, *but* большо́й, плохо́й, молодо́й
(stressed masc.)
but ма́ленький (velar rule)
but хоро́ший (non-paired rule)

Nom. fem. бе́лая
Nom. neut. бе́лое *but* хоро́шее (non-paired rule, unstressed о)

Acc. fem. бе́лую

Some proper names in Russian are adjectives in form, e.g., Толсто́й (like молодо́й), Достое́вский (like ма́ленький), Толста́я ('Ms. Tolstoy', like молода́я), etc.

PRACTICE 3

Write these people's last names in Russian, e.g. (Ms.) Portnoy →
Портна́я.

(Mr.) Tolstoy
(Mr.) Dostoevsky
(Ms.) Tolstoy
(Ms.) Dostoevsky
(Mr.) Portnoy

3.2 Special adjectives.

The new special adjectives in this lesson are чей 'whose', третий 'third' and possessives of the type ма́шина кни́га 'Masha's book'. We list here the Nominative/Accusative forms of all those you have had so far, plus э́тот 'this' and тво́й 'your'. In all of these forms the endings are identical to noun endings (though some of the masculine forms have peculiar stem changes, like the extra -т in э́тот and the -e- in че́й):

	my, mine	your, yours	your, yours	this/ that	whose	third	Masha's
Nom. m.	мо́й	тво́й	ва́ш	э́тот	че́й	тре́тий	ма́шин
Nom. f.	моя́	твоя́	ва́ша	э́та	чья́	тре́тья	ма́шина
Nom. n.	моё	твоё	ва́ше	э́то	чьё	тре́тье	ма́шино
Acc. f.	мою́	твою́	ва́шу	э́ту	чью́	тре́тью	ма́шину

Further examples of possessives are given in section 4, below.

3.3 Это vs. the special adjective э́тот/э́та/э́то/э́ту.

When the word э́то is used in a sentence like 'This *is* X', it does not agree with X. If, however, you want to say 'This X', then the word 'this' agrees with X, just like any other adjective.

(a) 'This is X.'

Э́то каранда́ш.	*This is* a pencil.
Э́то чёрный каранда́ш.	*This is* a black pencil.
Э́то ру́чка.	*This is* a pen.
Э́то моя́ ру́чка.	*This is* my pen.
Э́то кольцо́.	*This is* a ring.
Э́то Ната́ша.	*This is* Natasha.
Э́то Пе́тя.	*This is* Pete.

(b) 'this X'

Э́тот каранда́ш бы́л на столе́.	*This pencil* was on the table.
Э́та ру́чка была́ на столе́.	*This pen* was on the table.
Э́то кольцо́ бы́ло на столе́.	*This ring* was on the table.
Э́та ру́чка моя́.	*This pen* was mine.
Возьми́те э́тот каранда́ш.	Take *this pencil*.
Возьми́те э́ту ру́чку.	Take *this pen*.
Возьми́те э́то кольцо́.	Take *this ring*.

W 4. Possession

One way of expressing possession in Russian is to use the suffix -ин- with the stem of an a-declension name. The resulting word is an adjective which agrees with the noun.

name	*possessive*	
Са́ша	m. са́шин каранда́ш	Sasha's pencil
	f. са́шина кни́га	Sasha's book
	n. са́шино письмо́	Sasha's letter
ма́ма	ма́мина ви́лка	Mom's fork
Ле́на	ле́нин нож	Lena's knife
па́па	па́пина ды́ня	Dad's melon
Пе́тя	пе́тин слова́рь	Pete's dictionary
А́ня	а́нино вино́	Annie's wine

Possessive pronouns fall into two groups; (1) first and second person vs. (2) third person.

Group (1) consists of adjectives, i.e. they agree with the noun:

	my	*your*	*your*	*our*		
m.	мой	твой	ваш	наш	нож	my/your/our knife
f.	моя́	твоя́	ва́ша	на́ша	ло́жка	my/your/our spoon
n.	моё	твоё	ва́ше	на́ше	кольцо́	my/your/our ring

Group (2) consists of forms which do *not* show agreement.

m.	его́	её	их	нож	his/her/their knife
f.	его́	её	их	ло́жка	his/her/their spoon
n.	его́	её	их	кольцо́	his/her/their ring

To ask 'Whose X is this?' use the word чей 'whose' and make it agree with X:

Чей э́то слова́рь?	Whose dictionary is this?
- Мой.	Mine.
- Э́то мой слова́рь.	That's my dictionary.
- Э́тот слова́рь мой.	That dictionary is mine.
Чья э́то ды́ня?	Whose melon is this?
- Моя́.	Mine.
- Э́то моя́ ды́ня.	That's my melon.
- Э́та ды́ня моя́.	That melon is mine.
Чьё э́то кольцо́?	Whose ring is this?
- Моё.	Mine.
- Э́то моё кольцо́.	That's my ring.
- Э́то кольцо́ моё.	That ring is mine.

PRACTICE 4

Translate the words in parentheses into Russian. All of these items are special adjectives, except 'his, her, their' (sections 3.2, 3.3, and 4.). Then translate each sentence into English.

(Whose) э́то ды́ня?

Э́то (Yura's) ды́ня.

Возьми́те (this) ды́ню.

Кто́ е́л (my) ды́ню?

(Whose) э́то до́м?

Э́то (Masha's) до́м.

Э́то (your) лаборато́рия?

Да́, (mine).

(Whose) э́то кольцо́?

Э́то (his) кольцо́.

Э́то (her) кольцо́.

Э́то (my) кольцо́.

Э́то (Dad's) кольцо́.

(Whose) э́то кабине́т?

Э́то (his) кабине́т.

Э́то (her) кабине́т.

Э́то (my) кабине́т.

Э́то (Mom's) кабине́т.

W 5. Prepositional vs. Accusative Case

Nouns, along with the adjectives which modify them, have a
set of endings called *Prepositional case* endings. The term
prepositional is used to describe these endings because they
occur only when the noun is preceded by certain prepositions.
(Some prepositions take other cases.)

The prepositional case ending for most nouns is -e , e.g.,
Москва́ (Nominative) → в Москве́ (Prepositional) 'in Moscow'.

The contrast in meaning between Prepositional case and Accusative case was introduced in Lesson 2, Text Comment 6. In
the following sections we give further details on certain
prepositions, the Prepositional case endings of adjectives,
nouns, and pronouns, and some information on word order.

5.1 The prepositions в, на, о.

The meanings of the prepositions в, на, and о depend upon
the case of the following noun.

	Prepositional	Accusative
в	in, at (location)	in, into (motion)
на	on (location)	on, onto (motion)
о	about, concerning	against

Examples:

в Москве́   in Moscow   в Москву́   to Moscow

на столе́   on the table   на сто́л   on(to) the table

о столе́   about the table   о сто́л   against the table

(In the following discussion and exercises we will dispense
with the last example, 'against', because one doesn't often
have occasion to use it; it does illustrate the point, however: the meaning of words often depends on case endings.)

Further examples:

Ру́чка лежи́т на большо́м   The pen is lying on the large
   столе́.   table.
Кто́ положи́л ру́чку на   Who put the pen on the large
   большо́й сто́л?   table?

Он бы́л в го́роде.   He was in town.
Он ходи́л в го́род.   He went to town.

Он в теа́тре?   (Is) he in the theater?
Он в теа́тр?   (Is) he (going) to the theater?
Он говори́т о Большо́м   He's talking about the Bolshoy
   теа́тре.   theater.

PRACTICE 5

Translate the preposition as 'in,' *if the following noun is in the Prepositional case, and as* 'to,' *if the following noun is in the Accusative case.*

в Москве́	в Нью-Йо́рке
в Москву́	в Нью-Йо́рк
в Босто́н	в Аме́рику
в Босто́не	в Аме́рике

5.2 Variant forms of prepositions.

The prepositions в and о have variant forms, depending on what sounds the next word begins with.

в Москве́	in Moscow
во Флори́де	in Florida
о Москве́	about Moscow
об Аме́рике	about America

There are rules governing the occurrences of these variants. The rules for во are complex; for the time being, just note that во is used when the next word begins with certain clusters of consonants, e.g., во все́х газе́тах, во Фло́риде.

The rule for о vs. об is simple:

> о + consonant sound
> об + vowel sound

This is the same kind of rule you have for *a* vs. *an* in English; *a* pear vs. *an* orange. But note that a word beginning with the Cyrillic palatal indicators е я ё ю does not begin with a vowel sound, but with the consonant /y/ (as in *yes*); therefore, consistent with the above rules, the preposition о is used, not the variant об, e.g.,

	о его́ карандаше́	/ayivó.../	about his pencil
vs.	об э́том карандаше́	/abétam.../	about this pencil

о яйце   about the egg
vs.   об Аме́рике   about America

BUT: об икре́ (="абыкре́") about caviar
Note also: обо мне 'about me' and обо всём 'about everything'.

5.3 Prepositional case endings: adjectives and nouns

The adjective and noun endings for the Prepositional case
are:

	adjective	*noun*
masculine, neuter	-ом	-е
feminine	-ой	-е

о како́м столе́?
о како́й руке́?

The adjective endings -ом, -ой are written -ем, -ей
after stems ending in a palatalized consonant or when the
spelling rules require it (i.e., when unstressed after ц ш
ж щ ч; see 1.1 above) or when the stem ends in й (the sound
/y/; see Lesson 2.2), e.g., о на́шем столе́, о большо́м
столе́, о мое́м столе́ — note the two dots in мое́м which
indicate stress. The feminines мое́й and чье́й are irregular in that they have stressed -е́й (without the two
dots):

о мое́й ру́чке   about my pen

о чье́й ру́чке   about whose pen?

The noun endings are spelled -е. Notice that the letter е
is a palatal indicator. This means that all stems become
palatalized in the Prepositional case (all except those ending in ц ш ж, which are never palatalized — see 1.1 above).

Москва́   Plain /v/: /maskvá/

в Москве́   Palatalized /ɣ/: /maskɣé/

BUT: о яйце́   Non-paired plain /ts/: /yiytsé/

Spelling exception:

Nouns ending in -ий, -ия, and -ие have a Prepositional
case spelled -ии rather than the normal ending -е.

Nominative   *Prepositional*

masc.

ге́ний   о ге́нии   about a genius

пролета́рий   о пролета́рии   about the proletarian

коммента́рий   о коммента́рии   about the comment

fem.

лаборато́рия	о лаборато́рии	about the lab
Фра́нция	о Фра́нции	about France
Ита́лия	об Ита́лии	about Italy

neut.

зда́ние	о зда́нии	about the building
упражне́ние	об упражне́нии	about the exercise
коронова́ние	о коронова́нии	about the coronation

Some nouns are peculiar in that they require the preposition
на to mean *in*, *at*, *to*, rather than the expected в. The word
уро́к 'lesson, class (below the college level)' is one such
noun:

| Пе́тя на уро́ке. | Pete is in class/at a lesson. |
| Пе́тя не хо́дит на уро́к. | Pete doesn't come to class. |

When уро́к means 'lesson (in a textbook)', в is used.

| Э́то в пе́рвом уро́ке. | That's in lesson one/ in the first lesson. |
| Э́то в тре́тьем уро́ке. | That's in the third lesson. |

5.4 Prepositional case endings: pronouns

The third person and interrogative pronouns have Prepositional case forms which are like adjective endings:

	Nominative	*Accusative*	*Prepositional*
masc.	он	его́	о нём
neut.	оно́		
fem.	она́	её	о не́й
	кто́	кого́	о ко́м
	что́	что́	о чём

The forms of the other personal pronouns are:

я	обо мне́	about me
ты́	о тебе́	about you
вы́	о ва́с	about you
мы́	о на́с	about us
они́	о ни́х	about them

(Note the variant обо before мне́.)

Examples:

О ко́м ты говори́л?	*Who* were you talking about?
О не́й.	About *her*.
О нём.	About *him*.
О чём ты говори́л?	*What* were you talking about?
Что́ ты зна́ешь о чёрной икре́?	What do you know about black caviar?
— Я ничего́ не зна́ю о не́й.	I don't know anything about *it*.
Что́ ты зна́ешь о на́шем институ́те?	What do you know about our institute?
— Я ничего́ не зна́ю о нём.	I don't know anything about *it*.
Что́ ты зна́ешь о ру́сском вине́?	What do you know about Russian wine?
— Я ничего́ не зна́ю о нём.	I don't know anything about *it*.

5.5 Location and motion: где́, куда́.

Question words distinguish *location* and *motion* just as the Prepositional and Accusative cases do: где́ means 'located in what place, where?' and куда́ means 'to what place, whither?'.

Examples:

Где́ Пе́тя?	Where is Pete?
— В Москве́.	In Moscow.
vs. Куда́ улете́л Пе́тя?	Where did Pete fly off to?
— В Москву́.	To Moscow.
Где́ икра́?	Where is the caviar?
— На столе́.	On the table.
Куда́ ты положи́л икру́?	Where did you put the caviar?
— На сто́л.	On(to) the table.
Где́ ты была́?	Where were you?
— В музе́е.	At the museum.
Куда́ ты ходи́ла?	Where did you go?
— В музе́й.	To the museum.

English used to make this same distinction; 'whither' is now
archaic, but Russian куда́ is not.

PRACTICE 6

*Repeat Practice 5, but instead of trans-
lating, ask the question* где? *or* куда?
as appropriate, e.g. в Москве — Где?
                          в Москву — Куда?

5.6 Prepositional case and word order.

Review Lesson 2.6. Recall that the rule for word order is:
save the punch line (the short answer) till last. This applies to locational sentences as well (we will use a double
stress mark " for the heavily stressed word):

	Что́ на столе́?	What's on the table?
short:	— Кни́га.	A bo͞ok.
full:	— На столе́ кни́га.	There's *a* bo͞ok on the table.

Compare:

	Где́ кни́га?	Where's the book?
short:	— На столе́.	On the ta͞ble.
full:	— Кни́га на столе́.	*The* book is on the ta͞ble.

Further examples:

Что́ у него́ в руке́?	What does he have in his hand?
— Стака́н.	A gla͞ss.
— У него́ в руке́ стака́н.	He has *a* gla͞ss in his hand.

Где́ стака́н?	Where's the glass?
— У него́ в руке́.	In his ha͞nd.
— Стака́н у него́ в руке́.	*The* glass is in his ha͞nd.

Что́ лежи́т на столе́?	What's lying on the table?
— На столе́ лежи́т карандаш.	*A* pe͞ncil is lying on the table.

Где́ лежи́т каранда́ш?	Where is the pencil lying?
— Каранда́ш лежи́т на столе́.	*The* pencil is (lying) on the ta͞ble.

As you examine the English translation of the above examples,
you will see that the difference in Russian word order often
corresponds to the difference between the indefinite article
a and the definite article *the*.

RW 6. Vowel quality next to palatalized consonants: /e/.

In Lesson 2.7 we said that the vowel /i/ is very strongly
colored by the *preceding* consonant (вы vs. ви). The vowel
/e/ is very strongly colored by the *following* consonant.
Compare the sound of нéт vs. здéсь (/ņét/ vs. /ẓḍéş/)
(Lesson 1, Exercise 9). The /e/ of нéт sounds pretty much
like the vowel in English *bet*, but the /e/ of здéсь sounds
more like the vowel in *bait*, though not so drawled out. If
you know French or German the difference is like è vs. é or
bette vs. bete, resp. Examples:

/e/ before plain		/e/ before palatalized	
нéт	no	здéсь	here
вéс	weight	вéсь	all, entire
смотрéла	watched (f.)	смотрéли	watched
газéта	newspaper	Амéрика	America
éл	ate (m.)	éсть	to eat
éла	ate (f.)	éли	ate (pl.)
секрéт	secret	музéй	museum
ракéта	rocket	о ракéте	about the rocket

The last example above illustrates the importance of this
pronunciation feature in learning the Prepositional case:
since the noun ending -e palatalizes the preceding consonant (except for ш ж ц), the last vowel of the *stem* will be
colored by it. Compare the /e/ in the stem of the Nominative and Prepositional case forms of the following words:

университéт	об университéте	about the university
коллéга	о коллéге	about the colleague
кабинéт	о кабинéте	about the study
секрéт	о секрéте	about the secret
ракéта	о ракéте	about the rocket-ship
атмосфéра	об атмосфéре	about the atmosphere
мéл	о мéле	about the chalk
газéта	о газéте	about the newspaper
балéт	о балéте	about the ballet
билéт	о билéте	about the ticket
пакéт	о пакéте	about the package
пьéса	о пьéсе	about the play
сигарéта	о сигарéте	about the cigarette

RW 7. Infinitives.

The infinitive form of the verb (e.g. писа́ть) roughly corresponds to the English verb phrase with the word *to* (e.g. *to
write*).

| Óн меня́ учи́л писа́ть. | He taught me *to write*. |
| Кто́ тебя́ учи́л говори́ть по-ру́сски? | Who taught you *to speak* Russian? |

If you know the infinitive of a verb, you can form the past
tense, and vice versa. To get from the infinitive to the
past, substitute -л for -ть (чита́-ть → чита́-л); to
get from the past to the infinitive, do the reverse (чита́-л
→ чита́-ть). There are rare exceptions, e.g. е́сть,
е́ла 'eat'.

	Infinitive	*Past*
write	писа́ть	писа́ла
read	чита́ть	чита́ла
teach	учи́ть	учи́ла
put, lay	положи́ть	положи́ла
go	ходи́ть	ходи́ла
eat	е́сть	е́ла

Some verbs show a stress shift to the feminine ending:

be	бы́ть	бы́л	была́	бы́ли
take	взя́ть	взя́л	взяла́	взя́ли
pass	переда́ть	переда́л	передала́	переда́ли
drink	пи́ть	пи́л	пила́	пи́ли

PRACTICE 7

*Say the following past tense forms aloud;
then say the infinitive forms. Check your
answers with the list given above.
Translate into English.*

чита́ла	передала́
ходи́ла	писа́ла
взяла́	пила́
была́	положи́ла
е́ла (irregular!)	учи́ла

8. Summary of case endings.

#-*declension*	Adj.+*noun*		Examples
Nomin.-Accus.	-ый/-ой	-#	э́тот бе́лый (большо́й) сто́л
Prepositional	-ом	-е	э́том бе́лом столе́

o-*declension*			
Nomin.-Accus.	-ое	-о	э́то бе́лое вино́
Prepositional	-ом	-е	э́том бе́лом вине́

a-*declension*			
Nominative	-ая	-а	э́та бе́лая плане́та
Accusative	-ую	-у	э́ту бе́лую плане́ту
Prepositional	-ой	-е	э́той бе́лой плане́те

Moscovites reading the news in **front** of the American **embassy**.

УПРАЖНЕНИЯ

1. Review of imperative forms from Lesson 2.

Say these sentences, using the proper form of the verbs in parentheses.

1. _____ у него́ стака́н. (Ask for; formal)
2. _____ у неё стака́н. (Ask for; informal)
3. _____ икру́. (take; formal)
4. _____ письмо́. (take; informal)
5. _____ нож. (pass; informal)
6. _____ газе́ту. (read; formal)
7. _____ письмо́. (read; formal)
8. _____ кни́гу. (open; formal)
9. _____ вино́. (open; informal)
10. _____ пожа́луйста. (repeat; formal)
11. _____ пожа́луйста. (repeat; informal)
12. _____ его́, как его́ зову́т. (ask; formal)
13. _____ её, как её зову́т. (ask; formal)

2. Review. Lesson 2.5 (Accusative).

П: Са́ша, попроси́те у неё кни́гу. (Pointing to Masha.)
С: Ма́ша, переда́й, пожа́луйста, кни́гу.
М: Каку́ю кни́гу?
С: Э́ту.
М: Пожа́луйста.

П: Попроси́те у неё и ру́чку.
С: Переда́й, пожа́луйста, и ру́чку.
М: Вот, пожа́луйста.

С: Спаси́бо.

М: Э́то всё?

С: Да, э́то всё.

Substitute: нож, ло́жка, каранда́ш, кольцо́, мел, яйцо́, ка́мень, ды́ня, слова́рь, ви́лка

3. Imitate, then read these syllables aloud.

Remember to pronounce и as ы after non-paired ш ж (See Analysis 1.2). Also, pronounce е as э after ш ж ц.

тык	мын	ныт	нэт	шем
тик	мин	нит	нет	чем
шик	жин	шит	щет	жем
щик	чин	чит	жет	щем
цык	цын	жит	шет	цем
чик	щин	щит	чет	чем

Make the non-paired consonants high or low pitch, as required:

товáрищ	ещё
карандáш	хорошó
нáш	яйцó
бóрщ	положил
нóж	на ножé
тóже	о кольцé
óчень	ЦРУ
лóжка	учил
рýчка	лежит
читáть	лежý

Сáша хорóший товáрищ.
Нáш товáрищ ещё лежит на дивáне.
Óчень хорошó, что Сáша ещё хорошó ýчится.
Щи да кáша — пища нáша. (Russian soldiers' proverb:
'Cabbage soup and porridge is our fare', an expression of
proud resignation.)

4. Review of adjectives (Lesson 2.3.2).

Say these sentences aloud, using the proper form of the words
in parentheses.

1. Это _____ _____ стакáн. (my first)
2. Это _____ _____ стакáн. (my second)
3. Это _____ _____ письмó. (my first)
4. Это _____ _____ письмó. (my second)
5. Это _____ _____ лóжка. (his first)
6. Это _____ _____ лóжка. (his second)

5. See Analysis 3 on possessives.

П: Саша, это ваша ложка?

С: Нет, _   не моя.

П: Чья это ложка?

С: Это машина ложка.

Substitute nouns and names of people in the class. Switch
to ты. (П: Саша, спросите Машу, чья это ложка.)

6. Identify things as to whether they are big or little, black
   or white, good or bad. See Analysis 3 on adjectives.

П: Саша, какая это ручка?
С: Большая.
П: А эта?
С: Маленькая.

М: Маша, спросите Наташу, какой это стакан?
М: Наташа, какой это стакан?
Н: Большой.
М: А этот?
Н: Маленький.

П: Петя, спросите Борю...

Substitute familiar nouns.

7.   П: Маша, спросите Сашу, какой это флаг.

       М: Саша, какой это флаг?

       С: Это испанский флаг.

       М: Ты говоришь по-испански?

       С: {Да, говорю.
          {Нет, не говорю.

   Substitute: английский
                американский / по-английски
                французский
                советский/ по-русски, по-украински,
                немецкий 'German'   по-армянски...
                китайский 'Chinese'
                японский
                итальянский

Ⱃ 8. Identify these people. You'll need three words:

композитор   'composer'
писа́тель   'writer' (Pronunciation: palatalized -ль!)
учёный   'scholar, scientist' (an adjective in form)

Remember that some names are adjective (Analysis 3.1).

Spelling exception: in certain foreign words the letter e does
not represent palatalization of the preceding consonant, e.g.,
Вольтер is pronounced as though spelled Вальтэр. We will
write the letter э in parentheses after such words to indicate
this exceptional pronunciation.

П: Что́ вы зна́ете о Шек спи́ре?
С: Шекспи́р — писа́тель.

            Пу́шкин   Достое́вский
            Па́влов   Ри́мский-Ко́рсаков
            Солжени́цын   Пастерна́к
            Ньюто́н   Чайко́вский
            Да́рвин   Вольте́р (э)
            Бальза́к   Аристо́тель
            Толсто́й   Бетхо́вен
   Switch to ты and add nationality adjectives.

П: Ма́ша, спроси́те Са́шу, что он зна́ет о Шекспи́ре.
М: Са́ша, что́ ты зна́ешь о Шекспи́ре?
С: Шек спи́р — англи́йский писа́тель.

9. Dialog 2. Analysis 4,5.

Notice the unstressed word же in this conversation. It expresses mild impatience. It is pronounced as though it were a part of the preceding word.

П: Са́ша, э́то мо́й каранда́ш?

С: Не́т, э́то мо́й каранда́ш.

П: А где́ же мо́й каранда́ш?

С: Ва́ш каранда́ш лежи́т на столе́.

Substitute familiar nouns. Switch to ты:

П: Са́ша, спроси́те Ма́шу, че́й э́то каранда́ш.

С: Ма́ша, э́то мо́й каранда́ш?

М: Не́т, э́то мо́й каранда́ш.
С: А где́ же мо́й каранда́ш?
М: Тво́й каранда́ш лежи́т на столе́.

П: Ната́ша, че́й каранда́ш лежи́т на столе́?
Н: На столе́ лежи́т са́шин каранда́ш.

10. Pronunciation Exercise. Analysis 5.

Listed below are various place names. Read them aloud. Then put them in the following sentence.

Ма́ша была́ в ....

Prepositions are pronounced as though they were not printed with a space between them and the following word, e.g.,

в Аме́рике	= "ваме́рике"
в Москве́	= "вмаскве́"
в институ́те	= "вынститу́ти"
в Ки́еве	= "фки́иви"
во Флори́де	= "вафлари́ди"

Recall that ц ш ж are never palatalized (Analysis 1.2):

в Пари́же	= "фпари́жы"
в По́льше	= "фпо́льшы"

рестора́н	Флори́да (use во)	институ́т
Босто́н	Филаде́льфия	Аме́рика
Нью-Йо́рк	Сове́тский Сою́з	Индиа́на
Москва́	кино́ (indeclinable)	Ита́лия
Детро́йт (э)	Сорбо́нна	Испа́ния
Мадри́д	кре́мль (end-stress)	Эрмита́ж
Бе́лый До́м	Кана́да	
	Фра́нция (use во)	
	По́льша	

11. Read aloud and translate; see Analysis 5 on Prepositional vs. Accusative.

в Москве́	в Аме́рику	в январе́
в Москву́	в университе́те	в феврале́
в Смоле́нске	в Кремль	в ма́рте
во Владивосто́к	в Ита́лии	в апре́ле
во Фра́нцию	в Мадри́д	в ма́е
в Сове́тский Сою́з	в Аме́рике	в ию́не
в библиоте́ку	во Флори́ду	в ию́ле
на уро́к	в рестора́н	в а́вгусте
на уро́ке	в Сове́тском Сою́зе	в сентябре́
в уро́ке	в Ита́лию	в октябре́
в Кремле́	в Венесуэ́ле	в ноябре́
в институ́т	в Лу́вре	в декабре́
в Филаде́льфии	в Ло́ндон	

12. Read these words and phrases aloud in pairs, e.g.,

газе́та   о газе́те   'about the newspaper'

The e in the stem of the word газета sounds different from the e in the stem of the word газете ; see Analysis 6.

раке́та	о раке́те
кабине́т	о кабине́те
колле́га	о колле́ге
мёл	о ме́ле
биле́т	о биле́те
сигаре́та	о сигаре́те

13. Pronunciation exercise.

Use the preposition о before consonants (including the /y/-sound of word-initial е-, я-, ё-, ю-   ) and об before vowels. See Analysis 5.2. Repeat the last word in the teacher's sentence with the yes-no Question Intonation and follow the model.

П: Во́т на́ша газе́та.

С: Газе́та? Мы́ вчера́ говори́ли о газе́те|

П: Га́рвард большо́й университе́т.
   На на́шей плане́те то́лько одна́ раке́та.
   На на́шей плане́те хоро́шая атмосфе́ра.
   Это секре́т.
   Возьми́те мёл.
   Этот компози́тор написа́л то́лько один бале́т.
   Где́ на́ш обе́д?
   Где́ нахо́дится Югосла́вия?
   Во́т на́ш секре́тный институ́т.
   В институ́те больша́я аудито́рия.
   Это хоро́шее яйцо́.
   Это зю́зина плане́та.
   Это Большо́й теа́тр.

14. Dialog 2. Analysis 5.

   Read the following sentences aloud; fill in the blanks.

   1. Ру́чка лежи́т на _____ (большо́й сто́л)
   2. Я положи́л ру́чку на _____ (большо́й сто́л)
   3. Газе́та лежи́т на _____ (э́тот сто́л)
   4. Кто́ положи́л её на _____?(э́тот сто́л)

15. Dialog 2. Analysis 5.

   Answer the question with the proper case form of the phrase
   большо́й сто́л.

   П: Где́ икра́?
   С: На большо́м столе́.

   П: Что́ э́то?
   С: Большо́й сто́л.

   Где́ кольцо́?   Где́ ды́ня?
   Куда́ он положи́л икру́?   О чём он спроси́л?
   О чём он говори́т?   Что́ она́ взяла́?
   Куда́ вы́ положи́ли письмо́?   Где́ лежи́т бума́га?

   Now answer with the proper case form of моя́ газе́та . (See
   5.3 for the forms of мой)

16. Pronoun practice: о не́й/о нём (Analysis 5.4).

   Use the yes-no contour on your question.

   П: Что́ вы́ зна́ете о большо́й раке́те?
   С: О большо́й раке́те? Я́ ничего́ о не́й не зна́ю.
      чёрная икра́   больша́я ды́ня
      эюзина плане́та   америка́нский флаг
      секре́тный институ́т   америка́нский президе́нт
      секре́тный докуме́нт   америка́нская архитекту́ра
      ле́нин па́па   францу́зское вино́
      па́пина лаборато́рия   италья́нская пи́цца
      больша́я лаборато́рия
      па́пин институ́т   Сове́тский Сою́з
      Бе́лый д о́м   Пётр Пе́рвый
      Большо́й теа́тр

   Switch:

   Ма́ша: Са́ша, что́ ты́ зна́ешь о большо́й раке́те?
   Са́ша: О большо́й раке́те? Я́ ничего́ о не́й не зна́ю.

17. (a)

П: Cáша, кáжется, говорил о дирéкторе. Спросите
    егó, о кóм он говорил.

М: Cáша, о кóм ты говорил?

С: О дирéкторе.

М: Зачéм говорить о дирéкторе?

С: Просто тáк.

Substitute:

нáш дирéктор	космонáвт
президéнт	нáш космонáвт
нáш президéнт	дóктор
преподавáтель	нáш дóктор
нáш преподавáтель	Джóрдж Вашингтóн
генерáл	Пётр Пéрвый
нáш генерáл	Толстóй
агéнт	Достоéвский
нáш агéнт	
инженéр	
нáш инженéр	

(b) П: Cáша, кáжется, говорил о винé. Спросите егó,
    о чём он говорил.

М: Cáша, о чём ты говорил?

С: О винé.

М: Зачéм тебé винó?

С: Чтобы пить.

Substitute these nouns for ВИНО and select a suitable
verb in the last speech (ПИТЬ, есть, писáть, etc.)

дыня	вилка
большáя дыня	стакáн
икрá	
чёрная икрá	мéл
винó	бумáга
бéлое винó	яйцó
книга	лимóн
большáя книга	грейпфрýт
карандáш	вóдка
большóй карандáш	коктéйль (э)
рýчка	борщ
большáя рýчка	сýп

газéтə
пéтина газéтa

18. Translate. Dialogs 2,3.

(1) Where's the pen? The pen's lying on the table. It's
     lying on the table. Where's the black caviar? It's in
     my right hand. It's in my left hand. Put the caviar on
     the table. Put the pen on the table, please. Thank you.
     Whose glass is this? Put the glass on the table. On
     Which table? On the black table. Where's the wine?
     It's on the big table. Put it on the small table. Thank
     you.

(2) What were you talking about? About black caviar. About
     my right hand. About my left hand. About him. About
     her. Why? Just because. What do you need caviar for?
     To eat. What do you need my letter for? To read. What
     do you need to talk Russian for? I don't know. Just
     because.

19. Conversation topic. Dialogs 2,3.

Three students have a conversation. A asks B where things
are, who they belong to, and who put them there. (Avoid
things that "stand;" uses only things that "lie".) Student
C interrupts to ask B what he/she is talking about and what
he/she needs it for.

20. Dialog 4.

П: Са́ша, спроси́те Ма́шу, где́ она́ была́ вчера́, в
    рестора́не и́ли в теа́тре?

С: Ма́ша, где́ ты была́ вчера́?   В рестора́не?

М: Да, я ходи́ла в рестора́н.

С: Ка́к та́м бы́ло?

М: Та́м бы́ло хорошо́.

С: Что́ ты та́м де́лала?

М: Я е́ла икру́.

Substitute places and think up things to do (last line).

теа́тр, библиоте́ка, институ́т, лаборато́рия,
        кино́, университе́т, Большо́й теа́тр.

21. Ask the question где or куда (Analysis 5.5) as if you
    don't catch the last word of the teacher's statement. Use
    the yes-no Contour to render the meaning 'Please repeat — I
    didn't hear you'.

П: Ва́ня рабо́тает в институ́те.
С: Где́?
П: В институ́те.

П: Ва́ня ходи́л в библиоте́ку.
С: Куда́?
П: В библиоте́ку.

Пе́тя рабо́тал в большо́м институ́те.
На́дя лета́ла в Москву́. (лета́ла = flew)
Го́род Филаде́льфия нахо́дится в   Пенсильва́нии.
Пе́тя лета́л в Ло́ндон.
Приходи́те в наш институ́т.
Това́рищ дире́ктор рабо́тает в кабине́те.
Това́рищ Си́доров не ходи́л в институ́т.
Та́уэр нахо́дится в Ло́ндоне.
Она́ положи́ла каранда́ш на бума́гу.
Ва́ша икра́ на большо́м столе́.
Положи́те икру́ на большо́й сто́л.
Стака́н у него́ в пра́вой руке́.
Он положи́л кни́гу в раке́ту.

Now read the above sentences aloud and translate.

22. Dialog 4, Analysis 5.   Read aloud.

   1. _____ ты была́?   (Where)

   2. _____ ты ходи́ла? (Where)

   3. Я был в _____. (restaurant)

   4. Я ходи́л в _____. (secret institute)

   5. Ива́н Петро́вич смотре́л фильм в _____. (secret
                                                  institute)

   6. Моя́ сестра́ ходи́ла в _____. (library)

   7. Профе́ссор ходи́л _____. (home)

   8. Она́ чита́ла кни́гу в _____. (big library)

   9. Он смотре́л пье́су в _____. (big theater)

   10. Вы ходи́ли в _____? (secret library)

23. Translate. Dialog 4.

Where were you yesterday? In the restaurant. I was eating caviar. My brother was in the restaurant too. He was drinking wine. Why did you go to the restaurant? To eat and talk. Where were you yesterday? In the library. In the big library in the university. I was reading a book. I was reading a book about the White House. No, you weren't reading a book. You did nothing. Where were you yesterday? I was at the theater. I went to the theater. No, you didn't go to the theater. You went to the secret institute.

24. Conversation. Dialog 4, Active Word List.

Go around the class asking your neighbor where (s)he was yesterday and what (s)he did there. A asks B, then B asks C, then C asks D, etc. Go as fast as you can.

25.   П: Где ручка? (Having given Masha a pen.)

      М: Ручка у меня в правой/левой руке.

      П: Положите её на стол.

      М: На какой стол?

      П: На большой. Саша, где ручка?

      С: Ручка лежит на столе.

      П: На каком столе?

      С: На большом.

      П: Кто положил ручку на стол?

      С: Ручку на стол положила Маша.

      П: Чья это ручка?

      С: Это машина ручка.

Substitute: карандаш
кольцо
дыня
словарь
письмо

26. Analysis 5.6. Translate.

The pen is on the table.
There's a pen on the table.
There's a newspaper lying on the table.
The newspaper was put on the table by Masha. = Masha put the newspaper on the table.
Masha put a newspaper on the table.

27. Read aloud and translate. Ромéо (э), Отéлло(э).

Вчерá я ходи́л в теáтр. В теáтре бы́ло хорошó. Я
смотрéл óчень хорóшую пьéсу. Её написáл Шекспи́р.
Всé егó пьéсы хорóшие — Гáмлет, Отéлло, Мáкбет,
Ромéо и Джульéтта, Всё хорошó, что хорошó кончáется,
Ри́чард Вторóй, Ри́чард Трéтий, Гéнрих Четвёртый, Гéн-
рих Пя́тый, Гéнрих Шестóй, Корóль Лир, и так дáлее.

28. Translate. See Lesson 3, Text Comment 9, on pas-
    sive sentences.

Zyuzya was taught to fly.   Зю́зю учи́ли летáть.
Masha was taught to read.
Sasha was taught to write in Russian.
Natasha was taught to speak Italian.
Natasha was introduced by Masha.
Masha was introduced by Natasha.
This glass was put on the table by Natasha.
The caviar was eaten by Natasha.
The caviar was taken by Masha.
The spoon was put on the table by Sasha.

29. Dialog 5. Translate.

In what city is the White House located? In Washington.
That's in what country? In America. In what country is Moscow located? In the Совéтский Сою́з.

30. Answer in the affirmative (Да, я _____):

Вы́ знáете, гдé э́тот институ́т?
Вы́ говори́те по-ру́сски?
Вы́ понимáете?
Вы́ знáете мою́ сестру́?

Now ask these questions using ты́.

УРОК ЧЕТВЁРТЫЙ

ТЕКСТ

1. Как вы помните, в первом уроке Зюзя упала с неба[1] в квартиру Ивана Петровича Сидорова и его дочки Лены[2]. Лена увидела Зюзю и удивилась, но не испугалась. Лена и Зюзя познакомились. Лена позвала маму, Нину Степановну, и представила её Зюзе.

Потом Лена начала учить Зюзю говорить, читать и писать по-русски. Они говорили о разных предметах[3]: о карандаше, о ручке, о книгах[3] и письмах[3].

2. Потом Лена показывала Зюзе[4] картинки и спрашивала Зюзю о них[3]. На одной картинке был Пётр Первый, русский царь, на другой картинке был Джордж Вашингтон, первый американский президент, на третьей картинке была Валентина Терешкова, первая в мире женщина-космонавт. Потом Лена и Зюзя говорили о флагах: об английском флаге, об албанском и болгарском флагах.

3. В это время пришли Шура и Юра и принесли красное вино и чёрную икру. Шура и Юра — коллеги. Они работают в секретном институте, который делает ракеты. Иван Петрович тоже работает в этом институте. Шура и Юра пригласили Зюзю в секретный институт.

Во время завтрака Зюзя спрашивала Лену о вилке и ноже, о ложке и стакане. Оказалось, что Зюзин нож лежал справа от Зюзи. Зюзина вилка лежала слева от Зюзи, а Зюзин стакан стоял напротив Зюзи. Потом Иван Петрович открыл бутылку сухого красного вина, и все выпили вина[5].

4. В третьем уроке Зюзя, Иван Петрович, Шура и Юра поехали в секретный институт. В секретном институте Зюзя увидела лаборатории, аудитории и кабинеты. Потом Зюзю пригласили в кабинет директора института. Директор института попросил Зюзю рассказать о её планете. Зюзя согласилась.

В следующем уроке вы прочитаете первый рассказ Зюзи о её планете.

Vocabulary

From this point onward the words in these Vocabularies will be listed alphabetically and in their dictionary forms, except for highly irregular stem changes (like пришли́ 'came', infinitive: прийти́).

буты́лка bottle

вре́мя time (irregular neuter)

во вре́мя за́втрака during breakfast (Lit.,'at the time of breakfast)

вы́пить drink

друго́й other

испуга́ться be frightened

как as; how; like

карти́нка picture, small picture

кварти́ра apartment

кото́рый which

кра́сный red

мир world

напро́тив Зю́зи opposite Z., across from Z. (Genitive)

нача́ть begin

не́бо sky

но but

оказа́ться, что turn out that

от from

спра́ва от Зю́зи to the right of Z. (Genitive)

сле́ва от Зю́зи to the left of Z. (Genitive)

пое́хать go (by vehicle)

позва́ть call

познако́миться get acquainted

пока́зывать show

по́мнить remember

попроси́ть ask, request

пото́м then

предме́т object

предста́вить present, introduce

пригласи́ть invite

пришли́ came, arrived (*Infinitive:* прийти́)

принести́ bring

прочита́ть read

ра́зный various

расска́з story

с from

сле́дующий following, next

согласи́ться agree (to do it)

спра́шивать ask

стоя́ть stand

сухо́й dry

уви́деть see, catch sight of

удиви́ться be surprised

упа́сть fall

четвёртый fourth

COMMENTS

1. с не́ба

The word не́ба is the Genitive of не́бо. When the preposition с is followed by the Genitive, it means 'from, off of.'

2. 'of'

All of the words after кварти́ру are Genitive. The meaning is 'of': 'into the apartment *of* Ivan Petrovich Sidorov and (*of*) his daughter Lena'. (See Analysis 3.7)

3. Prepositional Plural.

The adjective + noun endings are -ых, -ах. The word них = 'them'.

The Prepositional Plural will be discussed in more detail in Lesson 6.

4. Dative

The form Зю́зе is Dative. The meaning here is 'to'.

Ле́на пока́зывала Зю́зе карти́нки. Lena showed pictures *to* Z.

5. 'some'

Вы́пили вина́ (Genitive) means 'They drank *some* wine.'
Вы́пили вино́ (Accusative) means 'They drank *the* wine.'

интересно ⟨ interestingly / it is interesting

ясно — interestingly

DIALOGS

1. Роди́тельный паде́ж[1]

    С: Како́го цве́та ва́ша плане́та?
    П: На́ша плане́та жёлтого цве́та.
       С одно́й стороны́[2] на ней океа́н.
       И с друго́й стороны́ на ней океа́н.

2а. Вопро́сы е́сть?

    С: У меня́ е́сть вопро́с. Мо́жно[3] зада́ть[4] вопро́с?
    П: Коне́чно, мо́жно.
    С: Како́го ро́да сло́во "студе́нт", мужско́го, же́нского или
       сре́днего?
    П: Сло́во "студе́нт" мужско́го ро́да.

2б. У меня́ не́т стака́на.

    С: Ма́ша, ты́ ещё не поста́вила стака́н на сто́л?
       Поста́вь, пожа́луйста, стака́н на сто́л.
    М: У меня́ не́т стака́на.
    С: Извини́. Я ду́мал, что у тебя́ е́сть стака́н.

3а. Его́ взяла́ Ма́ша.

    П: Где́ мо́й стака́н?
    С: Его́, ка́жется, не́т.
    П: Его́ наве́рно взяла́ Ма́ша.
    С: Не беспоко́йтесь[5], она́ его́ вернёт.

3б. Его́ брала́ Ма́ша.

    П: Где́ мо́й стака́н?
    С: Во́т о́н стои́т[6] на столе́.
    П: О́н стои́т не[7] на своём ме́сте.
    С: Его́ наве́рно брала́ Ма́ша.
    П: Хорошо́, что она́ его́ верну́ла.

4а. О́н пошёл в библиоте́ку.

    П: Где́ Са́ша?
    М: Его́ не́т. О́н пошёл в библиоте́ку.

4б. О́н ходи́л в библиоте́ку.

    П: Са́ша, где́ вы́ бы́ли?
    С: Я ходи́л в библиоте́ку.
    П: Хорошо́, что вы́ верну́лись[8].

5. Отку́да?

    П: Отку́да э́ти пи́сьма?
    С: Из Сове́тского Сою́за.
    П: От кого́?
    С: От мое́й сестры́.
                    ***
    П: Где́ вы́ родили́сь[8]?
    С: Я родила́сь/роди́лся в Сове́тском Сою́зе.

6. Вы́учите э́ти выраже́ния!

До́брое у́тро!
Как дела́?
Ничего́. А у тебя́?
кра́сный
зелёный
голубо́й
си́ний[9]

чётвёртый
пя́тый
шесто́й
седьмо́й
восьмо́й
девя́тый
деся́тый

Translation

1. Genitive case.

S: What color is your planet?
P: Our planet is yellow.
   On the one side there's an ocean on it.
   And on the other side there's an ocean on it.

2a. Are there any questions?

S: I have a question. Can (I) ask a question?
T: Of course (you) can.
S: What is the gender of (Lit., 'of what gender') the word, "студе́нт",
   masculine, feminine, or neuter?
T: The word, "студе́нт " is (of) the masculine gender.

2b. I don't have a glass.

S: Masha, haven't you put (Lit. 'stood') the glass on the table yet (ещё
   = yet)?
M: I don't have a glass.
S: Excuse [me], I thought you had a glass.

3 a. Masha took it.

T: Where's my glass?
S: It doesn't seem to be here.
T: Masha probably took it.
S: Don't worry, she'll return it.

3b. Masha took it.

T: Where's my glass?
S: There it is, standing on the table.
T: It's not (standing) in its (proper) place.
S: Masha probably took it.
T: It's a good thing she returned it.

4a. He went to the library.

T: Where's Sasha?
M: He's not here. He went to the library.

4b. He went to the library.

T: Sasha, where have you been?
S: I went to the library.
T: It's a good thing you returned.

5. Where from?

    T: Where are these letters from?
    S: From the Soviet Union.
    T: Who from?
    S: From my sister.
                 ***
    T: Where were you born?
    S: I was born in the Soviet Union.

6. Learn these expressions:

    Good morning.
    How are things?
    Not bad (Lit., 'nothing').   fourth
    And you (Lit., 'by you')?   fifth
    red   sixth
    green   seventh
    light blue   eighth
    dark blue   ninth
                          tenth

ACTIVE WORD LIST

Nouns

цве́т	color
ро́д	gender
вопро́с	question
плане́та	planet
сло́во	word
ме́сто	place
у́тро	morning
де́ло	business, affair
Ка́к дела́?	How are things?
океа́н	ocean
сою́з	union
сторона́	side
выраже́ние	expression

[vzīlá]

Verbs

бра́ть; бра́л, брала́, бра́ли	take
взя́ть; взя́л, взяла́, взя́ли	take
пойти́; пошёл, пошла́, пошли́	go
бы́ть; бы́л, была́, бы́ло, бы́ли	be
не́ был, не была́, не́ было, не́ были	
зада́ть; за́дал, задала́, за́дали	to ask (a question)
роди́ться; роди́лся, роди́лась,	be born
роди́ли́сь	
поста́вить; поста́вила	put (in a standing position)
поста́вь(те)	put (imperative form)
верну́ться; верну́лся, верну́лась	return, come back
.вернётся	will return, come back
верну́ть	return (something)
вернёт	will return (something)
ка́жется	it seems/apparently
стои́т/стоя́т	it/they stand, is/are standing

не беспокойтесь, не беспокойся   don't worry, don't trouble yourself
выучи.(те)   learn, commit to memory (*Imperative*)
извини(те)   excuse [me]

Adjectives

советский	Soviet
родительный	genitive
жёлтый	yellow
красный	red
зелёный	green
голубой	light blue
синий	dark blue
другой	other, another, different
мужской	masculine
женский	feminine
средний	neuter
добрый	good; kind
четвёртый	fourth
пятый	fifth
шестой	sixth
седьмой	seventh
восьмой	eighth
девятый	ninth
десятый	tenth
свой, своя, своё	one's own, (my, your, our, her, his, it's, their)
наш, наша, наше	our
один, одна, одно	one

Miscellaneous

с + Genitive	from, off of
с одной стороны	on one side
у	at, by
У меня есть книга.	I have a book. (Lit., 'By me there is a book.')
из	from, out of
от	from
откуда	where from
ничего	nothing
наверно	probably
можно	one can (I, you, he, etc., can)
конечно	of course
(pronounced as though spelled конешно)	
нет X (X = Genitive)	there is no X, there are no X.
У меня нет брата.	I don't have a brother. (Lit., 'By me there is no brother.')
есть X (X = Nominative)	there is X, there are X
У меня есть брат.	I have a brother. (Lit., 'By me there is a brother.')

COMMENTS

1. Роди́тельный паде́ж

The name for the genitive case is роди́тельный. The literal translation of the genitive phrase Како́го цве́та 'What color..? is 'Of what color'.

2. С одно́й стороны́

The preposition с (variant form со) plus the Genitive is usually translated 'from, off of', (see Text Comment 1):

Кни́га упа́ла со стола́. (Gen. of сто́л)   The book fell off of the table.
Зю́зя упа́ла с не́ба.(Gen. of не́бо)   Zyuzya fell from the sky.

With the noun сторона́ 'side', however, the translation may be 'on', as
in the Dialog: с одно́й/друго́й стороны́ 'on the one/other side'. See also
сле́ва 'on the left,' спра́ва 'on the right'.

3. Мо́жно

This word literally means 'one can, one may,' but in translating it you
should supply a subject like 'I can, you can, etc.' to make it sound less
stilted.

4. зада́ть вопро́с

In Lesson 2 (Active Word List, Comment 3) it was said that *ask* must be
translated спроси́ть in the sense of *inquire* and попроси́ть in the sense
of *request*.   A third way of translating it must be chosen for the sense
pose/put , as in 'to pose a question: зада́ть вопро́с.

In other words, Russian has no cover term like *ask* for the three verbs
inquire, request, pose.

5. не беспоко́йтесь

The familiar form is не беспоко́йся.

6. Third person forms of verbs: стои́т/стоя́т.

Verb forms ending in —т have third person subjects (Singular о́н, она́,
оно́; plural они́; or nouns). Singular vs. Plural is distinguished by the
vowel preceding —т : Sing. = и or е (ё), Plural = у/ю or а/я , depending
on the type of verb (to be discussed later, Lesson 5:3).

я	ты	он	вы	они	
стою́	стои́шь	стои́т	стои́те	стоя́т	
лежу́	лежи́шь	лежи́т	лежи́те	лежа́т	
зна́ю	зна́ешь	зна́ет	зна́ете	зна́ют	they know
понима́ю	понима́ешь	понима́ет	понима́ете	понима́ют	they understand
верну́	вернёшь	вернёт	вернёте	верну́т	they will return
напишу́	напи́шешь	напи́шет	напи́шете	напи́шут	they will write

7. Negation

This sentence means that the glass is there, but it's in the wrong place:
не на своём ме́сте.   The verb is not negated. Compare the sentence in
Lesson 3, Text comment 4:

Э́ту раке́ту сде́лали не на на́шей плане́те.	This rocketship wasn't made on our planet.

8. -ся verbs

The verbal particle -ся means that the verb is intransitive, i.e., it
cannot have an Accusative direct object.
Compare:

О́н вернётся.	He will return (= come back).
О́н вернёт кни́гу.	He will return the book (= give back).
О́н верну́лся.	He returned (came back).
О́н верну́л кни́гу.	He returned the book (gave back).
Она́ верну́лась.	She returned.
Она́ верну́ла кни́гу.	She returned the book.

As the last example shows, -ся has the variant -сь when a vowel precedes
(верну́ла - сь, верну́ли - сь).
Further examples:

Не беспоко́йтесь.	Don't bother.
Не беспоко́йте его.	Don't bother him.
Не беспоко́йся.	Don't bother.
Не беспоко́й его.	Don't bother him.
На́ша овца́ родила́сь в ма́рте.	Our ewe was born in March.
Сестра́ родила́ в ма́рте.	Our sister gave birth (bore a child) in March.

Russian speakers vary as to where they put the stress on the past tense
of this verb; we use   роди́лся, родила́сь, роди́лись.

Many Russian speakers pronounce -ся/-сь as though spelled -са/-с.
Infinitives with -ся are pronounced like a double цц, e.g., роди́ться
as though роди́цца.

9. си́ний, сре́дний

The stem final consonant of these adjectives is a palatalized n; the
palatal indicators и е я ю (rather than ы о а у) are used in all case
endings, e.g.,

сре́дняя	си́няя	Nom. Sg. f.
сре́днее	си́нее	Nom. Sg. n.
сре́днюю	си́нюю	Acc. Sg. f.
сре́днем	си́нем	Prep. Sg. masc/neut.

Э́тот каранда́ш си́него цве́та.	That pencil is dark blue. (Lit., 'of dark blue color')
Сло́во "вино́" — сре́днего ро́да.	The word вино́ is neuter. (Lit., 'of neuter gender')

There are very few such palatalized adjectives.

1. Nominative plural forms.

Masculine and feminine nouns have the ending -ы in the Nominative plural. Neuters have -а.

	Singular	Plural
masc.	стол	столы́
	стака́н	стака́ны
	конве́рт	конве́рты
fem.	плане́та	плане́ты
	бу́ква	бу́квы
	сестра́	сёстры
neut.	письмо́	пи́сьма
	кольцо́	ко́льца
	яйцо́	я́йца

These endings are spelled –и and –я , respectively, when the spelling rules require (i.e., when the stem final consonants are palatalized (дыня/ дыни, преподаватель/ преподава́тели) when the stem final consonant is the /y/ sound (музе́й/музе́и, упражне́ние / упражне́ния) or, in the case of –и , when the stem final consonant is к, г, х or ш, ж, ч, щ (ру́чка/ ру́чки, това́рищ/това́рищи).

Special adjectives are spelled with the palatal indicator и in all plural case forms, except for все́ 'all'.

все́ столы́	all (the) tables
э́ти столы́	these tables

The pronunciation of the first vowel (/e/) in э́ти is affected by this palatalization of /t̡/ in the plural forms (See Lesson 3.6). Compare:

/éta/ э́та кни́га (/e/ as in не́т)	this book
/ét̡i/ э́ти кни́ги (/e/ as in зде́сь)	these books

Ordinary adjectives have the ending -ые/ие (all genders):

хоро́шие, бе́лые { конве́рты (m.)
                    плане́ты (f.)
                    я́йца (n.)

Summary chart of Nominative endings:

Singular		Plural	
Adj. + Noun		Adj. + Noun	
masc. -ый -о́й	– #	-ые	-ы
fem. -ая	-а		-ы
neut. -ое	-о		-а

1.1 Stress shift in nouns.

For some nouns (by far the minority) there is a shift of stress as you go from singular to the plural (письмо́/пи́сьма). Most of these shifts are in short, one or two-syllable words. In some cases there are rules you can learn in order to help you with this problem, e.g., for almost all bisyllabic neuters the stress will shift:

Sing: stress on Stem　　　　──────→　　Plur: stress on Ending
　　　сло́во　　　　　　　　　　　　　　　　сло́ва
Sing: stress on Ending　　　──────→　　Plur: stress on Stem
　　　письмо́　　　　　　　　　　　　　　　пи́сьма

In order to describe stress shifts succinctly, we will use the capital letters S and E; S = stress on the Stem, E = stress on the Ending. The shift of stress on a word like сло́во/слова́ will be described as stress pattern SE, where the first letter stands for the singular cases and the second letter stands for the plural cases. Stress pattern ES is exemplified by письмо́/пи́сьма.

The stress symbol E must be understood to mean "stress on the Endings other than zero," of course, since you can't put stress on a zero ending. In such cases, stress falls on the immediately preceding syllable. Examples:

	Nom. Sg.	Prep. Sg.	Nom. Plur.
сто́л EE =	сто́л	столе́	столы́

Some nouns (very few) have a stress shift *within* the Singular and/or *within* the Plural forms, e.g.

Nom. Sg.　рука́
Acc. Sg.　ру́ку
Prep. Sg.　руке́

For such nouns we will use the symbol M (= Moveable stress). For feminine singular nouns M means that it is the Accusative case (and *only* the Accusative) which has a shift back to the stem (рука́ → ру́ку). We will give more details when you have learned more nouns and more case forms.

In the Active Word Lists from now on we will list the Nominative Plural forms if there is a shift in stress in the Plural, e.g., письмо́; пи́сьма, сло́во; слова́. The semi-colon means that the following word is Nom. Plur. and, unless otherwise stated, all the other plural case forms have stress on the same syllable. Case forms listed before the semi-colon are Singular; for example a word like сто́л (stress pattern EE) will be listed like this:

сто́л, стола́; столы́

The form just before the semi-colon is Genitive Singular (see section 3, below) and it shows that the endings are stressed in all the Singular cases; the form столы́ *after* the semi-colon shows that all the *plural* endings are stressed.

For words with stress pattern SS (stress on the stem throughout, which is the pattern for most Russian nouns) we will list only the Nominative Singular.

1.2 Irregular nouns.

Some masculine nouns have an irregular ending -а/-я instead of -ы in the Nominative Plural, e.g.

Sing.　　　　Plur.
профе́ссор　профессора́　　　professor

We will list such irregularities in the Active Word Lists the same way we do
for stress shift: the first form after the semi-colon will be the Nominative
Plural, e.g.,

профе́ссор; профессора́

     Some nouns, mostly masculine, have an irregular stem change as you go from
Singular (all cases) to Plural (all cases). E.g.,

	Singular	*Plural*
Stem	/brat-/	/braty-/
Nom.	бра́т	бра́тья /braty-a/
Prep.	бра́те	бра́тьях /braty-akh/

Again, the Active Word Lists will have the Nominative Plural form cited right
after the semi-colon; remember that such stem changes will characterize *all*
case forms in the Plural, — not just the Nominative.

1.3 The inserted vowel.

     When a noun ends in certain clusters of consonants, the vowel *e* or *o* is
inserted into the cluster if a zero ending follows. For example, the stem of
the word for *end* is конц-

в конце́ уро́ка   at the end of the lesson

The Nominative Singular ending is zero, and the vowel is inserted:

Э́то коне́ц уро́ка.   That's the end of the lesson.

You have not yet met any words with the inserted vowel *o* , but here is an
example :

щено́к, о щенке́   puppy

     Words having inserted vowels will be listed in the Active Word Lists with
the vowel (e) or (o) in parentheses, e.g., коне́ц (e).

Summary.
     Listed below are all the nouns you have met so far in the Active Word Lists
except for those nouns which have *no* peculiarity in their plural forms and with
the exception of a few which have peculiarities that you won't encounter in the
exercises in this book. This list includes the nouns with stress patterns other
than SS, the irregular plural stems, the irregular Nominative Plural endings,
and the occurrences of inserted vowels. These words are listed in the way the
Active Word List will cite them from now on — with singular forms before the
semi-colon, and plural forms after it. (We omit mention of case forms that
won't be discussed until future lessons.) In the center column you'll see an
indication of the kind of irregularity or stress pattern the noun has.

Active Word Listing	Type of irregularity	Gloss
де́ло; дела́	SE	business, affair
ме́сто; места́	SE	place
сло́во; слова́	SE	word
яйцо́; я́йца	ES	egg
письмо́; пи́сьма	ES	letter
страна́; стра́ны	ES	country
сестра́; сёстры	ES	sister
но́ж, ножа́; ножи́	EE	knife
сто́л, стола́; столы́	EE	table
паде́ж, падежа́; -жи́	EE	case
слова́рь, словаря́; -ри́	EE	dictionary
каранда́ш, -ша́; -ши́	EE	pencil
коне́ц(e), конца́; концы́	EE, (e)	end
рука́, ру́ку; ру́ки	MM	arm, hand
сторона́, сто́рону; сто́роны	MM	side
го́род; города́	SE, NP1 ending	city
до́м; дома́	SE, NP1 ending	house, building
профе́ссор; -ра́	SE, NP1 ending	professor
цве́т; цвета́	SE, NP1 ending	color
господи́н; господа́	SE, NP1 ending, Pl. stem	Mr.
бра́т; бра́тья	NP1 ending, Pl. stem	brother
ка́мень (e)	inserted vowel	stone
кольцо́	ES	

PRACTICE 1

Say these words aloud and give the Nominative Plural. Mark stress. Check your answers with the list above. If the word is not on the list, it will have the regular ending.

но́ж	письмо́	го́род	газе́та
ви́лка	рестора́н	стака́н	фла́г
ло́жка	рука́	профе́ссор	до́м
коне́ц	океа́н	бра́т	господи́н
конве́рт	теа́тр	сестра́	студе́нт
сло́во	ме́сто	фи́льм	каранда́ш
			слова́рь

2.   Есть.

This word means 'There is, There are,' e.g.,

Там есть па́рки?	*Are there* any parks there?
Есть.	Yes, *there are.*
Там есть сто́л?	*Is there* a table there?
Есть.	Yes, *there is.*
В на́шем го́роде есть па́рк.	There is a park in our town.
В Москве́ есть хоро́шие теа́тры.	There are good theaters in Moscow.
В на́шем институ́те есть лаборато́рии, аудито́рии, кабине́ты.	There are labs, lecture halls, and offices in our institute.
Вино́ есть?	Is there any wine?
Карандаши́ есть?	Are there any pencils?
Карандаши́ есть.	There are pencils (= We have pencils).

Don't use есть if some word other than the noun is in the punch line of
the sentence (i.e., bears the main stress). In the following example the word
хоро́шие is stressed, not па́рки ; therefore, the word есть is not used in
Russian and the phrase *there are* is not used in English:

В Москве́ хоро́шие па́рки.	Moscow has *nice* parks (= The parks in Moscow are *nice*.)

The more usual word order for this type of sentence is with хоро́шие in the
last position - this is the usual rule for word order: save the punch line
till last (Lesson 2.2.6):

Па́рки в Москве́ хоро́шие.	The parks in Moscow are *nice*.
Преподава́тели в на́шем университе́те хоро́шие.	The teachers in our university are *good*.

Compare:

В на́шем университе́те есть хоро́шие преподава́тели.	There are (some) good *teachers* at our university.

For more examples of есть , see section 3.6.
In the past and future tenses (was, were; will be) there is no problem:
you use the proper form of бы́л (past) or бу́дут /бу́дет (future) no matter
what word constitutes the punch line, e.g.,

Там бы́ли па́рки.	There were parks there.
Па́рки там бы́ли хоро́шие.	The parks there were good.
Там была́ чёрная икра́.	There was black caviar there.
В го́роде бу́дет секре́тный институ́т.	There will be a secret institute in the city.
Лаборато́рии бу́дут о́чень хоро́шие.	The labs will be very good.

PRACTICE 2

Change these sentences to past tense, using the proper form of би́л, била́, би́ло, би́ли.

Та́м е́сть па́рки?
Та́м е́сть па́рк?
Па́рки та́м хоро́шие?
Та́м е́сть хоро́шая преподава́тельница?
Карандаши́ е́сть?
На столе́ е́сть письмо́?

Now repeat, using the form бу́дем *(Singular) or* бу́дут *(Plural). Translate the resulting sentences.*

3.1 Genitive case: singular endings.

The genitive case is required in a wide variety of constructions. In this lesson we will discuss four of them. As you study them refer to this chart of endings; note that there is no difference between masculine and neuter — this is true of most of the case endings: masc. and neuter are identical in all cases except Nom. Sg., Nom. Pl., and Gen. Plur.

	Adj. + Noun	
masc./neut.	-ого	-а
fem.	-ой	-ы

Examples:

	Nominative singular	*Genitive singular*	
masc.	большо́й сто́л	большо́го стола́	of the big table
neut.	большо́е кольцо́	большо́го кольца́	of the big ring
fem.	больша́я газе́та	большо́й газе́ты	of the big newspaper

Pronunciation: all genitive endings in -ого/-его are pronounced as though spelled -ово/-ево , with the sound /v/ instead of /g/.

The spelling rules will effect the following changes (Lesson 3.1.2):

-ого → -его   -а → -я
-ой → -ей   -ы → -и

For example:

Nominative singular	*Genitive singular*
хоро́ший слова́рь	хоро́шего словаря́
хоро́шая газе́та	хоро́шей газе́ты
хоро́шая ды́ня	хоро́шей ды́ни

Special adjectives have the same endings as ordinary adjectives, except that мой, твой and чей have —ей instead of —ой in the feminine. This is the same irregularity you met in the Prepositional case.

твоей сестры́	your sister's
моей сестры́	my sister's
этой газе́ты	of this newspaper

The Genitive forms of the pronouns are:

Singular		Plural	
Nom.	Gen.	Nom.	Gen.
я́	меня́	мы́	на́с
ты́	тебя́	вы́	ва́с
о́н	} его́	они́	и́х
оно́			
она́	её		
кто́	кого́		
что́	чего́		

3.2 не́т

The word не́т is used in two ways:

(1) 'No'

— Вы́ бы́ли в Москве́?	Were you (Have you been) in Moscow?
— Не́т.	No.

(2) 'There is no X'

— Вино́ е́сть?	Is there any wine?
— Вина́ не́т.	There is no wine.

The word не́т in usage (2) functions as the negative counterpart of е́сть 'There is, There are' - see section 2, above. The element X in the не́т X construction is always in the Genitive case (Вина́).

Стака́н е́сть? — Не́т, стака́на не́т.	Is there a glass? No, there is no glass.
Икра́ е́сть? — Не́т, икры́ не́т.	Is there any caviar? No, there is no caviar.
В на́шем го́роде не́т хоро́шего па́рка.	There is no good park in our town.
Зде́сь не́т стола́.	There is no table here.

(We shall avoid the use of не́т with plurals for the time being; the forms of the Genitive plural will be presented in Lesson 7.)

Sometimes the translation 'There is no X' is awkward, but the meaning *absence* is clear:

Петра́ Ива́новича не́т.	Peter Ivanovich isn't here. (lit., There is no Peter Ivanovich.)
Его́ не́т.	He isn't here. (= He's absent.)
Ни́ны Серге́евны не́т.	Nina Sergeyevna isn't here.
Её не́т.	She isn't here.
На́шего преподава́теля не́т.	Our teacher isn't here.
Кого́ сего́дня не́т?	Who isn't here today?
Пе́ти не́т.	Pete isn't here.
Пра́вды не́т.	There is no truth (Truth doesn't exist.).
"Пра́вды" сего́дня не́т, а "Изве́стия" е́сть.	There is no Pravda today, but we have Izvestiya.

The past form of the нет construction is не́ бы́ло X, with stress on не́ ; since the element X is Genitive, there is no Nominative form for the verb to agree with and the verb is always in the neuter.

Вина́ не́ было.	There was no wine.
Стака́на не́ было.	There was no glass.
Икры́ не́ было.	There was no caviar.
Пе́ти вчера́ не́ было на уро́ке.	Pete wasn't at the lesson yesterday.
Меня́ то́же не́ было.	I wasn't here either. (I was also absent.)

The future form is не бу́дет:

Вина́ не бу́дет.	There will be no wine.
Стака́на не бу́дет.	There will be no glass.
Икры́ не бу́дет.	There will be no caviar.
Пе́ти за́втра не бу́дет на уро́ке.	Pete won't be at the lesson tomorrow.
Меня́ то́же не бу́дет.	I won't either.
Тебя́ не бу́дет?	Won't you be here/there? (Will you be absent?)

PRACTICE 3

Cover up the right-hand column and look at the words on the left. For each item say aloud the Russian for There is no X *or* X isn't here, *i.e. say the word in the Genitive Sing. form followed by* нéт. *Check your answers.*

стакáн	Стакáна нéт.
флáг	Флáга нéт.
Ивáн	Ивáна нéт.
кáмень	Кáмня нéт.
преподавáтель	Преподавáтеля нéт.
винó	Винá нéт.
письмó	Письмá нéт.
мéсто	Мéста нéт.
икрá	Икры́ нéт.
вилка	Вилки нéт.
ды́ня	Ды́ни нéт.
преподавáтельница	Преподавáтельницы нéт.
Сáша	Сáши нéт.
Мáша	Мáши нéт.
óн	Егó нéт.
онá	Еë нéт.
онó	Егó нéт.
они́	Их нéт.

Now repeat, replacing нéт *with* нé было *(past) and then* не бýдет *(future).*

3.3 Genitive with prepositions: из, от

Many prepositions are not changed in meaning by the choice of case forms because there is, for such prepositions, no choice at all: they are invariably followed by the Genitive case. The prepositions из 'from, out of' and от 'from, away from' are of this type.

Я́ из Москвы́.	I'm from Moscow.
Я́ из Ленингрáда.	I'm from Leningrad.
Вóт письмó от твоегó брáта.	Here's a letter from your brother.
Вóт письмó от твоéй сестры́.	Here's a letter from your sister.

The prepositions из and от can both be translated as 'from,' although they mean different things:

из	'from, out from the inside of something'
от	'from, away from alongside of something'

Normally, you use от 'from' with people (письмó от брáта), and из with things and places (Я́ из Москвы́.).

(You've also met the preposition с + Genitive; see Text Comment 1 and Dialog Comment 2. This preposition will be discussed later. For the time being, just learn с однóй стороны́ as a fixed expression.)

PRACTICE 4

Read the following sentences aloud, inserting the preposition
из *or* от, *as appropriate. Also, give the dictionary form*
(Nominative) of the noun that comes after it.

Во́т письмо́ ___ бра́та.
Во́т письмо́ ___ на́шего дире́ктора.
Во́т письмо́ ___ Владивосто́ка.
Во́т письмо́ ___ Москвы́.
Во́т письмо́ ___ сестры́.
Во́т письмо́ ___ на́шей сестры́.
Во́т письмо́ ___ на́шего пе́рвого президе́нта, Джо́рджа
            Вашингто́на.
Во́т письмо́ ___ на́шей ма́мы.
Во́т письмо́ ___ на́шего па́пы.

3.4 Pronouns with н- after prepositions.

The Genitive forms of the pronouns о́н, оно́, она́, они́ (его́, её, и́х)
have two meanings:

(1) Possessive meaning 'his, her, its, their'

Во́т письмо́ от его́ бра́та.   Here's a letter from *his* brother.
Во́т письмо́ от её сестры́.   Here's a letter from *her* sister.
Во́т письмо́ от и́х бра́та.   Here's a letter from *their* brother.

(2) Pronominal meaning 'him, her, it, them'

Спроси́те его́.   Ask *him*.
Спроси́те её.   Ask *her*.
Спроси́те и́х.   Ask *them*.

If a preposition precedes one of these words when used *pronominally*, they
are prefixed with н-.

Во́т письмо́ от него́.   Here's a letter from him.
Во́т письмо́ от неё.   Here's a letter from her.
Во́т письмо́ от ни́х.   Here's a letter from them.

Here are some examples of the Prepositional case of these pronouns:

На не́й (На плане́те) е́сть океа́н.   There's an ocean on it (on the
                                planet).

На нём (На столе́) стои́т стака́н.   There's a glass on it (on the
                                table).

В нём (В институ́те) нахо́дится   There's a large lab located in it
 большáя лаборато́рия.   (in the institute).

3.5 The preposition y.

The preposition y means 'by, near, at' and it is used very much like
French *chez*. It is always used with the Genitive case.

у Петра́   at Peter's place, chez Pierre
у Пе́ти   at Pete's

The context must often be used to render an appropriate translation of this preposition, because it means 'in a place normally associated with what we're talking about.' Thus, if you are talking to a Russian and comparing food in your two countries, you might say:

Икра́ у на́с нехоро́шая.	Caviar in our country isn't very good.

Further examples:

Она́ у до́ктора.	She's at the doctor's (office).
О́н у дире́ктора.	He's at the director's (office).
Они́ жи́ли у меня́.	They lived at my house/my place.

Don't use the word for 'house' (дом) when you want to say 'at somebody's house.' Just use the preposition y and the Genitive case of the person's name:

О́н у Са́ши.	He's at Sasha's house/place.

PRACTICE 5

Read these sentences aloud and supply the appropriate preposition to mean 'located in, at, on': в, у *or* на. *Translate, and give the Nominative form and identify which case is used. (the verb* живёт *means 'lives';* рабо́тает *means 'works'.)*

Она́ рабо́тает ___ институ́те.
Она́ живёт ___ жёлтой плане́те.
Она́ живёт ___ ма́мы.
Стака́н стои́т ___ столе́.
О́н рабо́тает ___ университе́те.
О́н живёт ___ на́шей плане́те.
Она́ живёт ___ на́шей сестры́.
Пе́тя живёт ___ на́шего бра́та.
Пе́тя живёт ___ него́.
Пе́тя живёт ___ бра́та.

There is one set of idiomatic expressions that doesn't follow the usage of y and от as described above: when you *take, borrow* or *steal* something *from* somebody, you use y (though you would expect от from what has been said). So when you learn the verb pair брать/ взять, you have to learn that y is used with them.

Я́ взя́л у бра́та ру́сский слова́рь.	I took a Russian dictionary *from* my brother.
Я́ взя́л у сестры́ ру́сский слова́рь.	I took a Russian dictionary *from* my sister.
Я́ бра́л у сестры́ ру́сский слова́рь.	I took (and returned) a Russian dictionary *from* my sister.

There are a number of special expressions like слева от 'to the left of'
and справа от 'to the right of' which take the genitive after от and it
doesn't matter whether the object is a person, place or thing — always use от
in these fixed expressions, not из or у.

слева от Ивана   to the left of Ivan
слева от стола   to the left of the table

3.6   To have and to have not.

In conversational Russian there is no verb 'to have'. The notion of *possession* is expressed by the preposition у plus the verb *be*, e.g.

У меня была дыня.   I had a melon.
У меня был словарь.   I had a dictionary.
У меня было яйцо.   I had an egg.
У меня были яйца.   I had eggs.

The preposition у is followed by the genitive case, as explained in 2.5
above. The у- phrase usually comes first in the sentence in this construction
(unlike the 'at'-construction, e.g. Она живёт у меня.). The thing possessed
(melon, dictionary, egg) is Nominative and the verb agrees with it.

'Will have' is expressed by the future form будет/будут 'will be'.

У него завтра будет русская икра.   He will have Russian caviar tomor-
                                                 row.
У него завтра будет урок.   He will have a lesson tomorrow.
У него завтра наверно будет   He'll probably have a letter tomor-
   письмо.   row.
У него завтра наверно будут   He'll probably have letters tomor-
   письма.   row.

'Have' in the present tense lacks a verb, as do all sentences with 'be' in
the present tense. The word есть may be used, in accordance with the discussion in section 2, above.

У меня есть ручка.   I have a pen.
У него есть словарь.   He has a dictionary.
У Пети есть вино.   Pete has wine.

As mentioned in 2, above, you don't use есть   when an attributive word
bears sentence stress:

У вас большая семья?   Do you have a big family?
OR: Семья у вас большая?   (I know you have a family; is it a
                                                 big one?)
vs. У вас есть семья?   Do you have a family?

In English we use the verb *have* with places and institutions, e.g. *Moscow
has* nice parks. With such nouns you should avoid the у- construction, because
it is used mostly with people; use в instead. (See example in 2, above.)

В Москве хорошие парки.   Moscow has nice parks.
 = Парки в Москве хорошие.   = The parks *in* Moscow are nice.
В нашем институте есть лабора-   Our institute has labs. (There
   тории.   are labs *in* our institute.)
В нашем городе есть парк.   Our town has a park. (There is a
                                                 park *in* our town.)

Another way of expressing possession in these latter two examples is to use у нас instead of the possessive adjective нашем.

У нас в институ́те е́сть лабора- то́рии.	Our institute has labs.
У нас в го́роде е́сть па́рк.	Our town has a park.

Similarly:

Что́ у него́ в руке́?	What does he have in his hand?
У на́с в Аме́рике икра́ нехоро́шая.	We have poor caviar in America.

The negative counterpart of есть was described in section 3.2 above; use нет/не́ бы́ло/не бу́дет plus genitive with the у- construction in accordance with that description, e.g.,

У меня́ не́т ру́чки.	I don't have a pen.
У него́ не́т словаря́.	He doesn't have a dictionary.
У Пе́ти не́т вина́.	Pete doesn't have (any) wine.
У ва́с не́т семьи́?	Don't you have a family?
У на́с в го́роде не́т па́рка.	We don't have a park in our town. (There is no park ...)
У него́ в руке́ ничего́ не́т.	He doesn't have anything in his hand.
У Са́ши не́т бра́та.	Sasha doesn't have a brother.
У Са́ши не́т сестры́.	Sasha doesn't have a sister.
У на́шей сестры́ не́т до́ма.	Our sister doesn't have a house.
У на́с сего́дня не́т икры́.	We don't have any caviar today.

PRACTICE 6

Read aloud the following sentences and insert either его́ *or* него́ *, as required. Translate. Then repeat with* её/неё

Во́т письмо́ от ___ .
Во́т письмо́ от ___ сестры́.
Во́т письмо́ от ___ бра́та.
Спроси́те ___ .
Спроси́те ___ профе́ссора.
На ___ плане́те не́т океа́на.
У ___ е́сть икра́.
У ___ не́т икры́.
Что́ у ___ в руке́?
Что́ вы зна́ете о ___ плане́те?
Я говори́л о ___ сестре́.
Где́ ___ стака́н?
Пе́тя стои́т сле́ва от ___ .
Я взя́л у ___ словарь.
Я взя́л у ___ бра́та словарь.
Я взя́л словарь у ___ профе́ссора.
Ми́ша живёт у ___ .
Ми́ша живёт у ___ бра́та.

PRACTICE 7

Change from negative to affirmative, e.g. У меня́ не́ было
ды́ни → У меня́ была́ ды́ня. *You have to change the noun
to nominative and make the verb agree with it.*

У меня́ не́ было словаря́.   вина́
                кольца́   кни́ги
                стака́на   икры́
                профе́ссора   ка́мня
                сестры́   стола́
                раке́ты   америка́нского фла́га
                ру́чки   францу́зского вина́
                ме́ла   большо́й ды́ни
                конве́рта

3.7 Genitive 'of'

The Genitive case often corresponds to the English preposition 'of' or
the possessive *'s*.

дире́ктор на́шего институ́та.   the director *of* our institute
кни́га моего́ бра́та   my *brother's* book

In Lesson 3.4 there was a discussion of possessives of the type са́шина
кни́га 'Sasha's book.' This type of possessive can be formed *only* from a-
declension nouns. If the noun is of another declension class, like брат in
the second example above, you must use the Genitive case: кни́га бра́та,
literally 'the book of my brother.' You can also use the Genitive of a- declension nouns if you want to, i.e., instead of се́стрина кни́га you can say
кни́га сестры́ for '(my) sister's book.'

Further examples:

в кабине́те президе́нта   in the president's office (= the
                               office *of* the president)
в конце́ семе́стра   at the end *of* the semester
теа́тры на́шей страны́   the theaters *of* our country
бра́тья моего́ профе́ссора   my professor's brothers (= the
                               brothers *of* my professor)

In some constructions the Genitive is used where *of* would sound stilted
in English.

Како́го цве́та ва́ша кни́га?   (Of) what color is your book?
Моя́ кни́га кра́сного цве́та.   My book is (of) red (color).
Како́го ро́да сло́во "кни́га"?   (Of) what gender is the word кни́га?
Сло́во "кни́га" - же́нского ро́да. The word кни́га is (of the)
                               feminine gender.

4. свой

The English sentence *Pete took his book* can mean two things: 'Pete took his (Pete's) book' or 'Pete took his (somebody else's) book.' In Russian there is no such ambiguity. The special adjective свой means 'belonging to the same person as the subject of the clause.'

Пе́тя взял свою́ кни́гу.	Pete took his (Pete's) book.
Пе́тя взял его́ кни́гу.	Pete took his (somebody else's) book.

Same goes for *her*:

Ма́ша взяла́ свою́ кни́гу.	Masha took her (own) book.
Ма́ша взяла́ её кни́гу.	Masha took her (somebody else's) book.

Same goes for *their*:

Они́ взя́ли свои́ кни́ги.	They took their (own) books.
Они́ взя́ли и́х кни́ги.	They took their (somebody else's) books.

If the noun refers to family members or parts of the body, you normally do not use any possessive word at all, e.g.,

Пе́тя лю́бит сестру́.	Pete likes (his own) sister.
Что́ у него́ в руке́?	What does he have in (his) hand?

The endings of свой are identical to those of мо́й: свой, своя́, своё, свою́, etc.

5. Aspect

Verbs have various *tense* forms, e.g. past, present, future. Verbs also have various *aspect* forms.

The term *aspect* is unfamiliar to most English-speaking students, despite the fact that English verbs have aspect as well as tense. For example, the forms *took* and *was taking* are both in the past tense; the difference between the two is one of aspect.

In Russian, verbs that specify an end-point are called *Perfective* verbs (like взять, 'take'); their partners are called *Imperfective* verbs (like брать, 'take').

Before reading the following section, review Dialogs 3 and 4, where these verbs are illustrated in context.

5.1 The Perfective Aspect specifies 'end-point'

(1) взял/брал

The infinitves of these verbs are, predictably, взять and брать. Both mean 'take.' Взять/взял is a Perfective verb; брать/брал is its Imperfective partner.

Use взял when you want to specify that the action has an end point. For example, Он взял кни́гу specifies that the book is gone — the end point of the action of 'taking' is that the object is no longer in its place. If, on the other hand, the book has been returned, then you can't use взять . In this situation it would not be appropriate to specify the end point of 'taking,' because the object is back in the owner's possession. You must use брать in this situation: Он брал кни́гу. Both sentences are translated 'He took the

book,' but they mean different things. Óн взял кни́гу implies Кни́ги
здесь не́т, while Óн бра́л кни́гу does not.

The two actions can be diagrammed in this way:

| взял | •————————→ | Perfective aspect |
| бра́л | •————————┐ ←————— | Imperfective aspect |

(2) пошёл/ходи́л

Пойти́/пошёл, пошла́ is a Perfective verb; ходи́ть/ходи́л is its Imperfective partner. The infinitive of пошёл (fem. пошла́) is irregular:
пойти́. Both can be translated 'go.'

The usage of these two verbs is roughly like that of взял/бра́л. Use
пошёл when you want to specify that the action has an end point. The end
point of someone's 'going' is that he is no longer here. Thus, Óн пошёл
means 'he took off;' it is roughly synonymous with Его́ не́т 'He's not here,'
just as Óн взял кни́гу implies Кни́ги здесь не́т. Óн пошёл в кино́
means 'He took off for the movies;' we don't know if he got to the movies or
not, but we do know that he is gone. On the other hand, Óн ходи́л в кино́
implies that he got there and returned. We can use the same diagram for
пошёл/ходи́л as for взял/бра́л:

| пошёл | •————————→ | Perfective aspect |
| ходи́л | •————————┐ ←————— | Imperfective aspect |

5.2 Terminology

Although it is not yet necessary for you to memorize the Russian grammatical terms for 'Perfective' and 'Imperfective aspect,' we are going to use
their Russian abbreviations in the Active Word Lists (for typographical reasons).
Thus, the capital Cyrillic letter C will stand for Perfective aspect
(соверше́нный ви́д) and the letters НС for Imperfective aspect (несовер-
ше́нный ви́д). This should be easy to remember, because the prefix не- on
несоверше́нный means 'non-' just like the *im-* on *Imperfective*.

Verbs from now on will be listed with these symbols:

взя́ть	C	take
бра́ть	НС	take
пойти́	C	go
ходи́ть	НС	go

6. Summary of case endings.

	Singular		*Plural*	
	Adj.	Noun	Adj.	Noun

#-declension

Nom.-Acc.	-ый/-о́й -#		-ые	-ы
Gen.	-ого	-а		
Prep.	-ом	-е		

o-declension

Nom.-Acc.	-ое	-о	-ые	-а
Gen.	} same as *#-declension*			
Prep.				

a-declension

Nom.	-ая	-а	-ые	-ы
Gen.	-ой	-ы		
Acc.	-ую	-у		
Prep.	-ой	-е		

Examples:

#-declension

	Singular	*Plural*
Nom.-Acc.	э́тот (бе́лый / большо́й) сто́л	э́ти бе́лые столы́
Gen.	э́того бе́лого стола́	
Prep.	э́том бе́лом столе́	

o-declension

Nom.-Acc.	э́то бе́лое ме́сто	э́ти бе́лые места́

a-declension

Nom.	э́та бе́лая плане́та	э́ти бе́лые плане́ты
Gen.	э́той бе́лой плане́ты	
Acc.	э́ту бе́лую плане́ту	
Prep.	э́той бе́лой плане́те	

Pronouns

Nom.	я́	ты́	мы́	вы́	о́н(о́)	она́	они́	что́	кто́
Gen.	меня́	тебя́	на́с	ва́с	его́	её	и́х	чего́	кого́
Acc.	меня́	тебя́	на́с	ва́с	его́	её	и́х	что́	кого́
Prep.	мне́	тебе́	на́с	ва́с	нём	не́й	ни́х	чём	ко́м

УПРАЖНЕНИЯ

1. Review. Geography.

(a) Answer affirmatively.

> П: Скажи́те, пожа́луйста, Бе́лый до́м нахо́дится в Вашингто́не?
> С: Да́, в Вашингто́не.
> П: Э́то в како́й стране́, в Аме́рике?
> С: Да́, в Аме́рике.

Substitute:

Кре́мль	Москва́	Сове́тский Сою́з
Лу́вр	Пари́ж	Фра́нция
музе́й Эрмита́ж	Ленингра́д	Сове́тский Сою́з
музе́й Пра́до	Мадри́д	Испа́ния
Пиза́нская ба́шня	Пи́за	Ита́лия
Эйфелева ба́шня	Пари́ж	Фра́нция
Сорбо́нна	Пари́ж	Фра́нция
Га́рвардский уни- версите́т	Кэ́мбридж	Аме́рика
Большо́й теа́тр	Москва́	Сове́тский Сою́з
Ватика́н	Ри́м	Ита́лия
Колизе́й	Ри́м	Ита́лия
автозаво́д "Форд"	Детро́йт	Аме́рика

(b) Now, without looking at the list, give the correct answer.

> П: Са́ша, скажи́те, пожа́луйста, где́ нахо́дится Бе́лый до́м?
> С: В Вашингто́не.
> П: Э́то в како́й стране́?
> С: В Аме́рике.

(c) Now give long answers, e.g.,

> С: Бе́лый до́м нахо́дится в Вашингто́не.
>   Вашингто́н нахо́дится в Аме́рике.

2. Review. Adjectives.

Read aloud.

1. _____ _____ ничего́ не де́лал. (the bad student)

2. Об _____ _____ _____ напи́шут во все́х газе́тах. (this bad student)

3. _____ до́м нахо́дится в Вашингто́не. (white)

4. Э́то _____ _____ _____. (my black caviar)

5. Студе́нтка ходи́ла в _____ _____. (big library)

6. _____ э́то письмо́? (whose)

7. _____ э́та газе́та? (whose)

8. _____ _____ бра́т писа́л _____ письмо́. (my little) (little)

9. Я́ е́ла _____ икру́. (black)

10. Расскажи́те о _____ икре́. (black)

3. Review. Verbs.

(a) Read aloud, inserting the proper past tense forms.

1. Я _____ газéту. (read)

2. Лéна _____ икрý. (took)

3. Ивáн Петрóвич _____ винó. (drank)

4. Письмó _____ Мáша. (read)

5. Сáша ничегó не _____. (did)

6. Я _____ упражнéния. (wrote)

7. Винó _____ ётот студéнт. (passed)

8. Меня _____ мóй преподавáтель. (taught)

9. Зюзя _____ секрéтный инститýт. (saw)

10. Вы _____ винó? (drank)

11. Вы _____ по-рýсски? (spoke)

12. Я _____ в ресторáн. (went)

(b) Insert the formal imperative forms. Then switch to the informal.

1. _____, пожáлуйста, об ётой кнѝге.(tell)

2. _____ письмó.(read)

3. _____ икрý. (pass)

4. _____ егó, кáк егó зовýт. (ask)

5. _____ у негó вѝлку. (ask for)

6. _____ кнѝгу на стóл. (put)

4.   Pronunciation Exercise: unstressed vowels (Lesson 1.4.2)

        Now that you are learning plural forms, which often have stress on
a different syllable from the singular, it is especially important to
observe the pronunciation rules for unstressed syllables.

    (a)   Read aloud:

Singular	*Plural*
сло́во (=сло́ва)	слова́ (=слава́)
ме́сто (=ме́ста)	места́ (=миста́)
де́ло (= де́ла)	дела́ (=дила́)
кольцо́ (=кальцо́)	ко́льца
но́ж	ножи́ (=нажи́)
сто́л	столы́ (=сталы́)
го́род (=го́рат)	города́ (=гарада́)
до́м	дома́ (=дама́)
паде́ж	падежи́ (=падижи́)
цве́т	цвета́ (=цвита́)
сестра́ (=систра́)	сёстры

    (b)   Read the following words aloud and observe the pronunciation
rules for unstressed vowels.

солда́т	сабота́ж
до́ктор	поэ́т
команди́р	о́пера
дире́ктор	меха́ник
генера́л	секу́нда
конце́рт	янва́рь
докуме́нт	телефо́н
коммуни́зм	телегра́мма
пропага́нда	колониали́зм

5.   Change from singular to plural (Analysis 1.)

    П: Что́ э́то?

    С: Э́то стака́н. Стака́ны у на́с хоро́шие.

    Substitute:

ру́чка	каранда́ш	сто́л
кольцо́	ды́ня	но́ж
кни́га	ви́лка	яйцо́
конве́рт	слова́рь	раке́та

6.   Genitive case (Analysis 3.7, Dialog 1.)

    П: Са́ша, вы́ зна́ете, како́го цве́та э́тот каранда́ш?

    С: Коне́чно, зна́ю. Э́тот каранда́ш - жёлтого цве́та.

        Substitute any nouns, singular or plural, and any colors. Then
switch to ты́ зна́ешь. Use the yes-no contour on зна́ешь.

    П: Са́ша, спроси́те Ма́шу, како́го цве́та э́та ру́чка.

    С: Ма́ша, ты́ зна́ешь, како́го цве́та э́та ру́чка?

    М: Коне́чно, зна́ю. Э́та ру́чка - зелёного цве́та.

M 7. More genitives (Dialog 2).

П: Какого рода слово "кольцо", мужского, женского, или
среднего рода?
С: Слово "кольцо" - среднего рода.

ручка, карандаш, письмо, студент, студентка, вопрос,
океан, союз, слово, институт, преподаватель, преподавательница

M 8. Intonation Practice

When you call somebody, use the question-word contour on their
name. Use the yes-no contour on можно. The word значит means 'means'.

П: Слово "окно" значит 'window.'
С: (имя-отчество), можно задать вопрос?
П: Конечно, можно.
С: Какого рода слово "окно"?
П: Слово "окно" - среднего рода.

Substitute words from previous texts, e.g.,
пауза, доклад, бутылка, завтрак, удовольствие, кабинет,
письмо, предмет, рассказ, аудитория, лаборатория,
упражнение, атмосфера, агент, ракета, Вашингтон,
Москва, спутник, хор, ...

M 9. Substitute items from the previous exercise.

П: Саша, спросите Машу, что значит слово "икра"?
С: Маша, что значит слово "икра"?
М: Слово "икра" значит *caviar*.

10. Writing practice (Analysis 1; also, Lesson 3.1.2)

Write the Nominative Plural of these words. None are irregular,
so if the word is unfamiliar you should be able to spell it correctly.
Mark stress as indicated by the capital letters.

коллега	товарищ	секрет
неделя	женщина	президент
кольцо ES	урок	отец (е) EE
место SE	гений	нож EE
статья EE	гараж EE	агент
царь EE	диван	лаборатория
спутник	упражнение	школа
камень (е)	поле SE	сэндвич

M 11. Genitive case (Analysis 3.2, Dialog 2)

Change the statement 'We have X' to 'We don't have X' as in the model.

У на́с е́сть икра́.   У на́с не́т икры́.
У на́с е́сть вино́.
У на́с е́сть слова́рь.
У на́с е́сть ло́жка.
У на́с е́сть до́м.
У на́с е́сть зелёная ды́ня.
У на́с е́сть чёрная икра́.
У на́с е́сть си́няя бума́га.
У на́с е́сть хоро́ший профе́ссор.
У на́с е́сть кра́сный фла́г.

M 12. Answer in the negative (Analysis 3.2, 3.6 and Dialog 2)

(a) На столе́ е́сть каранда́ш?
    Не́т, на столе́ не́т карандаша́.

(b) У ва́с е́сть каранда́ш?
    Не́т, у меня́ не́т карандаша́.

Substitute: ру́чка, ды́ня, ме́л, ...

Add colors: бе́лый, чёрный, кра́сный, ...

13. More genitive case (Analysis 3.2, 3.6)

Change from present to negative past as in the model.

У меня́ е́сть сове́тская газе́та.   У меня́ не́ было сове́тской
                                     газе́ты.
У э́той студе́нтки е́сть хоро́ший слова́рь.
У мое́й ма́мы е́сть чёрная икра́.
У на́шего профе́ссора е́сть кра́сный фла́г.
У э́того студе́нта е́сть хоро́шая раке́та.
У меня́ е́сть э́та кни́га.
У ни́х е́сть си́нее яйцо́.
На на́шей плане́те е́сть голубо́й океа́н.
В на́шем го́роде е́сть зелёный па́рк.
В Вашингто́не е́сть больша́я библиоте́ка.

14. Change the sentences in the above exercise to the negative future.

У меня́ е́сть сове́тская газе́та.   У меня́ не бу́дет сове́тской
                                     газе́ты.

15. Answer as in the model.

> Note the use of И in the meaning 'either.'

П: Где́ Са́ша?
С: Его́ не́т.
П: А вчера́?
С: Вчера́ его́ то́же не́ было.
П: А за́втра?
С: Его́ наве́рно не бу́дет и за́втра.
> 'He probably won't be here tomorrow, *either*.'

Substitute names of classmates and:

наш дире́ктор	ва́ша сестра́
мо́й оте́ц	моё письмо́
мо́й бра́т	ва́ш преподава́тель
э́тот студе́нт	э́та студе́нтка
наш профе́ссор	тво́й па́па
твоя́ ма́ма	америка́нский президе́нт
дире́ктор институ́та	дире́ктор ЦРУ

16. Сво́й vs. его́/её (Analysis 4.)

П: Ма́ша, возьми́те э́ту кни́гу в пра́вую ру́ку. (Points.)
М: (Takes it.)
П: Ната́ша, чью́ кни́гу она́ взяла́?
Н: Она́ взяла́ её кни́гу.⎫ if it's somebody else's book
         его́   ⎬
         свою́   if it's Masha's own book

Substitute: кольцо́, каранда́ш, ру́чка, ...

17. брать/взять (Analysis 5.1; Dialog 3)

> Ask the teacher what (s)he took the book for. Use взять if the teacher kept the book, but use брать if the book was returned to you.

(a) П: (Takes Sasha's book and keeps it.)
     С: Заче́м вы́ взя́ли мою́ кни́гу?
     П: Извини́те, я́ ду́мал, что э́то моя́ кни́га.

(b) П: (Takes Sasha's book and returns it.)
     С: Заче́м вы́ бра́ли мою́ кни́гу?
     П: Извини́те, я́ ду́мал, что э́то моя́ кни́га.

Substitute familiar nouns.

Switch to ты:

П: Ма́ша, возьми́те са́шину кни́гу.
М: (Does so.)
С: Заче́м ты взяла́...?
М: Извини́, я ду́мала...

П: Ната́ша, у ва́с е́сть вопро́с?
Н: Да́, е́сть. Кто́ взял са́шину кни́гу?
П: Не зна́ю. Спроси́те Са́шу.
Н: Са́ша, ты́ не зна́ешь, кто́ взял твою́ кни́гу?
С: Её взяла́ Ма́ша. Не беспоко́йся, она́ её вернёт.

18. The teacher takes somebody's book, perhaps Sasha's own book
    or somebody else's. (Analysis 4)

    П: Са́ша, что́ у меня́ в руке́?
    С: В како́й руке́?
    П: В пра́вой/ле́вой руке́.
    С: У ва́с в пра́вой/ле́вой руке́ кни́га.

    П: Ма́ша, о чье́й кни́ге он говори́т?
    М: О́н говори́т о свое́й/его́/её кни́ге.

19. Translate. (Dialogs 1-3)

  (a) What color is your planet? What color is your pencil? What color are
      your pens? Our pens are green. And yours? My pencils are dark blue.
      Where's my red book? It doesn't seem to be here. Where's my white chalk?
      It doesn't seem to be here. Don't worry, it's (lying) on the table. And
      my glasses? Don't worry, they are (standing) on the table.

  (b) Can I ask a question? Of course you can. Where's my Soviet flag? It
      doesn't seem to be here. Masha probably took it. Do you have a Soviet flag?
      No, I don't have a Soviet flag. Masha will probably return it. Where's
      Masha? She's not here. I don't know where she is. Who is she? She's
      a teacher at the university.

  (c) My black caviar is (standing) on the table. It's not in its (proper) place.
      May I ask a question? Please (do). Who took it? Masha took it. It's
      good she returned it. Yes, and it's good she didn't eat it.

20. Conversation.

    Student A has lost something and asks B where it is. B asks what color
    it is. The conversation may have either of two outcomes: (1) the item
    is gone, Masha having taken it away, or (2) the item is (standing/lying)
    on the table, not in its proper place, Masha having taken it and returned
    it.

21. Translate. (Dialog 4)

    Where's Sasha? He's not here. He went to the library. Where's Masha?
    She's not here. She went to the library too. Sasha and Masha are in
    the library.

    Where were you, Sasha? I went to the library. It's good that you came
    back. Where were you, Masha? I went to the institute. It's good you
    came back. What were you doing at the institute? I was watching a film.
    And what have you been doing? I've been thinking about you.

22. Conversation.

    Student A asks B where C is. B answers. Then C returns. They greet him
    and ask where he was and what he was doing there. His answer does not
    correspond with B's answer. B says, А я ду́мал(а), что ты бы́л в X.
    To which C replies, Я бы́л не в X, а в У.

23. Substitute the items listed (Analysis 3.3 , Dialog 5)

П: Откуда эти письма?
С: Из Советского Союза.
П: От кого?
С: От моей сестры.

из	*от*
наш институт	наш директор
наш университет	наш профессор
Гарвардский университет	наш преподаватель
Владивосток	мой брат
Москва	Саша
Бостон	моя сестра
Атланта	моя мама
Вашингтон	мой папа
Лондон	Иван Петрович
Париж	Нина Степановна

24. Use the statement contour on your answer.

П: Саша, в какой стране говорят по-итальянски, в Италии?
С: Да, в Италии.

П: Маша, в какой стране говорят по-итальянски?
М: В Италии.

Substitute names of languages and countries.

25. (Lesson 3.5)

П: Что вы знаете о Нью-Йорке?
С: Я ничего о нём не знаю.
П: А что вы знаете о Пенсильвании?
С: Я ничего о ней не знаю.

Select some names of states to substitute. Names of states and other foreign nouns ending in -o or -и are indeclinable, like кино.

Айдахо	Калифорния	Нью-Йорк
Айова	Канзас	Нью-Мексико
Алабама	Кентукки	Нью-Хэмпшир
Аляска	Колорадо	Огайо
Аризона	Коннектикут	Оклахома
Арканзас	Луизиана	Орегон
Вайоминг	Массачузетс	Пенсильвания
Вашингтон	Миннесота	Род-Айленд
Вермонт	Миссисипи	Северная Дакота
Виргиния	Миссури	Северная Каролина
Висконсин	Мичиган	Теннесси
Гавайи	Монтана	Техас
Делавар	Мэн	Флорида
Джорджия	Мэрилэнд	Юта
Западная Виргиния	Небраска	Южная Дакота
Иллинойс	Невада	Южная Каролина
Индиана	Нью-Джерси	

26. Answer factually. (Analysis 3.3 and Dialog 5)

Declinable names of states, cities, books, operas, etc. can be treated like any other noun, i.e., you can put the proper case ending on them as required by context (Я из Алабамы); alternatively, you can use the generic word (e.g. штат) in its correct case form, and leave the proper noun in the Nominative case (Я из штата Алабама).

П: Откуда вы?
С: Я из (state).

27. Answer in the affirmative (Dialog 5).

П: Откуда вы? Из Советского Союза?
С: Да, я из Советского Союза.
П: Вы там родились?
С: Да, я родился/родилась в Советском Союзе.

     Substitute names of cities, states and countries. Notice that you cannot hear the difference between the Gen. and Prep. of feminines (из Америки = в Америке) and you can't even see the difference if the next to last letter is и - (из Филадельфии = в Филадельфии).

Variation: Answer factually:

П: Откуда вы?
С: Я из _____.
П: Вы там родились?
С: Да/Нет, я родился в _____.

Switch to ты.

П: Маша, спросите Сашу, откуда он?

28. Reading practice.

     Read aloud and translate:

— Где работает Иван Петрович?
— Иван Петрович работает в секретной лаборатории в секретном институте.
— А где работает американский президент?
— Американский президент работает в Белом доме.
— А где работает советский президент?
— Советский президент работает в Кремле.
— В каком городе находится Белый дом?
— Белый дом находится в Вашингтоне.
— А в каком городе находится Кремль?
— Кремль находится в Москве.
— Вы были в Белом доме?
— Нет, я был в Вашингтоне, но (but) я не был в Белом доме.

29. Pronunciation exercise (Lesson 3.1.2)

When you say the word Шу́ра , round your lips in anticipation
of the у *before* you start saying ш.

Шу́ра
хорошо́
шо́к
шу́м
шу́тка

Do the same for these words beginning with л . Round your lips
before you start saying the word.

лу́чше   ло́жка
гало́шу   луна́
Ло́ндон   луна́тик 'sleepwalker'
Лу́вр

30. Пье́са 'a play'

Go back to Lesson 1, Text. Read the text aloud, each person
taking roles (Lena, Zyuzya, the father, etc.) as though you were
reading a script for an audition for a play. Try to get the intonation right.

31. Ten words are written on the blackboard.

(a) П: Ма́ша, чита́йте, пожа́луйста, пе́рвое сло́во.
    М: (чита́ет.)

Substitute numerals up to *tenth*.

    П: Са́ша, како́е э́то сло́во? (points.)
    С: Э́то пе́рвое сло́во.

Substitute бу́ква, then уро́к.

Masc nouns — Ивана = gen. (animate)
(accusative) — ресторан = nom. (inanimate)

УРОК ПЯТЫЙ

Рассказ Зюзи о её планете

Наша планета небольшая[1] и очень красивая. Она круглая и жёлтого цвета. На нашей планете всегда тепло, потому что у нас два солнца и две луны[2]. У нас растут апельсины, лимоны и дыни. Нам[3] не нужна тёплая одежда. Всё, что нам нужно, мы делаем сами.

Как я уже сказала, у нас две луны. Первая луна зелёного цвета. Она квадратная. На ней живут пенсионеры. Они работают и отдыхают. Врачи им[3] дают апельсины, лимоны и дыни. Каждый день врачи дают пенсионерам[3] по апельсину[3], по лимону[3] и по дыне[3].

Вторую луну мы сделали сами. Она круглая. На ней живут журналисты и атеисты. Журналисты передают по телевизору[3] новости[4] на планету[5]. Атеисты не верят в Бога.

На нашей планете — один большой океан, в океане острова. На каждом острове есть город[6], в каждом городе есть церковь[4], синагога и мечеть[4]. На нашей планете все верят в Бога. Все атеисты живут на второй луне.

Я родилась и жила на самом большом острове, в самом большом городе. Я училась в школе и в университете. Вначале я училась математике[3], но я бросила математику и начала учиться философии[3]. Когда я кончила учиться, я не знала, что делать. На нашей планете философы не нужны. У нас каждый человек — философ.

Наша планета небольшая. Мне[3] там было скучно. На зелёной квадратной луне мне тоже было скучно. И на луне, где живут журналисты, мне тоже было скучно. Я написала письмо моему богатому другу[3]. Я позвонила моим родителям[3]. Они мне[3] подарили билет на ракету. На этой ракете я прилетела на вашу планету.

Vocabulary

апельси́н orange
атеи́ст atheist
биле́т ticket
Бо́г God
бога́тый rich
бро́сить to throw; quit, give up, abandon
ве́рить to believe, have faith in
внача́ле at first, in the beginning
вра́ч doctor
всегда́ always
дава́ть to give
два́, две́ two
де́нь day
журнали́ст journalist
квадра́тный square
ко́нчить to end, finish
краси́вый beautiful
кру́глый round
лимо́н lemon
луна́ moon
матема́тика mathematics
мече́ть mosque
небольшо́й small, smallish
но́вость piece of news
  но́вости (plural) news
ну́жен needed, necessary
  На́м нужна́ оде́жда We need clothing (Lit., Clothing is necessary for us/ needed by us [Dative case]).
оде́жда clothing
о́стров island
  острова́ islands (irreg. plural)
отдыха́ть be resting
пенсионе́р pensioner

переда́ть to broadcast, transmit (also, 'to pass')
по
  Им даю́т по апельси́ну, по лимо́ну, и по ды́не. They give them an orange apiece, a lemon apiece and a melon apiece (Dative case).
по by
  передаю́т по телеви́зору (they) broadcast (by) television
подари́ть bestow; give as a gift
позвони́ть to call by phone
расту́т (*Infinitive* расти́) to grow
роди́тель parent
са́ми ourselves (yourselves, themselves)
са́мый most, -est (superlative)
  на са́мом большо́м о́строве on the biggest (Lit., 'most big') island.
синаго́га synagogue
ску́чно bored
  Мне́ ску́чно I'm bored (Lit., for me (Dative case) it is boring.)
со́лнце sun
телеви́зор television
тепло́ warm
учи́ться to study, pursue studies
фило́соф philosopher
филосо́фия philosophy
це́рковь church
челове́к person; man
шко́ла school (primary and secondary only — not higher education)

Нача́ть - веди
Нача́ла

COMMENTS

1. небольшо́й

This word means 'smallish, rather small', smaller than большо́й, but larger than ма́ленький.

2. два́, две́

Два́ is used with masculine and neuter nouns, две́ with feminine; the noun is in the Genitive *singular*.

3. Dative

There are many Dative case forms in this text. All are marked with this footnote number. See Analysis 2.

4. Fourth declension nouns

Fourth declension nouns all have -ь in the Nom. Sg. All fourth declension nouns are feminine.

но́вость	a piece of news
це́рковь	church
мече́ть	mosque

5. Accusative = direction

Note that планéту is Accusative; translate на as 'to'.

Передаю́т но́вости с луны́ на плане́ту. The news is broadcast from the moon to the planet.

6. Comma = 'and'

The English translation requires a conjunction here; in Russian it is optional.

A series of nouns or verbs may also appear without conjunctions, e.g.,

Та́м е́сть це́рковь, синаго́га, мече́ть. There's a church, synagogue *and* mosque there.

Они́ чита́ли, писа́ли, говори́ли. They were reading, writing *and* talking.

DIALOGS FOR MEMORIZATION

1. Да́тельный паде́ж

   С: Господи́н профе́ссор! Научи́те на́с да́тельному падежу́.
   П: В конце́ семе́стра все́м хоро́шим студе́нтам даду́т[1] по одному́ большо́му я́блоку и по одно́й большо́й ды́не.

2. Позвони́те!

   С: Да́й мне́, пожа́луйста, кра́сный каранда́ш.
   М: Заче́м тебе́ кра́сный каранда́ш?
   С: Мне́ ну́жен кра́сный каранда́ш, чтобы нарисова́ть кра́сную плане́ту.
   М: Хм...У меня́ не́т кра́сного карандаша́. Но[2] я позвоню́ са́шиному бра́ту и попрошу́ у него́ кра́сный каранда́ш. Ему́ роди́тели да́ли кра́сный каранда́ш.
   С: Спаси́бо, а я напишу́ сестре́. Е́й роди́тели ча́сто даю́т[1] карандаши́.
   М: Пожа́луй, я позвоню́ и мои́м роди́телям то́же.

3а. Хо́лодно.

   С: Зде́сь, по-мо́ему, хо́лодно. Кто́-то открыва́л окно́. Тебе́ не хо́лодно?
   М: Не́т, мне́ тепло́. Мне́ да́же жа́рко. Откро́йте, пожа́луйста, окно́.

3б. Слова́.

   тру́дно
   легко́
   ску́чно
   ве́село

4. Чтó вы́ дéлали вчерá?

П: Чтó вы́ дéлали вчерá на занятии[3]?
С: Мы́ читáли и переводи́ли. Я́ бóльше не[4] хочý читáть и переводи́ть. И Пéтя бóльше не хóчет. Мы́ бóльше не хоти́м.
П: Тогдá чтó вы́ бýдете дéлать?
С: Мы́ бýдем игрáть на флéйте.
П: Гдé вáша флéйта?
С: Я́ её положи́л[5] на стóл. Я́ всегдá кладý[5] вéщи на своё мéсто.

5. Вы́ читáли эту кни́гу?

П: Вы́ читáли эту кни́гу?
С: Дá, читáла.
П: Интерéсная кни́га?
С: Дá, óчень.
П: О чём эта кни́га?
С: О немéцком языкé.
П: Ктó её написáл[5]?
С: Её написáл профéссор Штрóтман.

6. Три́ медвéдя.[6]

Медвéдь: Ктó-то éл[5] мою́ кáшу.
Медвéдица: Ктó-то éл и мою́ кáшу.
Медвежóнок: Ктó-то éл и мою́ кáшу тóже, и всю́ съéл[5]!

7. Мéсяцы.

январь	апрéль	ию́ль	октябрь
феврáль	мáй	áвгуст	ноябрь
мáрт	ию́нь	сентябрь	декáбрь

Translation

1. Dative case
   S: Professor, sir!   Teach us the dative case.
   T: At the end of the semester all the good students will be given a big apple and a big melon apiece.

2. Phone !

   S: Please give me a red pencil.
   M: What do you want a red pencil for?
   S: I need a red pencil (in order) to draw a red planet.
   M: Hm...I don't have a red pencil. But I'll phone Sasha's brother and ask him for a red pencil. (His) parents gave him a red pencil.
   S: Thanks, and I'll write (my) sister. (Our) parents often give her pencils.
   M: Maybe (= I guess/ I think) I'll call my parents, too.

3. It's cold.
   S: I think (= in my opinion) it's cold (in) here. Somebody's been opening
      the window. Aren't you cold?
   M: No, I'm warm. I'm even hot. Please open the window.

4. What did you do yesterday?
   T: What did you do in class yesterday?
   S: We read and translated. I don't want to read and translate any more.
      Pete doesn't want to either. We don't want to any more.
   T: Then what are you going to do?
   S: We're going to (we will) play the flute.
   T: Where's your flute?
   S: I put it on the table. I always put things in their proper place.

5. Have you read this book?

   T: Have you (ever) read this book?
   S: Yes, I have.
   T: Is it (an) interesting (book)?
   S: Yes, very.
   T: What's the book about?
   S: About (the) German (language).
   T: Who wrote it?
   S: Professor Strothmann wrote it. (= It was written by Professor Strothmann.)

6. The three bears

   The (papa) bear: Somebody's been eating my porridge.
   The (mama) bear: Somebody's been eating my porridge, too.
   The (baby) bear: Somebody's been eating my porridge, too, and has eaten
                     it all up!

Active Word List

Nouns

вещь	(fourth conjugation) thing
окно́; о́кна	window
флéйта	flute
я́блоко; я́блоки	apple
ка́ша	porridge, kasha
заня́тие	class (in college)
медве́дица	she-bear
медве́дь	bear
медвежо́нок	cub
роди́тель	parent
мéсяц	month
янва́рь, января́	January
февра́ль, февраля́	February
ма́рт	March
апре́ль	April
ма́й	May
ию́нь	June
ию́ль	July
а́вгуст	August
сентя́брь, сентября́	September

окт́ябрь, октябр́я	October
но́ябрь, ноябр́я	November
деќабрь, декабр́я	December
яз́ык, языка́; языќи	language

Verbs (See Analysis 3 for the forms of verbs.)

д́ать; дала́, д́али (С)	(to) give
дад́ут	they give
нарисова́ть (С)	(to) draw
науч́ить (С)	(to) teach
науч́ите	teach (*Imperative*)
позвон́ить (С)	(to) call by phone
позвоню́	I will phone
позвон́ите	phone (*Imperative*)
съ́есть; съ́ела (С)	(to) eat up
дава́ть (НС)	(to) give
даю́т	they give
кл́асть (НС)	(to) put (in a lying position)
кладу́	I put, lay
открыва́ть (НС)	(to) open
хот́еть (НС)	(to) want
хочу́, х́очет, хот́им	I/he/we want
игра́ть (НС)	(to) play
переводи́ть (НС)	(to) translate

Adjectives

д́ательный	dative
интер́есный	interesting
нем́ецкий	German
хор́оший	fine, good
н́ужен, нужна́, н́ужно, нужн́ы	needed, necessary
три	three

Misc.

в́есело	happy; having a good time
ж́арко	hot; it is hot
легќо	easy; it is easy
сќучно	boring; it is boring
тепл́о	warm; it is warm
тр́удно	hard, difficult; it is difficult
х́олодно	cold; it is cold
ч́асто	often
б́ольше не + verb	any more
всегда́	always
д́аже	even
тогда́	then
кт́о-то	somebody
по-м́оему	in my opinion, I think
мы́	we
н́о	but
по (+ Dative case)	apiece, each
пожа́луй	maybe, I guess, I think perhaps

COMMENTS

1. дадýт (P) vs. даю́т (I)

The form дадýт, being Perfective, means future: 'they will give'.
The form даю́т, which occurs in the second dialog, means 'they give', Imperfective aspect. See Analysis 3.2 for the irregular forms of дáть.

2. нó

The range of meanings covered by the two English conjunctions *and/but* is covered by three words in Russian: и/а/нó. The word нó is used in cases where what follows is suprising or unexpected or strongly contrasting to what precedes. (See Lesson 2, Text Comment 1 on и and а .)

Compare:

Сáша у нáс учи́лся, нó ничегó не знáет.	Sasha studied at our university, but he doesn't know anything! (How suprising!)
vs. Сáша учи́лся в Мичигáне, а Пéтя в Техáсе.	Sasha studied in Michigan but (= and on the other hand) Pete studied in Texas.
vs. Сáша учи́лся в Москвé, Ми́ша в Ленингрáде, и Пéтя в Ки́еве.	Sasha studied in Moscow, Misha in Leningrad, and Pete in Kiev. (simple listing)

Russian нó is always translated into English 'but', but *but* is translated into Russian as either нó or а . Don't over-use нó — it's a strong word.

3. заня́тие vs. урóк

Generally speaking, 'class' is rendered by заня́тие on the college level and by урóк on the lower levels, but урóк can be used for private lessons, music lessons, and lessons in a textbook.

Вчерá у Пéти в шкóле бы́ли урóки рýсского языкá и матемáтики.	Yesterday, in school, Pete had lessons in Russian and in mathematics.
В университéте я бóльше всегó люби́ла заня́тия по филосóфии.	At the university, I liked best of all, classes in philosophy.
У моéй жены́ сейчáс урóк мýзыки.	My wife has her music lesson now.
Какóй урóк вы́ сейчáс изучáете? — Пя́тый.	What lesson are you studing now? — The fifth.

4. бо́льше не

The expression means 'not any more' or 'no longer'.

О́н здесь бо́льше не рабо́тает.	He doesn't work here any longer/ any more.
Они́ бо́льше не зову́т меня́ обе́дать.	They don't call me for dinner any more.
Они́ бо́льше не хо́дят в э́тот па́рк гуля́ть.	They don't go to this park to stroll around any more.

5. Aspect pairs

Here are the infinitive forms of the aspect pairs marked with the footnote number 5. See Analysis 5 for usage.

кла́сть (нс)/ положи́ть (с)   'put, lay'
писа́ть (нс)/ написа́ть (с)   'write'
е́сть (нс)/ съе́сть (с)   'eat'

6. три́

This numeral, like два́/две́, is followed by a Genitive singular noun:

оди́н медве́дь   (Nom.)
два́ медве́дя   (Gen. Sg.)
три́ медве́дя   (Gen. Sg.)

The tale of the Three Bears is somewhat revised here. See Ле́в Толсто́й for a different version.

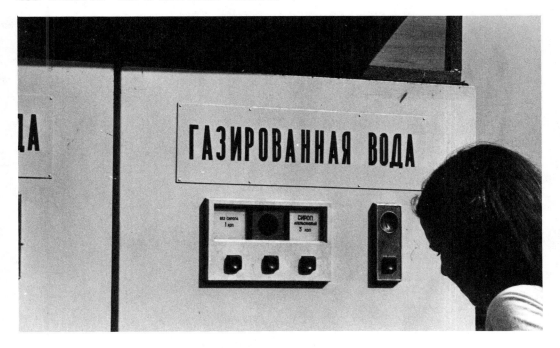

A sidewalk seltzer machine.
Without syrup, 1 kopeck; with orange syrup, 3 kopecks.

ANALYSIS

1. Accusative: animate vs. inanimate

Recall Lesson 2.5: the Accusative is like Nominative except for the a- declension (сестру́) and for nouns that refer to animate beings. (We are ignoring here the fourth declension; see Lesson 7.1.)

Nominative	*Accusative*
Это моя́ сестра́.	Я зна́ю твою́ сестру́.
Это хоро́ший ресто́ран.	Я зна́ю э́тот ресто́ран.
Это моё письмо́.	Я написа́ла э́то письмо́.

The Accusative ending for zero-declension nouns that refer to *animate beings* is the same as the Genitive ending:

Это мо́й бра́т.	Я зна́ю твоего́ бра́та.
Это това́рищ Си́доров.	Я зна́ю това́рища Си́дорова.

Compare the Accusative forms of inanimate nouns (=Nominative) and animate (=Genitive):

Inanimate (=Nominative)	*Animate(=Genitive)*
Я зна́ю ру́сский язы́к.	Я зна́ю э́того журнали́ста.
Я ви́дел тво́й слова́рь.	Я ви́дел твоего́ бра́та.
Она́ задала́ интере́сный вопро́с.	Она́ предста́вила своего́ преподава́теля.

Neuter animate nouns don't follow this rule, but very few neuters denote animate beings , anyway.

Plural nouns of *all* declension follow the same rule, but you should avoid plural animates for the time being, since you haven't yet been introduced to the rather complex set of Genitive Plural endings. Feel free to use *inanimate* nouns in the Acc. plural—they are identical to the Nominative forms discussed in Lesson 4.1.

	I (NC)	P (C)
past	писал	написал
inf	писать	написать. (письмо)
future	буду писать	напишу
present.	пишу.	

\|

```
┌─────────────────────────────────────────────────────┐
│                     PRACTICE 1                        │
├─────────────────────────────────────────────────────┤
```

*Translate the sentences. Then give the dictionary
forms (Nominative Singular) of the Accusative forms
in these sentences.*

Accusative Singular
Я зна́ю са́шиного бра́та.
Я зна́ю хоро́ший рестора́н.
Я зна́ю его́ сестру́.
Я зна́ю ва́шего преподава́теля.
Я зна́ю Ива́на Петро́вича.
Я зна́ю ру́сский язы́к.

Accusative Plural (inanimate only)
Я зна́ю э́ти рестора́ны.
Я писа́ла пи́сьма.
Я положи́ла карандаши́ на сто́л.
Они́ де́лают раке́ты.
Он задае́т глу́пые вопро́сы.
Попроси́те у него́ кни́ги.
Переда́йте ви́лки и ножи́.
Я зна́ю э́ти слова́.
Врачи́ и́м даю́т апельси́ны, лимо́ны и ды́ни.

2. Dative vs. Accusative

Some verbs may have two objects, e.g., *She gave me* (1) *the book*(2). In
English you can transform the *indirect object* to a phrase: *She gave the book
to me.* In Russian the indirect object is in the Dative case (мне in the following examples), and the direct object is in the Accusative:

Она́ мне́ дала́ кни́гу.   She gave *me* the book.
Она́ мне́ передала́ икру́.   She passed *me* the caviar.

2.1 Dative endings

The endings of the Dative case in the singular are:

masc., neut.	fem.
Adj. + Noun	Adj. + Noun
—ому —у	—ой —е

Note that the feminine endings are identical to the Prepositional case
endings of feminine nouns.

	masc.	fem.
Dat.	большо́му бра́ту	большо́й сестре́
Prep.	о большо́м бра́те	о большо́й сестре́

The usual spelling rules apply:

хоро́шему преподава́телю	to a good teacher
мое́й сестре́	to my sister

The plural forms do not distinguish gender:

Adj. +	Noun
-ым	-ам
мои́м э́тим	сёстрам врача́м

Врачи́ даю́т пенсионе́рам апельси́ны.   The doctors give retired people
                                         oranges.

The special adjective ве́сь, вся́, всё, все́ 'all' is peculiar in having
the vowel -e in plural forms (the others have -u): все́м студе́нтам   'to
all the students.' (vs. э́тим студе́нтам 'to these students').

You have already met most of the Dative pronoun forms:

Nom.	Dat.	Nom.	Dat.
я́	мне́	мы́	на́м
ты́	тебе́	вы́	ва́м
она́	е́й		
о́н оно́ }	ему́	они́	и́м
что́	чему́		
кто́	кому́		

The third person pronouns, as in other case forms, have endings like adjectives;compare:

Adjectives	*Pronouns*	
хоро́шему	ему́	'to him'
хоро́шей	е́й	'to her'
хоро́шим	и́м	'to them'

PRACTICE 2

Translate the sentences. Then underline the Datives and
write out their Nominative Singular forms (dictionary forms).

Я написа́ла письмо́ моему́ бога́тому бра́ту.
В секре́тном институ́те Зю́зе показа́ли лаборато́рии и
    кабине́ты.
Ле́на позвала́ ма́му, Ни́ну Серге́евну, и предста́вила её
    Зю́зе.
Всем хоро́шим студе́нтам даду́т по одному́ большо́му
    я́блоку и по одно́й большо́й ды́не.
Ка́ждый де́нь врачи́ даю́т пенсионе́рам по апельси́ну.
Я написа́ла письмо́ мое́й бога́той сестре́.
Ей роди́тели да́ли кра́сный каранда́ш.
    Роди́тели да́ли студе́нтам по одному́ я́блоку.

2.2 Verbs with Dative

There is no straight-forward one-to-one correspondence between English
indirect objects and Russian Datives. You must simply learn which verbs
take the Dative.

да́ть	to give something *to somebody*
переда́ть	to pass something *to somebody*
зада́ть вопро́с	to ask *somebody* a question
сказа́ть,	to tell something *to somebody*
рассказа́ть	to tell (a story) *to somebody*
написа́ть	to write something *to somebody*
предста́вить	to introduce somebody *to somebody*
позвони́ть	to phone *somebody* (make a call *to somebody)*
научи́ть	to teach somebody *something* (= to introduce somebody *to* a body of knowledge)

The last verb on the list is peculiar in that the person is Accusative and the
thing is Dative; usually it's the other way around, as the other verbs illustrate. With the related verb учи́ться 'to pursue a course of studies' (see
Text) the same is true: the name of the field of study is in the Dative
case, e.g.

Я учи́лся/учи́лась матема́тике.   I studied math.

PRACTICE 3

Do as you did in Practice 2.

Я позвони́ла мои́м роди́телям.
Кому́ вы позвони́ли?
Научи́те на́с да́тельному падежу́.
Чему́ ва́с научи́л Профе́ссор Петро́в?
Предста́вьте меня́ ва́шему бра́ту.
Напиши́те сестре́ письмо́.
Расскажи́те ва́шим студе́нтам о сове́тских теа́трах.
Он сказа́л все́м, что о́н ничего́ не понима́ет.

2.3 ну́жен + Dative

To express *need* in Russian you use an adjective, not a verb. The person who *needs* is in the Dative case; the thing needed is the Nominative subject:

Мне́ ну́жен каранда́ш.	I need a pencil (Lit. 'A pencil is necessary for me.').
Мне́ нужна́ ру́чка.	I need a pen.

The word ну́жен must *precede* the verb бы́ть:

Мне́ нужна́ была́ ру́чка.	I needed a pen. (Lit., 'A pen was necessary for me.')
Мне́ нужна́ бу́дет ру́чка.	I'll need a pen.

This adjective has the usual four endings, just like the Nominative of special adjectives, but it doesn't have the other case forms: ну́жен, нужна́, ну́жно, нужны́.

Ему́ нужна́ ви́лка.	He needs a fork.
Что́ е́й ну́жно?	What does she need?
Им ну́жно вино́.	They need wine.
Ва́м нужны́ э́ти ножи́?	Do you need those knives?
На́м не нужна́ тёплая оде́жда.	We don't need warm clothing.

PRACTICE 4

Say the following sentences aloud, inserting the proper form of ну́жен *. Watch out for the shifty stress. Translate.*

Мне́ нуж-

ме́л	карандаши́
ды́ня	словари́
ды́ни	ножи́
икра́	газе́та
кольцо́	ка́ша
бума́га	фла́г

Repeat in the past (ну́жен бы́л... *) and future (* ну́жен бу́дет...*).*

2.4 ску́чно + Dative

The word ску́чно 'It is boring' is often pronounced as though spelled ску́шно.

Ску́чно.	It's boring.
Та́м бы́ло ску́чно.	It was boring there.

The person experiencing the boredom is in the Dative case.

Мне́ ску́чно.	I'm bored (Lit. 'For me it is boring.')
Мне́ та́м бы́ло ску́чно.	I was bored there (Lit. 'For me it was boring there.')
Мне́ та́м бу́дет ску́чно.	I'll be bored there.

Many neuter forms work this way, e.g.

Хорошо́.	It's fine.
Мне́ хорошо́.	I'm fine.
Мне́ та́м бы́ло хорошо́.	I had a fine time there/ I felt comfortable there.
Мне́ та́м бу́дет хорошо́.	I'll have a fine time there.
Хо́лодно.	It's cold.
Вчера́ бы́ло хо́лодно.	It was cold yesterday.
Ва́м хо́лодно?	Are you cold?
Да́, мне́ о́чень хо́лодно.	Yes, I'm very cold.

PRACTICE 5

Say these sentences aloud. Then change to past tense. Notice that the verb is always neuter, because there is no Nominative subject for it to agree with.

Example: Сестре́ ску́чно.   →   Сестре бы́ло скучно.
        (My) sister is bored.   →   *(My) sister was bored.*

Бра́ту ску́чно.
Сестре́ ску́чно.
Преподава́телю ску́чно.
Преподава́тельнице ску́чно.
Э́тому студе́нту ску́чно.
Э́той студе́нтке ску́чно.
Э́тим студе́нтам ску́чно.
Мне́ ску́чно.
На́м все́м ску́чно.

Now change to future. Again, the verb form бу́дет *does not change.*

2.5 по + Dative

The preposition по is followed by the Dative case.

Он да́л студе́нтам по я́блоку.	He gave the students an *apple apiece*.

This preposition is used in a wide variety of meanings:

(1) with distributable things: *apiece, each*

Ка́ждый де́нь врачи́ даю́т пен-сионе́рам по апельси́ну, по лимо́ну и по ды́не.	Every day the doctors give the retired people an orange, a lemon and a melon *each*.

(2) with instruments: *on*

Журнали́сты передаю́т по телеви́зору но́вости.	Newsmen broadcast the news on TV.
Мы́ говори́ли по телефо́ну.	We spoke on the phone.

(3) with places: *around in, along*

Он ходи́л по па́рку.	He was walking around in the park.
Он ходи́л по у́лице.	He was walking around in the street (or better: up and down the street).

(4) with subject matter: *on, in*

уро́к по матема́тике	a lesson *on* math
заня́тие по программи́рованию	a college level class *in* programming
уче́бник по ру́сскому языку́	a textbook *on* Russian
ле́кция по филосо́фии	a lecture *on* philosophy

The words уро́к 'lesson' and уче́бник 'textbook' can also be followed by Genitive 'of': уро́к ру́сского языка́ 'Russian lesson.'

The preposition по is spelled with a hyphen in the set expressions:

по-мо́ему (Note stress; compare: моему́)	in my opinion
по-тво́ему	in your opinion
по-ва́шему	in your opinion
Ка́к по-тво́ему?	What's your opinion? What do *you* think?

PRACTICE 6

Read aloud. Then replace 'an X apiece' by 'one big X apiece,' e.g. по я́блоку → по одному́ большо́му я́блоку.
Pronounce по одному́ *as one word, as though spelled* паадному́.

Он да́л студе́нтам по ды́не.   ...ру́чке
                карандашу́   стака́ну
                ка́мню   ви́лке
                кни́ге   ножу́
                словарю́   письму́

3. The forms of the non-past tense

3.1 Verb conjugation

There are two sets of verb endings; they are identical except for the first vowel.

	Conjugation I 'put (lying)'		*Conjugation II* 'be standing'	
я	кладу́	-у	стою́	-ю
ты	кладёшь	-ёшь	стои́шь	-ишь
óн, она́, оно́	кладёт	-ёт	стои́т	-ит
мы	кладём	-ём	стои́м	-им
вы	кладёте	-ёте	стои́те	-ите
они́	кладу́т	-ут	стоя́т	-ят

Spelling:

(1) There is only one spelling peculiarity in verb endings: –шь is always spelled with –ь , even though ш is a non-paired consonant; the consonant is always pronounced plain, despite the presence of the palatal indicator –ь.

The remainder of the spelling conventions listed below all follow from the rules already presented.

(2) The two dots over the ё mark stress; therefore they are not used with stem-stressed verbs:

Conjugation I.	бу́ду	бу́дем	
	бу́дешь	бу́дете	
	бу́дет	бу́дут	'they will be'

(3) If the stem ends in a non-paired consonant, the usual rules apply; only –у and –ат are affected by these rules—the other endings, those with –е- and –и- are unaffected, and are always spelled as such.

Conjugation II.	лежу́	лежи́м	
	лежи́шь	лежи́те	
	лежи́т	лежа́т	'they are lying'

When you learn a verb, you must learn which set, or *conjugation* it belongs to. This is very easy to do, because the first vowel of the ending tells you which set it belongs to. Thus, лежи́т must belong to the second conjugation because the first letter of the ending –ит is и , like стои́т.

There are two pitfalls, however:

(1) The first person singular –у/–ю does *not* tell you which conjugation the verb belongs to: кладу́ is Conj. I, лежу́ is Conj. II.

(2) If you *hear* a verb rather than see it printed, and if the ending is unstressed, it is impossible to tell the difference between –ишь, –ит, –им, –ите on the one hand, and –ешь, –ет, –ем, –ете, on the other because unstressed е is pronounced as though spelled и (Lesson 1.4.2); observe the transcription of the following first and second conjugation stem-stressed verbs:

	I 'will be'		II 'go. come'	
я	бу́ду		хожу́	
ты	бу́дешь	/búḓish/	хо́дишь	/khóḓish/
óн	бу́дет	/búḓit/	хо́дит	/khóḓit/
мы	бу́дем	/búḓim/	хо́дим	/khóḓim/
вы	бу́дете	/búḓiṭi/	хо́дите	/khóḓiṭi/
они́	бу́дут		хо́дят	

The third person plural -ут/-ют , on the other hand, always sounds distinct from the second conjugation -ат/-ят. For this reason, among others, we use the third person plural from in citing verbs in the glossaries.

3rd Pl. forms:

	I		II	
stressed	кладу́т	/kladút/ put	говоря́т	/gavar̯át/ speak
unstressed	бу́дут	/búdut/ will be	хо́дят	/khó̯dat/ go
	понима́ют	/..áyut/ under-stand	попро́сят	/papró̯sat/ request

Pronunciation note:

In the above transcription of хо́дят we use the letter /a/ to represent the unstressed vowel, but in fast speech it can approach the vowel /i/ and sound almost like the singular form хо́дит . This is true of all unstressed 3rd plural forms of Conj. II.

These sets of endings are called the *non-past* endings, because 'past' is the one thing they do *not* mean. Their meaning can be either 'present' or 'future', depending on the verb stem they are attached to. If the verb stem is an Imperfective verb (See Lesson 4.4 on Aspect), the meaning is 'present'; if Perfective, 'future'.

Imperfective verbs		*Perfective verbs*	
пи́шут	they write, are writing	напи́шут	they will write
даю́т	they give, are giving	даду́т	they will give
кладу́т	they put, are putting	поло́жат	they will put

Listed below are the non-past forms you will need in the Exercises to this lesson. Some of them have not occurred in this form in previous dialogs, so you'll have to learn which conjugation they belong to; they are marked with an asterisk. Some of the verbs in this list have the first person singular listed after the 3rd Plural, e.g., хо́дят, хожу́ ; there are two reasons for this:

(1) some verbs have a change of consonant in the 1st Sing.;
(2) some verbs have a shift of stress to the 1st Sing. ending. The verb хо́дят/ хожу́ illustrates both these points (see above for a display of all 6 forms). For further explanation, see Lesson 6.6.

The letters in parentheses refer to aspect, as explained in Lesson 4:
C = Perfective, and HC = Imperfective.

Conjugation I

Infinitive	*Non-past*	
бы́ть	бу́дут	they will be
верну́ть (C)	верну́т	they will return
дава́ть (HC)	даю́т	they give, are giving
зна́ть (HC)	зна́ют	they know
класть (HC)	кладу́т	they put (lay), are putting
{ написа́ть (C)	*напи́шут напишу́	they/I will write
писа́ть (HC)	*пи́шут пишу́	they/I write, am writing
нарисова́ть (C)	*нарису́ют	they will draw
понима́ть (HC)	понима́ют	they understand
{ прочита́ть (C)	*прочита́ют	they will read
чита́ть (HC)	*чита́ют	they read, are reading

Conjugation II

Infinitive	*Non-past*	
ви́деть (НС)	*ви́дят ви́жу	they/I see
говори́ть (НС)	говоря́т	they speak, talk, say
лежа́ть (НС)	лежа́т	they lie, are lying
научи́ть (С)	*нау́чат научу́	they/I will teach
позвони́ть (С)	позвоня́т	they will phone
положи́ть (С)	*поло́жат положу́	they/I will put (lay)
поста́вить (С)	*поста́вят поста́влю	they/I will put (stand)
попроси́ть (С)	*попро́сят попрошу́	they will request
спроси́ть (С)	*спро́сят спрошу́	they will inquire
стоя́ть (НС)	стоя́т	they stand, are standing
ходи́ть (НС)	*хо́дят хожу́	they/I go

We will continue to list Imperative forms (used in giving commands) as separate words in the Active Word lists until their formation is discussed, but in the meantime observe that non-past forms may differ from Imperatives, quite often in the position of stress:

Положи́те ви́лку на сто́л!   Put the fork on the table! (Imperative)

Вы́ поло́жите ви́лку на сто́л?   Will you put the fork on the table? (non-past)

Научи́те на́с да́тельному падежу́!   Teach us the dative case!

Вы́ на́с нау́чите да́тельному падежу́? Will you teach us the dative case?

The Imperative may differ in other ways, too:

Не кла́дите ло́жки на сто́л!   Don't put the spoons on the table!

Вы́ кладёте ло́жки на сто́л?   Are you putting the spoons on the table?

In summary, learn the 3rd Plural non-past to identify what conjugation the verb belongs to; learn Imperatives (command forms) as separate words for the time being.

3.2 Irregular verbs

With respect to the non-past endings, there are only four irregular verbs in Russian. Of them you have had three: хоте́ть (I) 'want', да́ть (P) 'give' and е́сть (I) 'eat'.

хоте́ть:	я́ хочу́	мы́ хоти́м	
	ты́ хо́чешь	вы́ хоти́те	
	о́н хо́чет	они́ хотя́т	'they want'

This verb is irregular in all sorts of ways; it is a first conjugation verb in the singular forms, second in the plural; no other verb has this stress pattern: no other verb has -ч- in the singular vs. -т- in the plural.

да́ть:	я́ да́м	мы́ дади́м	
	ты́ да́шь	вы́ дади́те	
	о́н да́ст	они́ даду́т	'they will give'

As the English translation indicates ('*will* give') this verb is perfective, as is the derived verb переда́ть 'pass, hand; transmit'.

передам́	передади́м	
переда́шь	передади́те	
переда́ст	передаду́т	'they will pass'

The addition of a prefix (e.g. пере-) to a verb (e.g. да́ть) almost never affects the verb's ending or stress pattern. Therefore, a statement like 'The verb да́ть is irregular' should be taken to mean 'the simple verb (да́ть) and all prefixed forms thereof(переда́ть, зада́ть,...)'.

This point is illustrated also by the verb е́сть (I), whose Perfective partner съе́сть has the same irregular endings (съе́м 'I will eat', съе́шь, съе́ст , etc.)

е́сть			
	я́ е́м	мы́ еди́м	
	ты́ е́шь	вы́ еди́те	
	он́ е́ст	они́ едя́т	'they eat, are eating'

Pronunciation: recall the vowel coloring caused by neighboring palatalized consonants (Lesson 3.6); the /e/ of е́сть sounds different from the /e/ of ест.

Here are some examples of the irregular Perfective verb да́ть, даду́т (future meaning) and its regular Imperfective partner дава́ть, даю́т (present meaning):

Я да́м тебе́ бо́мбу.	I will give you a bomb.
Ты́ да́шь бо́мбу сестре́.	You will give the bomb to your sister.
Сестра́ переда́ст бо́мбу роди́телям.	Your sister will pass the bomb to your parents.
Я даю́ уро́ки англи́йского языка́.	I give English lessons.
Ты́ даёшь уро́ки болга́рского языка́.	You give Bulgarian lessons.
Зю́зе даю́т уро́ки матема́тики.	They give Zyuzya math lessons. Zyuzya is being given math lessons.

PRACTICE 7

Cover the right-hand columns and look at the left-hand column. For each verb listed there say the 1st Sing. (я), 3rd Sing. (она́) and 2nd Pl. (вы) forms, e.g.,

кладу́т → я́ кладу́, она́ кладёт, вы́ кладёте

Watch out for stress. Check your answers.   Translate Perfective verbs with **will**, *and Imperfective verbs with the English present tense, e.g.,*

положу́   *'I will put'*, *vs*   кладу́ *'I put'*

	я	она	вы
кладу́т	кладу́	кладёт	кладёте
верну́т	верну́	вернёт	вернёте
даду́т	да́м	да́ст	дади́те
даю́т	даю́	даёт	даёте
стоя́т	стою́	стои́т	стои́те
говоря́т	говорю́	говори́т	говори́те
лежа́т	лежу́	лежи́т	лежи́те
едя́т	е́м	е́ст	еди́те
зна́ют	зна́ю	зна́ет	зна́ете
понима́ют	понима́ю	понима́ет	понима́ете
пи́шут	пишу́	пи́шет	пи́шете
поло́жат	положу́	поло́жит	поло́жите
спро́сят	спрошу́	спро́сит	спро́сите
нау́чат	научу́	нау́чит	нау́чите
нарису́ют	нарису́ю	нарису́ет	нарису́ете

3.3 The forms of the Future tense

There are no new forms to learn to express future tense. The future of *Perfective* verbs is the non-past tense as illustrated above; the future of *Imperfective* verbs consists of the non-past forms of бу́дут 'they will be' plus the Imperfective infinitive (e.g. бу́дут де́лать 'they will do').

Compare the examples in the first group (Perfective) with those in the second (Imperfective); we will discuss the usage of the two aspects in the future in the future.

Perfective future:

Я позвоню́ са́шиному бра́ту.	I'll phone Sasha's brother.
Она́ за́втра позвони́т.	She'll call tomorrow.
Я попрошу́ у него́ каранда́ш.	I'll ask him for a pencil.
Студе́нты попро́сят преподава́теля научи́ть их да́тельному падежу́.	The students will ask the teacher to teach them the dative case.
Студе́нтам даду́т по ды́не.	The students will be given a melon apiece.
Я тебе́ да́м кра́сный каранда́ш.	I'll give you a red pencil.
Я напишу́ сестре́.	I'll write my sister (I'll get a letter off).

Imperfective future:

Что́ вы бу́дете де́лать?	What will you do? What are you going to do? What are you going to be doing?
Я бу́ду игра́ть на фле́йте.	I'm going to play (on) the flute (Not playing any particular piece, just playing).
Я бу́ду писа́ть сестре́.	I'll write my sister (I'll be writing my sister, I'll be in correspondence with her.)

4. ъ (твёрдый зна́к)

The symbol ъ , like ь , represents no sound of its own. Its function is to separate a consonant letter from a following palatal indicator so that the palatal indicator represents the sound /y/ rather than palatalization. Compare:

/y/-sound

съе́л is pronounced *as though* spelled: "сйе́л" /şyél/ ate up

vs. palatalization:

се́л is pronounced as written: "се́л" /şél/   sat down

This is the only position in which ъ is used—after consonant before vowel. Its function in this position is identical to that of ь (See Lesson 3.2.3):

польёт	*pronounced:* "палйо́т"	/paḷyót/	it will pour
полёт	*pronounced:* "палёт"	/paḷót/	flight

You can always tell how to pronounce these Cyrillic sequences aloud, but you can't tell how to spell them (with ъ or with ь ?) until you learn the prefixes of Russian; the spelling rule is: ъ after prefixes, ь elsewhere. The с- of съе́л is a prefix; compare:

е́л	=	"йе́л"	/yél/	ate, was eating
съе́л	=	"сйе́л"	/ş-yél/	ate up

(The с of сел 'sat down' is not a prefix—it is part of the root meaning 'sit', just like the s in English *sit*.)

Incidentally, the meanings of the words мя́гкий зна́к and твёрдый зна́к are 'soft sign' and 'hard sign'. Some scholars and teachers call palatalized consonants *soft consonants* and plain ones *hard consonants*.

5. Aspect: past involvement

This section contains a review of "round trips" and then expands that notion to past situations which represent simply involvement in activity (Imperfective) rather than specification of the end-point (Perfective).

5.1 Another "round trip" verb: открыва́ть (I)

The infinitive forms of the aspect pair 'to open' are:

открыва́ть (I)
откры́ть (P)

The past forms are regular; no stress shift; The past tense can be used in the meaning "round trip" (in a broad sense of the term) very much like ходи́ть (I) /пойти́ (P) 'go' and бра́ть (I) /взя́ть (P). (See Lesson 4.4)

Imperfective

Зде́сь хо́лодно.

-Кто́ открыва́л окно́?

It's cold in here. -Who opened the window? (The window is closed right now, but I can tell that somebody opened it at some time or other because its cold in here—Who's been opening the window?)

vs. Perfective

Кто́ откры́л окно́?

Who opened the window? (I see the result before me now: the window is open—who has opened it?)

Imperfective

Кто́ открыва́л вино́?

Who opened the wine? (Some of the wine has been drunk, or some of you people are drunk, though I'm not saying specifically that the cork is now out of the bottle. There is evidence, however, that it had been opened.)

vs. Perfective

Кто́ откры́л вино́?

Who opened the wine? (I see before me an uncorked bottle. It has not been re-corked—no "round trip")

Вино́ откры́л па́па.

Dad opened the wine.

In these examples the window and the cork have made a round trip where the Imperfective is used.

5.2 Simple involvement

The meanings of "round trip" verbs are such that the action can be reversed: you can reverse the act of going away by coming back; or the act of opening by closing. Other verbs have meanings that cannot be reversed: you can't unread a book, undrink wine, uneat kasha, unspeak words, untranslate a text, unshow somebody a laboratory, etc., etc. In fact, most verbs have meanings of this sort. How does the Imperfective/Perfective distinction apply to such verbs?

The meaning of Perfective Aspect is roughly the same for those verbs as for the Perfectives previously discussed: the end-point of the activity is specified; you've finished reading the book, drunk the wine up, eaten the kasha up, got the words spoken, completed the translation on time, wound up the tour of the lab, etc., etc.

The Imperfective, on the other hand, is used in all other situations. (This is true of all Perfective/Imperfective pairs: the Perfective is always the one with the more specific, definite meaning; Imperfective has all other meanings.) One of these other situations is 'simple involvement in the activity.'

Кто́ е́л (I) мою́ ка́шу?	Who's been eating my porridge?
Что́ вы́ де́лали (I) вчера́?	What did you do yesterday? What were you engaged in? What were you involved in? I'm not asking specifically what you got done.)
Я́ переводи́ла (I).	I did translations. (I was engaged in translating.)

Before giving examples contrasting Perfective vs. Imperfective uses, we shall list the verbs to be illustrated in their infinitive forms, with the past tense added only in cases where it is not predictable from the infinitive (these pairs will be used in the past tense in subsequent exercises):

Imperfective	Perfective	gloss
чита́ть	прочита́ть	read
писа́ть	написа́ть	write
де́лать	сде́лать	do; make
ви́деть	уви́деть	see
рисова́ть	нарисова́ть	draw
есть	съесть	eat/ eat up
е́ла	съе́ла	
пи́ть	вы́пить	drink/ drink up
пила́, пи́ли	вы́пил, вы́пила	
переводи́ть	перевести́	translate
	перевёл	
	перевела́	
	перевели́	

Examples:

(I) Кто́ е́л мою́ ка́шу?	Who's been eating my porridge?
vs. (P) Кто́ съе́л мою́ ка́шу?	Who ate up my porridge? (It's all gone.)

(I) Что́ ты́ де́лал вчера́?	What did you do yesterday?
Мы́ пи́ли вино́ и е́ли икру́.	We drank wine and ate caviar.
vs. (P) Где́ вино́?	Where's the wine?
Мы́ вы́пили вино́.	We drank up the wine.
А икра́?	And the caviar?
Съе́ли.	We ate (it all up).

(I) Кто́-то пи́л мою́ во́дку.	Somebody drank/has been drinking my vodka.
vs. (P) Кто́-то вы́пил мою́ во́дку.	Somebody drank (up) my vodka.

(I) Вы́ чита́ли Войну́ и Ми́р?	Have you (ever) read War and Peace?
vs. (P) Вы́ прочита́ли Войну́ и Ми́р?	Did you finish reading War and Peace? (I knew you were reading it—have you finished?)
	or: Have you read War and Peace? (I assigned it for today—did you get it done?)

(I) Скажи́те, пожа́луйста, вы́ чита́ли "Войну́ и Ми́р?"	Tell me please, have you (ever) read War and Peace? (Question out of the blue.)
vs. (P) Ва́ся! Ты́ прочита́л "Войну́ и ми́р"? Я́ хочу́ её верну́ть в библиоте́ку.	Vasya! Did you finish War and Peace? I want to return it to the library (Question with a certain implication: I expected to finish.)

In the last two sets of examples above, notice how the Perfective is associated with *expectation*. This illustrates the generalization that Perfectives are more explicit, definite, and specific than are Imperfectives.

Further examples:

(I) Я́ вчера́ переводи́ла ве́сь де́нь.	I translated (did translations) all day yesterday.
vs. (P) Я́ вчера́ перевела́ ве́сь те́кст.	Yesterday I got the whole text translated.

(I) Я́ вчера́ де́лал упражне́ния.	I did exercises yesterday (I was involved in doing exercises. Maybe I finished them, maybe I didn't; I'm just telling you what I was involved in.)
vs. (P) Мы́ сде́лали раке́ту са́ми.	We built the rocket ourselves. (This specific ship was built by us.)

(I) Кто́ писа́л на доске́?	Who's been writing on the blackboard? (I have no notion who it was and am not interested in what was written.)
vs. (P) Кто́ написа́л Войну́ и Ми́р?	Who wrote War and Peace? (I know this specific book was written at a particular time by a definite author; either I've forgotten this fact or I'm quizzing you.)

Finally, notice that negation of an action can often mean that you simply were not involved in any action; thus, negation very frequently triggers the Imperfective aspect, e.g.,

$$\begin{cases} \text{(I) Я ничего́ не переводи́ла.} & \text{I didn't translate anything.} \\ \textit{vs.} \text{ (P) Я перевела́ ве́сь те́кст.} & \text{I got the whole text translated.} \end{cases}$$

$$\begin{cases} \text{(I) Я ничего́ не писа́л.} & \text{I didn't write anything.} \\ \textit{vs.} \text{ (P) Я написа́л письмо́.} & \text{I got a letter written.} \end{cases}$$

Here are examples in the future tense:

$$\begin{cases} \text{(I) Я не бу́ду чита́ть.} & \text{I'm not going to do any reading.} \\ \textit{vs.} \text{ (P) Я прочита́ю ве́сь те́кст.} & \text{I'll get the whole text read.} \end{cases}$$

$$\begin{cases} \text{(I) Я не бу́ду рисова́ть.} & \text{I'm not going to draw.} \\ \textit{vs.} \text{ (P) Я нарису́ю кра́сную плане́ту.} & \text{I'll make a drawing of a red planet.} \end{cases}$$

6.   Pronunciation: sentence stress with the yes-no contour.

This rise-fall contour occurs with yes-no questions, as we discussed in Lesson 1.3.1. From the point of view of English, it is peculiar not only in its melody, but in its placement in the sentence. In English we usually put the rising question-intonation (with main stress) at the end of the sentence:

Did he go to s$^{ch^{oo}l^?}$

In Russian you normally put the rise-fall contour (with main stress) on the verb:

О́н ход$^{и́л}$ в ш$_{ко́}$ду?   Did he go to school (and return)?

If you put the main stress at the end of the sentence on something other than the verb, the sentence asks about this item specifically:

О́н ходи́л в ш$^{ко́}$лу?   Did he go to *school*? (Is it to
                                                 school that he went? I thought he
                                                 went somewhere else.)

Similarly:

Вы́ чи$^{та́ли}$ э́ту книгу?   Did you read this book?

Вы́ попроси́ли его́ верну́ть кни́гу?   Did you ask him to return the book?
Вы́ говори́те по-ру́сски?   Do you speak Russian?
Вы́ на́с нау́чите да́тельному падежу́?   Will you teach us the Dative case?

7. Summary of case endings.

	Singular		*Plural*	
	Adj.	*Noun*	*Adj.*	*Noun*
#-declension				
Nom.	-ый/-о́й	-#	-ые	-ы
Gen.	-ого	-а		
Dat.	-ому	-у	-ым	-ам
Acc.	= *Nom./Gen.*			
Prep.	-ом	-е		

o-declension

= *#-declension except for:*

Nom.	-ое	-о	-ые	-а

a-declension

Nom.	-ая	-а	-ые	-ы
Gen.	-ой	-ы		
Dat.	-ой	-е	-ым	-ам
Acc.	-ую	-у		
Prep.	-ой	-е		

Examples:

#-declension

	Singular	*Plural*
Nom.	ве́сь э́тот { бе́лый / большо́й } сто́л	все́ э́ти бе́лые столы́
Gen.	всего́ э́того бе́лого стола́	
Dat.	всему́ э́тому бе́лому столу́	всем э́тим бе́лым стола́м
Acc.	= *Nom./Acc.*	
Prep.	всём э́том бе́лом столе́	

o-declension

Nom.	всё э́то бе́лое ме́сто	все́ э́ти бе́лые места́

a-declension

Nom.	вся́ э́та бе́лая плане́та	все́ э́ти бе́лые плане́ты
Gen.	все́й э́той бе́лой плане́ты	
Dat.	все́й э́той бе́лой плане́те	всем э́тим бе́лым плане́там
Acc.	всю́ э́ту бе́лую плане́ту	
Prep.	все́й э́той бе́лой плане́те	

Pronouns

Nom.	я́	ты́	мы́	вы́	о́н (о́)	она́	они́	что́	кто́
Gen.	меня́	тебя́	на́с	ва́с	его́	её	и́х	чего́	кого́
Dat.	мне́	тебе́	на́м	ва́м	ему́	е́й	и́м	чему́	кому́
Acc.	меня́	тебя́	на́с	ва́с	его́	её	и́х	что́	кого́
Prep.	мне́	тебе́	на́с	ва́с	нём	не́й	ни́х	чём	ко́м

УПРАЖНЕНИЯ

1. **Review. Translate.**

   Where are these letters from? From the Soviet Union. Where are you from? From America. From what city? From what state? From New York. And where are your brothers from? They're from the Soviet Union. They were born in Moscow. Who are those letters from? From my professor. He is in Leningrad.

2. **Conversation.**

   Student A asks B where letters, wine, rings, flags, rockets, canteloupes, brothers, sisters, Mom, Dad, etc. are from (from what country, city, state, secret institute, etc.). When B answers, he asks if A knows where that is located.

3. **Quiz.**

   Substitute any city name for X and answer factually:

   В како́м шта́те нахо́дится X?
   В како́й стране́ нахо́дится X?

4. **Review of Nominative plural forms. Read aloud.**

   1. Где́ _____? (red pens)

   2. Где́ _____?(light blue books)

   3. Я́ ви́дел _____. (dark blue glasses)

   4. У неё бы́ли _____. (green eggs)

   5. Где́ _____? (our brothers)

   6. _____ ходи́ли в теа́тр. (our professors)

5. **Review of case forms.**

   1. Я́ роди́лся в _____. (Soviet Union)

   2. Мы́ ходи́ли в _____. (a/one good restaurant)

   3. Мо́жно зада́ть _____? (a question)

   4. Вы́ за́дали о́чень _____. (good question)

   5. Мо́жно зада́ть ещё _____? (a/one question)

   6. У меня́ не́ было _____. (a read pen)

   7. На на́шей плане́те не́т _____. (a blue ocean)

   8. Не́т _____. (white wine)

   9. В _____ ничего́ не́т. (our city)

   10. _____ э́та кни́га? (whose)

   11. _____ э́ти кни́ги? (whose)

   12. Она́ говори́ла о _____. (light blue planet)

   13. Кто взял _____? (my book)

   14. Он верну́лся из _____. (America)

6.   Review of pronouns.

Put these pronouns in the proper case form.

1. Мы́ говори́ли о _____.   (он)

2. О _____ вы́ говори́ли? (кто)

3. _____ не́ было? (кто)

4. _____ не́ было. (она)

5. Ка́к _____ зову́т? (ты)

6. На _____ е́сть океа́н. (она)

7. На _____ лежи́т письмо́.   (он)

8. О́н ви́дел _____. (он)

9. Она́ _____ взяла́. (она)

10. Я́ понима́ю _____. (он)

11. Во́т письмо́ от _____. (он)

12. Я́ взя́л слова́рь у _____. (она)

7.   Review of past tense forms.

Change from о́н to она́, then to они́.

П: О́н ходи́л в рестора́н.
C₁: Она́ то́же ходи́ла в рестора́н.
C₂: Они́ ходи́ли в рестора́н.
П: О́н бы́л в рестора́не.
   О́н не бра́л э́ту кни́гу.
   О́н взя́л стака́ны.
   О́н за́дал интере́сные вопро́сы.
   О́н переда́л вино́.
   О́н да́л на́м зелёные карандаши́.
   О́н верну́лся из Сове́тского Сою́за.
   О́н смотре́л секре́тный фи́льм.

8.   Accusative case, Analysis 1.

Put the words listed below in proper form in the sentence 'I know X.'

П: Ива́н Петро́вич
C: Я́ зна́ю Ива́на Петро́вича.
П: да́тельный паде́ж
C: Я́ зна́ю да́тельный паде́ж.

его́ бра́т   его́ сестра́
его́ профе́ссор   э́тот профе́ссор
э́тот преподава́тель   э́тот язы́к
э́та преподава́тельница   э́та кни́га
э́тот теа́тр   э́тот студе́нт
э́та студе́нтка   э́та ру́сская кни́га
э́тот ру́сский теа́тр   э́тот ру́сский профе́ссор
э́то ру́сское сло́во   америка́нский президе́нт
да́тельный паде́ж   францу́зский язы́к

9. Accusative case, Analysis 1, Dialog 2.

      One student asks another for a colored pencil or pen. The other
student supplies an answer from the list of animate and inanimate nouns
(plus a color, where appropriate).

C: Máша, дай мне красный карандаш/красную ручку.
M: Зачем тебе красный карандаш/красная ручка?
C: Чтобы нарисовать красную планету.

наша преподавательница   наша мама
эта студентка   этот студент
этот стакан   наш ресторан
наш профессор   Иван Петрович
(color) планета   (nationality) флаг
наш преподаватель   наш дом

10. Dative case. Analysis 2.1, Dialog 2.

      Repeat Dialog 2, but switch брат and сестра and make the
appropriate changes in the pronouns, i.e., say сашиной сестре instead
of сашиному брату . Then substitute преподаватель/преподавательница
for брат/сестра.

11. Analysis 2.

      One student asks another to distribute things. Use any familiar nouns
(вилка, ложка, карандаш,...) Notice that Masha uses the вы form
положите to her friends—she can't use ты because it is singular and
she's talking to them both at once.

П: Саша, попросите Машу дать студентам ножи.
C: Маша, дай Васе и Пете по одному большому ножу.
M: Пожалуйста. (Does so.)
   Положите ножи на стол.

Now expand the converstion by adding the following:

В. и П.: Куда?
M: Справа от карандаша (ручки/ложки/...)

12. Dative vs. Accusative. Analysis 2, Dialog 2.

      One student asks another where somebody is. The second student has
to think up an animate noun or somebody's name.

C: Ты не знаешь, где преподаватель?
M: Не знаю. Позвони директору и спроси его.
C: А где директор?
M: Не знаю. Позвони X и спроси его.
C: А где X ?
M: Не знаю. Позвони...

13. Dative vs. Accusative. Analysis 2, Dialog 2.

Make a possessive adjective from your classmates' names. Go around the class as fast as you can.

C: Ма́ша, ты́ не зна́ешь, где́ ната́шин бра́т?
M: Не зна́ю. Позвони́ ди́миному бра́ту и спроси́ его́.
C: Ва́ня, ты́ не зна́ешь, где́ ди́мин бра́т?
B: Не зна́ю. Позвони́ пе́тиному бра́ту и спроси́ его́.
C: О́ля, ты́ не зна́ешь, где́ пе́тин бра́т?
O: Не зна́ю. Позвони́...

Repeat, substituting сестра́ for бра́т.

14. Translate. Dialog 1, 2.

Give me a read pencil, please. I need a red pencil. Why do you need a red pencil? I don't have a red pencil. I have a white pencil. I need a red pencil to draw a red house. I need a red pencil to draw a red general. I'll call (my) sister. (My) parents gave her a red pencil. I'll write my parents. I need a good book. Why do you need a good book? To read. Call a good student. At the end of the semester all good students were each given a good book.

15. Conversation.

Student A asks B for something. B wants to know what its for, but he doesn't have one anyhow, and A should call somebody or write. The conversation ends when A says that all the good students will be given one each.

16. Dative. Analysis 2, Dialog 3.

Answer in the affirmative, using the proper Dative pronoun (ему́, е́й, or и́м).

П: Ва́шему бра́ту ску́чно?
C: Да́, ему́ ску́чно.

Твоему́ бра́ту ску́чно?   Студе́нтам ску́чно?
Твое́й сестре́ ску́чно?   Э́тому студе́нту ску́чно?
Твои́м бра́тьям ску́чно?   Э́той студе́нтке ску́чно?
Преподава́телю ску́чно?

Substitute: ве́село, жа́рко, хо́лодно, тепло́.

17. Analysis 2, Dialog 3.

> Answer with different neuter form, as in the model:

П: Вам не хо́лодно?
С: Не́т, мне́ тепло́.

Ва́м э́то не тру́дно?   Ва́м не ску́чно?
Ва́м пло́хо? ("Are you feeling ill?")   Ва́м жа́рко?
Ва́м   неприя́тно чита́ть э́ти те́ксты?   Ва́м э́то легко́?
Ва́м интере́сно чита́ть по-ру́сски?   Ва́м ве́село?
Ва́м не хо́лодно?   Ва́м тепло́?

18. The verb дать. Analysis 3.2.

> Substitute for я́блоко:

П: Что́ ва́м да́ст профе́ссор?
С: О́н на́м да́ст по одному́ большо́му я́блоку.

яйцо́   кольцо́
но́ж   слова́рь
ло́жка   ви́лка
италья́нский фла́г   ру́сский слова́рь
ру́сская кни́га

19. The verb да́ть. Analysis 3.2.

> Two students discuss the professor's intentions vis-à-vis the dative case. Substitute the items listed below for я́блоко   and ды́ня.

С: Ма́ша, ка́к по-тво́ему: профе́ссор на́с нау́чит да́тельному
        падежу́?
М: Да́. В конце́ семе́стра о́н на́м да́ст по одному́ большо́му
        я́блоку и по одно́й большо́й ды́не.

яйцо́/кни́га
но́ж/ ло́жка
италья́нский слова́рь/раке́та
ру́сский слова́рь/ру́сская газе́та

20. Play the roles of Dialog 4 and substitute the following instruments for флéйта:

гита́ра   guitar   труба́   trumpet
скри́пка   violin   кларне́т   clarinet
бараба́н   drum   гобо́й   oboe
роя́ль   (grand) piano   аккордео́н   accordion

Also substitute different imperfective verbs for чита́ли и переводи́ли
(писа́ли, е́ли, пи́ли,...)

21. Imperfective infinitives. Analysis 5.

Supply an appropriate *Imperfective* infinitive to replace читать (есть, пить, писать).

П: Вот книга.
     Что вы хотите делать?
С: Я хочу *читать* книгу.

Substitute:

вино	водка
каша	яйцо
газета	упражнения
лимонад	апельсины
флейта	грейпфрут
суп	письмо

22. Analysis 5, Dialog 4.

Answer the question, substituting verbs from the preceding exercise for читали и переводили.

П: Что вы делали вчера?
С: Мы читали и переводили.
П: Маша, вы тоже читали и переводили?
М: Да, но я больше не хочу читать и переводить. И Петя больше не хочет. Мы больше не хотим.

23. Analysis 5 (Aspect) and 1 (Accusative).

Note the use of the Imperfective буду рисовать with negation and of the Perfective нарисую to mean 'future'. The form нарисуйте is the Imperative (command) form.

П: Какой это камень?
С: Это чёрный камень.
П: Нарисуйте его.
С: Я не буду рисовать такой неинтересный камень. Я нарисую профессора.

Substitute for профессор: брат, сестра, яйцо, директор, президент, министр, карандаш, журналист, стакан, генерал, планета, атеист, дыня, икра.

Substitute other colors as well.

24. Dialog 5.

Play the roles of Dialog 5 and substitute as many language names as you can for the line О немецком языке. Or use real textbooks. If you use science books, many of the sciences end in -ия, with stress on the preceding syllable: биология, философия, химия, история, психология; the word for 'literature' is литература.

25. Dialog 6.

Three people re-enact the scene from The Three Bears, with variations.
Substitute е́л for пи́л where necessary.

П: Кто́-то пи́л моё вино́.
С: Кто́-то пи́л и моё вино́.
М: Кто́-то пи́л и моё вино́ то́же, и всё вы́пил!

икра́   бо́рщ
су́п   апельси́н
ды́ня   апельси́ны
во́дка   я́блоко
я́блоки   лимо́ны

26. More verbs. Analysis 3.

Answer 'I will' by using the appropriate form of the Perfective
(future) verb in the question. Watch out for stress shift and/or
consonant alternation and irregular verbs.

П: Вы́ им дади́те по я́блоку?
   Вы́ поло́жите скри́пку на сто́л?
   Вы́ прочита́ете "Войну́ и ми́р?"
   Вы́ напи́шете письмо́?
   Вы́ нарису́ете кра́сную плане́ту?
   Вы́ за́втра та́м бу́дете?
   Вы́ дади́те ему́ македо́нский фла́г?
   Вы́ е́й передади́те икру́?
   Вы́ ему́ задади́те вопро́с?

27. More verbs. Analysis 3.

Give the answer 'I also X' and translate, e.g.,

Они́ чита́ют. → Я́ то́же чита́ю.

Они́ едя́т икру́.
Они́ съедя́т икру́.
Они́ хотя́т е́сть икру́.
Они́ им даду́т икру́.
Они́ им расска́жут об икре́.
Они́ напи́шут об икре́.

Repeat with О́н то́же X, and then Вы́ то́же X.

28. Translate.

   (1) Dialog 4. What did you do yesterday in class? We talked Russian.
       I don't want to talk Russian anymore. Masha doesn't want to talk
       Russian anymore. The students don't want to talk Russian anymore.
       May I ask a question? Of course you may. What do you want to do?
       We want to read books.

   (2) Dialog 5. Did you read this book? I read it. Is it interesting?
       Yes, very. What's it about? About one doctor. Who wrote it?
       Chekhov. Did you read this letter? I read it. Is it interesting?
       No, not very. Who's it from? From my brother and sister. Where
       are they? In the Soviet Union. Where were they born? In Moscow.

29. Conversation.

   Students A asks B what (s)he was doing yesterday. B answers (wrote letters,
   translated plays, etc.) but doesn't want to do it anymore. A changes the
   subject and asks whether B has read this book (Read a play, seen a film,
   etc.).

30. Review of plural forms, Lesson 4.1.

   Answer in the negative and supply an adjective with a contrary
   meaning(хоро́ший/плохо́й, большо́й/ма́ленький, интере́сный/ску́чный).

   П: Са́ша, Пётр Ива́нович хоро́ший профе́ссор?
   С: Не́т, плохо́й.
   П: Ма́ша, о́н говори́т о хоро́шем профе́ссоре?
   М: Не́т, о плохо́м. У на́с все́ профессора́ плохи́е.

   Continue around the class:

   Пётр Ива́нович хоро́ший преподава́тель?
   Ни́на Степа́новна хоро́шая преподава́тельница?
   Ната́ша плоха́я студе́нтка?
   Ва́ня плохо́й студе́нт?
   Влади́мир Ильи́ч хоро́ший коммуни́ст?
   Леони́д Ильи́ч хоро́ший президе́нт?
   Мо́царт плохо́й композитор?
   О́н хоро́ший музыка́нт?
   Э́то хоро́ший слова́рь?
   "Пра́вда" хоро́шая газе́та?
   Э́то ску́чное упражне́ние?
   Э́то ма́ленький медве́дь?
   Э́то большо́й теа́тр?
   Э́то интере́сная кни́га?

31. Months and numerals.

    Answer factually. The word гóда means 'of the year'.

(a) П: Какóй пéрвый мéсяц гóда?
    С: Пéрвый мéсяц гóда — январь.

(b) П: Вы родились в мáрте?
    С: Нéт, я родился не в мáрте, а в мáе.
    П: Май — э́то какóй мéсяц? Четвёртый?
    С: Нéт, мáй — э́то не четвёртый, а пя́тый мéсяц.

32. Months.

        Answer factually.

    П: В какóм мéсяце прáзднуется францýзская револю́ция?
        (прáзднуется = 'is celebrated')
    С: В ию́ле.

    Substitute: америкáнская револю́ция
                 большевистская револю́ция
                 октя́брьская револю́ция
                 кубинская револю́ция
                 дéнь рождéния Джóрджа Вашингтóна
                 дéнь рождéния Аврáама Линкóльна

33. Names of cases.

        Answer the teacher's question as to what case the noun is in.
    (родительный, дáтельный, винительный или предлóжный?)

    П: Какóй падéж—от моегó *брáта*?
    С: Родительный.
    П: Какóй падéж—о моём *брáте?*
    M: Предлóжный.
    П: Какóй падéж—   1. от моегó брáта
                           2. о моём брáте
                           3. моемý брáту
                           4. Я́ знáю вáшего брáта.
                           5. Я́ знáю францýзский язы́к.
                           6. (substitute сестрá for брат in all the above)
                           7. в Москвé
                           8. в Москвý
                           9. по одномý я́блоку
                          10. мою́ мáму
                          11. моемý преподавáтелю

34.   Answer as in the model. Watch out for the stress on the negative
не (*not* on the verb) in the masculine form Я не́ был... The feminine
form is what you'd expect: Я не была́, with no stress on the negative
particle.

П: Вы́ бы́ли в Бе́лом до́ме?
С: Не́т, я бы́л в Вашингто́не, но́ я не́ был в Бе́лом до́ме.

Большо́й теа́тр
Кре́мль
Эрмита́ж
Сорбо́нна
музе́й Пра́до
Пентаго́н
Га́рвардский университе́т
ло́ндонский та́уэр

35. Analysis 6. (Intonation)

       One student asks a question of another; the second answers as in
the model. A third student translates the answer into English. The high
pitch of the yes-no question occurs on the verb in all of these questions
(marked ∥).

Model:

−Ты́ позвони́ла са́шиному бра́ту?
−Не́т, я ему́ сейча́с позвоню́.

1. Ты́ позвони́л (а) са́шиной сестре́?
2. Ты́ нарисова́л (а) са́шиного бра́та?
3. Ты́ положи́л (а) кни́гу на сто́л?
4. Ты́ спроси́л (а) са́шиного бра́та, где́ икра́?
5. Ты́ позвони́л (а) са́шиному бра́ту?
6. Ты́ спроси́л (а) са́шину сестру́, где́ икра́?
7. Ты́ написа́л (а) са́шиной сестре́?

Repeat, but use the name Ната́ша instead of вы́ , e.g.,

−Ната́ша позвони́ла са́шиному бра́ту?
−Не́т. Она́ ему́ сейча́с позвони́т.

36. **Italics in Cyrillic.** Italics are based on Cyrillic script; the tricky ones are: б/*б*, в/*в*, г/*г*, д/*д*, и/*и*, and т/*т*.

Regular: а б в г д е ё ж з и й к л м н о п р с т у ф х ц ч ш щ ъ ы ь э ю я
Italic: *а б в г д е ё ж з и й к л м н о п р с т у ф х ц ч ш щ ъ ы ь э ю я*

Read the following passages aloud and translate.

а. Кто́ кого́ рису́ет?

Генера́л рису́ет журнали́ста. Журнали́ст рису́ет ло́шадь*. Ло́шадь рису́ет соба́ку*. Соба́ка рису́ет преподава́теля. Преподава́тель рису́ет свою́ жену́*. Жена́ преподава́теля рису́ет себя́*. Коне́ц.

*Glossary

ло́шадь	horse
соба́ка	dog
жена́	wife
себя́	(her)self

б. Ва́ся и А́ся друзья́*, но они́ о́чень ра́зные* лю́ди*. Ва́се всегда́ хо́лодно. Ему́ бы́ло хо́лодно, когда́* всем бы́ло тепло́. Все́ говори́ли: "Ка́к здесь тепло́! В э́той ко́мнате* о́чень тепло́." А Ва́ся сказа́л: "Мне́ хо́лодно."

А́се всегда́ тепло́. Ей бы́ло тепло́, когда́ всем бы́ло хо́лодно. Все́ говори́ли: "Ка́к здесь хо́лодно! В э́той ко́мнате о́чень хо́лодно." А А́ся сказа́ла: "Ва́м хо́лодно, а мне́ тепло́." Ва́се всегда́ хо́лодно, но он тёплый челове́к. А́се всегда́ тепло́, но она́ холо́дный челове́к. Ва́ся и А́ся о́чень ра́зные лю́ди, но они́ друзья́.

*Glossary

друзья́	friends (irreg. plural of друг)
ра́зные	different, varied, various
лю́ди	people (irregular plural of челове́к)
когда́	when
ко́мната	room

УРО́К ШЕСТО́Й

ТЕ́КСТ: РАЗГОВО́Р МЕ́ЖДУ ДИРЕ́КТОРОМ ИНСТИТУ́ТА И МИНИ́СТРОМ

Дире́ктор: Това́рищ мини́стр, Зю́зя написа́ла[1] пе́рвый расска́з о свое́й плане́те, и я его́ прочита́л[1]. Ску́чная плане́та. Кли́мат как в Гре́ции, о́браз жи́зни как в Швейца́рии. Похо́же на капитали́зм.

Мини́стр: Хм... Что она́ уме́ет де́лать[2]?

Дире́ктор: Уме́ет чита́ть, писа́ть[2]. По-ру́сски говори́т без акце́нта[3]. И э́то всё. Вое́нный потенциа́л у неё, по-мо́ему, незначи́тельный.

Мини́стр: О вое́нном потенциа́ле я тебя́ не спра́шивал[2]. Что ещё[4] ты зна́ешь о её плане́те?

Дире́ктор: Плане́та не о́чень интере́сная. У них два со́лнца и две луны́. Одна́ луна́ кру́глая, друга́я квадра́тная. На одно́й луне́ живу́т пенсионе́ры, на друго́й — атеи́сты и журнали́сты. На плане́те все ве́рят[2] в Бо́га. У них всегда́ тепло́, расту́т[2] апельси́ны, лимо́ны и ды́ни. Тёплая оде́жда им не нужна́. Всё, что им ну́жно, они́ де́лают[2] са́ми. Зю́зе там бы́ло ску́чно, и она́ прилете́ла[1] к нам.

Мини́стр: Интере́сно... Что ещё ты зна́ешь о Зю́зе? Како́е у неё образова́ние?

Дире́ктор: Она́ занима́лась[2] матема́тикой, бро́сила[5], начала́[1] занима́ться[2] филосо́фией и други́ми предме́тами.

Мини́стр: Како́й филосо́фией, маркси́стско-ле́нинской[6]?

Дире́ктор: Ду́маю, что нет,[7] това́рищ мини́стр. Они́ все ве́рят в Бо́га. В ка́ждом го́роде на её плане́те есть це́рковь, синаго́га и мече́ть.

Мини́стр: Хм... А матема́тику она́ хорошо́ зна́ет?

Дире́ктор: На́ши матема́тики разгова́ривали с ней, они́ говоря́т, что она́ ничего́ не зна́ет.

Мини́стр: Ты ей[8] ве́ришь? Мо́жет быть, она́ вас обма́нывает?

Дире́ктор: Я никогда́ никому́ не[9] ве́рю, това́рищ мини́стр. Э́то моя́ рабо́та. Но по-мо́ему, Зю́зя говори́т пра́вду[10]. По-мо́ему, она́ про́сто наи́вный тури́ст.

Мини́стр: Наи́вный тури́ст... Э́то интере́сно. Тури́сту ну́жен па́спорт[11], а у Зю́зи па́спорта нет. Америка́нцы о ней всё равно́ ско́ро узна́ют... Ты сказа́л[1] Си́дорову, что гуля́ть[1] Зю́зе мо́жно то́лько под зо́нтиком?

Дире́ктор: Сказа́л, това́рищ мини́стр.

Мини́стр: Его́ до́чка... как её зову́т...

Дире́ктор: Ле́на, това́рищ мини́стр.

Мини́стр: Да, Ле́на — она́ Зю́зе расска́зывала[2] о на́шей стране́, кака́я она́ больша́я и интере́сная?

Дире́ктор: Расска́зывала, това́рищ мини́стр.

Мини́стр: Хорошо́. Тепе́рь[12] пусть Ле́на ей расска́жет о самолётах и аэропо́ртах. Мо́жет быть, Зю́зя захо́чет[1] полете́ть[1] в Сре́днюю А́зию на самолёте.

Vocabulary

А́зия Asia
акце́нт accent
америка́нец American
аэропо́рт airport
без without

вое́нный military, war (adj.)
Гре́ция Greece
гуля́ть take a walk, take a
  stroll
жизнь life
  о́браз жи́зни way of life,
  lifestyle
занима́ться (НС) (+ Instrumental)
  to work on, be busy (with), study
захоте́ть (C) want
зо́нтик umbrella
к (+ Dative) to (motion towards)
капитали́зм Capitalism
кли́мат climate
маркси́стско-ле́нинский
  Marxist-Leninist
матема́тик mathematician
ме́жду between
мини́стр minister
мо́жет бы́ть maybe, perhaps
найвный naive

незначи́тельный insignificant
  meaningless (cf. зна́чит 'it means')
никогда́ never
обма́нывать to deceive
о́браз way, form, shape, image
образова́ние education, formation
  (cf. о́браз)
па́спорт passport
под under
полете́ть (C) to fly
потенциа́л potential
похо́жий resembling, alike, similar to
пра́вда truth
пусть let
равно́ same, equal
  Всё равно́ all the same, nevertheless
  Мне́ всё равно́. It's all the same
  to me/ I don't care.
разгова́ривать to talk, converse
  (cf. разгово́р)
разгово́р conversation
самолёт airplane
ско́ро soon
ску́чный boring
тепе́рь now
тури́ст tourist
Швейца́рия Switzerland

COMMENTS

1. Perfective Verbs

This footnote number will be used throughout this Text to comment on Perfective aspect forms, listed below in order of their occurrence.

написа́ла...прочита́л	'she *has* written...I *have* read' is a better translation in this context than 'wrote...read.'
прилете́ла	(and here she is; no round trip).
бро́сила	gave up
начала́	began to study (*began* here is a point in time; the activity that you begin to be engaged in is not. Therefore, you *always* use Imperfective *after* verbs meaning 'begin.').

узна́ть	get to know, find out, learn, recognize. Cf. зна́ть (HC) 'to know.'
сказа́л	told (In other contexts, 'said,' e.g. Он сказа́л, что ему́ ску́чно.) Cf. говори́л(HC), said (repeatedly), spoke, talked.
расска́жет Пу́сть она́ расска́жет о плане́те.	tell (future) Let her tell (her story) about the planet. (The Perfective here means 'get this particular story told' not 'tell stories any old time about it,' which would be Imperfective. (See Comment 2).
захо́чет	will want to, will take it into her head to
полете́ть	to fly, set off (by air). (This is like пойти́ - no round trip. See Lesson 4.5.1).

2. Imperfective Verbs

Non-past forms that obviously have present meaning are marked with footnote #2 but aren't listed below because there is no contrast between Perfective and Imperfective in such cases; only Imperfective can be used.

уме́ет де́лать/писа́ть/ чита́ть	'knows how to, can do/write/ read (in general, no endpoint).'
не спра́шивал	'didn't ask, wasn't asking.' (Note Imperfective with negation).
занима́лась	'studied, was studying' (then бро́сила, *Perfective*, 'gave up').
занима́ться	(See начала́ in Comment 1 above).
разгова́ривали	'conversed, talked' (at length, continuously; no end-point specified).
гуля́ть мо́жно	'(she) is permitted to walk' (on various occasions, generally).
расска́зывала	'tell' (about) — like разгова́ривала above. See расска́жет (C) in Comment 1.

3. акце́нт

This word means 'foreign/non-standard accent', not just 'accent'. There-fore you cannot use   хоро́ший   with it to translate 'She has a good accent'. Use у неё хоро́шее произноше́ние 'pronunciation'.

4. ещё

When used with a question word, ещё is translated 'else', e.g.,

Что́ ещё ты зна́ешь?	What *else* do you know?
Кто́ ещё пришёл?	Who *else* came?
Кому́ ещё ты написа́л?	Who *else* did you write to?

When used with a verb, (including the zero verb *is*) it is translated 'still', e.g.,

О́н ещё рабо́тает?	Is he *still* working?
О́н ещё в кабине́те.	He's *still* in the office.

When used with a noun it is translated 'another' in the sense of *one more*, e.g.,

У меня́ ещё оди́н вопро́с.	I have *another* (one more) question.
Да́й ещё стака́н.	Give me *another* (an additional) glass.

Compare друго́й, which means 'another' in the sense of *a different one*:

Да́й друго́й стака́н.	Give me *another* (a different) glass.

5. Ellipsis

The term *ellipsis* is used for incomplete sentences where an expected sen-tence part is omitted.

Бро́сила.	(She) gave up (math).
Зна́ю.	(I) know.
Куда́ ты?	Where are you (going)?
В библиоте́ку.	(I'm going) to the libe.
Кому́ ты пи́шешь?	Who are you writing to?
— Сестре́.	(I'm writing) to (my) sister.
Ты́ е́й сказа́л, что за́втра не бу́дет уро́ка?	Did you tell her there won't be any lessons tomorrow?
Сказа́л.	I did. (I) told (her so).

The fact that Russian has noun and verb endings allows the language to make more use of ellipsis (without loss of information) than is the case in English. Even so, ellipsis often results in ambiguity, resolvable only by context.

6. Compound -o-

There are fewer compounds in Russian than in English. One way of forming them in Russian is with the vowel -o- , as in

маркси́стско-ле́нинская филосо́фия	'Marxist-Leninist philosophy'
а́нгло-ру́сский слова́рь	'English-Russian dictionary'
сове́тско-фи́нский догово́р	'Soviet-Finnish treaty'
ру́сско-япо́нская война́	'Russo-Japanese war'
самолёт	'airplane'
сам 'self' + лет 'fly'	
аэропо́рт	'airport'

Some compounds have no joining vowel:

Ленингра́д = го́род Ле́нина	'Leningrad' = 'Lenin city'

But:

Волгогра́д	'Volgograd' = 'Volga city'
Краснодо́н	'Krasnodon' = 'Red Don (city)'

7. Ду́маю, что нет.

Note the absence of не with the verb. Translation: 'I don't think so' or, more literally, 'I think not'. (See Lesson 4, Dialog Comment 7).

8. ве́рить + Dative

To believe *something/somebody* is ве́рить + Dative:

Я *э́тому* не ве́рю.	I don't believe that.
Я *ему́* не ве́рю.	I don't believe him.

Compare *to believe in something/somebody*: ве́рить в + Acc.

Во *что́* ты ве́ришь?	What do you believe in?
Я ве́рю в *Бо́га*.	I believe in God.

9. n-tuple negation

Negation is not just double (Lesson 2, Text Comment 5), but n-tuple.

Я *никогда́ никому́* не ве́рю.	I never believe anybody (Lit., I don't never believe nobody).
Я *никогда́ нигде́ ничего́* тако́го не ви́дел.	I never saw anything like it anywhere.

10. Пра́вда

Also the name of a newspaper. Another newspaper name: "Изве́стия" "The News". Old joke: В "Пра́вде" нет изве́стий и в "Изве́стиях" нет пра́вды.

11. Па́спорт

Not only tourists need passports. Soviet citizens need internal passports
for a variety of purposes: getting a place to live in a town, getting a job,
travelling. Some classes of citizens don't automatically get passports, e.g.,
collective farm workers.

12. тепе́рь vs. сейча́с

Use тепе́рь   sparingly; it has a narrower usage than сейча́с. Тепе́рь
implies a   contrast with the past, that something or other has preceded, e.g., we've done so and so, so and so, and *now* — we'll do so and so.

Большой Харитоневский переулок (Great Kharitonevskii Lane)
The Moscow street will figure later in our story.

DIALOGS FOR MEMORIZATION

1. Творительный падеж

   С: Господин профессор, почему[1] вы так мало интересуетесь
      творительным падежом[2]?
   П: Это неправда. Когда я гулял[3] по парку с моей второй
      женой[2] /с моим вторым мужем[2]/, мы занимались и творительным
      падежом[2] и всеми остальными падежами[2].

2. Передайте привет

   П: Кем[2] работает Надежда Константиновна?
   С: Врачом[2].
   П: А её муж?
   С: Учителем[2].
   П: Что он преподаёт?
   С: Физику и математику.
   П: Передайте им от меня привет.
   С: Обязательно передам.

3. Разговор по телефону

   П: С кем[2] вы только что говорили[5] по телефону?
   С: С Петром Ильичом[2], а потом с его женой[2].
   П: С какой женой[2]? Он не женат[6].
   С: Вы ошибаетесь. У Петра Ильича[4] две[7] жены. Я разговаривал
      с его второй женой[2].
   П: Я думал[8], вы разговаривали с другим Петром Ильичом[2],
      у которого[9] нет жены.

4. Три медведя

   Медведь сидел за большим столом[2] и ел кашу большой ложкой[2].
   Медведица сидела за маленьким столом[2] и ела кашу маленькой
   ложкой[2].
   А медвежонок? Медвежонок сидел под столом[2] и ничего не ел.
   Ему было скучно.

5. Куда? Где?

   Куда положить книгу?   Под стол.
   Где лежит книга?   Под столом[2].
   Куда поставить стул?   Между столами[2].
   Где стоит стул?   Между столами[2].

6. Анкета: Слова:

   имя   гражданин   четырнадцатый
   отчество   гражданка   пятнадцатый
   √ фамилия   передадут   шестнадцатый
   гражданство   живут   семнадцатый
   место рождения   замужем   восемнадцатый
   √ профессия   одиннадцатый   девятнадцатый
   √ адрес   двенадцатый   двадцатый
                                 тринадцатый   двадцать первый

Translation

1. *The Instrumental case.*

   S: Professor, sir, why are you so uninterested in the instrumental case?
   T: That's not so. When I was walking in the park with my second wife
      /with my second husband,/we studied both the instrumental case and all
      (of) the other (Lit. 'remaining') cases.

2. *Say hello!*

   T: What does Nadezhda Konstantinovna do? (more literally *as whom* or *as
      what* does she work?)
   S: She's a doctor. (Lit. 'As a doctor.')
   T: And her husband?
   S: He's a school teacher.
   T: What does he teach?
   S: Physics and mathematics.
   T: Say hello to them for me. (Lit. 'Transmit to them greetings from me.')
   S: I'll be sure to. (обязáтельно = 'without fail')

3. *Telephone conversation*

   T: Who were you just talking to on the phone? (Lit. 'with whom?')
   S: With Peter Ilyich, and then with his wife.
   T: What wife? He isn't married.
   S: You're mistaken. Peter Ilyich has two wives. I was talking to his
      second wife.
   T: I thought you were talking to another Peter Ilyich who doesn't have a
      wife.

4. *The Three Bears*

   The bear was sitting at a big table (and was) eating kasha with a big spoon.
   The she-bear was sitting at a small table (and was) eating kasha with a
      small spoon.
   And the cub? The cub was sitting underneath the table and wasn't eating any-
      thing. He was bored.

5. *Where to?*

Where (shall I) put the book?	— Under the table.
Where is the book (lying)?	— Under the table.
Where (shall I) put the chair?	— Between the tables.
Where is the chair (standing)?	— Between the tables.

6. *Questionnaire:*   *Words:*

First name	citizen (male)
Patronymic	citizen (female)
Last name	(they) will pass, hand, send, transmit
Citizenship	(they) live
Place of birth	married (said of a woman)
Profession	
Address	

Active Word List

Nouns

анкета	questionnaire
телефон	telephone
по телефону	on the phone, by phone
стул; стулья	chair
парк	park
врач, врача; врачи	doctor
гражданин; граждане	citizen (male)
гражданка	citizen (female)
жена; жёны	wife
муж; мужья	husband
учитель; учителя	teacher
адрес; адреса	address
гражданство	citizenship
имя, имени; имена (neuter, irreg.)	name (first)
математика	mathematics
отчество	patronymic
правда	truth
привет	greetings
профессия	profession
разговор	conversation
рождение	birth
фамилия	name (last)
физика	physics

Verbs

передать, передадут (С) (Irreg. like дадут)	pass, hand, send, transmit
поставить, -ставят, -ставлю (С)	put (in a standing position)
преподавать, -дают (НС)	teach
гулять, гуляют (НС)	stroll
думать, думают (НС)	think
жить, живут; жила, жили (НС)	live
заниматься, занимаются (НС) (+ Instrumental)	be busy (with), be occupied (with), study
интересоваться, интересуются (НС) (+ Instrumental)	be interested (in)
ошибаться, ошибаются (НС)	be mistaken, make mistakes
работать, работают (НС)	work
разговаривать, разговаривают(НС)	talk, converse
сидеть, сидят, сижу (НС)	be sitting

Adjectives

который	which
остальной	remaining
творительный	instrumental

одиннадцатый	eleventh
двенадцатый	twelfth
тринадцатый	thirteenth
четырнадцатый	fourteenth
пятнадцатый	fifteenth
шестнадцатый	sixteenth
семнадцатый	seventeenth
восемнадцатый	eighteenth
девятнадцатый	nineteenth
двадцатый	twentieth
двадцать первый	twenty first

Other

мало	little, few
обязательно	without fail
потом	then, next
две	two (feminine form)
за (+ Instrumental)	behind (location)
за столом	at the table
за (+ Accusative)	behind (direction)
когда	when
между	between
под (+ Instrumental)	under (location)
под (+ Accusative)	under (direction)
почему	why
только	only
только что	just
женат	married (said of a man)
замужем	married (said of a woman)

COMMENTS

1. зачем vs. почему

зачем asks 'What future benefits will result from the action?' It is future-oriented, like English 'what for'.

Зачем ты это сделал?	What did you do that for? Why did you do that? What did you expect to get out of it?

почему asks 'What prior or attendant circumstances motivated the action?' It is past-oriented, like English 'how come', 'how did it come about?' .

Почему ты это сделал?	Why did you do that? What impelled you to do that?

Do not equate these two words with English 'why, what for' — English speakers often use them interchangeably, while Russian speakers maintain a firm distinction between зачем and почему.

Compare:

Зачем ты ходил в кино?	Why did you go to the movies? What did you go to the movies for?

| Заче́м о́н проигра́л втору́ю па́ртию? | What did he lose the second game for? (Implication: he did it on purpose.) |
| Почему́ о́н проигра́л втору́ю па́ртию? | Why did he lose the second game? How come? (Explain how circumstances caused the loss; maybe he's a poor player or was distracted.) |

The answer to заче́м typically begins with что́бы '(in order) to'; the answer to почему́ typically begins with потому́ что 'because'.

Заче́м вы́ занима́етесь твори́тельным падежо́м?	What are you studying the instrumental case for?
— Что́бы лу́чше говори́ть по-ру́сски.	— In order to speak Russian better.
Почему́ мы́ ещё не занима́лись твори́тельным падежо́м?	Why haven't we studied the instrumental case yet?
— Потому́ что у на́с не́ было вре́мени.	— Because we didn't have time.

2. Instrumental

Instrumental case forms are marked with this footnote number throughout the dialogs. See Analysis 1.

3. Aspect: гуля́л

Since the Imperfective Aspect is used in such a variety of situations (any situation where end-point is not specified), it is sometimes subject to more than one interpretation. We simply don't know whether Когда́ я гуля́л... here means 'When I was strolling...(e.g. yesterday afternoon)' or 'When I used to stroll (on frequent occasions).' Without further context, either interpretation is possible.

4. Patronymics

Women's patronymics are formed by adding -овна/-евна to the father's first name.

Father	Daughter
Ива́н	Мари́я Ива́новна
Серге́й	Мари́я Серге́евна
Пётр	Мари́я Петро́вна

For a few names, like Илья́, the suffix -и́нична is used:

Илья́	Мари́я Илью́нична

In conversational style the unstressed -овна/-евна is abbreviated in pronunciation (not spelling), e.g., as though spelled Ива́нна, Се́ргевна.

Men's patronymics are formed with -ович/-евич (for Илья́: —Ильи́ч).

Father	Son
Ива́н	Ива́н Ива́нович (= Ива́ныч)
Серге́й	Ива́н Серге́евич (= Сирге́ич)
Пётр	Ива́н Петро́вич (= Питро́ич)

Patronymics are nouns, and have the same endings as the noun classes you have learned.

Don't use the abbreviated forms when speaking slowly or formally.

If you don't know somebody's patronymic, it's quite proper to ask them directly: Ка́к ва́ше и́мя-о́тчество? 'What is your first name and patronymic?'

5. 'talk to'

In English you can say *I talked/spoke "with" him* or *"to" him*, with very little difference in meaning. In Russian you must use с 'with' + Inst. to render this meaning Я́ с ни́м говори́л/разгова́ривал. In this context it doesn't matter very much whether you use говори́л or разгова́ривал. The important thing is to *not* use the Dative — it means something different with говори́л (i.e., 'told, said') and it doesn't occur at all with разгова́ривал. For details, see Lesson 9.2.1.

6. 'be married'

Said of a man: о́н жена́т; said of a woman: она́ за́мужем; said of a couple: они́ жена́ты.

7. две + Gen.

Recall that a noun is in the Gen. *Singular* after два́, две́, три́ and четы́ре.

8. что omission

Standard literary Russian rarely allows two contiguous clauses without a joining word like что or кото́рый. The sentence Я́ ду́мал вы́ разгова́ривали... is conversational style for Я́ ду́мал, что вы́ разгова́ривали, with что omitted. If you omit it, you can't make a pause between the two clauses.

9. кото́рый

This word refers back to a noun and is an adjective meaning 'which' or 'who'. It agrees with the noun in gender and number, but its case form depends on its role in its own clause. Thus, кото́рого here is masculine singular because it comes after Петро́м Ильичо́м (Inst. Sg. Masc.), but it is Genitive because it is being used with the preposition у. Compare the sentence in the dialog with the following sentence, where it goes with a feminine noun:

Я́ ду́мал, вы́ разгова́ривали с друго́й Наде́ждой Константи́новной (Inst.), у кото́рой (Gen.) не́т му́жа.	I thought you were talking to another Nadezhda Konstantinovna who doesn't have a husband.

Further examples:

Nom. Возьми́те кни́гу, кото́рая лежи́т
     на столе́.

Take the book which is lying on
     the table.

Acc. Где́ кни́га, кото́рую я́ тебе́
     дала́?

Where's the book I gave you?

Acc. Где́ стака́н, кото́рый я́ тебе́
     дала́?

Where's the glass I gave you?

Acc. Где́ кольцо́, кото́рое я́ тебе́
     дала́?

Where's the ring I gave you?

Prep. Где́ кольцо́, о кото́ром мы́
      говори́ли?

Where's the ring we were talking
      about (= about which we were
      talking)?

Dairy store

ANALYSIS

1. Instrumental Case

The instrumental case is so called because one of its typical uses is to indicate the instrument by which something is done:

Чём о́н пи́шет?	What's he writing *with*?
О́н пи́шет *кра́сным карандашо́м.*	He's writing *with* a red pencil.
Она́ пи́шет *пра́вой руко́й.*	She writes *with* her right hand.

It also occurs with the meaning 'as' (О́н рабо́тает до́ктором), with various prepositions (с бра́том), and as the object of certain verbs (О́н интересу́ется грамма́тикой).

In the following sections we shall list the Instrumental endings and illustrate these uses.

1.1 Instrumental endings.

Singular:

masc., neut.	fem.
Adj. + Noun	Adj. + Noun
-ым -ом	-ой -ой

Plural:

Adj. + Noun
-ыми   -ами

О́н интересу́ется	He's interested in...
твори́тельным падежо́м.	the Instrumental case.
ру́сской грамма́тикой.	Russian grammar.
ру́сскими падежа́ми.	Russian cases.

If you know the difference between adjective and noun, these endings are quite distinct from all other case endings. However, notice that the Instrumental *noun* ending -ОМ is like the Prep. *adjective* ending:

Inst.	кра́сным карандашо́м	with a red pencil
Prep.	о кра́сном карандаше́	about a red pencil

Also, the Inst. adjective ending -ой (fem.) is just like three other cases: Genitive, Dative and Prepositional; the Adjective and Noun combination -ой+ -ой, however, is quite distinct:

Gen.	-ой	-ы	э́той же́нщины	that woman's
Dat.	-ой	-е	э́той же́нщине	to that woman
Prep.	-ой	-е	об э́той же́нщине	about that woman
Inst.	-ой	-ой	с э́той же́нщиной	with that woman

The Instrumental case forms of pronouns are listed below; note the similarity with adjective endings:

Nom.	Inst.	Nom.	Inst.
я́	мно́й	мы́	на́ми
ты́	тобо́й	вы́	ва́ми
о́н } óнó }	и́м	они́	и́ми
она́	е́й		
чтó	чéм		
ктó	кéм		

Special adjectives have the masc./neut. ending -им (э́тим), except for вéсь 'all, whole,' which has the Inst. form всéм (see Section 3, below).

PRACTICE 1

Cover the right column; read aloud, then check. Change the nouns in these phrases to pronouns, e.g., 'with Peter' → 'with him'.

                                                    ANSWERS

1. с му́жем   с ни́м
2. с жено́й   с не́й
3. с профе́ссором   с ни́м
4. с профессора́ми   с ни́ми
5. с А́нной Степа́новной   с не́й
6. с Петро́м Ива́новичем   с ни́м
7. с мое́й пе́рвой жено́й   с не́й
8. с мои́м пе́рвым му́жем   с ни́м
9. с на́шими генера́лами   с ни́ми
10. с преподава́тельницей   с не́й

1.2 'by means of'

Do not use a preposition to express this meaning.

О́н пи́шет мое́й ру́чкой.	He's writing *with* my pen.
Она́ взяла́ кни́гу пра́вой руко́й.	She picked up the book *with* her right hand.
Мы́ рису́ем карандаша́ми.	We're drawing *with* pencils.
Лю́ди ду́мают голово́й, а рабо́тают рука́ми.	People think *with* their heads and work *with* their hands.
Су́п едя́т ло́жкой, а мя́со — ви́лкой и ножо́м.	Soup is eaten *with* a spoon, but meat (is eaten) *with* a fork and knife.

PRACTICE 2

Add the adjectives такóй плохóй *to these sentences, i.e. change from 'I don't want to write with a pencil' to 'I don't want to write with such a bad pencil.'*

Я не хочý писáть карандашóм.
  мéлом.
  рýчкой.
Я не хочý éсть вИлкой.
  лóжкой.
  ножóм.

1.3 'as'

Another meaning of the Instrumental is 'as, in the capacity of'.

Кéм вы рабóтаете?	What do you do? = What's your profession?
Я рабóтаю врачóм.	I'm a doctor. (Lit. 'I work in the capacity of a doctor')
А вáша женá?	And your wife?
Медсестрóй.	(She's) a nurse.

PRACTICE 3

With many of the liberal professions and high positions you don't use рабóтает *+ Inst., just as you don't say 'He works as a king.' With the following list of professions make the sentence* Он рабóтает *+ Inst. only with those having an asterisk; otherwise use* Он *+ Nom., e.g.,* Он музыкáнт.

*врáч	*механик	президéнт
*учитель	композитор	*медсестрá
профéссор	*журналист	преподавáтель

1.4 With prepositions: с, под, за, мéжду

The meaning of the preposition C/CO depends on what case follows it; with Genitive it means 'from, off of' (See Lesson 4, Text Comment 1); with Instrumental it means 'with, accompanying'.

Gen.	Зюзя упáла с *нéба.*		Zyuzya fell *from* the sky.
	Медвежóнок упáл со *стýла.*		The bear fell *off* the chair.
Inst.	Медвежóнок гулял с *медвéдем* и *медвéдицей* по пáрку.		The baby bear was walking *with* the pappa and mamma bear in the park.

Further examples:

Врач сиде́л с *жено́й* в па́рке.	The doctor was sitting in the park *with* his wife.
Они́ разгова́ривали с *учителя́ми*.	They were talking *with* the teachers.
Учителя́ разгова́ривали по телефо́ну с *мини́стром*..	The teachers were talking on the telephone *with* the minister.
Мини́стр жи́л с *балери́ной*.	The minister was living *with* a ballerina.
Мини́стр ду́мал, что балери́на ему́ изменя́ет с *одни́м. гражда́нином* Швейца́рии.	The minister thought she was deceiving him (being unfaithful to him) *with* a citizen of Switzerland.
Но́ о́н ошиба́лся: она́ ему́ изменя́ла с *граждани́ном* Гре́ции, кото́рый роди́лся в Швейца́рии.	But he was mistaken: she was being unfaithful to him *with* a citizen of Greece who was born in Switzerland.
С *удоево́льствием.*.	Sure. Certainly. (Lit. 'with pleasure')

The meaning of под depends on the following case, much like в and на; with Instrumental it means '(located) under, underneath' and with Accusative it means '(motion) under'.

Examples:

Ле́на и её дру́г гуля́ли под *больши́м зо́нтиком.*.	Lena and her friend were taking a walk under a large umbrella.
Вра́ч Ивано́ва и её му́ж гуля́ли под *дождём*.	Dr. Ivanora and her husband were walking in (Lit. 'under') the rain.
Compare:	
Ви́лка упа́ла под *сто́л. (Acc.)*	The fork fell under the table (*motion*).
vs.	
Ви́лка лежи́т под *столо́м. (Inst.)*	The fork is lying under the table (*position*).

The preposition за is like под: use Instrumental for location, Accusative for direction.

Examples:

О́н бро́сил ви́лку за *сто́л. (Acc.)*	He threw the fork to the other side of (Lit. 'beyond')the table.
Ла́мпа стои́т за *столо́м. (Inst.)*	The lamp is (standing) on the other side of (Lit. 'beyond') the table.
Де́ти убежа́ли за *до́м. (Acc.)*	The children ran behind the house.
Бори́с Миха́йлович и его́ жена́ живу́т за́ *го́родом. (Inst.)*	Boris Mikhailovich and his wife live in the suburbs (Lit. beyond the city).
Все́ врачи́ е́дут за́ *го́род.(Acc.)*	All the doctors are driving to the suburbs.
За *до́мом (Inst.)* у ни́х е́сть ма́ленький огоро́д.	Behind their house they have a small vegetable garden.

Some prepositions such as ме́жду 'between' invariably take the Instrumental case, whether or not motion is involved.

Она́ поста́вила стака́н *ме́жду* на́шими таре́лками.	She put (stood) the glass *between* our plates.
Стака́н стои́т *ме́жду* на́шими таре́лками.	The glass is (standing) *between* our plates.
Во́т грани́ца *ме́жду* По́льшей и Сове́тским Сою́зом.	There's the border *between* Poland and the Soviet Union.
Ме́жду на́ми, о́н ма́ло зна́ет о зю́зиной плане́те.	(Just) *between* us, he doesn't know much about Z's planet.
разгово́р *ме́жду* дире́ктором и мини́стром.	a conversation *between* the director and the minister

---

PRACTICE 4

Put the words listed below in this sentence:

Я́ гуля́л по па́рку с (мо́й)(второ́й)_____.

    му́ж
    жена́
    студе́нт
    студе́нтка
    вра́ч

PRACTICE 5

Put the words listed below in this sentence (use plural forms throughout):

О́н разгова́ривал с на́шими _____.

студе́нт	сестра́
учи́тель	жена́
профе́ссор	учи́тельница
бра́т	студе́нтка
му́ж	роди́тели

1.5 Verb objects

The objects of most verbs are Accusative. Such verbs are said to be *transitive* verbs. Verbs that take no object, or an object in a non-accusative case, are said to be *intransitive*.

You have already been introduced to some verbs that govern the Dative case (e.g. Позвони́те *мне́.* 'Call me.')

Here are some verbs that govern the Instrumental case:

интересова́ться (НС)	be interested in
занима́ться (НС)	be busy with, occupied with; study

Examples:

Я о́чень интересу́юсь ру́сским
  языко́м.
Я занима́юсь ру́сским языко́м.
На́ши студе́нты интересу́ются
  теа́тром и кино́. (Indeclinable)

I'm very interested in the Russian
  language.
I'm studying Russian.
Our students are very interested
  in theater and cinema.

Translate the following sentences:

Че́м вы́ интересу́етесь?
-Фи́зикой.
Е́сли вы́ интересу́етесь фи́зикой,
  почему́ вы́ занима́етесь ру́сским
  языко́м?
В ру́сском языке́ е́сть твори́тельный
  паде́ж, а я́ всегда́ хоте́л занима́ться
  твори́тельным падежо́м.
Каки́м падежо́м вы́ занима́етесь?
-Твори́тельным.
Профессора́ интересу́ются цве́том
  плане́ты.
"Я о́чень интересу́юсь ва́шим де́лом,"
  сказа́л генера́л.
Ты́ ма́ло интересу́ешься фи́зикой.
Ната́шины роди́тели ма́ло интересу́ются
  Сове́тским Сою́зом.
Студе́нты ру́сского языка́ ма́ло ин-
  тересу́ются твори́тельным падежо́м.

PRACTICE 6

*Put the words in parentheses in the Instrumental and trans-
late.*

     Медве́дь жи́л с _____(жена́) в одно́м большо́м до́ме.
_____(кто́) рабо́тал медве́дь? Медве́дь рабо́тал _____
(профе́ссор) в университе́те. _____(что́) о́н интересо-
ва́лся? О́н интересова́лся _____ (матема́тика) . О́н
писа́л кни́ги. _____(что́) о́н и́х писа́л? _____(каран-
да́ш). Где́ о́н и́х писа́л? За _____(сто́л). Коне́чно.
Под _____(сто́л) не́ было ме́ста.

2. Pronouns with н-: review.

Recall Lesson 4.3.4. Here are further examples of third person pronoun forms with н- (after prepositions) and without н- (not after prepositions).

Этот карандаш плохо́й. Я не могу́ *им* писа́ть.	This pencil is bad. I can't write with it.
Этот флейти́ст плохо́й. Я не хочу́ с *ним* игра́ть.	That flautist is poor. I don't want to play with him.
Мой люби́мый предме́т—ру́сский язы́к. Когда́ вы на́чали *им* занима́ться?	My favorite subject is Russian. When did you start studying it?
Са́ша меня́ научи́л твори́тельному падежу́. Когда́ вы на́чали с *ним* занима́ться?	Sasha taught me the Instrumental case. When did you start studying with him?
Мой люби́мый предме́т—биоло́гия. Когда́ вы на́чали *ей* занима́ться?	Biology is my favorite subject. When did you start studying it?
Я рабо́таю в библиоте́ке с Ма́шей.	I'm working in the library with Masha.
Когда́ вы на́чали с *ней* рабо́тать?	When did you start to work with her?

3. Prepositional Plural.

The plural endings are:

Adj. + Noun	
-ых	-ах

о тру́дных вопро́сах   about difficult questions

The usual spelling rules apply:

о на́ших ды́нях   about our melons
на больши́х плане́тах   on large planets
в мои́х лаборато́риях   in my labs

Watch out for stem changes; if the Nominative Plural has a stem different from the singular, so will all the other plural cases.

Nom. Sg.	Nom. Pl.	Prep. Pl.
брат	бра́тья *(Irreg. stem)*	бра́тьях
сестра́	сёстры *(ES stress)*	сёстрах
сло́во	слова́ *(SE stress)*	слова́х

Quiz   PRACTICE 7

This is a review of the case forms you have had so far. Answer these questions with the word сестра́ *in its proper case form e.g.,*

Кого́ вы ви́дели в па́рке?   —Сестру́.

О кого́ вы бы́ли вчера́?
О ко́м вы говори́ли?
С ке́м вы гуля́ли по па́рку?
Кому́ вы позвони́ли?
Кто́ е́л мою́ ка́шу?
О ко́м вы ду́маете?
Кому́ вы пи́шете?

Кого́ вы спроси́ли об э́том?
У кого́ вы попроси́ли икру́?
Кому́ вы за́дали э́ти вопро́сы?
С ке́м вы разгова́ривали?
Кому́ вы переда́ли ка́шу?

Now answer the questions with the two words са́шина сестра́ *; then with* са́шин вра́ч.

---

4. The forms of весь.

This special adjective has endings like all the other special adjectives (э́тот, мо́й, ва́ш, etc.) except that it has -e- where the others have -и-.

	весь 'all, whole'	Other Special Adj.
Inst. Sg. masc./neut.	всём	э́тим, мои́м...
Nom. Pl.	все́	э́ти, мои́...
Dat. Pl.	все́м	э́тим, мои́м...
Inst. Pl.	все́ми	э́тими, мои́ми...
Prep. Pl.	все́х	э́тих, мои́х...

Все сиде́ли *весь* де́нь за столо́м.   *Everybody* sat at the table *all* day.
О́н *всё* зна́ет.   He knows *everything*.
Всем студе́нтам даду́т по ды́не.   *All* the students will be given a
                                            melon apiece.

Она́ *всем* интересу́ется.   She's interested in *everything*.
Она́ *все́ми* интересу́ется.   She's interested in *everybody*.

Prepositions with variants in -о (с/со, в/во etc.) use these variants when вс- follows; the preposition о uses the variant обо.

Они́ говори́ли *обо* всём.   They talked about **everything**.
Они́ говори́ли *обо* всёх *со*   They talked about everybody with
  все́ми студе́нтами.   with all the students.
во все́х больши́х газе́тах   in all the big newspapers

PRACTICE 8

Fill in the blanks with the proper form of все *'all, everybody.'*
Translate.

____ бы́ли в Москве́.
Я ча́сто ду́маю о ва́с ____.
Она́ говори́ла со ____ студе́нтами.
Она́ позвони́ла ____ студе́нтам.
Она́ ____ интересу́ется.
Она́ гуля́ла по па́рку со ____ свои́ми студе́нтами.
Она́ задала́ э́тот вопро́с ____ свои́м студе́нтам.
Она́ написа́ла ____ упражне́ния.
На́м ____ ску́чно.

Now use the proper singular forms; remember that the neuter form
все́ *can mean 'everything.'*

Она́ съе́ла ____ икру́.
Она́ вы́пила ____ вино́.
Она́ съе́ла ____.
Она́ ____ зна́ет.
Она́ ____ интересу́ется.
Она́ говори́ла обо ____.
Она́ смотре́ла ____ фи́льм.
Во ____ стране́ не́т тако́го институ́та.
Она́ гуля́ла по ____ го́роду.

---

5.   Aspect: Imperfective contexts.

5.1   Imperfective and plurality

There is an affinity between Imperfective aspect and plurality. Compare:

(1) О́н ча́сто писа́л (НС) мне́ пи́сьма.   He often wrote me letters.
(2) О́н мне́ написа́л (С) письмо́.   He wrote me a letter. (He got a
                                                   letter written)

In (1) there is no definite end-point; he wrote a number of letters a number of times. In (2) there is an end-point, a finished letter.

This affinity is somewhat vague; it is a statistical fact rather than a grammatical rule. It is quite normal to have plurals with Perfectives; e.g.

О́н написа́л (С) пи́сьма.   He wrote the letters.

But notice that the English translation contains the article *the*, which renders the meaning of definiteness in much the same way that the Perfective написал renders the meaning of end-point (a kind of definiteness). The translation 'He wrote letters' would be wrong; this sentence in Russian has an *Imperfective* verb: Он писал письма. The reason that Perfectives go with singular nouns more often than with plurals has less to do with grammar than with real life; when someone wants to sit down and write a letter, or eat a bowl of porridge, or do a Russian lesson or get something done, it is more likely that it will be one thing rather than many things, though there is no rule against writing more than one letter at a time, eating any number of bowls of kasha, or doing six lessons at a sitting.

Return now to example (1) and observe the element of plurality in the adverb часто 'often, frequently, many times'. The affinity of such adverbs with Imperfective aspect is very strong. In fact, it can be stated as a rule, at least for the past tense:

> Use the Imperfective aspect to
> describe repeated or habitual
> actions in the past, not the
> Perfective aspect.

In the following examples note the expressions like часто 'often', всегда 'always', каждый раз 'every time', etc., all of which force you to use the Imperfective form.

Когда я *занимался* русским языком, мы каждый день *читали* по-русски, *писали* упражнения и *переводили* тексты с русского языка на английский.

When I studied Russian, we read in Russian, wrote exercises, and translated texts from Russian into English *every day.*

Я часто *хожу* к врачу.

I *often* go to the doctor.

Каждый раз, когда я *говорю* с ним по телефону, я *передаю* привет его жене.

Every day when I talk to him on the phone I send regards to his wife.

Учителя и врачи часто *ошибаются*, и не всегда *говорят* правду.

Teachers and doctors *often* make mistakes, and don't *always* tell the truth.

Каждый день я *ставлю* лампу под стол, и каждый день, когда меня нет дома, она *ставит* лампу на стол. Когда я *прихожу* домой, я каждый раз *нахожу* лампу на столе, а не под столом.

Every day I put the light under the table, and *every day*, when I'm not at home, she puts the light on the table. *When(ever)* I come home, *every time* I find the light on the table, not under the table.

Почему он всё время *открывает* рот и ничего не *говорит*?

Why does he *always* open his mouth and never say anything?

Потому что он не *умеет разговаривать* с дамами.

Because he doesn't know (in general, always) how to converse with ladies.

5.2 Imperfective: on-going action

In comment 3 to the Dialogs it was noted that Я гуля́л по па́рку can be variously translated, 'I (often) *walked* in the park' or 'I *was walking* in the park (yesterday)'. The latter translation is what we mean by *on-going* action. The sentence can be disambiguated by a larger context or by the addition of adverbs, e.g.

Я ча́сто гуля́л(НС) по па́рку.	I *often* walked (used to walk) in the park.
vs. Когда́ я гуля́л(НС) по па́рку, я уви́дел(С) дире́ктора институ́та.	As (when) I was walking in the park, I saw (caught sight of) the director of the institute.

The second example above is not ambiguous even though there is no adverbial of time in it. The reason there is no ambiguity is that the verb in the second clause (уви́дел) is Perfective. This makes it clear that the situation is not a repeated one. Compare:

Когда́ я гуля́л(НС) по па́рку, я всегда́ ви́дел(НС) та́м дире́ктора институ́та.	When I walked (used to walk) in the park I always saw (I always used to see/I would always see) the director of the institute there.
Когда́ я писа́ла(НС) письмо́, мне́ позвони́л (С) Ви́тя.	As (when) I was writing the letter, Vitya called me.
Когда́ я говори́л(НС) с профе́ссором, кто́-то взя́л (С) мою́ кни́гу.	As (when) I was talking to the professor, somebody took my book.
Когда́ я занима́лся (НС) в библиоте́ке, кто́-то съе́л (С) всю́ мою́ чёрную икру́.	As (when) I was studying in the library, somebody ate up all my black caviar.

Here are some more examples of Imperfectives without a sufficiently large context to make a precise translation possible; hints at possible contexts are given in English.

Кто́-то е́л мою́ ка́шу.	Somebody has been eating my kasha. ...ate (but didn't eat it up) ...was eating ...used to eat
Что́ ты де́лал?	What did you do? ...were you doing (when I saw you)
Я чита́л "Войну́ и ми́р."	I read War and Peace (at some time or other). ...was reading

6. Non-past verb forms (continued)

6.1 Consonant alternations in Conjugation II

The stem-final consonant of Conj. II verbs changes in the 1 sg. form according to a regular pattern. The change from -с- to -ш- in они́ спро́сят → я спрошу́, is not an irregularity: *all* II verb stems ending in -с- predictably undergo this alternation of -с- to -ш-.

These alternations also occur in English word-pairs, although our spelling system does not reflect it:

Russian			English	
т→ч	отве́тят→отве́чу	'answer'	t→ch	create→creature
д→ж	ви́дят→ви́жу	'see'	d→j	verdant→verdure
з→ж	во́зят→вожу́	'convey'	z→zh	please→pleasure
с→ш	спро́сят→спрошу́	'ask'	s→sh	face→facial
ст→щ	пу́стят→пущу́	'let go'	st→shch	quest→question

In addition to the above set of alternations, all Conj. II verbs ending in a labial consonant add -л- in the 1 Sg.:

п → пл	ку́пят →	куплю́	'will buy'
б → бл	лю́бят →	люблю́	'like, love'
м → мл	ко́рмят →	кормлю́	'feed'
в → вл	ста́вят →	ста́влю	'put, stand'

Listed below are the verbs of this sort you have had thus far:

д→ж   ходи́ть, хо́дят, хожу́
       сиде́ть, сидя́т, сижу́
       ви́деть, ви́дят, ви́жу
       переводи́ть, -во́дят, -вожу́

с→ш   спроси́ть, спро́сят, спрошу́
       попроси́ть, -про́сят, -прошу́

в→вл   поста́вить, -ста́вят, -ста́влю
        предста́вить, -ста́вят, -ста́влю

Verbs like пи́шут/пишу́ are *not* of the above type, even though they do have an alternation of consonants (cf. -с- in писа́ть); the difference is that -ш- here runs throughout *all* the non-past forms, not just the 1 Sg. Besides, they are Conjugation I, not II. There are few such verbs; we'll discuss them later.

6.2 Stress patterns

There are 3 possible stress patterns for the non-past. (The only exceptions are 3 of the 4 irregular verbs of Russian.)

S = Stem stressed	E = End stressed	M = Movable stress
я зна́ю	я говорю́	я хожу́
ты зна́ешь	ты говори́шь	ты хо́дишь
о́н зна́ет	о́н говори́т	о́н хо́дит
мы́ зна́ем	мы́ говори́м	мы́ хо́дим
вы́ зна́ете	вы́ говори́те	вы́ хо́дите
они́ зна́ют	они́ говоря́т	они́ хо́дят

Movable stress affects only one ending: stress shifts to the 1 Sg. ending:
There are no other patterns.

The verbs you have had so far with M-stress are:

(на)писа́ть, пи́шут, пишу́
(на)учи́ть, у́чат, учу́
положи́ть, поло́жат, положу́
попроси́ть, -про́сят, -прошу́
спроси́ть, спро́сят, спрошу́
сказа́ть, ска́жут, скажу́
рассказа́ть, -ска́жут, -скажу́
смотре́ть, смо́трят, смотрю́
ходи́ть, хо́дят, хожу́
переводи́ть, -во́дят, -вожу́

PRACTICE 9

The following verbs are not from your active vocabulary, but
you should be able to give the first person singular (я)
according to the pattern of consonant alternations described
above. The letters S, E, and M will serve as a guide to the
position of stress.

они́ полетя́т	E	they will fly off
они́ приглася́т	E	they will invite
они́ лю́бят	M	they love
они́ ло́вят	M	they are catching
они́ во́зят	M	they haul
они́ чи́стят	S	they clean
они́ ку́пят	M	they will buy
они́ познако́мятся	S	they will get acquainted
они́ встре́тят	S	they will meet

7. Summary of case endings.

	Singular		Plural	
	Adj.	*Noun*	*Adj.*	*Noun*
#-declension				
Nom.	-ый/-о́й	-#	-ые	-ы
Gen.	-ого	-а		
Dat.	-ому	-у	-ым	-ам
Acc.	*= Nom./Gen.*			
Inst.	-ым	-ом	-ыми	-ами
Prep.	-ом	-е	-ых	-ах

o-declension

= #-declension except for:

Nom.	-ое	-о	-ые	-а

a-declension				
Nom.	-ая	-а	-ые	-ы
Gen.	-ой	-ы		
Dat.	-ой	-е	-ым	-ам
Acc.	-ую	-у		
Inst.	-ой	-ой	-ыми	-ами
Prep.	-ой	-е	-ых	-ах

Examples:

#-declension

	Singular	Plural
Nom.	ве́сь э́тот {бе́лый / большо́й} сто́л	все́ э́ти бе́лые столы́
Gen.	всего́ э́того бе́лого стола́	
Dat.	всему́ э́тому бе́лому столу́	все́м э́тим бе́лым стола́м
Acc.	*= Nom./Gen.*	
Inst.	все́м э́тим бе́лым столо́м	все́ми э́тими бе́лыми стола́ми
Prep.	все́м э́том бе́лом столе́	все́х э́тих бе́лых стола́х

o-declension

Nom.	всё э́то бе́лое ме́сто	все́ э́ти бе́лые места́

a-declension

Nom.	вся́ э́та бе́лая плане́та	все́ э́ти бе́лые плане́ты
Gen.	все́й э́той бе́лой плане́ты	
Dat.	все́й э́той бе́лой плане́те	все́м э́тим бе́лым плане́там
Acc.	всю́ э́ту бе́лую плане́ту	
Inst.	все́й э́той бе́лой плане́той	все́ми э́тими бе́лыми плане́тами
Prep.	все́й э́той бе́лой плане́те	все́х э́тих бе́лых плане́тах

Pronouns

Nom.	я́	ты́	мы́	вы́	о́н(о́)	она́	они́	что́	кто́
Gen.	меня́	тебя́	на́с	ва́с	его́	её	и́х	чего́	кого́
Dat.	мне́	тебе́	на́м	ва́м	ему́	е́й	и́м	чему́	кому́
Acc.	меня́	тебя́	на́с	ва́с	его́	её	и́х	что́	кого́
Inst.	мно́й	тобо́й	на́ми	ва́ми	и́м	е́й	и́ми	че́м	ке́м
Prep.	мне́	тебе́	на́с	ва́с	нём	не́й н́их	чём	ко́м

1. Review: places.

Recall the institutions listed in Lesson 4, Exercise 1. Answer questions
based on that exercise according to this model. Watch out for the stress:
нé был vs. не былá.

П: Вы́ бы́ли в Ватикáне?
С: Нéт, я́ бы́л в Ри́ме, нó я́ нé был в Ватикáне.
П: Вы́ бы́ли в Бéлом дóме? в Кремлé? в Сорбóнне? в Колизéе?
    в Большóм теáтре?...

2. Review: verb practice.

Translate. Then change all the sentences from они́ to я́ ; then to óн ;
then to ты́ ; All these verbs are Imperfective, so the non-past means
"present".

Они́ всегдá кладу́т вéщи на своё мéсто.
Они́ говоря́т по-ру́сски.
Они́ читáют по-ру́сски.
Они́ знáют Петрá Ивáновича.
Они́ ви́дят Петрá Ивáновича.
Они́ даю́т студéнтам кни́ги.
Они́ пи́шут пи́сьма.
Они́ хóдят в теáтр.
Они́ стоя́т на столé.
Они́ лежáт на столé.
Они́ хотя́т читáть.
Они́ едя́т кáшу.

The following verbs are all Perfective, so the non-past means "future".

Они́ полóжат вéщи на своё мéсто.
Они́ постáвят стакáны на стóл.
Они́ напи́шут письмó.
Они́ спрóсят егó, кáк егó зову́т.
Они́ попрóсят у негó словáрь.
Они́ прочитáют газéту.
Они́ верну́т кни́ги в январé.
Они́ нарису́ют ракéту.
Они́ бу́дут в ресторáне.
Они́ даду́т студéнтам кни́ги.

3.   Review: "also".

Translate these sentences. Then reword the second and third members of each triplet using either то́же or и...то́же as required by the context. (See Lesson 2, Dialog Comment 1.) Note that all these verbs are Perfective, so the non-past meaning is "future".

Model:

а) Кто́-то поста́вил стака́ны на сто́л.
б) Пожа́луй, я *то́же* поста́влю стака́ны на сто́л.
в) Пожа́луй, я поста́влю *и* вино́ на сто́л *то́же*.

1а) Кто́-то да́л студе́нтам по одному́ я́блоку.
б) Пожа́луй, я да́м студе́нтам по одному́ я́блоку.
в) Пожа́луй, я да́м профессора́м по одному́ я́блоку.

2а) Кто́-то позвони́л Петру́ Ива́новичу.
б) Пожа́луй, я позвоню́ Петру́ Ива́новичу.
в) Пожа́луй, я позвоню́ Ни́не Степа́новне.

3а) Кто́-то попроси́л у Пе́ти кра́сный каранда́ш.
б) Пожа́луй, я попрошу́ у Пе́ти кра́сный каранда́ш.
в) Пожа́луй, я попрошу́ у Пе́ти жёлтый каранда́ш.

4а) Кто́-то написа́л письмо́ Президе́нту.
б) Пожа́луй, я напишу́ письмо́ Президе́нту.
в) Пожа́луй, я напишу́ кни́гу   президе́нту.

5а) Кто́-то прочита́л э́то письмо́.
б) Пожа́луй, я прочита́ю э́то письмо́.
в) Пожа́луй, я прочита́ю друго́е письмо́.

6а) Кто́-то нарисова́л на́шу раке́ту.
б) Пожа́луй, я нарису́ю на́шу раке́ту.
в) Пожа́луй, я нарису́ю твою́ раке́ту.

7а) Кто́-то положи́л фле́йту на слова́рь.
б) Пожа́луй, я положу́ фле́йту на слова́рь.
в) Пожа́луй, я положу́ икру́ на слова́рь.

8а) Кто́-то за́дал вопро́с о я́блоках.
б) Пожа́луй, я зада́м вопро́с о я́блоках.
в) Пожа́луй, я зада́м друго́й вопро́с о ды́нях.

9а) Кто́-то переда́л ды́ню.
б) Пожа́луй, я переда́м ды́ню.
в) Пожа́луй, я переда́м ка́шу.

10а) Кто́-то попроси́л у Са́ши ды́ню.
б) Пожа́луй, я попрошу́ у Са́ши ды́ню.
в) Пожа́луй, я попрошу́ у Са́ши ка́шу.

11а) Кто́-то спроси́л Са́шу, где́ нахо́дится Кре́мль.
б) Пожа́луй, я спрошу́ Са́шу, где́ нахо́дится Кре́мль.
в) Пожа́луй, я спрошу́ Са́шу, где́ нахо́дится Бе́лый до́м.

4. Language names and names of peoples.

П: На како́м языке́ говоря́т *кита́йцы*?
С: Кита́йцы говоря́т на *кита́йском языке́*.
П: Говоря́т, что ваш бра́т зна́ет *кита́йский язы́к*.
С: Да́, он хорошо́ говори́т *по-кита́йски*. Он преподава́тель
    кита́йского языка́ в университе́те.

Names of Peoples	*Adjectives*	
кита́йцы	кита́йский	Chinese
францу́зы	францу́зский	French
испа́нцы	испа́нский	Spanish
италья́нцы	италья́нский	Italian
не́мцы	неме́цкий	German
поля́ки	по́льский	Polish
ру́сские	ру́сский	Russian
англича́не	англи́йский	English
америка́нцы	америка́нский	American
япо́нцы	япо́нский	Japanese
ара́бы	ара́бский	Arabian

5. Analysis 1, Dialog 1.

    Answer the teacher's question with the name of a language.

П: Че́м вы занима́етесь?
С: Я занима́юсь *ру́сским языко́м*. Я о́чень интересу́юсь *ру́сским
    языко́м*.

    Substitute: англи́йский язы́к, испа́нский....
    Switch to ты and go around the class as follows:

М: Че́м ты занима́ешься?
С: Я занима́юсь *ру́сским языко́м*. Я о́чень интересу́юсь *ру́сским
    языко́м*.
М: А я́ интересу́юсь то́лько *италья́нским языко́м*.

6. Repeat the above, but make these substitutions:

    (1) names of cases (вини́тельный, да́тельный...)
    (2) names of fields of study or occupation:

фи́зика	хи́мия
матема́тика	биоло́гия
му́зыка	филосо́фия
о́пера	исто́рия
гимна́стика	психоло́гия
спо́рт (Singular)	геоло́гия
теа́тр	социоло́гия
кино́ (Indeclinable)	дерматоло́гия

    (3) the plural form дела́ 'business, affairs', with a modifier, e.g. дела́
         (дела́ми) моего́ бра́та, дела́ мое́й сестры́, са́шины дела́, ма́шины
         дела́...

7. Analysis 1, Dialog 2.

Go around the class asking one another about Пётр Петро́вич .
Answer as fast as you can, without repeating the profession or places in
italics. Before you start the conversation, say these names of professions
aloud; note the consistent stress shift in words like геоло́гия: гео́лог.

биоло́гия	био́лог	фи́зика	фи́зик
социоло́гия	социо́лог	матема́тика	матема́тик
психоло́гия	психо́лог	исто́рия	исто́рик
филосо́фия	фило́соф	хи́мия	хи́мик

Others: врач, профе́ссор, учи́тель, преподава́тель, меха́ник,
генера́л, медсестра́ (nurse) ....

П: Кем рабо́тает Пётр Петро́вич?
С: Он рабо́тает учи́телем. (Он био́лог.)
П: А его́ жена́?
С: *Врачо́м.* (Она́ фи́зик.)
П: Где они́ живу́т?
С: В *Москве́.*
П: Переда́йте им от меня́ приве́т.
С: Обяза́тельно переда́м.

8. Analysis 1. Answer factually.

П: Чем занима́ются фи́зики?
С: Фи́зикой.

Substitute with items from the preceding exercise.

9. Analysis 1.

The verb занима́ться can refer to a habitual activity (e.g., a profession) or an on-going activity (as in *What were you doing yesterday?*).
The latter usage is illustrated in this exercise. The word за́втра in the
third speech means 'tomorrow'. Substitute fields of study or activity
from the preceding exercises.

П: Чем вы́ занима́лись вчера́?
С: Я занима́лась/занима́лся *фи́зикой.*
П: А за́втра?
С: За́втра я́ бу́ду занима́ться *му́зыкой.*

10. Translate. Dialog 2.

What does Nadezhda Konstantinovna do? She's a doctor. And her husband?
He's a doctor too. What does Boris Mikhailovich do? He's a professor,
he teaches mathematics. He also teaches physics. And his wife? She's
a professor too. She teaches physics. What do you do? I'm a school
teacher. Tell him hello from me. I'll be sure to ("without fail").
Tell them hello from me. Tell her hello from me.

11. Conversation. Dialog 2.

A asks B what C and her husband do, what city they live in, what country
that city is located in, and what language they speak. A says that he
too is interested in or studies those professions and languages. The
conversation ends when A asks B to give his regards to the C's in that
language. (If you can make C a real person, so much the better.)

12. Analysis 3.

The word сегодня (pronounced сиводня) in the first speech means
'today'.

П: О чём пишут сегодня в *советских* газéтах?
С: В *советских* газéтах пишут о *советском* президéнте.

Substitute nationality adjectives: америкáнский, итальянский, францýзский, немéцкий...

Then substitute the following in place of президéнт: математика,
библиотéка, университéты.

13. Answer factually.

П: На каких языкáх вы говорите?
С: Я говорю по-____ и по-____.

Switch to ты and go around the class.

14. Analysis 3.

Answer factually, using a plural form where possible (some places, like Бе́лый до́м, are one-of-a-kind, so you'll have to use a singular form for them).

П: Где́ рабо́тают профессора́?
С: Профессора́ рабо́тают в университе́тах.
П: Где́ рабо́тает на́ш президе́нт?
С: На́ш президе́нт рабо́тает в Бе́лом до́ме.

Substitute:

профе́ссии	*места́ рабо́ты*
меха́ник	гара́ж EE
вра́ч	поликли́ника
астроно́м	обсервато́рия
библиоте́карь	библиоте́ка
актёр	теа́тр
учи́тель	шко́ла
космона́вт	ко́смос
на́ш президе́нт	Бе́лый до́м
сове́тский президе́нт	Кре́мль EE
акроба́т	ци́рк
америка́нский сена́тор	Сена́т

If somebody makes a mistake, add the following speech:

М: Не́т, Са́ша, ты́ ошиба́ешься. По-мо́ему, профессора́ рабо́тают не в гаража́х, а в университе́тах.

15. Dialog Comment 10.

Insert the proper form of the word кото́рый 'which, who'. Translate.

Я́ ви́дел стака́н, _____ стои́т на столе́.
Я́ ви́дел бума́гу, _____ лежи́т на столе́.
Я́ ви́дел письмо́, _____ лежи́т на столе́.
Где́ до́м, в _____ ты́ живёшь?
Где́ страна́, в _____ ты́ живёшь?
Где́ вра́ч, _____ не хо́чет рабо́тать?
Где́ вра́ч, _____ я́ вчера́ позвони́л?
Где́ вра́ч, _____ я́ вчера́ ви́дел?
Где́ вра́ч, с _____ я́ вчера́ говори́л?
Где́ медсестра́, _____ не хо́чет рабо́тать?
Где́ медсестра́, _____ я́ вчера́ позвони́л?
Где́ медсестра́, с _____ я́ вчера́ говори́л?
Где́ медсестра́, _____ я́ вчера́ ви́дел?

16. Translate. Dialog 3.

Hello. (Алло́) Is this Sasha? No, this is his wife, Masha. I want
to talk to ("with") Sasha. To ("with") whom? Sasha's not here. When
he comes back, give him my regards.

Who were you talking to on the phone? Is he married? Is she married?
Are they married? I was talking to a teacher (fem.) who doesn't have a
husband,...who works at the university,...about whom they wrote in the
newspapers,...to whom we gave the books,...who I phones yesterday,...
with whom I talked yesterday. You are mistaken. It's his second wife
who works at the university....

17. Conversation.

This is like the previous conversation, except that it is a report of a
telephone conversation and has a great confusion over marital status and
precise identification of just who B is (which wife/husband?). Use
кото́рый   as often as possible.

A talks to B on the phone. Then C asks A who B is, where (s)he works,
studies, lives, etc.

18. Ask where something/somebody is, using the verbs стои́т, лежи́т, сиди́т,
as befits the situation. Dialogs 4 and 5.

C: Где́ сиди́т Ната́ша?
M: За столо́м.
C: За каки́м столо́м?
M: За больши́м столо́м.

Similarly, Где́ лежи́т кни́га?(на столе́) . Где́ стои́т стака́н?(на
столе́). Substitute familiar objects and names of classmates.

19. Analysis 2 and 3.

      Read the following sentences; supply the proper form of the word for 'him'. Then repeat with 'her', then 'them'.

П: Саша, прочитайте, пожалуйста, первую фразу.
С: Я прочитаю первую фразу с большим удовольствием, господин профессор! (Читает)

1. Я с ___ ходил в кино.
2. Я ___ очень интересуюсь.
3. Вот от ___ письмо.
4. Вы ___ знаете?
5. Я много думал о ___.
6. ___ не было в ресторане.
7. Я с ___ разговаривал по телефону.
8. Когда вы ___ позвонили?
9. У ___ есть яблоко.
10. ___ скучно говорить об этом.
11. Я пил вино вместе с ___.
12. Вы ___ видели?
13. Вы ___ научили творительному падежу?
14. У ___ есть красные карандаши?
15. Как ___ зовут?
16. Спросите ___, где наш преподаватель.
17. Скажите ___, что вина нет.
18. ___ скучно.

20. Dialog 4, Analysis 1.

(a) Answer the question Чем едят X? 'What is X eaten with?' using the words вилка, нож, or ложка. If none are appropriate, say руками.

П: Чем едят бифштекс?
С: Бифштекс едят вилкой и ножом.

Substitute: суп, дыня, икра, борщ, яблоки, каша

(b) Supply any of the instruments in the preceding exercise and explain why, as in the model. The word for 'because' is потому что , pronounced without any stress on что: патамушта.

П: Маша, спросите Сашу, чем он ест.
М: Саша, чем ты ешь?
С: Я ем ножом.
М: А почему ты ешь ножом?
С: Потому что у меня нет вилки.

You can vary the exercise by supplying a food name, e.g. Чем он ест суп?

Substitute the usual instruments (вилка, ложка, нож, рука) and go around the class.

There are differences in customs as to how things are eaten. In Russia:

Торт (cake) едят ложкой, а не вилкой.
Дыню едят руками, а не ложкой.

21. Analysis 1, Dialog 4.

Explain why you are writing with a certain kind of instrument by saying
you lack the appropriate kind, as in the model.

С: Ма́ша, почему́ ты пи́шешь *таки́м больши́м карандашо́м?*
М: Я пишу́ *больши́м карандашо́м,* потому́ что у меня́ нéт *ма́ленького
карандаша́.*

Substitute various colors, e.g. Почему́ ты пи́шешь кра́сным карандашо́м?
and then use ру́чка instead of каранда́ш. Then change the sentence to:

С: Ма́ша, почему́ ты éшь тако́й большо́й ло́жкой?

Ask her also about her big fork and knife.

22. Analysis 4.

Complete the sentences   with the proper form of вéсь.   Translate.

1. Я всегда́ говорю́_____.   the whole truth
2. Я хочу́ жи́ть ка́к _____.   everybody
3. _____ бы́ло на столé.   everything
4. Я хочу́ жи́ть вмéсте со _____.   everybody
5. _____ ску́чно.   everybody
6. _____ вéсело.   everybody
7. Я _____ зна́ю.   everything
8. Пéтя тебé ска́жет обо _____.   everything

23. Analysis 3.

Change to prepositional plural.

Мы́ говори́ли о зелёной ды́не.
Мы́ ду́мали о его́ письмé.
Мы́ ду́мали о хоро́шей сторонé вопро́са.
Мы́ разгова́ривали о си́нем океа́не.
Мы́ не хотéли ду́мать о ва́шем дéле.
Мы́ не ду́мали о кра́сном я́блоке.
Мы́ не говори́ли о его́ бра́те.
Мы́ не хотéли говори́ть об э́той совéтской газéте.
Мы́ не писа́ли об э́том плохо́м врачé.
Мы́ писа́ли о хоро́шей странé.

24. Dialog 4.

Go around the class, each person adding another noun.

Медвéдь ходи́л по па́рку.
(a) Медвéдь ходи́л по па́рку с *карандашо́м* в рука́х.
(b) Медвéдь ходи́л по па́рку с *карандашо́м и словарём* в рука́х.
(c) Медвéдь ходи́л по па́рку с *карандашо́м, словарём и кни́гой*
в рука́х.

When you get stuck, say: Я бо́льше не хочу́ говори́ть об э́том медвéде.
Я хочу́ говори́ть о друго́м медвéде.
and start again.

25. Put the word in parentheses in the Instrumental case.

Analysis 1, Dialogs 4, 5.

1. Врач говорил со ____.   (свои братья)
2. ____ он писал?   (что)
3. Михаил Михайлович работает ___.   (учитель)
4. Медвежонок сидел за ___.   (стол)
5. Между ___, все профессора в этом
    университете плохие.   (мы)
6. Почему вы занимаетесь ___?   (немецкий язык)
7. Между ___, я мало интересуюсь ___.   (мы/творительный падеж)
8. Где машин муж? Он лежит под ___.   (стол)
9. Почему вы интересуетесь ___?   (это)

26. Translate. (Dialog 5)

Where's the bear? The bear is (sitting) at the table. Where's the baby
bear? Under the table. Why? He's bored. Where's the book (lying)?
The book is (lying) on the table. Where's the glass (standing)? The
glass is (standing) on the table. Where should I put the book? On the
table. Where should I put the glass? On the table. No, you're mistaken; under the table.

27. Conversation.

One person puts things in various places. A second person asks a
third where he put it and asks a fourth where it is standing or lying.

C: Маша, куда он поставил книгу? (standing on end)
M: Он поставил книгу на стол.
C: Наташа, где книга?
H: Книга стоит на столе.

Use в, на, под, and между.

28. Analysis 5.

    You are asked whether you got something done (Perfective verb). Answer with an Imperfective verb, saying that you don't want to do it any more. Your answer will contain a plural object, unless of course it is a word that doesn't have a plural, like каша, икра, etc.

П: Саша, вы написали письмо?
С: Нет, я больше не хочу писать письма.

Similarly:

    Вы написали упражнение?
    Вы прочитали это письмо?
    Вы съели кашу?
    Вы съели яйцо?
    Вы написали книгу?
    Вы прочитали книгу?
    Вы прочитали словарь?
    Вы съели икру?
    Вы взяли у него икру?
    Вы положили книги на своё место?
    Вы положили нож на стол?
    Вы положили карандаш на стол?
    Вы нарисовали стол?
    Вы нарисовали стул?
    Вы нарисовали портрет брата?
    Вы прочитали газету?

29. Analysis 5.

    Again you are asked whether you got something done (Perfective verb). This time you explain that while you were doing it (on-going activity: Imperfective verb), you were interrupted by the telephone (Perfective).

П: Саша, вы написали письмо?
С: Нет. Когда я его писал, мне позвонили.

Ask the same questions as in the preceding exercise.

30. Put the word in parentheses in the proper case (mixed cases).

    1. ____ в вашей стране очень скучно. (мы)
    2. Я работал вместе с ____. (этот врач)
    3. Миша съел ____. (красная дыня)
    4. Мы часто звоним ____. (сестра)
    5. С ____ ты работаешь? (кто)
    6. В ____ ты занимаешься? (какая библиотека)
    7. О ____ вы говорите? (что)
    8. В этом словаре нет ____. (это слово)
    9. Когда мы гуляли по парку, мы видели ____. (белый медведь)
    10. Саша учится ____. (физика)
    11. Маша учится ____. (немецкий язык)
    12. Мы всё занимаемся ____. (эта проблема)
    13. В этой стране всё едят ____. (ложки и вилки)
    14. Ваня рисует ____. (красный карандаш)
    15. Ваня рисует ____. (наш врач)

31. Разгово́р и перево́д.

   С: Ка́к ва́ше и́мя-о́тчество?
   М: Меня́ зову́т_____.
   С: Скажи́те мне́, (name), почему́ вы́ _____.
   М: _____.

   write with a green pencil   / I don't have a green pen
   don't tell the whole truth   / I don't know the whole truth
   are studying the Instrumental case   / I still don't know the Inst. case
   are interested in my affairs   / I'm not interested in your affairs.
                                          I'm interested in the instrumental
                                          case.

   are sitting under the table   / I don't know. I was bored.
   called my wife on the telephone   / I don't know. I was bored.
   called my husband on the telephone   / I don't know. I was happy.

   Continue making up your questions and answers. Use the following
   verbs: живу́т, занима́ются, интересу́ются, рабо́тают (ке́м), сидя́т.

32. Анкета. Dialog 6.

  a) Read quickly, translate.

   А: Мо́жно зада́ть вопро́с?
   Б: Мо́жно.
   А: Скажи́те, пожа́луйста, ке́м вы́ рабо́таете.
   Б: Я́ рабо́таю врачо́м.
   А: Гдé вы́ живёте?
   Б: Я́ живу́ в Москве́.
   А: Гдé вы́ роди́лись?
   Б: Я́ роди́лся в Ленингра́де.
   А: О́чень прия́тно бы́ло поговори́ть с ва́ми. До свида́ния.

  b) Translate.

   Can I ask a question? Certainly. Tell me, please, what you do for a
   living. I'm a doctor. I'm a teacher. I don't work, I'm a student.
   Where were you born? I was born in New York. We all were born in New
   York, but my sister was born in London. It was nice talking to you.
   Goodbye. I don't want to talk with you anymore. I'm bored.

33. Conversation topics.

   (a) A is applying for something—perhaps a visa—and asks B questions
        from a questionnaire. Use вы́.
   (b) Change (a) to a personal inquiry between friends. Use ты́.

34. Composition.

   Write a brief autobiography. Use the following verbs and expressions:
   зову́т   у меня́
   занима́ться   бра́т
   роди́ться в   сестра́
   сейча́с живу́ в   живу́т в

УРО́К СЕДЬМО́Й

ТЕ́КСТ А: ЧТО́ ДЕ́ЛАТЬ[1]? ЗЮ́ЗЕ СКУ́ЧНО

Ле́на: Па́па, я хочу́ погуля́ть.

Па́па: Иди́, погуля́й.

Ле́на: Зю́зя то́же хо́чет погуля́ть. Мы хоти́м погуля́ть вме́сте.

Па́па: Хм... Куда́ вы хоти́те пойти́?

Ле́на: Я не зна́ю. Нам всё равно́. Про́сто погуля́ть по у́лице. Зю́зе надое́ло[2] сиде́ть до́ма.

Па́па: Ты себе́ представля́ешь[3], что бу́дет? Соберётся толпа́, начну́т задава́ть вопро́сы...

Ле́на: Зю́зя хо́чет пойти́ погуля́ть. Она́ же[4] не в тюрьме́, она́ у нас в гостя́х.

Па́па: Ну, заче́м таки́е слова́ говори́ть: в тюрьме́. Вот, предлага́ю тебе́ компроми́сс: иди́те ве́чером[5], когда́ темно́ и ма́ло люде́й на у́лице.

Ле́на: Да, но сего́дня ве́чером[5] и но́чью[5] бу́дет идти́ дождь.

Па́па: Отку́да[7] ты зна́ешь, что сего́дня ве́чером бу́дет идти́ дождь?

Ле́на: По ра́дио передава́ли.

Па́па: Ничего́[6], я тебе́ дам мой большо́й зо́нтик.

ТЕ́КСТ Б: ПРОГУ́ЛКА ПОД ДОЖДЁМ

Ве́чер. На у́лице[8] уже́ темно́, идёт дождь. Ле́на и Зю́зя гуля́ют под дождём с больши́ми зо́нтиками в рука́х. Ле́на расска́зывает Зю́зе о Сре́дней А́зии. Сре́дняя А́зия похо́жа на зю́зину плане́ту. Э́то са́мое тёплое ме́сто в Сове́тском Сою́зе. Там всегда́ тепло́, да́же зимо́й. Там расту́т апельси́ны, лимо́ны и ды́ни. Там мно́го мече́тей. —"А церкве́й? А синаго́г?" — спра́шивает Зю́зя. — "Я не зна́ю," — говори́т Ле́на. — "Я хочу́ ви́деть Сре́днюю А́зию," — говори́т Зю́зя. — "Э́то нетру́дно." — говори́т Ле́на. — "Туда́ лета́ют самолёты. Тебе́ на́до пойти́ в аэропо́рт и купи́ть биле́т на самолёт."

ТЕ́КСТ В: ВТОРО́Й РАЗГОВО́Р В БЕ́ЛОМ ДО́МЕ

Дире́ктор: Господи́н президе́нт, как вы зна́ете, на́ши спу́тники непреры́вно фотографи́руют не́которые райо́ны Москвы́. Вчера́шние фотогра́фии о́чень интере́сные. Из до́ма, в кото́ром живёт Ива́н Петро́вич Си́доров, вы́шла его́ дочь Ле́на и како́е-то стра́нное живо́тное[10]. Был уже́ ве́чер, бы́ло темно́, шёл дождь. На у́лице пе́ред до́мом бы́ли то́лько аге́нты КГБ. Ле́на и живо́тное погуля́ли полчаса́ и верну́лись домо́й. Са́мое гла́вное[9]: живо́тное свобо́дно говори́т по-ру́сски.

Президе́нт: Интере́сно. Как оно́ вы́глядит?

Дире́ктор: Вы́глядит стра́нно. Вот хоро́шая фотогра́фия.

Президе́нт: Действи́тельно, стра́нное живо́тное. Каки́е гипо́тезы об э́том живо́тном?

Дире́ктор: Мы ду́маем, что э́то пассажи́р той[11] раке́ты, о кото́рой я вам говори́л сего́дня у́тром.

Президе́нт: Ого́![12] ТАСС по-пре́жнему ничего́ не передава́ло?

Дире́ктор: Не́т. Мы́ уве́рены, что ру́сские хотя́т скры́ть э́ту исто́рию.
Президе́нт: Почему́ вы в э́том уве́рены?
Дире́ктор: Они́ изобрели́ зо́нтик, кото́рый блоки́рует ла́зеры на́ших
           спу́тников[13] . Они́ ещё не зна́ют, что мы́ уже́ научи́лись
           фотографи́ровать че́рез таки́е зо́нтики. Ле́на и её дру́г
           гуля́ли под таки́м зо́нтиком.
Президе́нт: У меня́ сего́дня ве́чером пре́сс-конфере́нция. Я могу́
           объяви́ть э́ту но́вость.
Дире́ктор: У меня́ про́сьба: не говори́те о фотогра́фиях.
Президе́нт: Хорошо́, не бу́ду[14] .

Vocabulary

биле́т ticket
   биле́т на (+ Acc.) ticket to/for
блоки́ровать (НС) block
ве́чер evening, night (before
   bedtime)
вчера́шний yesterday's
вы́глядеть look (= have the physical
   appearance)
вы́йти (С) exit from, go/come out of
   Irreg. past: вы́шел (е)
гипо́теза hypothesis
гла́вный main, principle
го́сть guest
   бы́ть в гостя́х be a guest, be
   visiting
   пойти́ в го́сти visit
   Она́ у на́с в гостя́х. She's our
   guest/ She's a guest at our
   place
действи́тельно yes, as a matter
   of fact, indeed, really
до́ждь rain
   идёт до́ждь it's raining; it rains
   бу́дет идти́ до́ждь it will rain
же (emphatic particle)
живо́тное animal
задава́ть (НС) pose, ask (questions)
зима́ winter
   зимо́й in the winter
идти́ (НС) go
   иди́ (imperative) go
   Иди́ погуля́й. Go (Go ahead)
   take a walk.
   бу́дет идти́ до́ждь it will rain
изобрести́ (С) invent
   Past: изобрёл
исто́рия story; history
како́й-то some, some kind of
компроми́сс compromise
купи́ть (С) buy

ла́зер laser, ray, beam
лета́ть (НС) fly
лю́ди (plural only) people
мо́чь be able
на́до (+ Dative) must, have to
   тебе́ на́до you must/ have to
надое́сть be sick and tired of
научи́ться (С) learn
не́который certain
непреры́вно constantly, uninterrupt-
   edly
нетру́дный not difficult, pretty
   easy
но́чь night
ну́ well! well then!
объяви́ть (С) announce
пассажи́р passenger
пе́ред (+ Inst.) before, in front of
по-пре́жнему as before
погуля́ть (С) take a walk
под (+ Inst) under
   под дождём in the rain (Lit.,
   'under')
пойти́ (С) go
   пойти́ погуля́ть to set out for a
   walk
полчаса́ (for) a half hour
предлага́ть (НС) propose,
   suggest
представля́ть себе́ (НС) imagine
пре́сс-конфере́нция press
   conference
прогу́лка walk
про́сьба request [of   проси́ть]
ра́дио radio
райо́н region
свобо́дный free, fluent
себя́ oneself; myself, yourself,
   etc.
скры́ть hide, conceal

собра́ться, соберу́тся (С)
  gather, collect
   собере́тся толпа́. There will be
  a crowd.
стра́нный strange
тёмный dark
толпа́ crowd
то́т that, those
туда́ there

тюрьма́ jail
уве́ренный sure
  уве́рен sure
   Я уве́рена. I'm certain (fem.).
у́лица street
фотографи́ровать photograph
фотогра́фия photograph
че́рез (+ Acc.) through

COMMENTS

1. Что́ де́лать?

'What is to be done?' 'What can we do?' Note the use of the infinitive to form whole sentences.
Что́ де́лать? is the title of several famous books (Черныше́вский , Ле́нин).

2. надое́ло

Note the Dative: *Мне́ надое́ло чита́ть.* 'I'm fed up/sick and tired of reading'.

3. представля́ть себе́ (НС)

The verb представля́ть is the Imperfective partner of предста́вить 'introduce, present', as in Предста́вьте ва́шего дру́га 'Introduce (present) your friend.' When used with the Dative form себе́ 'to one's self', however, it has the meaning: 'imagine' (Lit., 'represent to one's self, in one's mind'). The sentence in the text can be translated most idiomatically with *can* in English: 'Can you imagine what will happen?!' (Lit., 'what will be').

4. же

This particle is pronounced as part of the preceding word and is never stressed; its vowel is pronounced like the last vowel in *sofa*. It often expresses contrast or impatience: 'After all! — she's not in jail!'.

5. Сего́дня ве́чером

ве́чер 'evening, night (until bedtime)' Inst. ве́чером 'in the evening' сего́дня ве́чером 'tonight, this evening' (Lit., 'today in the evening') но́чь 'night' сего́дня но́чью (4th declension Instrumental) 'tonight'.

6. Ничего́

Lit., 'nothing', e.g., Я ничего́ не ви́дела I didn't see anything/ I saw nothing.' This word is used idiomatically to mean 'OK, It's OK, Never mind' Как дела́? — Ничего́. 'How are things? — OK/Fine/Not bad.' In the text you can translate it as 'Never mind' or 'That's OK!'

7. Откуда

Откуда ты́ зна́ешь? 'How do you know?' Don't use как in this question.

8. на у́лице/на дворе́

Lit., 'on the street.' City folk use this expression to mean 'outside'. На у́лице темно́. 'It's dark outside.' Country folk are more likely to say На дворе́ темно́. (дво́р 'yard, courtyard').

9. са́мый

The adjective са́мый is used to form the superlative (*most*, *-est*): те́плый 'warm' → са́мый те́плый 'warmest'.

The adjective гла́вный 'main, principal, chief' is used in the neuter form to mean 'the main *thing*.' The sentence in Текст Б can be translated as follows:

Са́мое гла́вное: живо́тное свобо́дно   The main thing is: the animal
   говори́т по-ру́сски.   speaks Russian fluently.

10. живо́тное

This word has neuter adjective endings (cf. тру́дное сло́во 'a difficult word') but is used as a noun: 'animal'.

Э́то стра́нное живо́тное.   That's a strange animal
Они́ говори́ли о стра́нном живо́тном.   They were talking about a strange
                                     animal.

It can also be used as an ordinary adjective, e.g.,

живо́тное ца́рство   the animal kingdom
живо́тный органи́зм   animal organism

11. то́т...кото́рый

When the special adjective то́т is followed by кото́рый 'which, that, who' the best translation is usually '*the*...which:' 'the passenger of *the* rocketship about which I spoke to you.'

12. ого́!

The letter г in this word stands for a sound much like the *h* in the English *Oho!*

13. Genitive plural

На́ших спу́тников = '*of* our satellites,' Genitive Plural of спу́тник.

14. бу́ду (говори́ть): ellipsis.

Хорошо́, не бу́ду = 'All right, I won't.' The form бу́ду alone means 'I will be', but in the text here it is short for Я́ не бу́ду говори́ть о фотогра́фиях I won't talk about the photographs.'

DIALOGS FOR MEMORIZATION

1. Роди́тельный паде́ж мно́жественного числа́.

   С: Господи́н профе́ссор, почему́ у на́с ещё не́ было роди́тельного
   падежа́ мно́жественного числа́?
   П: Со сле́дующей неде́ли, мно́го дней[1] и ноче́й[1] , мно́го часо́в[1]
   и мину́т[1]   мы бу́дем занима́ться роди́тельным падежо́м.

2. Что́ де́лать?

   С: Что́ де́лать? Я пригласи́ла госте́й на обе́д, а у на́с не́т ни
   стака́нов, ни ло́жек, ни ви́лок, ни ноже́й, ни таре́лок.
   М: Э́то ничего́. Вино́ мо́жно пи́ть пря́мо из буты́лок, а е́сть
   мо́жно рука́ми.

3. Идёт до́ждь.

   С: Во́т, чёрт![2] Опя́ть до́ждь идёт.
   М: Не руга́йся[3]. У на́с о́сенью ка́ждый де́нь до́ждь идёт.
   С: Мне́ надое́л э́тот до́ждь. Когда́ он ко́нчится?
   М: Когда́ начнётся зима́. Зимо́й у на́с идёт сне́г.

4. Времена́ го́да.   *neuter*

   П: Како́е вре́мя го́да вы бо́льше всего́ лю́бите: зи́му, весну́, ле́то,
   и́ли о́сень?
   С: Я всё времена́ го́да о́чень люблю́ — и зи́му, и весну́, и ле́то и
   о́сень.

5. Ка́к ску́чно!

   П: Что́ вы бу́дете де́лать сего́дня ве́чером?
   С: Занима́ться да́тельным падежо́м еди́нственного числа́.
   П: А за́втра ве́чером?
   С: Занима́ться да́тельным   падежо́м мно́жественного числа́.
   П: Бо́же мо́й![2.]   Ка́к вы мно́го рабо́таете!

6. Отведи́ Ва́сю в шко́лу.

   М: Отведи́ Ва́сю в шко́лу.
   С: Не могу́.
   М: Почему́?
   С: Потому́ что я иду́ к врачу́.
   М: К како́му[4] врачу́ ты идёшь?
   С: К Петру́ Ильичу́. Я всегда́ хожу́ к одному́ и тому́ же[5] врачу́.
   М: Отведи́ Ва́сю к врачу́.
   С: Ва́се не ну́жно к врачу́[6]. Ва́се ну́жно в шко́лу.

Pf.	one way идти́	Impf.
		none one way ходи́ть
пойти́		
пойду́т	иду́т	хо́дят
пошёл	шёл	

7. Ко́мпас

Нью-Йо́рк к восто́ку от Канза́са.
Калифо́рния к за́паду от Канза́са.
Теха́с к ю́гу от Канза́са.
Се́верная Дако́та к се́веру от Канза́са.
Канза́с — посереди́не Аме́рики.
Миссиси́пи нахо́дится на ю́ге.
Ве́тер сего́дня с ю́га.

Translation

1. Genitive Plural

   S: Professor, sir, why haven't we had the genitive plural yet?
   T: From next week (on), many days and nights, (and) many hours and minutes, we will be studying the genitive case.

2. What's to be done?

   A: What am I gonna do?! I invited guests for dinner and we don't have any glasses or spoons or forks or knives or plates.
   B: That's OK (= Think nothing of it.) (We) can drink wine right out of the bottles and eat with our hands.

3. It's raining.

   A: Dammit! It's raining again.
   B: Don't swear. We have rain every day in the fall.
   A: I'm sick and tired of (= fed up with) this rain. When is it going to end?
   B: When the winter begins (Lit., 'will begin' — *Perfective*). In winter we have snow.

4. The seasons (Lit., 'times of the year').

   T: What season do you like best (Lit., 'most of all'), winter, spring, summer, or fall?
   S: I like all the seasons very much — winter, spring, summer and fall.

5. How boring!

   T: What are you doing (Lit., 'will you be doing') tonight (Lit., 'today in the evening')?
   S: Studying the dative singular.
   T: And tomorrow night? (Lit., 'tomorrow in the evening).
   S: Studying the dative plural.
   T: My goodness! You really work hard! [Lit. 'How much...!']

6. Take Vasya to school.

    A: Take Vasya to school.
    B: I can't.
    A: Why?
    B: Because I'm going to the doctor.
    A: Which doctor are you going to?
    B: To Peter Ilyich. I always go to (one and) the same doctor.
    A: Take Vasya to the doctor.
    B: Vasya doesn't have to go to the doctor. Vasya has to go to school.

7. The Compass

    New York is to the east of Kansas.
    California is to the west of Kansas.
    Texas is to the south of Kansas.
    North Dakota is to the north of Kansas.
    Kansas is in the middle of America.
    Mississippi is located in the south.
    The wind today is from the south.

ACTIVE WORD LIST

Nouns

ко́мпас	compass
буты́лка (о)	bottle
таре́лка (о)	plate
восто́к	east
дако́та	Dakota
за́пад	west
Калифо́рния	California
Канза́с	Kansas
Миссиси́пи	Mississippi
Нью-Йо́рк	New York
обе́д	dinner
се́вер	north
Теха́с	Texas
шко́ла	school
юг	south
Бо́г	God
го́сть	guest
чёрт; че́рти	devil
весна́; вёсны	spring
ве́тер (е)	wind
ве́чер	evening
вре́мя вре́мени; времена́ *neuter*	time
год	year
де́нь	day
до́ждь дождя́	rain
зима́ зи́му; зи́мы	winter
зимо́й	in the winter
ле́то	summer
мину́та	minute
неде́ля	week

— мя nouns
(neuter)

имя = udder (similarly)

но́чь; но́чи, ноча́м (*4th declension*)	night
о́сень (*4th declension*)	fall, autumn
о́сенью (Inst.)	in the fall
пого́да	weather
сне́г	snow
ча́с; часы́	hour
число́ (e); чи́сла	number; date

Verbs

отвести́ отведу́т; отвёл, отвела́	take, lead
отвело́, отвели́ (C)	
отведи́	take (*Imperative*)
пригласи́ть (C)	invite
ко́нчиться (C)	end, finish
надое́сть (C); надое́л	be fed up
(= е́сть, е́л)	
Мне́ надое́л X.	I'm fed up with X.(X=masc.)
Мне́ надое́ла X.	I'm fed up with X.(X=fem.)
нача́ться, начну́тся (C)	begin, start
люби́ть (HC)	love
идти́ иду́т (HC)	go, come
мо́чь (HC)	be able
я́ могу́ мы́ мо́жем	
ты́ мо́жешь вы́ мо́жете	
о́н мо́жет они́ мо́гут	
руга́ться (HC)	swear

Adjectives

восто́чный	eastern
еди́нственный	singular (cf. оди́н)
за́падный	western
мно́жественный	plural (cf. мно́го)
се́верный	northern
сле́дующий	following
то́т	that
ю́жный	southern

Misc.

то́т же	same
за́втра	tomorrow
опя́ть	again
пря́мо	right; directly
сего́дня	today
же	*emphatic particle*
к	toward
мно́го	many
ни...ни	neither...nor
ну́жно	it is necessary
посереди́не + Gen.	in the middle of
(Pronounced "пасриди́ни" with	
one syllable dropped)	

COMMENTS

1. Genitive Plural

See discussion in the Analysis.

2. чёрт!

Lit., 'devil'. Equivalent in force to English 'Dammit!' or 'Damn!' Not a very nice word, but not foul, either.

Бо́же мо́й! in Dialog 5 is a mild expletive, much like French *Mon Dieu!* It's use is not considered swearing, so you wouldn't say Не ругайтесь! to somebody who used it, just as *Oh boy* or *My goodness* isn't swearing.

3. не руга́йся

This is an imperative form with -ся. The polite form has the variant -сь because the verb ends in a vowel:

руга́й + те + сь → руга́йтесь.

4. Pronunciation: к како́му.

Don't put a vowel in between the contiguous к's. Pronounce it either as a long, double кк (especially in slow deliberate speech), or as a single к. The same problem crops up with к кому? 'to whose place, to whom?' Beware! — you often can't hear the preposition.

Similarly, in dialog 7, if the last words were с се́вера 'from the north', you would have the same problem with double consonants.

5. то́т же 'same'

You can say either 'one and the same X' (оди́н и то́т же стака́н) or simply 'the same X' (то́т же стака́н). The special adjective то́т has the same forms as ве́сь 'all, whole', i.e., it has -e- where э́тот has -и-:

Nom. Pl.	все́	те́ же	э́ти
Prep. Pl.	о все́х	о те́х же	об э́тих
Instr. Plur.	все́ми	те́ми же	э́тими

6. Ellipsis with ну́жно.

The ellipsis in this sentence consists of the absence of the verb 'to go'. With ну́жно and на́до ellipsis is preferable to the full form Ему́ не ну́жно *ходи́ть* к врачу́ because the full form is ambiguous — it can mean 'He mustn't/He shouldn't' as well as 'He doesn't have to.'

1. The fourth declension: F II nouns.

In Lesson 1 Analysis 1 three of the four declensional classes of Russian were presented: #-nouns (masc.), о-nouns (neut.) and а-nouns (mostly feminine). The fourth declension nouns are all feminine and we will refer to them as *F II nouns* (feminine, group II), to distinguish them from а-nouns, F I). You met a few of them in Lesson 5 (see Text Comment 4).

All F II nouns end in мя́гкий зна́к , even after non-paired consonants, where мя́гкий зна́к does not affect the pronunciation.

Examples:

но́чь	night	до́чь	daughter
но́вость	piece of news	о́сень	autumn
ма́ть	mother	мече́ть	mosque

Just because a noun ends in -ь doesn't mean it's F II, as there are also masculine #-declension nouns ending in -ь (e.g., слова́рь, ка́мень, etc.).

However, sometimes you can identify F II by recognizing the suffix -ость, which is always F II, e.g. но́вость (root нов- 'new' + ость). (The word го́сть 'guest', contains the letters -ость , but they do not constitute a suffix here—the word is masculine.)

Another way to tell if a noun is F II is when it ends in a non-paired consonant before -ь , like но́чь ; masculine nouns ending in a non-paired consonant do not have -ь , e.g. това́рищ, му́ж, но́ж, мя́ч 'ball', etc.

A third way to determine the gender of a noun ending in -ь is to recognize the suffix -тель, which is always masculine (*not* F II), e.g.,

учи́ть	to teach	→	учи́тель	teacher
писа́ть	to write	→	писа́тель	writer
чита́ть	to read	→	чита́тель	reader

Otherwise, you must look the word up in the dictionary to find out whether it is masculine (like ка́мень) or F II (like о́сень). The active word lists from now on will mark F II nouns with the letter ж (for же́нский ро́д).

Here is a sample paradigm:

	Singular		Plural	
	animate	*inanimate*	*animate*	*inanimate*
	'mouse'	'fall'		
N	мы́шь (SM)	о́сень (SS)	мы́ши	о́сени
G	мы́ши	о́сени	мыше́й	о́сеней
D	мы́ши	о́сени	мыша́м	о́сеням
A	мы́шь	о́сень	мыше́й	о́сени
I	мы́шью	о́сенью	мыша́ми	о́сенями
P	мы́ши	о́сени	мыша́х	о́сенях

Remarks:

(1) Animate vs. inanimate is relevant only in the plural, where, like all nouns, Acc. = Gen. for animates and Acc. = Nom. for inanimates. In the singular Acc. = Nom. regardless of animacy.

(2) Non-accusative cases: in the singular the Instrumental -ью is quite distinctive; the other singular cases are all -и ; the plural endings are like other nouns (see Analysis 2, below, for Gen. Plural).

(3) Spelling rules: the only endings affected are the ones beginning with -я-
as illustrated above; я → а after ч щ ш ж . Endings beginning with -и-
are always spelled -и- (don't worry about nouns ending in -ц- , because
there don't happen to be any such nouns.)

The endings of the word мáть are just like those illustrated above, but
the stem is irregular in that the syllable -ep- (cf. moth*er*) is missing in
the Nom.-Acc. Singular. The stress pattern is SM.

N	мáть	мáтери
G	мáтери	матерéй
D	мáтери	матеря́м
A	мáть	= Gen.
I	мáтерью	матеря́ми
P	мáтери	матеря́х

The word дóчь has the same peculiarity (cf. daught*er*); in addition, the
Inst. Plural ending is irregular. The stress pattern is SM.

N	дóчь	дóчери
G	дóчери	дочерéй
D	дóчери	дочеря́м
A	дóчь	= Gen.
I	дóчерью	дочерьми́
P	дóчери	дочеря́х

(There are two words for 'daughter': дóчь and дóчка . Дóчь is more
formal, дóчка is more normal. Similarly, мáть vs. мáма.)

PRACTICE 1

Examine these nouns and mark them with ж *if they are feminine,*
м if masculine, or ? if it is impossible to tell without the
aid of a dictionary. Check your answers below.

1	рóжь	7	кúсть	13	óсень
2	нóж	8	напряжённость	14	плюмáж
3	тýш	9	жúзнь	15	представи́тель
4	тýшь	10	писáтель	16	зя́ть
5	мнóжественность	11	декáбрь	17	секрéтность
6	мóлодость	12	нóчь	18	преподавáтель

Answers: 1 ж, 2 м, 3 м, 4 ж, 5 ж, 6 ж, 7 ?, 8 ж, 9 ?,
10 м, 11 ?, 12 ж, 13 ?, 14 м, 15 м, 16 ?, 17 ж, 18 м

---

2. Stress pattern M (nouns)

Very few nouns have this pattern. In the Singular it affects only F I
nouns, in which stress is shifted from the ending to the initial syllable in
the Accusative, e.g. рукá, рýку 'hand, arm' бородá, бóроду 'beard.'
In the plural, (all declensions) it affects the Nominative (and Accusative of
inanimate) the same way, e.g., рýки vs. рукáм, рукáми, рукáх; бóроды vs.
бородáм, бородáх, бородáми. The MM stress paradigm looks like this, with
dashes for syllables:

	Singular	*Plural*
N	- - ´	´ - -
G	- - ´	- - ´
D	- - ´	- - ´
A	´ - -	= Nom. or Gen.
I	- - ´	- - ´
P	- - ´	- - ´

If the Gen. Plural has a zero ending, as F I nouns do (see below), then the stress falls on the last available syllable:

N	борода́	бо́роды
G	ы́	боро́д
D	е́	борода́м
A	бо́роду	= Nom.
I	о́й	а́ми
P	е́	а́х

Examples of pattern SM can be found in section 1, above. (мы́шь, ма́ть, до́чь).

3.   Genitive and Accusative Plural

3.1 Genitive Plural

There are three noun endings: **-ов, -ей** and **-#** (zero). The choice depends on two things: (1) the Nominative Singular *ending* and (2) the final consonant of the Plural *stem*.

The rule for **-#** vs. the other two (**-ов/-ей**) is neat: if the Nom. Sg. has zero, Gen. Pl. won't, and vice versa:

	Nom. Sg.	*Gen. Pl.*
Endings	-#	-ов / -ей
	-а / -о	-#

	Nom. Sg.	*Gen. Pl.*
Examples	сто́л	столо́в
	слова́рь	словаре́й
	кни́га	кни́г
	сло́во	сло́в

Or, if you want to think of it in terms of gender, masculines have Gen. Pl. **-ов** or **-ей** , while feminines (I) and neuters have Gen. Pl. **-#** (zero), and feminines (II) have **-ей.**

Further examples:

	Nom. Sg.	*Gen. Pl.*
masc.	{ стака́н учи́тель	стака́нов } учителе́й }
neuter	окно́ (о)	о́кон
fem. I	газе́та	газе́т
fem. II	но́чь	ноче́й

The choice between **-ов** and **-ей** for masculines depends on the final consonant of the stem. If it is a paired *plain* consonant, the ending is **-ов** ; if paired *palatalized* (i.e. ending in **-ь**), **-ей**.

Examples:

plain	стака́н	стака́нов
palatalized	писа́тель ка́мень (е)	писа́телей камне́й

Observe the inserted vowel before Gen. Pl. zero ending; it works just like the inserted vowel before Nom. Sg. zero ending, e.g., ви́лка (о)→ ви́лок, ло́жка(е) → ло́жек, письмо́ (е) → пи́сем.

PRACTICE 2

Cover the right-hand column. Look at the dictionary forms on the left and write down the Genitive Plural form. Observe the stress pattern and the inserted vowel (before zero ending).

бо́мба	бо́мб
ви́лка (о)	ви́лок
ло́жка (е)	ло́жек
кни́га	кни́г
окно́ (о) ES	о́кон
ме́сто SE	ме́ст
письмо́ (е) ES	пи́сем
сло́во SE	сло́в
уро́к	уро́ков
фи́льм	фи́льмов
конве́рт	конве́ртов
учи́тель SE	учителе́й
словы́рь EE	словаре́й
сто́л EE	столо́в
ру́чка (е)	ру́чек
де́нь (е)	дне́й
ка́мень(е) SM	камне́й
ве́тер(е)	ве́тров

If the stem final consonant is *non-paired* (see Lesson 3.1), the choice between **-ов** and **-ей** for masculines is as follows:

stem final consonant	Gen. Pl. ending
ц й (=/y/)	-ов , -ев , -ёв
ш ж щ ч	-ей

Spelling problems arise only in the case of stem final ц and the sound /y/. We will repeat here the rules given in Lesson 2.2, 3.1 and 3.2 as they apply to **-ов**. (The ending **-ей** causes no problem—it is always spelled **-ей**).

(1) After ц the vowel /o/ is spelled о when stressed, е when unstressed.

оте́ц (е)	отцо́в	father
америка́нец (е)	америка́нцев	American

(2) The sound /y/ is represented in Cyrillic by й at the end of the word (Nom. Sg.) and by palatal indicators before a vowel (Gen. Pl. **-ев** , but with two dots if stressed: **-ёв**):

музе́й	музе́ев	museum
сло́й (ЕЕ)	слоёв	layer

PRACTICE 3

Write the Gen. Plural forms as in Practice 2 and check your answers. All these nouns are masculine, so your choice is between **-ов** *(* **-ев** *,* **-ёв** *) and* **-ей**.

слова́рь ЕЕ	словаре́й
каранда́ш ЕЕ	карандаше́й
семе́стр	семе́стров
оте́ц (е) ЕЕ	отцо́в
америка́нец (е)	америка́нцев
конве́рт	конве́ртов
но́ж ЕЕ	ноже́й
фла́г	фла́гов
чита́тель	чита́телей
до́м SE	домо́в
коне́ц (е) ЕЕ	концо́в
медве́дь	медве́дей
паде́ж ЕЕ	падеже́й
музе́й	музе́ев
трамва́й	трамва́ев
сло́й ЕЕ	слоёв

When the zero ending is added, you have to remember the basic spelling rules for palatal indicators and for spelling the /y/-sound. We will review them here:

(1) The palatal indicators и е я ё ю represent palatalization of the preceding consonant plus the sounds /i e a o u/; when no vowel follows the consonant, the мягкий знак is used to represent palatalization. Therefore you should expect -ь to replace the -я of feminines whose stem ends in a palatalized consonant:

Nom. Sg.		Gen. Pl.	
ды́ня	/diṇa/	ды́нь	/diṇ/

(2) The sound /y/ is represented by the palatal indicators и е я ё ю when a vowel follows, and by й elsewhere. Therefore you should expect -й to replace the -я of feminines and the -е of neuters whose stem ends in /y/:

	Nom. Sg.	Nom. Pl.	Gen. Pl.
feminine	лаборато́рия	лаборато́рии	лаборато́рий
	/labarato̧riy-a/	/labarato̧riy-i/	/labarato̧riy-#/
neuter	сочине́ние	сочине́ния	сочине́ний
	/sachiṇeṇiy-a/	/sachiṇeṇiy-a/	/sachiṇeṇiy-#/

These uses of -ь and -й should not be considered to be irregular endings. They are not endings at all; they are the expected manifestations of the rules for Gen. Pl. endings (-# zero) and the spelling rules. The fact remains, however, that the ending -# (zero) is the most difficult ending to learn to spell!

PRACTICE 4

Cover the right-hand column and write the Gen. Pl. forms as in the preceding Practices. This list contains all genders (including F II) and it contains nouns that require -ь or -й as just discussed. It also contains nouns you haven't met yet, but they all follow the rules.

ды́ня	ды́нь
лаборато́рия	лаборато́рий
заня́тие	заня́тий
упражне́ние	упражне́ний
выраже́ние	выраже́ний
профе́ссия	профе́ссий
пу́ля	пу́ль
мече́ть (ж)	мече́тей
преподава́тель	преподава́телей
де́ло	дел
неде́ля	неде́ль
до́ждь EE	дожде́й
ме́сяц	ме́сяцев
ве́чер SE	вечеро́в
не́мец (е)	не́мцев
купе́ц (е) EE	купцо́в
бо́й SE	боёв
ру́бль EE	рубле́й

In some nouns the sound /y/ occurs in the Plural stem only (for Singular
vs. Plural stem changes see Lesson 4.1). An example of this is бра́т-бра́тья
/brátya/ (for the spelling of /y/ with -ь + palatal indicator, see Lesson
3.2.1). In such cases the above rules for Gen. Pl. apply as expected: the
ending is -ев (-ёв if stressed).

Nom. Sg.	Nom. Pl.	Gen. Pl.
бра́т	бра́тья	бра́тьев
сту́л	сту́лья	сту́льев

Genitive forms like бра́тьев should not be considered to be irregular; it
is not the particular *case* form that is irregular, it is rather the plural
stem , — in *all* plural cases.

There are some irregularities in stress in the Gen. Pl.

Nom. Sg.	Nom. Pl.	Gen. Pl.
сестра́ ES	сёстры	сестёр (you'd expect stress on the first syllable)

Some nouns have irregular Gen. Pl. endings.

Nom. Sg.	Nom. Pl.	Gen. Pl.
ра́з	разы́	ра́з (you'd expect -ов)
му́ж	мужья́	мужей (you'd expect it to be like бра́т/бра́тья/бра́тьев)

One noun has и for the inserted vowel rather than e or o ,

Nom. Sg.	Nom. Pl.	Gen. Pl.
яйцо́	я́йца	яйц

Summary of Genitive Plural noun endings:

Nom. Sg.	Gen. Pl.
-a, -o	-#
-#	-ов, -ей

Summary of all plural endings:

	Adj. +		Noun		
		m.	F I	n.	F II
Nom.	-ые +	-ы	-ы	-a	-и
Gen.	-ых +	-ов/-ей	- #	-#	-ей
Dat.	-ым +		-ам		
Acc.=Nom/Gen					
Inst.	-ыми +		-ами		
Prep.	-ых +		-ах		

As the above chart shows, adjectives have the vowel **-ы-** in all Plural
endings; the Gen. and Prep. endings are identical, but the Adj. + Noun *combination* **-ых -ах** is distinctly Prepositional; **-ых** plus anything else (**-ов, -ей, - #**) is Genitive.

PRACTICE 5

*Here are some combinations of plural adjective plus noun.
Label them as to what case they are in. Then write down
the dictionary form (nominative Singular) of the noun.*

1 хоро́шие словари́	9 хоро́шие ды́ни
2 хоро́ших карандаше́й	10 хоро́ших ножа́х
3 хоро́ших веще́й	11 хоро́ших веща́х
4 хоро́ших лаборато́рий	12 хоро́шим врача́м
5 хоро́ших упражне́ний	13 хоро́шими ру́чками
6 хоро́шими карандаша́ми	14 хоро́ших домо́в
7 хоро́ших фла́гах	15 хоро́ших раке́т
8 хоро́ших мест	

Answers:

1)NP1 of слова́рь , 2)GP1 of каранда́ш, 3) GP1 of ве́щь ,
4)GP1 of лаборато́рия , 5)GP1 of упражне́ния ,
6)IP1 of каранда́ш , 7)PP1 of фла́г , 8)GP1 of ме́сто ,
9)NP1 of ды́ня , 10)PP1 of но́ж, 11)PP1 of ве́щь , 12)DP1 of
вра́ч, 13)IP1 of рука́, 14)GP1 of до́м, 15)GP1 of раке́та .

3.2 Accusative Plural.

There are no distinctive endings for this case. Animate nouns have endings
identical to the Genitive; inanimate nouns have endings identical to the Nominative. Compare:

Я зна́ю э́тих *враче́й*.(вра́ч)   I know these *doctors.*
vs.   э́ти *языки́*.(язы́к)   I know these *languages.*

Я зна́ю э́тих *студе́нток*.(студе́нтка)I know these *students* (fem.).
vs.   э́ти *кни́ги*.(кни́га)   I know these *books.*

4. Instrumental and time

Seasons of the year and times of the day are expressed by the Instrumental case.

Nom. Sg.	Inst.	
зима́	зимо́й	in (the) winter(time)
весна́	весно́й	in (the) spring(time)
ле́то	ле́том	in (the) summer(time)
о́сень	о́сенью	in (the) fall
у́тро	у́тром	in the morning
де́нь	днём	in the afternoon/daytime
ве́чер	ве́чером	in the evening, at night
но́чь	но́чью	at night(time), by night

Evening and *night* are divided up differently than in English. Но́чь 'night' is after bedtime, so the sentence Что́ вы́ де́лали вчера́ но́чью means 'What did you do yesterday during the time when most people are asleep?' Normally, you would use вчера́ ве́чером to say 'last night' and сего́дня ве́чером to say 'tonight' (before bedtime). Ве́чер is used at sunset or after the evening meal, so ве́чер is used in a situation like 'I'll see you tonight (= this evening) at the theater.' Some speakers of English use 'tonight' to refer to various times between noon and sunset; if you're one of them, don't use either ве́чер or но́чь — use the proper form of де́нь (in the sense of 'afternoon, late afternoon.')

To say *at* a certain time of day *yesterday*, don't use the word for 'last' as you do in English.

вчера́ у́тром	yesterday morning
вчера́ днём	yesterday afternoon
вчера́ ве́чером	yesterday evening, last evening
вчера́ но́чью	yesterday in the nightime, last night

And use сего́дня , not the word for 'this.'

сего́дня у́тром	this morning
сего́дня днём	this afternoon
сего́дня ве́чером	this evening, tonight
сего́дня но́чью	today at nighttime, tonight

The word за́втра is used like the English *tomorrow* in these expressions:

за́втра у́тром	tomorrow morning
за́втра днём	tomorrow afternoon
за́втра ве́чером	tomorrow evening, night
за́втра но́чью	tomorrow at night, tomorrow night (after bedtime)

5. Prepositions meaning 'to/at/from'

5.1 The three series.

There are three series of prepositions having the meanings *motion to* ('to, onto'), *location* ('in, at') and *motion from*('from, off of, out of'). The three series are: в/в/из, к/у/от, and на/на/с. Most of these you have learned already (see Lesson 4.3.3). The general rule is to use в/в/из with bounded or enclosed places (like cities, boxes, bottles...), к/у/от with people, and на/на/с with things having surfaces on which things can be located (tables, floors, roofs, mountains). This is not a complete description of how to use these prepositions, but it will suffice for the moment.

Examples:

в/в/из

в Москву́ (Acc.)	to Moscow
в Москве́ (Prep.)	in Moscow
из Москвы́ (Gen.)	from Moscow
в институ́т (Acc.)	to the institute
в институ́те (Prep.)	in/at the institute
из институ́та (Gen.)	from/out of the institute

у/к/от

к Са́ше (Dat.)	to Sasha('s place)
у Са́ши (Gen.)	at "
от Са́ши (Gen.)	from "
к врачу́ (Dat.)	to the doctor('s office)
у врача́ (Gen.)	at "
от врача́ (Gen.)	from "
Óн пошёл к врачу́.	He's left for the doctor's office.
Óн сейча́с у врача́.	He's now at the doctor's office.
Óн верну́лся от врача́.	He's returned from the doctor's office.

Зю́зе та́м бы́ло ску́чно, и она́ прилете́ла *к на́м.*	Zyuzya was bored there, and she came *to us / to our planet/ to our country.*
Сейча́с она́ живёт *у на́с.*	Now she lives *with us/ on our planet/ in our country.*
Во́т письмо́ *от на́с.*	Here's a letter *from us.*

If you combine a place name with a person you can use both series:

Я ходи́л к бра́ту в кабине́т.	I went to my brother's office.
Вчера́ ве́чером о́н пришёл ко мне́ в кабине́т.	He came to my office last evening.
О́н сейча́с у дире́ктора в кабине́те.	He's now in the director's ;office.

(The above combinations sound better than a possessive genitive like Я ходи́л в кабине́т *бра́та*.)

на/на/с

на плане́ту	(Acc.)	to the planet
на плане́те	(Prep.)	on the planet
с плане́ты	(Gen.)	from the planet
на сто́л	(Acc.)	on/onto the table
на столе́	(Prep.)	on the table
со стола́	(Gen.)	off of the table

There are, of course, nouns for which you could use either the в/в/из series or the на/на/с series, depending on what you want to say, e.g.,

Ру́чка лежи́т *на газе́те*.	The pen is lying *on* the newspaper.
Я чита́л *в газе́те*, что луна́ кру́глая.	I was reading *in* the newspaper that the moon is round.

Similarly,

на столе́	on the table
в столе́	in the table (drawer)

PRACTICE 6

Fill in the proper preposition. Translate. Say what case the noun is in.

Кни́га лежи́т ____ столе́.
Она́ положи́ла кни́гу ____ сто́л.
____ како́й плане́те ты́ живёшь?
Зю́зя прилете́ла ____ на́м ____ друго́й плане́ты.
Она́ вчера́ ходи́ла ____ врачу́.
Она́ живёт ____ сестры́.
____ кого́ э́то письмо́?
Вы́ ____ Москвы́?
Вы́ бы́ли ____ Москве́?
Са́ша пошёл ____ библиоте́ку?
Са́ша сейча́с ____ библиоте́ке.
Са́ша верну́лся ____ библиоте́ки.
Ма́ша сейча́с сиди́т ____ преподава́теля ____ кабине́те.
Она́ ходи́ла ____ преподава́телю ____ кабине́т.

5.2 Points of the compass.

As we mentioned above in 5.1, our description of the use of the three series is not a hard-and-fast rule. The fact that у/к/от are used with people does not mean that they cannot be used with things or places. For example, if you use к with a place, it means "towards," e.g., к па́рку 'towards the park' vs. в парк 'into the park.' We will not be asking you, in the Exercises, to use these prepositions in any contexts other than those described in 5.1 except for points of the compass.

When you locate two places with respect to points of the compass, use к/от e.g.,

Ки́ев нахо́дится к ю́гу от Москвы́.   Kiev is located to the south of Moscow.

Otherwise, use the на/на/с series.

на се́вер/юг/восто́к/за́пад	*to* the north, south, east, west
на се́вере/ю́ге/восто́ке/за́паде	*in* the north, south, east, west
с се́вера/ю́га/восто́ка/за́пада	*from* the north, south, east, west
Он живёт на восто́ке.	He lives in the east.
Отку́да вы́? С ю́га?	Where are you from? From the south?

Put negatively: you can't use the в/в/из series with these particular nouns.

6. Verb stems.

Verbs have two stems, a past stem (from which the infinitive as well as the past tense is formed) and a non-past stem.

	past stem	*non-past stem*	
	писа-	пиш-	'write'
past	писа́л	я пишу́	
	писа́ла	ты́ пи́шешь	
	писа́ло	о́н пи́шет	
	писа́ли	мы́ пи́шем	
infinitive	писа́ть	вы́ пи́шете	
		они́ пи́шут	
	зна-	знай-	'know'
past	зна́л	я зна́ю	
	зна́ла	ты́ зна́ешь	
	зна́ло	о́н зна́ет	
	зна́ли	мы́ зна́ем	
infinitive	зна́ть	вы́ зна́ете	
		они́ зна́ют	

6.1 Citation forms.

So far we have been citing only one or another of the two stems in vocabularies and word lists, depending on which stem occurred in the text. From now on we will list both stems, using the infinitive (dictionary form) and 3 Pl. as citation forms:

знáть, знáют   'know'

If the non-past has M-stress, we will include the 1 Sg to remind you:

писáть, пи́шут, пишý 'write'

We will also remind you of Conj. II consonant alternation in the 1 Sg form, even though it's regular (Lesson 6.6.1):

сидéть, сидя́т, сижý   'be sitting, sit'

Hyphens will frequently be used instead of printing out words in full, e.g.,

писáть, пи́шут, -шý
сидéть, -дя́т, -жý

A few verbs have M-stress in the past tense. Pattern M in past tense forms is characterized by a shift to the feminine ending (neut. is always stressed like the plural):

EM взя́ть, возьмýт; взя́л, взяла́, взя́ло, взя́ли 'take'
EM брáть, берýт; брáл, брала́, брáло, брáли 'take'
SM бы́ть, бýдут; бы́л, была́, бы́ло, бы́ли 'be'

Instead of listing all four forms, we will cite only the fem. and plural forms for verbs with patterns M or E in the past tense; this will give you enough information to distinguish the two. Again, hyphens will be used to abbreviate forms; the stress mark on the hyphen means that the stem is stressed. Thus, the three verbs illustrated above will be cited this way:

взя́ть, возьмýт; взяла́, -́ли
брáть, берýт; брала́, -́ли
бы́ть, бýдут; была́, -́ли

In a few cases it is necessary to learn the maaculine form; note, for example, the vowel -ё- in these verbs:

EE отвести́, -ведýт; отвёл, отвела́, отвело́, отвели́
EE пойти́, пойдýт; пошёл, пошла́, пошло́, пошли́

In such cases the masc. will be cited:

отвести́, -ведýт; отвёл, -ла́,-ли́
пойти́, пойдýт; пошёл, пошла́, пошли́

Prefixed forms of irregular verbs will simply be cross-referenced to the simple verb, i.e., instead of spelling out all the forms передáть, передáм, передáшь, передáст, передади́м, передади́те, передадýт etc., we will cite it this way:

передáть (= дáть)   pass, transmit, broadcast

Similarly:

захотéть (= хотéть)   want, get a desire to

In Lesson 8 we will match up the two stems of most of the verbs you've met thus far. For now, it is sufficient for you to learn the citation system, and get accustomed to some of the non-predictable stem changes, e.g. отвести́, отведу́т; отвёл, отвела́, отвели́ — see the Active Word List in this Lesson.

6.2 Consonant alternation in Conjugation I

In this lesson the non-past of the verb 'can, be able' was cited in full:

могу́	мо́жем
мо́жешь	мо́жете
мо́жет	мо́гут

Obviously, the -г- of the citation form мо́гут alternates with -ж- in four other forms. This is not an irregularity— *all* Conj. I verbs with a stem final г have ж in these forms. Similarly, к alternates with ч , e.g.,

теку́	течём	
течёшь	течёте	
течёт	теку́т	'flow'

Therefore, you don't have to memorize all 6 forms of such verbs, and we will cite only the 3 Pl., as usual.

Incidentally, the alternations г→ж and к→ч show up elsewhere in the language. Notice the adjectival suffix -н- in these words:

ю́г	→ ю́жный	south/southern
восто́к	→ восто́чный	east/eastern

This phenomenon is also quite regular:

кни́га/кни́жный	bookish, pertaining to books
кни́жный магази́н	book store
библиоте́ка/библиоте́чный	pertaining to the library
рука́/ручно́й	hand
ручно́й тру́д	handwork, handicraft
бума́га/бума́жный	pertaining to paper
бума́жная фа́брика	paper mill
я́блоко/я́блочный	pertaining to apples
я́блочный со́к	apple juice

```
┌─────────────────────────────────────────────────────────────┐
│                        PRACTICE 7                             │
├─────────────────────────────────────────────────────────────┤
```

*Cover the right-hand column. On the left are the citation
forms of some verbs. Write the non-past* вы *form (e.g.,*
пи́шете*) and the past* вы *form (e.g.,* писа́ли *). Mark
stress.*

де́лать, -а́ют	де́лаете, де́лали
жи́ть, живу́т; жила́, жи́ли	живёте, жи́ли
лежа́ть, -а́т	лежи́те, лежа́ли
ви́деть, -дят, -жу	ви́дите, ви́дели
пи́ть, пью́т; пила́, пи́ли	пьёте, пи́ли
отвести́, -веду́т; -вёл,	отведёте, отвели́
-вела́, -вели́	
написа́ть, -пи́шут, -шу́	напи́шете, написа́ли
мо́чь, мо́гут, -гу́; мо́г,	мо́жете, могли́
могла́, могли́	
стри́чь, стригу́т; стри́г,	стрижёте, стри́гли
стри́гла	
ста́вить, -вят, -влю	ста́вите, ста́вили
учи́ть, у́чат, учу́	у́чите, учи́ли
кла́сть, кладу́т; кла́ла	кладёте, кла́ли

6.3 Predictable verbs.

Usually if you know one stem you can predict what the other
one will be, i.e., you only have to memorize one stem. This is
true for all but about 200 verbs. (English has about the same
number of exceptional "strong" verbs of the type *sing/sang/sung*.)
Of these 200 or so, many are seldom used, so your learning problem is considerably smaller than that.

The two verbs listed at the beginning of this section illustrate a predictable type (зна́ть/зна́ют) and a non-predictable
type (писа́ть/пи́шут). There are 6 groups of predictable verbs.
The rule for predicting the stem partner of the зна́ть/зна́ют
group is:

$$\boxed{\text{-ают} \longrightarrow \text{-ать}}$$

This rule is to be read: "If the non-past form is -ают, the infinitive form will be -ать. Notice that the prediction runs
only in one direction; if you start with an infinitive in -ать,
you can't be sure that the non-past will be -ают. For example,
the non-past of лежа́ть 'lie, be lying' is лежа́т (Conj. II)
not -ают (Conj. I).

Here are some examples of verbs of the predictable -ают
group you have met so far:

де́лают	→	де́лать (I)	do; make
игра́ют	→	игра́ть (I)	play
лета́ют	→	лета́ть (I)	fly
обе́дают	→	обе́дать (I)	dine
чита́ют	→	чита́ть (I)	read

There are three apparent exceptions to this rule, of which
you have had one: the verb stem -давáть 'give'. (The other two
are -ставáть and -знавáть.)

даю́т	давáть (I)	(NOT: дáть (P)!)	give
передаю́т	передавáть (I)	(NOT: передáть (P)!)	pass; transmit, broadcast
преподаю́т	преподавáть (I)		teach

This stem is stressed on the ending: даю́, даёшь, etc. None
of the predictable -ают → -ать verbs are stressed on the ending,
a fact which may help you to remember the non-predictable status of
давáть/даю́т.

In Lesson 8 we will give the rules for the other 5 predictable
groups.

7. Aspect: One-way verbs.

The difference between Он ходи́л в кино́ 'He went to the
movies (and returned)' and Он пошёл в кино́ 'He went to the
movies/He set out for the movies' was discussed in Lesson 4.5.1.
Now look at the verb in Шёл до́ждь 'It was raining', literally
'Rain was going.' If you used the Perfective Пошёл до́ждь
instead of the Imperfective it would have the same aspectual meaning as
in Он пошёл в кино́ 'He set out for the movies" namely 'It
started raining, the rain came.' If you used the Imperfective
verb ходи́л the sentence would have the ridiculous meaning of
the rain making a round trip. The special Imperfective form шёл,
on the other hand, specifies that the motion is in one direction
only, and it fits the situation 'It was raining,' with the rain-
drops coming in one direction from the clouds to the earth.

There are a dozen or so such One-Way   Imperfectives in the
language. All have to do with motion of some sort: go, fly,
crawl, lead, convey, carry, swim, etc. None have prefixes — if you put a
prefix on a One-way verb, it may mean something other than "One-way".

In Lesson 6.5.1 the Imperfective was said to be used for habitual or repeated actions, e.g., Он чáсто брáл кни́ги в
библиотéке 'He often took books out of (Lit., 'in') the
library.' Now the question is, how do you say 'It often rained'?
Which Imperfective do you use, ходи́л or шёл? In other words,
which feature takes precedence, repeatedness or one-wayness?
The answer is: one-wayness; use шёл.

Óсенью чáсто шёл до́ждь.   It often rained in the fall.

If the repeated action is *not* one-way, then you *can't* use шёл:

Он чáсто ходи́л в кино́.   He often went to the movies
                                  (the assumption being that
                                  he returned each time,
                                  naturally).

Thus, the rule for using past Imperfectives for repeated actions
holds good, but for verbs of motion you have to choose between
two different Imperfectives: one-way Imperfective for motion in
one direction, the other Imperfective for anything else.

Further examples:

Сего́дня бу́дет идти́ до́ждь.	It will rain today.
Вчера́ шёл до́ждь.	It rained yesterday. OR: It was raining yesterday.
Когда́ я́ её встре́тил вчера́, она́ шла́ к врачу́.	When I met her yesterday, she was going (one way, was on her way) to the doctor.
Вчера́ она́ ходи́ла к врачу́.	She went to the doctor's yesterday.
Весно́й у на́с ча́сто идёт до́ждь.	It often rains in our area in the spring.
Зимо́й мы́ ча́сто хо́дим в теа́тр.	We often go to the theater in wintertime.
У меня́ зимо́й бу́дет мно́го свобо́дного вре́мени. Я́ ча́сто бу́ду ходи́ть в теа́тр.	I'll have a lot of free time (this) winter. I'm going to go to the theater often.

Compare:

К како́му врачу́ ты́ идёшь?	What doctor are you going to (= are you on your way to)?
vs. К како́му врачу́ ты́ хо́дишь?	What doctor are you going to (do you go to nowadays, on a regular basis, repeatedly)?

Another type of action which is *not* one-way (and where шёл *cannot* be used) is aimless motion, e.g. walking around in the park. That's why the verb гуля́ть 'to walk around for pleasure' has no special one-way Imperfective.

О́н гуля́л по па́рку.	He was strolling in the park.
О́н ча́сто гуля́л по па́рку.	He often strolled in the park.

If you wanted to use the verb 'go, walk' instead of 'stroll', you would have to choose ходи́л, not the One-way verb шёл:

О́н ходи́л по па́рку.	He was walking in the park.
О́н ча́сто ходи́л по па́рку.	He often walked in the park.

Similarly, the general ability to walk must be ходи́л, as no directionality is involved:

Когда́ мне́ бы́л то́лько оди́н го́д, я́ уже́ ходи́л.	When I was only one year old, I was already walking (I could walk.)

Now compare the use of ходи́л with the One-way verb шёл:

О́н вчера́ ходи́л в па́рк.	Yesterday he went to the park (one round trip).
О́н ча́сто ходи́л в па́рк.	He often went *to* (*into*) the park (frequent round trips).
Я́ его́ ви́дел, когда́ о́н шёл в па́рк.	I saw him when he was going *to* (on his way to) the park.

Она́ вчера́ ходи́ла по па́рку.	She was walking(around) *in* the park.
Она́ ча́сто ходи́ла по па́рку.	She often walked(around) *in* the park.
Она́ шла́ в па́рк.	She was going(was on her way) *to* the park.
Óн ходи́л по у́лице.	He was walking (around) in the street (perhaps up and down the street).
Óн шёл по у́лице.	He was walking down the street (in one direction).

Compare пошёл (P) vs. ходи́л (I) vs. шёл (I-One-way):

Куда́ óн пошёл? Его́ нéт.	Where did he go? He's not here. (Where did he set out for?)
Куда́ óн ходи́л? Сла́ва Бо́гу, что верну́лся во́-время!	Where did he go? Thank goodness he came back in time! (Single round trip)
Куда́ óн обы́чно ходи́л, когда́ у него́ бы́ло свобо́дное вре́мя?	Where did he usually go when he had free time? (Repeated trips.)
Куда́ óн шёл, когда́ ты́ его́ ви́дела?	Where was he going when you saw him? (One-way)

Summary

Unprefixed verbs of motion make a three-fold aspectual distinction; P vs. I, vs. I-One-way, while other verbs have no more than a two-fold distinction, P vs. I.

		Verbs of motion			Other verbs	
Action		I-OW	I	P	I	P
. — .	end-point			пошёл		взял
⊂⟹	round trip		ходи́л		брал	
aimless	aimless		ходи́л			
......	repeated	шёл	ходи́л		брал	
∿∿∿∿	on-going	шёл	ходи́л		брал	

It's clear from the above chart where your difficulties lie: the bottom two rows force a choice between шёл and ходи́л for both on-going and repeated actions. Here's a rule of thumb which is statistically accurate, but which may get you into trouble if you're not careful:

Repeated action: use ходи́л.

> Óн ча́сто ходи́л в кино́.   He often *went* to the movies.

On-going action: use шёл.

> Óн ме́дленно шёл по у́лице, когда́ я его́ уви́дел.   He *was walking* slowly down the street when I caught sight of him.

As the chart indicates, aimlessness requires no choice of verbs: use ходи́ть , e.g.,

Óн ме́дленно ходи́л по у́лице.   He *was walking* slowly down (or maybe *up and down*) the street.

The citation forms of the three verbs 'to go' are:

ходи́ть, хо́дят, хожу́   (I)
идти́, иду́т ; шёл, шла   (I-OW)
пойти́, пойду́т ; пошёл, пошла́   (P)

PRACTICE 8

Label the italicized verbs with the symbols used in the above summary chart (.___ / ... / ⮂ etc.) and translate the sentences. If the verb denotes a One-way action, write the abbreviation OW. Note that sometimes you may need more than one symbol, e.g., for repeated round trips (... ⮂).

Врач *пошёл* в рестора́н и не верну́лся.
Врач *ходи́л* в рестора́н. (ambiguous)
Óн ча́сто *ходи́л* в рестора́ны.
Когда́ я его́ ви́дел, óн *шёл* в рестора́н.
Пе́тя *пошёл* в шко́лу и не верну́лся.
Пе́тя вчера́ *ходи́л* в шко́лу.
Пе́тя *взял* кни́гу и не верну́л.
Пе́тя *брал* э́ту кни́гу вчера́ в библиоте́ке.
Роди́тели *иду́т* к врачу́.
Роди́тели ча́сто *хо́дят* к врачу́.
Вчера́ у́тром роди́тели *ходи́ли* к врачу́.
Весно́й роди́тели ча́сто *ходи́ли* к врачу́.
Я ви́дел роди́телей, когда́ они́ *шли* к врачу́.

8. Pronunciation: voiced щ ; assimilation.

There is no letter in the Cyrillic alphabet to represent the
voiced counterpart of щ . The letter щ is pronounced as a long,
palatalized /ṣhṣh/ (high pitched), and its voiced counterpart can
be written /ẓhẓh/ in English transcription. This sound occurs
in very few words, one of which is до́ждь, Gen. дождя́, Inst.
дождём: /dóṣhṣh ‚daẓhẓhá daẓhẓhóm/. Many Russians, however,
pronounce this word as it is spelled: /dóshṭ dazhḍá dazhḍóm/,
with /ḍ/ instead of /ẓhẓh/.

There is another situation in which voiced /ẓhẓh/ may occur:
when щ is followed by another voiced consonant, assimilation may
take place (see Lesson 2, Dialog Comment 2). Just as Ка́к дела́?
is pronounced in fast speech as though spelled "ка́гдела́" so
това́рищ бы́л   will have the sequence /...ẓhẓh + b.../ instead of
/...ṣhṣh + b.../.

There are two consonants having voiced counterparts which
never appear as independent sounds in particular words — they are
always the result of assimilation: ц /ts/ and ч /ch/ are voiced
to /dz/ and /j/ (= Eng. *jury*) when a voiced consonant follows, e.g.
оте́ц бы́л /aṭédzbíl/ 'father was,' мяч бы́л /ṃájbíl/ 'the ball
was.' This assimilation takes place only in fast connected speech,
not in a slow, deliberate style.

Большо́й Теа́тр и о́чень большо́й Ле́нин. The sign reads: Long
live the 63rd anniversary of the Great October Socialist Revolution

9.   Summary of case forms.

	Singular		Plural	
	Adj	Noun	Adj	Noun
# declension (masc)				
Nom	-ый/-ой	-#	-ые	-ы
Gen	-ого	-а	-ых	-ов/ей
Dat	-ому	-у	-ым	-ам
Acc	*=Nom/Gen*		*=Nom/Gen*	
Inst	-ым	-ом	-ыми	-ами
Prep	-ом	-е	-ых	-ах
о-declension (neuter)				
=#declension except for:				
Nom	-ое	-о	-ые	-а
Gen				-#
a-declension (fem I)			*=# decl. except for:*	
Nom	-ая	-а		
Gen	-ой	-ы		-#
Dat	-ой	-е		
Acc	-ую	-у		*=Nom/Gen*
Inst	-ой	-ой		
Prep	-ой	-е		
ь-declension (fem II)			*=# decl. except for palatal indicators*	
Nom	-ая	-#(ь)		-и
Gen	-ой	-и		-ей
Dat	-ой	-и		-ям
Acc	-ую	-#(ь)		*=Nom/Gen*
Inst	-ой	-ью		-ями
Prep	-ой	-и		-ях

N	весь	э́тот	{ бе́лый большо́й	сто́л	всё	э́ти	бе́лые	столы́
G	всего́	э́того	бе́лого	стола́	все́х	э́тих	бе́лых	{ столо́в камне́й
D	всему́	э́тому	бе́лому	столу́	все́м	э́тим	бе́лым	стола́м
A	= *Nom./Gen.*				=*Nom./Gen.*			
I	все́м	э́тим	бе́лым	столо́м	все́ми	э́тими	бе́лыми	стола́ми
P	все́м	э́том	бе́лом	столе́	все́х	э́тих	бе́лых	стола́х
N	всё	э́то	бе́лое	ме́сто				места́
G								ме́ст
N	вся́	э́та	бе́лая	плане́та				плане́ты
G	все́й	э́той	бе́лой	плане́ты				плане́т
D	все́й	э́той	бе́лой	плане́те				
A	всю́	э́ту	бе́лую	плане́ту	=*Nom./Gen.*			
I	все́й	э́той	бе́лой	плане́той				
P	все́й	э́той	бе́лой	плане́те				
N				мече́ть				мече́ти
G				мече́ти				мече́тей
D				мече́ти				мече́тям
A				мече́ть	=*Nom./Gen.*			
I				мече́тью				мече́тями
P				мече́ти				мече́тях

Here are two sample paradigms illustrating nouns ending in a palatalized consonant (слова́рь and ды́ня) and adjectives ending in non-paired consonants (хоро́ший and ру́сский —see Lesson 3.1 for spelling rules):

	Singular			*Plural*		
N	хоро́ший	ру́сский	слова́рь	хоро́шие	ру́сские	словари́
G	хоро́шего	ру́сского	словаря́	хоро́ших	ру́сских	словаре́й
D	хоро́шему	ру́сскому	словарю́	хоро́шим	ру́сским	словаря́м
A	хоро́ший	ру́сский	слова́рь	хоро́шие	ру́сские	словари́
I	хоро́шим	ру́сским	словарём	хоро́шими	ру́сскими	словаря́ми
P	хоро́шем	ру́сском	словаре́	хоро́ших	ру́сских	словаря́х
N	хоро́шая	ру́сская	ды́ня	хоро́шие	ру́сские	ды́ни
G	хоро́шей	ру́сской	ды́ни	хоро́ших	ру́сских	ды́нь
D	хоро́шей	ру́сской	ды́не	хоро́шим	ру́сским	ды́ням
A	хоро́шую	ру́сскую	ды́ню	хоро́шие	ру́сские	ды́ни
I	хоро́шей	ру́сской	ды́ней	хоро́шими	ру́сскими	ды́нями
P	хоро́шей	ру́сской	ды́не	хоро́ших	ру́сских	ды́нях

Pronouns: See Lesson 6.7 for the complete set of forms.

УПРАЖНЕНИЯ

1. Review: кото́рый.

Read aloud and translate, inserting the proper form of кото́рый.

1. Я написа́л письмо́ врача́м, _____ рабо́тали вме́сте со мной
    в Нью Йо́рке.
2. Врачи́, _____ я написа́л письмо́, ча́сто руга́ются.
3. Кни́гу, о _____ ты говори́л, я взяла́ в библиоте́ке.
4. Кни́ги, о _____ ты говори́л, я брала́ в библиоте́ке.
5. Где студе́нты, с _____ я так мно́го разгова́ривала ле́том?
6. Студе́нты, у _____ я жила́ ле́том, все́ интересова́лись теа́тром
    и кино́.
7. Теа́тр, в _____ мы вчера́ ходи́ли, называ́ется Большо́й Теа́тр.
8. Мы́ говори́м об институ́те, в _____ рабо́тают мои́ друзья́
    Шу́ра и Юра.

2 . Review numerals. Dialog 4 and Lesson 6, Dialog 6.

Go around the class.

C: Каку́ю симфо́нию Чайко́вского ты бо́льше всего́ лю́бишь,
    пе́рвую, втору́ю, тре́тью, четвёртую, пя́тую, шесту́ю
    или седьму́ю?

M: Я все́ симфо́нии Чайко́вского о́чень люблю́— и пе́рвую, и
    втору́ю, и тре́тью, и четвёртую, и пя́тую и шесту́ю, но о́н.
    никако́й седьмо́й симфо́нии никогда́ не писа́л.

    Substitute Бра́мс, Ма́лер, Шу́берт, Бетхо́вен, etc., but watch out
    for Мо́царт and Га́йдн.

3. Review of cases: read aloud and translate:

1. Я интересу́юсь _____. (all the remaining students)
2. Я позвони́л _____. (the remaining students)
3. Вра́ч сиде́л за _____. (big table)
4. О́н то́лько что _____ в библиоте́ку. (went, set out for)
5. Ты́ ви́дел _____? (that general)
6. Они́ ходи́ли в _____. (a small restaurant)
7. Они́ бы́ли в _____. (a small restaurant)
8. Они́ пошли́ _домо́й_. (home)
9. Я зна́ю _____. (your sister)
10. С _____ вы́ разгова́ривали? (whom)
11. С _____. (your doctors)
12. С _____. (them)
13. Это письмо́ от _____. (them)

4. Review colors.

Identify pencils or crayons of various colors.

П: Cáша, возьмúте э́тот карандáш. Пишúте, пожáлуйста.
    Мáша, чéм Cáша пúшет?
М: Жёлтым карандашóм.
П: Какóй рукóй?
М: Прáвой рукóй/ Лéвой рукóй.

5. Review: non-past.

Read aloud and translate.

(a) Imperfective Non-past = "present"

1. Чтó ты́ _____ о нём? (think)

2. Всé _____ о Бéлом дóме. (are talking)

3. Гдé вы́ _____? (are sitting)

4. Я́ _____ знáть прáвду. (want)

5. Я́ не _____ её. (see)

6. Учителя́ _____ математúкой. (are interested in)

7. Онú _____ за столóм. (are sitting)

8. Гдé вы́ _____? (live)

9. Óн не _____. (is mistaken)

10. Я́ _____ математúку. (teach)

11. Чтó ты́ _____? (are eating)

(b) Perfective non-past = "future"

1. Мáша _____ емý привéт. (will give)

2. Волóдя _____ кнúгу на мéсто. (will put)

3. Медвежóнок _____ всю кáшу. (will eat)

4. Я́ _____ врачý. (will call)

5. Э́та студéнтка _____ вác. (will draw)

6. Cáша _____ кнúгу в библиотéку. (will return)

(c) Practice the above sentences with various subjects (я́, ты́, óн(á), мы́, вы́, онú).

6.   Conversation.

(a) Read aloud and translate.

      А: Что́ ты́ нарисова́л?
      Б: Это го́род, где́ я живу́.
      А: Где́ твой до́м?
      Б: Во́т здесь.
      А: А что́ нахо́дится спра́ва от твоего́ до́ма?
      Б: Спра́ва от моего́ до́ма нахо́дится рестора́н.
      А: А что́ э́то сле́ва?
      Б: Это шко́ла.
      А: А что́ напро́тив твоего́ до́ма?
      Б: Океа́н.

(b) Translate.

      What did you draw? That's the city where I live. What's that? That's
      my house. And that? That's a theater. What's to the left of the theater?
      The university. What's to the right of the university? A restaurant.
      What's across from the restaurant? The ocean.

(c) Draw a map of a small town and hold a conversation like the one above.

7.   Numerals. Dialog 1 and review.

      П: Како́е э́то упражне́ние?
      С: Это седьмо́е упражне́ние.
      П: А сле́дующее?
      С: Сле́дующее восьмо́е упражне́ние.
      П: А сле́дующее?

      (Stop when you get to 29th.)

8.   Genitive Plural (Analysis 3, Dialogs 1,2)

          Say the phrase meaning 'many X's' for each of the following
      nouns. Use Genitive Plural.

      Model: сло́во → мно́го сло́в

      сторона́   ды́ня   неде́ля
      де́ло   заня́тие   го́род
      яйцо́ (й)   упражне́ние   институ́т
      рестора́н   музе́й   оте́ц (е)
      америка́нец (е)   коне́ц (е)   каранда́ш
      преподава́тель   учи́тель   ка́мень (е)
      число́ (е)

9.   Genitive Plural. Analysis 3.

      П: Са́ша, спроси́те Ма́шу, у неё е́сть карандаши́?
      С: Ма́ша, у тебя́ е́сть карандаши́?
      М: Не́т, у меня́ не́т карандаше́й.
      С: Извини́. Я ду́мал, что у тебя́ е́сть карандаши́.

10. Genitive Plural. Analysis 3.

   П: Давайте поговорим о нашем городе.
   П: В нашем городе нет домов.
   С: В нашем городе нет домов и нет парков.
   М: В нашем городе нет домов, парков и театров...

   Go as far as you can (libraries, schools, universities, newspapers
   etc.). When you get stuck say:

   В нашем городе ничего нет. Мне надоело о нём говорить.
   Давайте поговорим о нашем доме.

   С: В нашем доме нет ручек.
   М: В нашем доме нет ручек и карандашей...

   Continue with books, letters, dictionaries, chalk and so on. When
   you get stuck say:

   В нашем доме ничего нет. Мне скучно о нём говорить.

11. Genitive Plural. Analysis 3.

   П: Где в вашем городе секретные институты?
   С: В нашем городе нет секретных институтов.

   зелёные парки   большие библиотеки
   приятные места   интересные газеты
   интересные места   большие дома
   большие театры   хорошие врачи
   французские рестораны   хорошие профессора
   секретные институты   весёлые студенты
   хорошие музеи   китайские рестораны

12. Genitive Plural. Analysis 3.

   П: Попросите у Маши *карандаш*.
   С: Маша, дай мне, пожалуйста, *карандаш*.
   М: У нас нет *карандашей*.
   С: Что делать? Мне очень нужен *карандаш*.

   Replace карандаш with the following. Watch the form of нужен.

   дыня   яблоко   бумага
   бутылка (о)   газета   нож
   вилка (о)   стакан   яйцо (й)
   словарь   письмо (е)   тарелка (о)
   ложка (е)

13. Accusative plural. Analysis 3.2

Put the Nom. plural words listed below into the sentence 'I know X.'

Я зна́ю _____.

э́ти студе́нты	э́ти кни́ги
э́ти теа́тры	э́ти студе́нтки
э́ти языки́	э́ти пье́сы
э́ти профессора́	э́ти медве́дицы
э́ти преподава́тели	его́ сёстры
э́ти па́рки	его́ бра́тья
э́ти врачи́	его́ го́сти

14. Plural practice. Mixed cases.

Make the italicized phrases plural.

1. Я позвони́л *бра́ту*.
2. Я отвела́ *моего́ го́стя* в университе́т.
3. У неё не́ было *большо́й буты́лки*.
4. Мы́ говори́ли об *э́том жёлтом до́ме*.
5. *Ва́шего го́стя* я ещё не ви́дела.
6. С *ва́шим го́стем* я мно́го часо́в разгова́ривала об *америка́нском президе́нте*.
7. В Аме́рике не́т *хоро́шего словаря́* кита́йского языка́.
8. Переда́йте приве́т *сестре́*.

15. Conversation. Dialog 2.

(a) Translate.

What am I going to do? I invited guests to dinner, and we don't have any glasses. Who did you invite? I invited the doctors. Doctors don't need glasses. We don't have any meat. Doctors don't need meat. They don't eat meat. We don't have any caviar. Doctors don't need caviar. Why did you invite the doctors? I don't know. It doesn't matter. You can drink wine right from the bottles.

(b) For everything that A says (s)he lacks, B says it isn't needed. The conversation ends when B says (s)he is also having a dinner and has invited all the animate nouns (s)he can think of and has lots of (мно́го) all the things A lacks.

16. Dialogs 3 and 4. Analysis 4.

    П: Скажи́те, пожа́луйста, кака́я во *Флори́де* о́сень?
    С: Во Флори́де о́сенью ча́сто идёт *до́ждь*.

    П: Скажи́те, пожа́луйста, кака́я в *Финля́ндии* о́сень?
    С: В Финля́ндии о́сенью ча́сто идёт *сне́г*.

Substitute for places: на се́вере, на ю́ге, в Калифо́рнии, в Кана́де, в Ленингра́де, в Я́лте, в Сиби́ри.

For contrast, substitute зима́, весна́, ле́то for о́сень.

17. Не́т. Analysis 3.

Make the following sentences past, then future. All of them take the past of не́т:

1. В университе́те не́т студе́нтов.
2. В э́том го́роде не́т музе́ев.
3. На столе́ не́т таре́лок.
4. В Аме́рике не́т плохи́х профессоро́в.
5. Ле́том не́т сне́га.

18. Cross-examination (Analysis 4).

    П: Скажи́те, пожа́луйста, когда́ вы́ познако́мились *с генера́лом*?
    С: Я познако́милась с ни́м *весно́й*.

Substitute for генера́л: anybody
Substitute for весна́: о́сень, зима́, ле́то, но́чь, ве́чер, де́нь, у́тро

19. Cross-examination (continued).

    П: Скажи́те, пожа́луйста, когда́ вы́ познако́мились с генера́лом?
    С: Я познако́милась с ни́м *весно́й*.
    П: А что́ вы́ де́лали вме́сте *ле́том*?
    С: Мы́ ничего́ вме́сте не де́лали. *Ле́том* генера́л бы́л *во Флори́де*.
    П: Непра́вда! Ва́с ви́дели вме́сте в *Калифо́рнии*.

Substitute seasons for весна́ . Make sure the next season follows. Use any pair of American states or foreign countries.

20. The seasons. Dialog 4. Analysis 4.

Change the dialog below in the following way:

хо́лодно → тепло́,   зима́ → весна́
тепло́   → жа́рко,   весна́ → ле́то
жа́рко   → идёт до́ждь, ле́то → о́сень

Get through the seasons as fast as you can.

П: Хо́лодно.
С: Да́, я́ о́чень люблю́ зи́му.
П: Почему́?
С: Я́ люблю́ рабо́тать зимо́й, когда́ хо́лодно.
П: Зима́ ско́ро ко́нчится.
С: Да́, ско́ро начнётся весна́.

21. Conversation. Dialogs 3 and 4.

(a) Read aloud and translate.

А: Како́е вре́мя го́да вы бо́льше всего́ лю́бите, зи́му, весну́, ле́то
    или о́сень?
Б: Я́ бо́льше всего́ люблю́ о́сень.
А: Кака́я у ва́с о́сень?
Б: У на́с о́сенью хо́лодно. Ка́ждый де́нь идёт до́ждь.
А: Почему́ же вы лю́бите о́сень?
Б: Я́ люблю́ чита́ть.

(b) Translate.

Which time of the year do you like best? I like spring best. I like
summer best. I don't like fall. I don't like winter. What kind of
winter do you have? What kind of spring do you have? Our spring is warm.
It rains every day. Our winter is cold. It doesn't rain in the winter,
it snows. It snows every day. When does your winter start? In November.
When does it end? In April. What kind of summer do you have? Our
summer is hot. What do you do in the summer? I don't do anything. I
like the summer because I like to stroll.

(c) A and B exchange opinions about the seasons and find out what they are
like in their home towns.

22. отку́да vs. от кого́ = из vs. от (Analysis 5)

(a) Check the statement you hear by asking for a repetition; this requires
the yes-no intonation contour on the question-words.

П: Э́то письмо́ из *Москвы́*.
С: Отку́да? Из Москвы́?
П: Да́, из Москвы́.
П: Э́то *письмо́* от *мои́х роди́телей*.
С: От кого́? От ва́ших роди́телей?
П: Да́, от мои́х роди́телей.

Substitute: Ленингра́д, мо́й бра́т, мои́ бра́тья, ру́сские профессора́,
   моско́вские учителя́, Босто́н, мо́й дру́г, мои́ друзья́, мои́ сёстры,
   Сове́тский Сою́з

Now say the following sentence, substituting the above words and supplying
из or от , as appropriate. Э́то письмо́ (from) _____.

23. Dialog 5, Analysis 4 and 6.

Answer these question with either у́тром, днём, or ве́чером. (There's nothing to do но́чью except sleep, and you don't know how to do that in Russian yet.) Answer as follows: eat in the morning, work in the afternoon, and play in the evening/at night.

П: Когда́ вы бу́дете *есть ка́шу?*
С: Я бу́ду е́сть ка́шу *у́тром.*
П: Когда́ вы бу́дете рабо́тать?
                     игра́ть на фле́йте?
                     писа́ть упражне́ния?
                     гуля́ть по па́рку?
                     е́сть я́блоки?
                     е́сть ды́ни?
                     чита́ть кни́ги?
                     ду́мать о ру́сском языке́?
                     ду́мать обо мне́?
                     е́сть я́йца?

Now repeat, adding these two lines:

П: Вы лю́бите е́сть ка́шу?
С: Да́, я е́м ка́шу ка́ждый де́нь.

The last line requires you to know the non-past of these verbs; all of these verbs are of the -ают/-ать type (Analysis 6.3) except е́сть and писа́ть.

Variation: change from вы to она́ and then to они́.

24. The verb мо́чь. Analysis 6.2.

П: *Вы* идёте в теа́тр сего́дня ве́чером?
С: Не́т, сего́дня ве́чером *я* не *могу́* идти́ в теа́тр.

Change the question to я́, ты́, она́, мы́, они́, and change the response accordingly.

25. Verbs. Dialog 6, Analysis 7.

П: Ма́ша, где́ вы бы́ли вчера́ ве́чером? *У врача́?*
М: Да́, я вчера́ ве́чером ходи́ла *к врачу́.*

Substitute:

вра́ч	университе́т
теа́тр	на́ш бра́т
Ива́н	на́ш профе́ссор
Ива́н Петро́вич	на́ша преподава́тельница
сестра́	на́ша сестра́
библиоте́ка	медве́дь
шко́ла	па́рк

Now repeat, adding the following lines:

П: Вы ви́дели Са́шу?
М: Да́, я его́ ви́дела, когда́ я шла́ *к врачу́.*

26. Verbs. Dialogs 6, Dialog Comment 5, Analysis 7.

(a) Change the subject of the following sentence to ты, о́н, мы́, вы́, они́.

   Я отведу́ Ва́сю в шко́лу.

(b) Do the following dialog, changing subjects again.

   П: Ты́ отведёшь Ва́сю в шко́лу?
   С: Я́ не могу́.
   П: Почему́?
   С: Потому́ что я́ иду́ к врачу́.

   Substitute: она́, мы́, вы́, они́.

(c) Practice the following dialog, changing subjects.

   П: В како́й рестора́н вы́ идёте?
   С: Я́ иду́ в рестора́н "Три́ медве́дя". Я́ всегда́ хожу́ в оди́н и
      то́т же рестора́н.

(d) Substitute:

   городска́я библиоте́ка
   учи́тель, кото́рый живёт в на́шем до́ме.
   учи́тельница, у кото́рой я́ бы́л вчера́.

27. Translate. Dialog 6.

   Take Vasya to school. Take Vasya and Musya to school.   Take the professors
   to the secret institute. I can't. Why? I'm going to the doctor. I'm
   going to the university. I'm going to Boris's. I always go to the same
   doctor. I always call the same doctor. I always read the same book. I
   always invite the same guests. Take Vasya to the doctor. I can't. Why?
   Vasya doesn't have to go to the doctor. Vasya has to go to school.

28. Conversation.

(a) Read aloud and translate.

   А: Что́ ты́ бу́дешь де́лать сего́дня ве́чером?
   Б: Я́ бу́ду занима́ться. А ты́?
   А: Я́ пойду́ в кино́. Не хо́чешь пойти́ в кино́ со мно́й?
   Б: Спаси́бо, я́ с удово́льствием пойду́. Я́ не хочу́ бо́льше занима́ться.

(b) Translate into Russian.

   Hi! Good morning. How are things? Fine. What are you doing this evening?
   I'm going to study. What else (А что́ ещё..) are you going to do? I'm
   going to play the flute. I'm going to read. I'm going to write a letter,
   and you? I'm going to the theater. Where else are you going? I'm going
   to a restaurant. I'm going to Peter Ivanovich's. Don't you want to come
   with me? Of course! Thanks! I'll be glad to come. I don't want to
   study. I don't want to write letters any more.

(c) A and B have a conversation like the one indicated. Then they have a
   similar one referring to yesterday ('What did you do yesterday?').

29. Ко́мпас (Analysis 5.2, Dialog 7).

Где́ Ташке́нт? Ташке́нт к восто́ку от на́с.
Где́ Ленингра́д?
Где́ Та́ллин?
Где́ Москва́?

30. Map questions. Dialog 7. Analysis 5.2.

Get a map of the USSR and find places.

Где́ нахо́дится Чёрное Мо́ре? Чёрное Мо́ре нахо́дится к ю́гу от Москвы́.
Где́ нахо́дится Москва́?
Где́ нахо́дится Ленингра́д?
Где́ нахо́дится Фи́нский зали́в?

Make up all the questions you like, but avoid NW, NE, SSE, etc.

31. Conversation. Dialog 7.

(a) Translate.

Where do you live? In the south. In the north. In the east. In the west.
Today the wind is from the south. You are mistaken. The wind today is
from the north. In the south it is raining. In the north it's snowing.
In the north in the winter it snows every day. Dammit! It's snowing
again. I'm cold.

(b) A and B ask each other about which seasons they like, and why. Then they
ask each other where they are from, where that place is located, and what
it's like there. The conversation ends when A notices that the wind seems
to be from a certain direction and that it's cold (or raining, or snowing)
and B says 'Let's go to the library and study Russian.'

Пиво — Beer

Two Leningrad intellectuals, a writer and a poet, against a
typical Leningrad fascade. The writer died in Jerusalem in 1980;
the poet is living in Texas and working on a four volume
anthology of Leningrad poets. The sign in full would read
женский зал парикмахерская (beauty parlor). Мужской зал
of the same парикмахерская would be 'barber shop.'

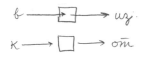

УРОК ВОСЬМОЙ

ТЕКСТ А: СРЕДА ВЕЧЕРОМ, ПРЕСС-КОНФЕРЕНЦИЯ В БЕЛОМ ДОМЕ

Спикер: Дамы и господа, Президент Соединённых Штатов Америки.

Аплодисменты. Все встают[1]. Президент подходит к микрофону, здоровается. Все садятся.

Президент: Дамы и господа[2]. Я думал, что буду[3] говорить сегодня о наших новых планах борьбы с инфляцией. Однако, сегодня утром я узнал очень важную новость, и я хочу объявить её немедленно. Вчера на Землю прилетела из космоса ракета. Она приземлилась ненадолго в Москве, и улетела обратно. Сегодня утром я узнал, что один пассажир этой ракеты остался в Москве. Человечество уже давно ждало этого момента[4], думало и мечтало о нём. Сегодня этот момент наступил. Мы установили контакт с другой цивилизацией, вернее - другая цивилизация установила контакт с нами. Я счастлив[5], что, как Президент Соединённых Штатов, я могу объявить эту новость американскому народу. Я буду рад[5] ответить на[6] ваши вопросы.

Джон Грин, Лос-Анжелес Таймз: Почему ракета приземлилась в Москве, а не в Вашингтоне?

Президент: Не знаю. Может быть потому, что у нас была ещё ночь, а в Москве уже было утро.

Гарри Браун, Балтимор Сан: Как выглядит этот гость из космоса?

Президент: Не знаю.

Гарри Браун: Почему вы покраснели, господин Президент?

Президент: Здесь очень жарко. Следующий вопрос.

Ричард Блэк, Филадельфия Энквайрер: Господин Президент, что вы знаете об этом загадочном пассажире этой загадочной ракеты?

Президент: Почти ничего. Я уже вам сказал всё, что знаю.

Уильям Уайт, Чикаго Трибьюн: Господин Президент, почему Телеграфное Агентство Советского Союза не объявило эту новость?

Президент: Не знаю. Завтра утром я буду говорить по телефону с Советским Президентом, и я задам ему этот вопрос.

Уильям Уайт: Пожалуйста, передайте мне его ответ, господин президент.

Президент: Обязательно передам[7], Билл.

Уильям Уайт: Спасибо, господин Президент.

Все смеются. Пресс-конференция окончена.

ТЕ́КСТ Б: ЧЕТВЕ́РГ: СТАТЬЯ́ В ГАЗЕ́ТЕ ПРА́ВДА
ОТ ЦЕНТРА́ЛЬНОГО КОМИТЕ́ТА КОММУНИСТИ́ЧЕСКОЙ ПА́РТИИ
СОВЕ́ТСКОГО СОЮ́ЗА ВСЕМУ́ СОВЕ́ТСКОМУ НАРО́ДУ.

Дороги́е това́рищи! Истори́ческий моме́нт, кото́рого[4] уже́ давно́ жда́ло всё прогресси́вное челове́чество, наступи́л. Вчера́ на Зе́млю прилете́л из ко́смоса представи́тель друго́й цивилиза́ции. Далеко́ не случа́йно[8], раке́та из ко́смоса приземли́лась в Москве́, в столи́це пе́рвого в ми́ре социалисти́ческого госуда́рства. На э́той раке́те прилете́ла к нам това́рищ Зю́зя. Сего́дня това́рищ Зю́зя почётный гость сове́тского наро́да и сове́тского госуда́рства. Во второ́й полови́не дня состои́тся встре́ча в Кремле́ ме́жду това́рищем Зю́зей и Пе́рвым Секретарём Центра́льного Комите́та КПСС, Президе́нтом Сою́за Сове́тских Социалисти́ческих Респу́блик това́рищем Петро́м Ильичём Бли́нчиковым.

Vocabulary

АГЕ́НТСТВО	agency	ОТВЕ́Т	answer
АППЛОДИСМЕ́НТЫ	applause	ОТВЕ́ТИТЬ	answer
БОРЬБА́	struggle	ПА́РТИЯ	party
ВА́ЖНЫЙ	important	ПЛАН	plan
ВЕРНЕ́Е	rather	ПОДХОДИ́ТЬ	approach, go up to
ВСТАВА́ТЬ	get up, rise	ПОКРАСНЕ́ТЬ	blush, turn red
ВСТРЕ́ЧА	meeting, encounter	ПОЛОВИ́НА	half
ГОСУДА́РСТВО	state	ПОЧЁТНЫЙ	respected, honored
ДАВНО́	for a long time	ПОЧТИ́	almost
ДАЛЕКО́	far, far off	ПРЕДСТАВИ́ТЕЛЬ	representative
ДА́МА	lady	ПРИЗЕМЛИ́ТЬСЯ	land
ДОРОГО́Й	expensive; dear	ПРОГРЕССИ́ВНЫЙ	progressive
ЖДА́ТЬ	wait (for), await	РЕСПУ́БЛИКА	republic
ЗАГА́ДОЧНЫЙ	mysterious	СЕКРЕТА́РЬ	secretary
ЗДОРО́ВАТЬСЯ	greet	СЛУЧА́ЙНО	by chance, by accident
ЗЕМЛЯ́	earth	СМЕЯ́ТЬСЯ	laugh
ИНФЛЯ́ЦИЯ	inflation	СОЕДИНЁННЫЙ	united
ИСТОРИ́ЧЕСКИЙ	historical, historic	СОСТОЯ́ТЬСЯ	take place
КОМИТЕ́Т	committee	СОЦИАЛИСТИ́ЧЕСКИЙ	Socialist
КОММУНИСТИ́ЧЕСКИЙ	communist		
		СПИ́КЕР	speaker
КОНТА́КТ	contact	СРЕДА́	Wednesday
КО́СМОС	cosmos, outer space	СТАТЬЯ́	article
МЕЧТА́ТЬ	dream	СТОЛИ́ЦА	capital
МИКРОФО́Н	microphone	СЧАСТЛИ́ВЫЙ	happy
МОМЕ́НТ	moment	ТЕЛЕГРА́ФНЫЙ	telegraph
НАРО́Д	people	УСТАНОВИ́ТЬ	establish
НАСТУПИ́ТЬ	come	ЦЕНТРА́ЛЬНЫЙ	central
НЕМЕ́ДЛЕННО	immediately	ЦИВИЛИЗА́ЦИЯ	civilization
НЕНАДО́ЛГО	for a short while	ЧЕЛОВЕ́ЧЕСТВО	humanity
НО́ВЫЙ	new	ЧЕТВЕ́РГ	Thursday
ОДНА́КО	however	ШТАТ	state (of the USA)
ОКО́НЧИТЬ	finish, end		
ОСТА́ТЬСЯ	remain, stay behind		

COMMENTS

1. вставáть, встаю́т

The stem -ставáть, -стаю́т is one of the three verb stems in which the syllable -ва- is in the past stem but not in the non-past. See Analysis 2.4.

2. господи́н, господá

Two remarks on this word: two of the endings are irregular: Nom. plur. -a instead of -ы and Gen. Plur. -# instead of -ов; also, the syllable -ин- occurs throughout the singular cases but not in the plural.

	Sing.	Plur.
N	господин	господá
G	господи́на	госпóд
D	господи́ну	господáм
A	=G	=G
I	господи́ном	господáми
P	господи́не	господáх

There is a small group of nouns that drop -ин- in the plural. Most of them denote members of social, religious or national groups, and almost all have Nom. Pl. in -e, like граждани́н, грáждане 'citizen', e.g.

Nom. Sg.	Nom. Pl.	Translation
англичáнин	англичáне	Englishman
армяни́н	армя́не	Armenian
христиани́н	христиáне	Christian
боя́рин	боя́ре	boyar

3. Future 'would'

English grammar requires that a future form like 'I *will* speak' be converted to *would* in clauses after verbs of speaking and thinking, e.g., 'I thought I *would* speak.' Russian has no such rule; thus,

Я бýду говори́ть о нáших плáнах.   I *will* speak about our plans.

Я дýмал, что бýду говори́ть о нáших плáнах.   I thought I *would* speak about our plans.

4. ждáть когó/чегó

This verb may take either the Accusative or Genitive case; in this text the object э́того момéнта is the Genitive of э́тот момéнт.

5. счáстлив, рáд

These are *short adjectives*, discussed further in Dialog Comment 6.

6. отве́тить на вопро́с

This phrase means 'to answer a question'. Leave на untranslated. See Dialog Comment 4 for details.

7. передава́ть (I) / переда́ть (P)

For the sentence Переда́йте мне́ его́ отве́т the best
translation is 'Pass his answer *on* to me.' The principal meaning of the prefix пере- is 'trans- , across,' but it will have
various translations in English depending on the verb it's tack-
ed onto and depending on the context. Further examples of
пере-:

Переда́йте, пожа́луйста, икру́. Pass the caviar, please.
Ра́дио Москва́ передаёт   Radio Moscow is broadcasting
   сего́дняшние но́вости.   (transmitting) today's news.
Переда́йте приве́т му́жу.   Give my regards to your hus-
                                band.

Переведи́те э́ту фра́зу на   Translate this sentence into
   англи́йский язы́к.   English.
О́н перешёл у́лицу.   He crossed the street.

8. далеко́ не случа́йно

A recurrent phrase in Soviet newspaper jargon: 'It is by no
means accidental that...it is no accident that...it is far from
accidental that...:

Далеко́ не случа́йно, что   It is no accident that the
   америка́нские империали́сты   American imperialists again
   сно́ва на́чали говори́ть об   have started to talk about
   усиле́нии ро́ли НАТО.   strengthening the role of
                                NATO.

DIALOGS FOR MEMORIZATION

1. СУЩЕСТВИ́ТЕЛЬНЫЕ.

        С: Господи́н профе́ссор, каки́е есть существи́тельные[1] в ру́сском языке́?

        П: Я с удово́льствием отве́чу на[2] ваш вопро́с. В ру́сском языке́ есть одушевлённые и неодушевлённые существи́тельные.

2. ВИНИ́ТЕЛЬНЫЙ ПАДЕ́Ж.

        С: Господи́н профе́ссор, дава́йте изуча́ть[3] вини́тельный паде́ж.

        П: Како́го числа́, еди́нственного и́ли мно́жественного?

        С: Мно́жественного.

        П: Вы уже́ зна́ете э́тот паде́ж. Он тако́й же[4], как имени́тельный.

        С: А е́сли э́то одушевлённое существи́тельное?

        П: Хм...в тако́м слу́чае...

        С: Почему́ вы красне́ете?

        П: Здесь жа́рко.

3а. ПОЗНАКО́МЬТЕСЬ![5]

        Н: Ты, ка́жется, знако́ма[6] с профе́ссором Бороди́ным?[7] Я мно́го слы́шала о нём и хоте́ла бы[8] с ним познако́миться.

        М: Пойдём, я тебя́ ему́ предста́влю.
Серге́й Ива́нович, разреши́те вам предста́вить мою́ подру́гу, Ни́ну Беля́еву[9]. Ни́на, э́то Серге́й Ива́нович Бороди́н.

        Б: Очень прия́тно.

        Н: Очень прия́тно.

3б.   М: Ну, как тебе́ понра́вился[10] профе́ссор Бороди́н?

        Н: Ничего́, интере́сный, ка́жется, челове́к.

4. Дни́ неде́ли

        В понеде́льник[11] начина́ется неде́ля,
        За понеде́льником идёт вто́рник,
        За вто́рником идёт среда́,
        За средо́й идёт четве́рг,
        За четверго́м идёт пя́тница,
        За пя́тницей идёт суббо́та,
        За суббо́той идёт воскресе́нье,
        В воскресе́нье конча́ется неде́ля.

5. Како́е сего́дня число́?

П: Скажи́те, пожа́луйста, како́е сего́дня число́?
С: По-англи́йски снача́ла называ́ют ме́сяц, а пото́м число́, а по-ру́сски?
П: А по-ру́сски наоборо́т.
С: Сего́дня тридца́тое января́.
М: А я́ ду́мала, что сего́дня три́дцать пе́рвое[12] января́.
Н: А я́ ду́мала, что сего́дня пе́рвое февраля́.
Ю: А я́ ду́мал , что сего́дня второ́е февраля́.

6. В авто́бусе.[13]

С: Куда́ ты́ е́дешь?[14]
М: На по́чту[15], за газе́тами и конве́ртами[16].   А ты́?
С: Я́ е́ду на рабо́ту.
М: Где́ ты́ рабо́таешь?
С: На фа́брике[17] и́мени Ле́нина. А ты́?   *gen имя name.*
М: На заво́де[17] Фо́рда.

7. Пого́да.

С: Ты́ не слы́шал по ра́дио, кака́я сего́дня бу́дет пого́да?
М: Сего́дня бу́дет я́сно, со́лнечно и тепло́, ве́тер с ю́га.
С: А за́втра?
М: За́втра бу́дет о́блачно и хо́лодно, ве́тер с се́вера.
С: Како́й здесь ужа́сный кли́мат. Мне́ совсе́м не нра́вится. *at all.*
М: А ты́ отку́да?
С: Я́ из Калифо́рнии.

Translation

1. Nouns.

S: Professor, sir, what kind of nouns are there in Russian?
T: I'll be glad to answer your question. Russian has animate and inanimate nouns.

2. The accusative case.

S: Professor, sir, let's study the accusative case.
T: What number, singular or plural?
S: Plural.
T: You already know that case. It's just like the nominative.
S: But what if the noun is animate?
T: Hm...in that case...
S: Why are you blushing?
T: It's hot in here.

3a. Get Acquainted!

   N: You're acquainted with Professor Borodin, aren't you? I've heard
      alot about him and would like to meet him.
   M: Let's go, I'll introduce you to him. Sergei Ivanovich, permit me to
      introduce my friend Nina Belyayev. Nina, this is Sergei Ivanovich
      Borodin.
   B: Pleased to meet you.
   N: Pleased to meet you.

3b. M: Well, how did you like Professor Borodin?
    N: OK, he seems to be an interesting person.

4. The days of the week.

   The week begins on Monday,
   After Monday comes Tuesday,
   After Tuesday comes Wednesday,
   After Wednesday comes Thursday,
   After Thursday comes Friday,
   After Friday comes Saturday,
   After Saturday comes Sunday,
   And the week ends on Sunday.

5. What's the date today?

   T: Excuse me (Lit., 'Tell me, please'), what's the date today?
   S: In English you name the month first, then the date: how about
      Russian?
   T: In Russian it's vice-versa.
   S: Today is January thirtieth.
   M: But I thought that today is January thirty first.
   N: But I thought that today is February first.
   Y: But I thought that today is February second.

6. On the bus.

   S: Where are you going?
   M: To the post-office, for newspapers and envelopes. How about you?
   S: I'm going to work.
   M: Where do you work?
   S: At the Lenin factory. And you?
   M: At the Ford plant.

7. The weather.

   S: Did you hear on the radio what the weather's going to be today?
   M: It will be clear, sunny, and warm today; wind from the south.
   S: And tomorrow?
   M: Tomorrow it will be cloudy and cold; wind from the north.
   S: What awful climate here! I don't like it at all.
   M: Where are you from?
   S: I'm from California.

ACTIVE WORD LIST

Nouns

ра́дио (ра́дио...)	radio
авто́бус	bus
заво́д (на)	plant
по́чта (на)	post office
фа́брика (на)	factory
подру́га	girl friend
челове́к	man, person, human being
воскресе́нье	Sunday
вто́рник	Tuesday
кли́мат	climate
понеде́льник	Monday
пя́тница	Friday
рабо́та (на)	work
слу́чай	case
среда́ сре́ду; сре́ды сред -а́м	Wednesday
суббо́та	Saturday
три́дцать тридцати́ (ж)	thirty
четве́рг четверга́; -и́	Thursday

Verbs

отве́тить -́тят -́чу С	answer
разреши́ть -ша́т -шу́ С	permit, allow
познако́миться -́мятся -́млюсь С	meet, become acquainted with
понра́виться -́вятся -́влюсь С	please, like
изуча́ть -а́ют НС	learn, study
называ́ть -а́ют НС	call; name
е́хать е́дут НС	go (by vehicle)
конча́ться -а́ются НС	end, finish
красне́ть НС	blush, turn red
начина́ться -а́ются НС	begin
нра́виться -́вятся -́влюсь НС	please, like
слы́шать -́ат НС	hear

Adjectives

знако́м	familiar
имени́тельный	nominative
неодушевлённый	inanimate
одушевлённый	animate
существи́тельное	noun
тако́й	such
тридца́тый	thirtieth
ужа́сный	awful, terrible

Misc.

о́блачно	cloudy
снача́ла	at first, at the beginning
со́лнечно	sunny
я́сно	clear
бы́	*particle*
дава́йте	let's
е́сли	if
наоборо́т	on the contrary
совсе́м	completely
уже́	already

Palace of Marriage Registration - брак means marriage.
The place to go for a socialist ritual.

1. и́мя существи́тельное

   This phrase means literally 'substantive name' (и́мя 'name') and is the
term for *noun*.   It is often abbreviated to существи́тельное , which is not
much of an abbreviation. As a result of this abbreviation the Russian word
for *noun* is an adjective, neuter gender: существи́тельное, -ого...
plural существи́тельные, -ых...

2. отве́тить кому́ на что́

   To answer a person, use Dative (кому́); to answer a thing use на plus
Accusative (на что́).

Они́ мне́ отве́тили.	They answered me.
Они́ отве́тили на письмо́.	They answered the letter.
на вопро́с.	They answered the question.

See text:

Я бу́ду ра́д отве́тить на ва́ши
вопро́сы.
> I'll be glad to answer your
> questions.

      Warning: you can't use the verb отве́тить to say 'answer the telephone'
or 'answer the door' — these are English idioms and, if you stop and think
about it, are rather peculiar. In Russian you 'go to' the telephone or 'lift
the receiver'.

Я подошёл к телефо́ну. }
Я сня́л тру́бку.   }   I answered the phone.

3. изуча́ть/учи́ться/занима́ться

   These three verbs can, on occasion, all be translated as 'study'. All
are imperfective. They differ in meaning and in verb government.

изуча́ть, -а́ют (I) что́   — Accusative object obligatory. *To make a
serious study of some field of knowledge.*

Что́ ты изуча́ешь?	What are you studying?
— Я изуча́ю ру́сский язы́к.	I'm studying Russian.
исто́рию ру́сского языка́.	...the history of the Russian language.
хи́мию.	chemistry
жи́знь Бетхо́вена.	the life of Beethoven.

учи́ться, у́чатся, учу́сь (I) чему́ — Dative, object optional.
To pursue a course of studies, be learning.

— Я учу́сь.	I study/ am studying/ am a student.
— Я учу́сь в университе́те.	I study at (attend) the university.
— Я учу́сь ру́сскому языку́.	I'm studying/learning Russian (take a Russian course).

занима́ться, -а́ются (I) чем — Instrumental object optional.
To be engaged in, busy with, work with

Что́ ты сейча́с де́лаешь?	What are you doing now?
— Я занима́юсь. Не меша́й!	I'm studying. Don't bother me.
— Я сего́дня занима́юсь ру́сским языко́м.	I'm studying Russian today.
— Я занима́юсь ру́сским языко́м в университе́те.	I study Russian at the university.
— Я занима́юсь спо́ртом.	I'm into sports.

4. тако́й же

The word тако́й means 'such an X' or 'an X like that', e.g.

Я не люблю́ таки́е упражне́ния.	I don't like such exercises/exercises like that.

When unstressed же is added, the phrase means 'the *same* kind of X, having the *same properties* as X', e.g.

Вини́тельный паде́ж тако́й же как имени́тельный.	The accusative case is just like (identical to) the nominative.
Она́ така́я же, как её ма́ть.	She's just like her mother.
Он тако́й же у́мный, как профе́ссор Бороди́н.	He is just as smart as professor Borodin.

5. Познако́мьтесь!

This imperative form 'get acquainted' can be used in introducing people; say each person's name (if you remember them) and then say Познако́мьтесь, пожа́луйста. If you have forgotten people's names, you can use this word and let them say their own names.

6. Short adjectives.

Знако́ма is a short adjective, like рад 'glad' and сча́стлив 'happy' See Text Comment 5. Short adjectives have four endings: m., n., f., and plur.

m.	рад	"glad"	сча́стлив	'happy'	знако́м 'acquainted'
f.	ра́да		сча́стлива		знако́ма
n.	ра́до		сча́стливо		знако́мо
pl.	ра́ды		сча́стливы		знако́мы

Short adjectives are never used to modify nouns (e.g. a *happy man*); they are used only as predicates (e.g. That man *is happy*).

Я с ним знако́м.	I *am* acquainted with him.
Они́ о́чень сча́стливы.	They *are* very happy.
Мы о́чень ра́ды, что она́ у́чится ру́сскому языку́.	We *are* very glad she's studying Russian.

7. Family names in -ин

The Instrumental ending -ым on Бородины́м is adjectival rather than nominal (compare: профе́ссором). Family names in -ин and -ов (Ле́нин, Бороди́н, Че́хов, Смирно́в...) have a mixed declension; some of the endings are like nouns, some like adjectives. See Analysis 1.5 for the full display.

8. хоте́л бы

The particle бы (always unstressed) plus the -л- form of the verb renders the meaning 'would'. Compare:

Я хочу́ с ним познако́миться,	I want to meet him.
Я бы хоте́л с ним познако́миться.	I would like to meet him.

This construction is the Russian conditional and subjunctive, to be discussed in a later lesson. For now, just learn хоте́л (а) бы as a set expression.

9. Patronymic usage

Masha introduces Nina without patronymic because of their youth — they are probably students, and the professor would not be expected to address her with и́мя-о́тчество.

10. понра́виться

Note the literal translation of this sentence:

Ка́к тебе́ понра́вился профе́ссор Бороди́н?	How did Borodin strike you? (= How did Borodin appeal to you?) (= How did you like Borodin?)

Since Бороди́н is the subject of the sentence, the verb agrees with it; compare the feminine and plural forms:

Мне́ о́чень *понра́вилась* его́ жена́.	I like his wife very much. (Lit., His wife appealed to me.)
Они́ ва́м *понра́вились*?	Did you like them?

The forms тебе́, мне́, ва́м are Dative.

11. Prepositions with days of the week.

On a day is *в* plus Accusative:

В четве́рг.	On Thursday.
Во вто́рник.	On Tuesday.
В сре́ду.	On Wednesday.

Recall that months work differently: в + *Prep.*, e.g., в *ма́рте*.

In this dialog note the use of the Instrumental in the expression *идти́ за* X. Thus, X идёт за Y means 'X follows Y' (Lit., 'X comes after Y').

12. Compound Ordinal numerals

You have learned the ordinal numerals up to *twentieth*. Above that numeral, Russian works like English: use the numeral twenty (thirty, forty, etc.) plus the ordinals already learned (first, second, etc.).

двадца́тый	twentieth
два́дцать пе́рвый	twenty first
два́дцать второ́й	twenty second
два́дцать тре́тий	twenty third
два́дцать четвёртый...	twenty fourth...
тридца́тый	thirtieth
три́дцать пе́рвый	thirty first
три́дцать второ́й	thirty second
три́дцать тре́тий	thirty third
три́дцать четвёртый...	thirty fourth...

13. Prepositions with vehicles.

To express location *in* or *on* a vehicle, use в plus Prepositional; to express *by* (vehicle), use на plus Prepositional or use Instrumental.

Óн сиди́т в авто́бусе.	He's sitting in the bus (He's on the bus).
Óн е́дет туда́ на авто́бусе. Óн е́дет туда́ авто́бусом.	He's going there by bus (on a bus).

Similarly for маши́на 'car', самолёт 'airplane', etc.

{ Óн сиди́т в маши́не.	He's sitting in the car.
{ Óн е́дет на маши́не.	He's going by car.
{ Óн сиди́т в самолёте.	He's sitting in the airplane.
{ Óн лети́т на самолёте.	He's going (flying) by plane.

14. е́хать

The verb е́хать, е́дут means the same thing as идти́, иду́т except that you cannot use идти́, иду́т if some means of locomotion other than your own self is involved (e.g. a bus, car, horse, bicycle, etc.).

Я иду́ на по́чту.	I'm going to the post office (under my own steam, on foot).
Я е́ду на по́чту.	I'm going to the post office (not on foot).

15. на nouns

With certain nouns you cannot use the preposition series в/в/из, e.g. the points of the compass (see Lesson 7.5). Instead, you must use the на/на/с series. In this lesson there are some more на-nouns:

по́чта	post-office
заво́д	plant
фа́брика	factory
рабо́та	work
неде́ля	week

Examples:

на фа́брике	at the factory
на фа́брику	to the factory
с фа́брики	from the factory
на рабо́ту	to work
на э́той неде́ле	this week

16. за 'to fetch'

To go somewhere *to fetch* something is за plus Instrumental.

Я е́ду на по́чту за конве́ртами.　　　I'm going to the post office for (to fetch) envelopes

The usual translation is 'for', but beware of this English preposition: it has many meanings and many different translations.

Он ходи́л в магази́н за вино́м.　　　He went to the store for wine.

17. заво́д vs. фа́брика

Although we translate заво́д as 'plant' and фа́брика as 'factory', these designations are arbitrary: which one of the two you use depends entirely on what goods are manufactured there.

автомоби́льный заво́д	automobile plant
тексти́льная фа́брика	woolen mill (textile mill)
стеклозаво́д	glass works
пивова́ренный заво́д	brewery
обувна́я фа́брика	shoe factory
сталелите́йный заво́д	steel mill
часова́я фа́брика	clock works
ме́бельная фа́брика	furniture factory

ANALYSIS

This analysis is a review of the forms of Russian adjectives, nouns and verbs. In Lesson 7, we summarized almost all the declensional endings of Russian adjectives, nouns, and pronouns. In this lesson we give rules for stress and we list exceptions for nouns and verbs. The verbs you have had will be brought together with their aspect partners, and all verbs will be cited in their full forms — i.e., with both past and non-past stems.

1.1 Review of adjective and noun forms.

The complete set of regular endings for adjectives and nouns was given in Lesson 7.9.

1.2 Citation conventions and types of irregularity.

In Section 1.4 we will list all of the irregular nouns that have occurred in Active Word Lists through Lesson 8. The list includes not only irregular endings and stems, but also nouns having inserted vowels and stress patterns other than pattern SS.

Before examining the list you may want to review Lesson 4.1, where the conventions for citing nouns were introduced. Remember that the *semi-colon* separates singular (on the left) from plural forms (on the right), e.g.

Nom. Sg.	*Acc. Sg.*	;	*Nom. Pl.*	*Gen. Pl.*	*Dat. Pl.*
рука́	ру́ку	;	ру́ки	ру́к	рука́м

The above citation form means that the word рука́ has stress pattern MM; the full paradigm would look like this:

N	рука́	*ру́ки*
G	руки́	ру́к
D	руке́	рука́м
A	*ру́ку*	*ру́ки*
I	руко́й	рука́ми
P	руке́	рука́х

The other thing to remember is that the letters (о) (е) (ё) in *parentheses* stand for inserted vowels before the zero ending (Nom. Sg. or Gen. Pl., as the case may be):

де́нь (е) implies дня́, дню́, etc.
медвежо́нок (о) implies медвежо́нка, медвежо́нку etc.
окно́ (о) ; о́кна implies Gen. Pl. о́кон
письмо́ (е); пи́сьма implies Gen. Pl. пи́сем
ру́чка (е) implies Gen. Pl. ру́чек
таре́лка (о) implies Gen. Pl. таре́лок

You have met most of the major types of irregularities of Russian nouns. Here is a summary of them:

(1) Plural stems (mostly masculine)

брáт; брáтья implies брáтьев, брáтьям, брáтьями, брáтьях

(2) Nom. Plur. endings (mostly masculine)

профéссор; профессорá (with -a instead of the expected -ы)
я́блоко; я́блоки (with -и instead of the expected -a)

(3) Gen. Pl. endings

мýж; мужья́ мужéй (you would expect it to be like брáтья, брáтьев)

(4) Gen. Pl. stress

сестрá (ё) ; сёстры сестёр сёстрам (this does not fit any of the
    normal stress patterns)

(5) Combinations of the above

граждани́н; грáждане граждáн (Irregular Plural stem, Nom. Pl. ending,
    and Gen. Pl. ending.)

Some nouns are indeclinable, i.e., they have no case endings. They are listed with *three dots*, like this:

кино́ (кино́...)

Two nouns deserve special mention: и́мя 'name' and врéмя 'time'. You'd expect them to be feminine, but they're not; they are neuter. The endings do not correspond to those of the normal declension classes. Their case forms have the extra syllable -ен- (just as до́чь and мáть have the extra syllable -ер- ; see Lesson 7.1). There are about a dozen such neuter nouns ending in -мя . Here is the full display of the paradigm:

'time'

Sg.	*Pl.*
врéмя	временá
врéмени	времён
врéмени	временáм
врéмя	временá
врéменем	временáми
врéмени	временáх

1.3 на nouns

There is a type of irregularity that has nothing to do with stress, stems, or endings: for certain masculine nouns you must learn to use the preposition series на/на/с 'at/to/from' rather than в/в/из. (See Lesson 7.5.2 on points of the compass). For such nouns we will print the word на right after it, e.g.,

се́вер (на) implies на се́вере, на се́вер, с се́вера.
рабо́та (на) implies на рабо́те, на рабо́ту, с рабо́ты.

Although the на nouns are included in the list in section 1.4, they are also listed here for your convenience:

се́вер	north
юг	south
восто́к	east
за́пад	west
заня́тие	class
по́чта	post office
фа́брика	factory
заво́д	plant

Sometimes the use of на/на/с vs. в/в/из depends on which of several meanings the word has:

уро́к: на уро́ке	lesson (class): in class
BUT: в уро́ке	in the lesson (in a textbook)
рабо́та: на рабо́те	work (place): at work
BUT: в рабо́тах Шопенга́уера	in Schopenhauer's works (writings)

Also, the use of на/на/с may depend upon the verb, e.g.,

переводи́ть с ру́сского (языка́) на англи́йский (язы́к)	to *translate from* Russian *to* English
BUT: В ру́сском языке́ е́сть мно́го интере́сных сло́в.	In Russian there are a lot of interesting words.

1.4 Complete list of irregular nouns, Lessons 1-8.

This list is arranged alphabetically so you can use it for reference. It contains not only irregular forms, but also three kinds of nouns which are not normally considered irregular: nouns with an inserted vowel, nouns with stress patterns other than SS, and на nouns. Although nouns of these three types are not irregular, you nevertheless have to learn these facts about them before you can use them in all their forms.

а́дрес; адреса́
бра́т; бра́тья
буты́лка   (о)
весна́   (е); вёсны
ве́тер   (е)
ве́чер; вечера́
ве́щь; ве́щи вещей -а́м   (ж)
ви́лка   (о)
восто́к   (на)
вра́ч врача́; -и́
вре́мя вре́мени вре́менем; времена́
  времён -а́м   (сред. род)
го́д го́да в (-у́) го́ды -о́в -а́м
го́род; города́
господи́н; господа́ госпо́д -а́м
го́сть; го́сти -е́й -я́м
граждани́н; гра́ждане, гра́ждан
гражда́нка   (о)   *gen. pl.*
дека́брь декабря́
де́ло; дела́
де́нь   (е)
до́ждь дождя́; -и́
до́м; дома́
жена́; жёны
заво́д   (на)
за́пад   (на)
зима́ зи́му; зи́мы
и́мя и́мени и́менем; имена́ имён
  -а́м   (сред. род)
ка́мень   (е); ка́мни камне́й -я́м
карандаш́ -а́; -и́
кольцо́   (е) ко́льца коле́ц ко́льцам
коне́ц   (е) конца́; -ы́

ло́жка   (е)
медвежо́нок   (о); медвежа́та
  медвежа́т
ме́сто; места́
му́ж; мужья́ муже́й
неде́ля   (на)

но́ж ножа́; -и́
но́чь; но́чи ноче́й -а́м
ноя́брь -ря́
окно́   (о); о́кна
октя́брь -ря́
паде́ж падежа́; -и́
по́чта   (на)
профе́ссор; -ра́
рабо́та   (на)
ра́з; разы́ ра́з -а́м

рука́ ру́ку; ру́ки ру́к -а́м
ру́чка   (е)`
се́вер   (на)
сентя́брь -ря́
сестра́   (ё); сёстры сестёр сёстрам
слова́рь словаря́; -и́
сло́во; слова́

сне́г сне́га; снега́
среда́ сре́ду; сре́ды
сто́л стола́; -ы́
сторона́ сто́рону; сто́роны сторо́н -а́м
страна́; стра́ны
студе́нтка   (о)
сту́л; сту́лья
таре́лка   (о)
уро́к   (на)
фа́брика   (на)
февра́ль -ля́

цве́т цве́та; цвета́
ча́с ча́са; часы́
четве́рг четверга́; -и́
число́   (е); чи́сла
ю́г   (на)
я́блоко; я́блоки
язы́к языка́; языки́
яйцо́   (е); я́йца яи́ц я́йцам
янва́рь -ря́

дочь
мать
чёрт , черти
лето   SE

1.5 Mixed declension: names in -ин/-ов.

All family names in -ин and -ов have endings that are a mixture of noun endings (masc. except for I Sg.) and special adjective endings (all fem., all Plur., and Inst. Sg. masc.).

	masc. (noun-like except I Sg)	*fem.* (like special adj.)	*plur.*
N	Бородин́ (Mr. B)	Бородина́ (Ms. B)	Бородины́ (the B's)
G	-а́	-о́й	-ы́х
D	-у́	-о́й	-ы́м
A	-а́	-у́	-ы́х
I	-ы́м	-о́й	-ы́ми
P	-е́	-о́й	-ы́х

PRACTICE 1

Listed below are the answers to this Practice, so don't look at them until you have followed the instructions and written down your own answers on a separate sheet of paper. Examine the list of irregular nouns and write down each word that has a stress pattern other than SS. Label each word with the symbols SE, ES, EE, MM, SM, MS, or Irreg. Remember that a word like сто́л стола́; столы́ *has pattern EE despite the fact that the Nom. Sg.* сто́л *is stressed on the stem; this is because the ending is zero, and in such cases "End stress" has no place to go other than on the stem.*

а́дрес SE	ка́мень SM	сестра́ ES Irreg.
весна́ ES	каранда́ш EE	слова́рь EE
ве́чер SE	кольцо́ ES	сло́во SE
ве́щь SM	коне́ц EE	сло́н EE
вра́ч EE	ле́то SE	сне́г SE
вре́мя SE	ме́сто SE	среда́ MM
го́д SM	му́ж SE	сто́л EE
го́род SE	но́ж EE	сторона́ MM
господи́н SE	но́чь SM	страна́ ES
го́сть SM	ноя́брь EE	февра́ль EE
граждани́н SS Irreg.	окно́ ES	хо́р SE
дека́брь EE	октя́брь EE	цве́т SE
де́ло SE	паде́ж EE	ча́с SE
до́ждь EE	профе́ссор SE	четве́рг EE
до́м SE	ра́з SE	число́ ES
жена́ ES		язы́к EE
зима́ MS	рука́ MM	яйцо́ ES Irreg.
и́мя SE	сентя́брь EE	янва́рь EE

PRACTICE 2

*As in Practice 1, don't peek at the answers listed below.
Go through the noun list again; this time write down all
the nouns that have an irregular stem change (ignore stress
and ignore irregular endings).*

брáт; брáтья
врéмя врéмени...;
господи́н; господá...
граждани́н; грáждане...
и́мя и́мени...
медвежóнок; медвежáта...
мýж; мужья́...
сту́л; сту́лья
чёрт; чéрти (two stem changes: ё to e and plain т to
                   palatalized т)
яйцó: the й of the Gen. Plur. might be considered a
       stem change.

PRACTICE 3

*Cover the forms on the right. Look at the Nom. Sg. form on the left
and say it aloud; then say the Gen. Sg., Nom. Pl. and Gen. Pl., e.g.,
бра́т → бра́та; бра́тья бра́тьев. All of these nouns exhibit a stress
pattern other than SS, an irregular stem or an irregular ending.
Identify the peculiarity.*

кольцó	→ кольцá; кóльца колéц
окнó	→ окнá; óкна óкон
мéсто	→ местá; местá мéст
я́блоко	→ я́блока; я́блоки я́блок
лóжка	→ лóжки; лóжки лóжек
рукá	→ руки́; ру́ки ру́к
и́мя	→ и́мени; именá имён
врáч	→ врачá; врачи́ врачéй
áдрес	→ áдреса; адресá адресóв
сестрá	→ сестры́; сёстры сестёр
слóво	→ слóва; словá слóв
язы́к	→ языкá; языки́ языкóв

2.1 Review of verb forms.

When you learn the forms of a verb you have to ask three things:

(1)   What *conjugation* does the verb belong to?

   Answer: Learn the 3 Pl. form (see Lesson 5.3.1).

(2)   What are its past and non-past *stems*?

   Answer: Learn the Infinitive in addition to the 3 Pl. For most verbs
   you can predict one stem from the other (see Lesson 7.6.3 and
   section 2.3 of this lesson). For a fair number of verbs, however,
   you must memorize the two stems, along with their stress patterns,
   e.g. писа́ть пи́шут пишу́ 'write' (see section 2.4 below).

(3)   What is its *aspect partner*?

   Answer: Look it up in a dictionary or in a list (see section 2.2 below).
   Later on we will give information as to how aspect pairs are
   formed, but for now you will have to memorize partners like
   написа́ть (С) писа́ть (НС) 'write'.

The purpose of this review is to match up the past and non-past stems of
all the verbs you have met and to match up the aspect partners of a selected
number of verbs you have met in one form or another.

Before presenting these lists of forms, we shall briefly review the two
conjugations, the regular consonant alternations, and the four irregular verbs.

The personal endings for each conjugation are illustrated below; for details
see Lesson 5.3.1.

Conjugation I		*Conjugation II*	
я́ кладу́	мы́ кладём	я́ говорю́	мы́ говори́м
ты́ кладёшь	вы́ кладёте	ты́ говори́шь	вы́ говори́те
о́н кладёт	они́ кладу́т	о́н говори́т	они́ говоря́т

The consonant alternations in the 1st Person Singular of Conjugation II
verbs (спро́сят, спрошу́) are listed below; for details, see Lesson 6.6.1.

т	→ ч	п	→ пл
д	→ ж	б	→ бл
з	→ ж	м	→ мл
с	→ ш	в	→ вл
ст	→ щ		

The alternations г → ж and к → ч in Conjugation I verbs (могу́, мо́жешь,
мо́жет, мо́жем, мо́жете, мо́гут) were discussed in Lesson 7.6.2.

Three of the four irregular verbs of Russian were presented in Lesson 5.3.2.
We list them here along with the fourth one бежа́ть 'to run'.

да́ть 'give'		е́сть 'eat'	
я́ да́м	мы́ дади́м	я́ е́м	мы́ еди́м
ты́ да́шь	вы́ дади́те	ты́ е́шь	вы́ еди́те
о́н да́ст	они́ даду́т	о́н е́ст	они́ едя́т

хоте́ть 'want'

я хочу́	мы хоти́м
ты хо́чешь	вы хоти́те
о́н хо́чет	они́ хотя́т

бежа́ть 'run'

я бегу́	мы бежи́м
ты бежи́шь	вы бежи́те
о́н бежи́т	они́ бегу́т

Any prefixed form of these verbs will have the same irregularities, e.g. переда́ть (С) 'transmit; pass' переда́м , etc.

2.2 Aspect pairs.

For many verbs you have met only one partner of an aspect pair, e.g. отвести́ (С) 'take, lead off (to)' but not отводи́ть (НС); for others you have met both, e.g., написа́ть (С) and писа́ть (НС) 'write'. The following list includes all the pairs you've met, plus a number of new partners; the latter are marked with an asterisk.

The list is divided into four groups:

(1) The suffix -ыва-.

      All verbs with this suffix are Imperfective.

      Examples: расска́зывать, спра́шивать.

(2) -ить/-ать,

      Given a pair of verbs, one ending in -ить, the other in -ать , the former will be Perfective and the latter Imperfective.

      Example: отве́тить (С), отвеча́ть (НС)

(3) Prefixes

      Given a pair of verbs, one with a prefix, the other without, the one with the prefix will be the Perfective partner.

      Example: написа́ть (С), писа́ть (НС)

      Note: unprefixed verbs are almost all Imperfective; да́ть and бы́ть are exceptions to this generalization.

(4) Others.

Perfective	Imperfective	Gloss
Group (1)		
откры́ть	открыва́ть	open
рассказа́ть	*расска́зывать	tell (narrate)
спроси́ть	*спра́шивать	ask (inquire)
Group (2)		
ко́нчиться	конча́ться	end
отве́тить	*отвеча́ть	answer
*ошиби́ться	ошиба́ться	be mistaken
повтори́ть	*повторя́ть	repeat
пригласи́ть	*приглаша́ть	invite
разреши́ть	*разреша́ть	permit
Group (3)		
написа́ть	писа́ть	write
понра́виться	нра́виться	appeal to (like)
съе́сть	е́сть	eat
*вы́пить	пи́ть	drink
нарисова́ть	*рисова́ть	draw
позвони́ть	*звони́ть	phone
попроси́ть	*проси́ть	ask (request)
поста́вить	*ста́вить	put (standing)
*прочита́ть	чита́ть	read
*сде́лать	де́лать	do; make
*уви́деть	ви́деть	see
Group (4)		
положи́ть	кла́сть	put (lying)
взя́ть	бра́ть	take
сказа́ть	говори́ть	say, tell
да́ть	дава́ть	give
зада́ть	*задава́ть	ask (a question)
переда́ть	*передава́ть	pass; broadcast
отвести́	*отводи́ть	take (lead) off to
*перевести́	переводи́ть	translate
нача́ться	начина́ться	begin

*For the past and non-past forms of the new verbs marked with an asterisk, see sections 2.3 and 2.4, below.

PRACTICE 4

Cover the second and third columns of the above list; look at the Perfective in column 1 and say the Imperfective and translate. Then cover the Perfective and test yourself. Then cover both aspects and say them aloud as you look at the gloss.

2.3 Past and non-past stems: Predictable verbs.

Sections 2.3 and 2.4 will match up the past and non-past stems of all the verbs you've had so far.

As we noted earlier (Lesson 7.6.3), verbs may be either *predictable* (given the non-past stem, you can predict the past stem, or vice-versa) or *non-predictable*. Below we list the six classes of predictable verbs, The first three rules work in both directions. The fourth and fifth rules work only in the direction 3 Pl. → infinitive: given the 3 Pl. -ают you can predict the infinitive -ать, but not the other way. The sixth rule works only in the direction infinitive → 3 Pl.: given an infinitive in -ить you can predict a 3 Pl. -ят, but not the other way.

The six classes of predictable verbs are as follows:

1.	infinitive	↔	non-past
	-овать	↔	-уют

You have had three such verbs:

рисова́ть, рису́ют (НС) 'draw'
нарисова́ть, -рису́ют (С) 'draw'
интересова́ться, интересу́ются (НС) 'be interested in'

The one seeming exception to this rule is здоро́ваться 'greet (one another)', which occurs in the Text of this lesson. The 3 Pl. is здоро́ваются (not -уют). The reason is that the sequence -ова- as it occurs in this word is not the suffix -ова, but part of the root здоро́в 'healthy'.

2.	infinitive	↔	non-past
	-нуть	↔	-нут

You have had two such verbs:

верну́ть, верну́т (С) 'return (something)'
верну́ться, верну́тся (С)'return, come back'

3.	infinitive	↔	non-past
	-ывать	↔	-ывают

You have had five such verbs:

называ́ть, называ́ют (НС) 'call, name'
открыва́ть, открыва́ют (НС) 'open'
разгова́ривать, разгова́ривают (НС) 'talk, converse'
спра́шивать, спра́шивают (НС) 'ask, inquire'
расска́зывать, расска́зывают (НС) 'tell (narrate)'

4.	non-past	→	infinitive
	-ают	→	-ать

Example: зна́ют → зна́ть

Note that you cannot predict in the other direction: an infinitive in
-ать will not always match up with a non-past in -ают . For example, the
non-past of лежа́ть is лежа́т (not -ают); писа́ть is пи́шут (not -ают);
рисова́ть is рису́ют (not -ают).

You have met the following verbs of the -ают → -ать type:

де́лать, де́лают (НС)	do; make
сде́лать, сде́лают (С)	do; make
изуча́ть, изуча́ют (НС)	study
гуля́ть, гуля́ют (НС)	walk; stroll
ду́мать, ду́мают (НС)	think
занима́ться, занима́ются (НС)	study, be busy (with)
игра́ть, игра́ют (НС)	play
конча́ться, конча́ются (НС)	end
начина́ться, начина́ются (НС)	start
ошиба́ться, ошиба́ются (НС)	be mistaken
рабо́тать, рабо́тают (НС)	work
руга́ться, руга́ются (НС)	swear, curse
зна́ть, зна́ют (НС)	know
понима́ть, понима́ют (НС)	understand
чита́ть, чита́ют (НС)	read
прочита́ть, прочита́ют (С)	read
отвеча́ть, отвеча́ют (НС)	answer
повторя́ть, повторя́ют (НС)	repeat
приглаша́ть, приглаша́ют (НС)	invite
разреша́ть, разреша́ют (НС)	permit

The verb дава́ть даю́т (НС) is an exception to this rule, as are all prefixed forms of this verb:

задава́ть, задаю́т (НС)	ask (a question)
передава́ть, передаю́т (НС)	pass; broadcast
преподава́ть, преподаю́т (НС)	teach

(Do not confuse these Imperfectives with their Perfective partners да́ть, зада́ть,
переда́ть— all having the irregular non-past да́м, да́шь,etc.)

There are only two other exceptions to this rule, -става́ть and -знава́ть,
which you will meet later.

5.

non-past	→	infinitive
-еют	→	-еть

You have met only one such verb:

краснеть, краснеют   blush, turn red

Note that this rule works only in the direction -еют → -еть ; you cannot
predict in the other direction, because an infinitive in -еть may be like
смотре́ть, смо́трят (not -еют).

Exceptions to this rule are rare.

6.

infinitive	→	non-past
- V -ить	→	-ят

Example: говори́ть → говоря́т   speak, talk, say

The -V- in this formula stands for a stem vowel, i.e., the prediction won't work for monosyllables like пить, пьют 'to drink' or for prefixed monosyllables.like выпить, выпьют 'to drink up', where the vowel is part of a prefix (вы-), not the stem.

In the course of time you will learn to recognize the prefixes of Russian verbs; there are about 15 common ones, most of them identical to prepositions. In the following list of polysyllabic -ить verbs we put a hyphen between the prefix and the root so that you can identify the prefixes and see how the prediction rule works. We also print the 1 Sg. of these verbs so that you can see the consonant alternation and stress pattern.

учить, учат, учу (НС)	teach
вы-учить, выучат, выучу (С)	learn
на-учить, научат, научу (С)	teach
звонить, звонят, звоню (НС)	phone
по-звонить, позвонят, позвоню (С)	phone
по-ложить, положат, положу (С)	put (lying)
просить, просят, прошу (НС)	ask (request)
по-просить, попросят, попрошу (С)	ask (request)
с-просить, спросят, спрошу (С)	ask (inquire)
ставить, ставят, ставлю (НС)	put (standing)
по-ставить, поставят, поставлю (С)	put (standing)
пред-ставить, представят, представлю (С)	introduce
при-гласить, пригласят, приглашу (С)	invite
раз-решить, разрешат, разрешу (С)	permit
кончиться, кончатся, кончусь (С)	end
по-знакомиться, познакомятся, познакомлюсь (С)	get acquainted
нравиться, нравятся, нравлюсь (НС)	appeal to (like)
по-нравиться, понравятся, понравлюсь (С)	appeal to (like)
по-вторить, повторят, повторю (С)	repeat
любить, любят, люблю (НС)	like, love
бес-покоиться, беспокоятся, беспокоюсь (С)	be disturbed
ходить, ходят, хожу (НС)	go
на-ходиться, находятся, нахожусь (НС)	be located
говорить, говорят, говорю	talk, say, tell
пере-водить, переводят, перевожу (НС)	translate
от-водить, отводят, отвожу (НС)	take (lead) off to
родиться, родятся, рожусь (С)	be born
от-ветить, ответят, отвечу (С)	answer

There are very few exceptions to this rule; you have met one of them:

ошибиться, ошибутся; ошибся, ошиблась (С)	be mistaken

With very rare exceptions predictable verbs of all types are stem-stressed in the past tense. The one exception you've met is:

родиться, -ятся, -жусь; родился, родилась, родились (С)	be born

More about stress in section 2.4 below.

Summary of Prediction Rules

Rule	Example
1. -овать ↔ -уют	рисова́ть ↔ рису́ют
2. -нуть ↔ -нут	верну́ть ↔ верну́т
3. -ывать ↔ -ывают	открыва́ть ↔ открыва́ют
4. -ают → -ать	зна́ют → зна́ть
5. -еют → -еть	красне́ют → красне́ть
6. -V-ить → -ят	говори́ть → говоря́т

Practice 5

*Cover all but the left-hand column. All the infinitives
listed here are of predictable types. Say the 3 Pl., 1 Sg.
and past feminine, e.g.* говори́ть → говоря́т говорю́
говори́ла. *Then translate; remember to translate Perfective non-past as future tense in English. Watch out for
stress: the* -ить *verbs are tricky in this respect.*

звони́ть	-ня́т	-ню́	-ни́ла
позвони́ть	-ня́т	-ню́	-ни́ла
открыва́ть	-ва́ют	-ва́ю	-ва́ла
рисова́ть	-су́ют	-су́ю	-сова́ла
спроси́ть	-́сят	-шу́	-си́ла
поста́вить	-́вят	-влю́	-́вила
положи́ть	-́жат	-жу́	-жи́ла
верну́ть	-ну́т	-ну́	-ну́ла
верну́ться	-ну́тся	-ну́сь	-ну́лась
расска́зывать	-́зывают	-́зываю	-́зывала
разгова́ривать	-́ривают	-́риваю	-́ривала
нарисова́ть	-су́ют	-су́ю	-сова́ла
интересова́ться	-су́ются	-су́юсь	-сова́лась
спра́шивать	-́шивают	-́шиваю	-́шивала
ходи́ть	-́дят	-жу́	-ди́ла
люби́ть	-́бят	-блю́	-би́ла
отве́тить	-́тят	-́чу	-́тила
переводи́ть	-́дят	-жу́	-ди́ла

2.4 Past and non-past stems: non-predictable verbs

We list here all the non-predictable verbs you have met so far. They are listed by conjugation. Irregular verbs are excluded (see section 2.1 above). The abbreviation ОН (<u>однонаправленный</u>) means "One-way verb".)

Conjugation I

брáть берýт; бралá брáли (НС)	take
бы́ть бýдут; былá бы́ли	be
взя́ть возьмýт; взялá взя́ли (С)	take
давáть даю́т давай!	give
Similarly: задавáть	ask (a question)
передавáть	pass; broadcast
преподавáть	teach
éхать éдут (НС/ОН)	go (by vehicle)
жи́ть живýт; жилá жи́ли (НС)	live
звáть зовýт; звалá звáли (НС)	call
идти́ идýт; шёл шлá шли́ (НС/ОН)	go
клáсть кладýт; клáла (НС)	put (lying)
казáться кáжутся кажýсь (НС)	seem
Similarly: сказáть скáжут скажý (С)	tell, say
рассказáть (С)	tell (narrate)
мóчь мóгут могý; мóг моглá могли́(НС)	can, be able
начáться начнýтся; начался́ началáсь начали́сь (С)	start
отвести́ отведýт; отвёл отвелá отвели́ (С)	take (lead) off to
Similarly: перевести́ (С)	translate
откры́ть открою́т (С)	open
ошиби́ться ошибýтся; оши́бся оши́блась	be mistaken
писáть пи́шут (НС)	write
Similarly: написáть (С)	write
пи́ть пью́т; пилá пи́ли (НС)	drink
Similarly: вы́пить вы́пьют; вы́пила (С)	drink
пойти́ пойдýт; пошёл пошлá пошли́ (С)	go

Conjugation II

There are only two kinds of non-predictable second conjugation verbs: one has an infinitive in -еть the other in -ать/-ять . The ending -ать/-ять occurs only after ч ж ш щ   or vowel letter, the ending -еть after other consonants.

ви́деть ви́дят ви́жу (НС)	see
Similarly: уви́деть (С)	see
смотрéть смóтрят смотрю́ (НС)	look
сидéть сидя́т сижý (НС)	sit
лежáть лежáт лежý (НС)	lie
слы́шать слы́шат слы́шу (НС)	hear
стоя́ть стоя́т стою́ (НС)	stand

2.5 Stress prediction rule

If a verb consists of more than one syllable (excluding prefixes) you can predict the stress pattern from the two citation forms (the infinitive and 3 Pl.).

Non-past Rule:

If the stress falls on different syllables, the non-past will have Movable stress (M).

писа́ть   пи́шут
я   пишу́
ты пи́шешь
он пи́шет
мы пи́шем
вы пи́шете
они пи́шут

Compare verbs with stress on the *same* syllable:

говори́ть говоря́т	ви́деть ви́дят
я говорю́	я ви́жу
ты говори́шь	ты ви́дишь
он говори́т	он ви́дит
мы говори́м	мы ви́дим
вы говори́те	вы ви́дите
они говоря́т	они ви́дят

Past Rule:

Stress falls on the same syllable in the past as in the infinitive.

E.g.,   писа́ть пи́шут → писа́ла
         говори́ть говоря́т → говори́ла
         ви́деть ви́дят → ви́дела

(These rules won't work for monosyllables. In general, beware of monosyllabic verb stems: most of them are non-predictable with regard to both stem changes and stress patterns.)

Despite the reliability of these rules (and despite the reliability of the 1 Sg. consonant alternation rules for Conjugation II verbs), we will continue to cite the 1 Sg. in Active Word Lists and in the Active Word Index at the back of the book; we will do this for all Conjugation II verbs and for all Conjugation I verbs that have pattern M in the non-past.

Practice 6

Go back to Practice 5 and cover up the third column. Look at the first two columns (infinitive and 3 Pl.) and say the 1 Sg. aloud. You should be able to predict the stress in all these verbs. Note that verbs in -овáть regularly have stress on the syllable -ý- in all forms of the non-past.

2.6 -ся verbs

The suffix -ся/сь means that the verb is intransitive. Most verbs that have -ся occur also without -ся , in which case they are transitive. Listed below are useful pairs of such verbs. New partners are marked with *.

Transitive (Acc. object or infinitive)   *Intransitive (No Acc. object)*

вернýть, вернýт (C) return (something) Óн вернýл *кнúгу*.	вернýться, вернýтся (C) return (come/go back) Óн вернýлся из Москвы́.
*интересовáть, -сýют (НС) interest somebody Это *меня́* интересýет.	интересовáться, -сýются (НС) be interested in something Я э́тим интересýюсь. (э́тим = Inst.)
*начинáть, -áют (НС) begin, start (something) Óн начинáет *рабóту*.	начинáться, -áются (НС) begin, start Рабóта начинáется сегóдня.

*начáть, -нýт; нáчал,
  началá, нáчали (C)
begin, start (something)
Óн зáвтра начнёт *рабóтать*.
	начáться, -нýтся; началcя́, -áсь,
	  -úсь (C)
	begin, start
	Рабóта начнётся зáвтра.

*кончáть, -áют (НС) finish (something) Óн кончáет свою́ *рабóту*.	кончáться, -áются (НС) end, be finished Рабóта кончáется сегóдня.
*кóнчить, ⌐чат, ⌐чу (C) finish (something) Óн кóнчил свою́ *рабóту*.	*кóнчиться, ⌐чатся, ⌐чусь (C) end, be finished Рабóта кóнчилась.
*познакóмить, ⌐мят, ⌐млю (C) acquaint Óн *нáс* вчерá познакóмил.	познакóмиться, ⌐мятся, ⌐млюсь (C) get acquainted Мы́ вчерá познакóмились.
*беспокóить, -óят, -óю (НС) disturb Я́ *вáс* беспокóю?	беспокóиться, -óятся, -óюсь (НС) be disturbed Я́ óчень беспокóюсь.

Note the difference in the translation of учи́ть and учи́ться :

учи́ть, -́чат, -чу́ (НС)   учи́ться, -́чатся, -чу́сь (НС)
teach   study, pursue a course of studies
Ле́на учи́ла Зю́зю чита́ть.   Где́ вы́ у́читесь?

The following verbs have occurred only with -ся ; variants without -ся either don't exist or have different meanings.

нра́виться   (НС)
понра́виться (С)   appeal to, like (with Dative)
занима́ться (НС)   study, be busy with (with Inst.)
находи́ться (НС)   be located
роди́ться   (С)   be born
каза́ться   (НС)   seem

Recall the rule for -ся *vs.* -сь :   -ся after consonant, -сь after vowel, e.g.,

past: верну́ться
              верну́лся *верну́лась, верну́лись, верну́лось*

non-past: *верну́сь*   вернёмся
              вернёшься   *вернётесь*
              вернётся   верну́тся

Practice 7

Cover the following translations. Write a translation of the sentences at the beginning of this section. Then check your answers. Be sure to translate non-past Perfectives as future tense in English.

Transitive	*Intransitive*
He returned the book.	He returned (came back).
That interests me.	I'm interested in that.
He's starting (beginning) work.	Work starts (begins) today.
He'll start working tomorrow.	Work starts tomorrow.
He's finishing his work.	Work ends today.
He finished his work.	The work is finished.
He acquainted us (=introduced) yesterday.	We met (got acquainted) yesterday.
Am I (not) disturbing you?	I'm very disturbed.
Lena taught Zyuzya to read.	Where do you study (=go to school)?

2.7 Summary: alphabetical reference list of verbs.

This list includes verbs from Dialogs 1-8, plus those introduced in Analyses.

беспоко́ить -о́ят -о́ю НС
беспоко́иться -о́ятся -о́юсь НС
бра́ть беру́т; брала́ бра́ли НС
бы́ть бу́дут С
верну́ть С
верну́ться С
взя́ть возьму́т; взяла́ взя́ли С
ви́деть -дят -жу НС
вы́пить -пьют; вы́пила С
вы́учить вы́учат -у С
говори́ть -ря́т -рю́ НС
гуля́ть -я́ют НС
дава́ть даю́т дава́й! НС
да́ть да́м да́шь да́ст дади́м дади́те
  даду́т да́й!; дала́ да́ли С
де́лать -ают НС
ду́мать -ают НС
е́сть е́м е́шь е́ст еди́м еди́те
  едя́т е́шь!; е́ла НС
е́хать е́дут НС/ОН
жи́ть живу́т; жила́ жи́ли НС
задава́ть -даю́т дава́й! НС
зада́ть (= дать); за́дал задала́
  за́дали С
занима́ться -а́ются НС
зва́ть зову́т; звала́ зва́ли НС
звони́ть -ня́т -ню́ НС
зна́ть -а́ют НС
игра́ть -а́ют НС
идти́ иду́т; шёл шла́ шли́ НС/ОН
извини́ть -ня́т -ню́ С
изуча́ть -а́ют НС
интересова́ть НС
интересова́ться НС
каза́ться ка́жутся НС
кла́сть кладу́т; кла́ла НС
конча́ть -а́ют НС
конча́ться -а́ются НС
ко́нчить -чат -чу С
ко́нчиться -чатся -чусь С
красне́ть -е́ют НС
лежа́ть -жа́т -жу́ НС
люби́ть -бят -блю́ НС
мо́чь мо́гут могу́; мо́г могла́
  могли́ НС
надое́сть (= есть) С
называ́ть -а́ют НС
написа́ть -пи́шут -шу́ С
нарисова́ть С
научи́ть нау́чат -чу́ С
находи́ться -дятся -жу́сь НС
нача́ть -ну́т; на́чал начала́ на́чали С
нача́ться начну́тся; начался́
  начала́сь начали́сь С
начина́ть -а́ют НС
начина́ться -а́ются НС
нра́виться -вятся -влюсь НС

отвести́ -веду́т; -вёл -вела́ -вели́ С
отве́тить -тят -чу С
отвеча́ть -а́ют НС
отводи́ть -дят -жу́ НС
открыва́ть -а́ют НС
откры́ть -кро́ют С
ошиба́ться -а́ются НС
ошиби́ться -бу́тся; оши́бся оши́блась С
перевести́ -веду́т; вёл вела́ вели́ С
переводи́ть -во́дят -жу́ НС
передава́ть -даю́т -дава́й! НС
переда́ть (= дать); пе́редал
  передала́ пе́редали С
писа́ть пи́шут -шу́ НС
пи́ть пью́т пе́й!; пила́ пи́ли НС
повтори́ть -ря́т -рю́ С
повторя́ть -я́ют НС
позвони́ть-ня́т -ню́ С
познако́мить -мят -млю С
познако́миться -мятся -млюсь С
пойти́ пойду́т; пошёл -шла́ -шли́ С
положи́ть -жат -жу́ С
понима́ть -а́ют НС
понра́виться -вятся -влюсь С
попроси́ть -сят -шу́ С
поста́вить -вят -влю С
предста́вить -вят -влю С
преподава́ть -даю́т -дава́й! НС
пригласи́ть -сят -шу́ С
приглаша́ть -а́ют НС
проси́ть -сят -шу́ НС
прочита́ть -а́ют С
рабо́тать -ают НС
разгова́ривать НС
разреша́ть -а́ют НС
разреши́ть -ша́т -шу́ С
рассказа́ть -ска́жут -жу́ С
расска́зывать НС
рисова́ть НС
роди́ться -дятся -жу́сь; роди́лся
  родила́сь роди́ли́сь С/НС
руга́ться -а́ются НС
сде́лать -ают С
сиде́ть -дят -жу́ НС
сказа́ть ска́жут -жу́ С
слы́шать -шат НС
смотре́ть -ря́т -рю́ НС
спра́шивать НС
спроси́ть -сят -шу́ С
ста́вить -вят -влю НС
стоя́ть стоя́т стою́ НС
съе́сть (= есть) С
уви́деть -ят -жу С
учи́ть у́чат учу́ НС
ходи́ть -дят -жу́ НС
хоте́ть хочу́ хо́чешь хо́чет хоти́м
  хоти́те хотя́т НС
чита́ть -а́ют НС

3.   Review of prepositions: spatial relationships

The preposition series в/в/из , на/на/с, and у/к/от were discussed
in Lessons 4.3.3 and 7.5. Here we will add some information on the series
у/к/от and introduce some additional prepositions to fill out the picture
('over, alongside, in front, behind').

The series у/к/от has been used, thus far, with people:

у жены́	*at* my wife('s place)
к жене́	*to* my wife('s place)
от жены́	*from* my wife('s place)

When these prepositions are used with things rather than people, they have
similar meanings but different English translations:

у окна́	*by* the window
к окну́	*towards* the window
от окна́	*away from* the window

Examples:

О́н стоя́л у окна́.	He was standing by the window.
О́н шёл к окну́.	He was walking toward the window.
О́н шёл от окна́.	He was walking away from the window.

The new prepositions are:

из-под + Gen.	out from under
ря́дом с + Inst.	alongside
пе́ред + Inst.	in front of
позади́ + Gen.	behind

Examples:

О́н взя́л стака́н из-под стола́.	He took the glass out from under the table.
Ла́мпа стои́т ря́дом со столо́м.	The lamp is alongside the table.
О́н стои́т перед столо́м.	He's standing in front of the table.
О́н стои́т позади́ стола́.	He's standing behind the table.

All of the spatial relationships you've studied thus far are presented
below in a diagram. To help you learn the cases that follow these prepositions it may be worthwhile noting certain generalizations:

(1)   Motion to a goal is Accusative (except for к + Dative): в, на, под
(2)   Motion away from a source is Genitive: с, из, от, из-под
(3)   The locations are varied:

в, на	plus Prepositional
под, ря́дом с, пе́ред	plus Instrumental
у, позади́	plus Genitive

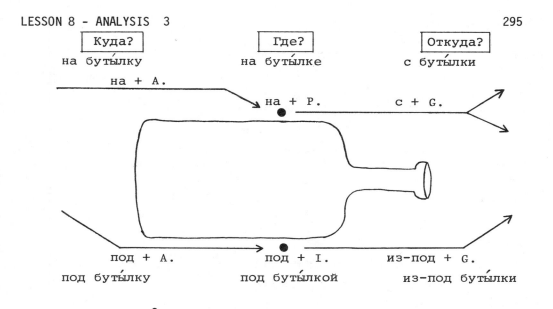

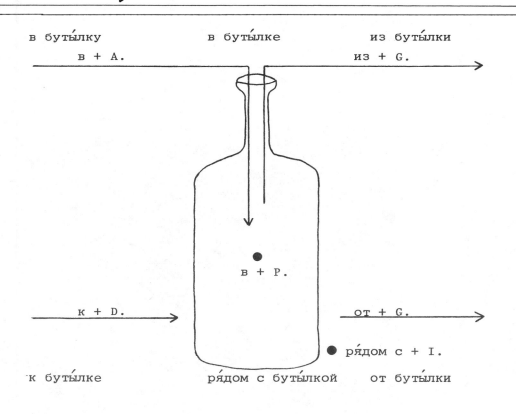

Examples (all with masculine / neuter nouns):

1. в го́роде   в го́род   из го́рода

2. { на столе́   на сто́л   со стола́ }
    { на восто́ке   на восто́к   с восто́ка }

3. { у окна́   к окну́   от окна́ }
    { у бра́та   к бра́ту   от бра́та }

4. под столо́м   под сто́л   из-под стола́

5. ря́дом со столо́м

6. перед столо́м

7. позади́ стола́

Translations:

1. in the city   in to the city   from/out of the city

2. { up on the table   on to the table   **from** off the table }
    { in the east   to the east   from the east }

3. { by the window   towards the window   away from the window }
    { at(my) brother's   to(my) brother's   from(my) brother's }

4. under the table   under the table   from under the table

5. alongside the table

6. in front of the table

7. behind the table

Wedding Palace No. 1. Division of ZAGS (Bureau of Statistics).
Перерыв is lunch break. Выходные are days off.

1. Review. Какой vs. который = question word vs. joining word.

   Insert the proper form of the proper one of these words. Translate.

   1. Врач, _____ я хожу, живёт в этом доме.

   2. К _____ врачу ты ходишь?

   3. К врачу, о _____ я тебе говорил.

   4. Студент, с _____ я люблю разговаривать, пьёт вино прямо из бутылки.

   5. О _____ студенте ты говоришь?

   6. Я говорю о студенте, _____ пьёт прямо из бутылки.

   7. _____ студентам дадут по яблоку?

   8. Всем студентам, _____ хорошо играют на флейте, дадут по яблоку.

   9. Студент, _____ знает папа, опять играет на флейте.

   10. Студент, _____ знает папу, опять играет на флейте.

   Repeat items 4-10 substituting студентка for студент.

2. Review. Prepositions.

   Read these sentences aloud, inserting the proper preposition. Translate.

   1. Студенты сидели вместе _____ столом.

   2. Северная Каролина находится _____ северу _____ Южной Каролины.

   3. Это письмо _____ Петра Ивановича.

   4. Откуда твой брат? Он _____ Ленинграда.

   5. Куда ты идёшь? Я иду _____ Петру Ивановичу.

   6. Откуда ты идёшь? _____ Петра Ивановича.

   7. Где ты был? _____ Петра Ивановича.

   8. Где он живёт? _____ востоке.

3. Review of Genitive Plural.

   П: По-моему, у вас на столе лежат *мои письма*.
   С: Вы ошибаетесь. У меня на столе нет *ваших писем*.

   Substitute for мои письма (be sure to change лежат to лежит when the subject is singular): мой словарь, мой карандаш, мой медвежонок, моя ложка, моя вилка, моя тарелка, моя ручка, мои бумаги, моя газета.
   You may continue by going around the room and making substitutions from the nouns you know.

4. Review: the compass.

Substitute the points of the compass in this sentence.

Ве́тер за́втра у́тром бу́дет с *се́вера*.

Now do the same in the following:

На́ш го́род нахо́дится к *се́веру* от Босто́на.

5. Dialog 1, Dialog Comment 2. Review Fem. II nouns.

П: Мо́жно ва́м зада́ть вопро́с?
С: Пожа́луйста. Я́ с удово́льствием отве́чу на ва́ш вопро́с.
П: Како́го ро́да сло́во *но́чь*?
С: Сло́во *но́чь* — же́нского ро́да.
П: У меня́ ещё оди́н вопро́с.
С: Пожа́луйста.
П: Ка́к бу́дет твори́тельный паде́ж э́того существи́тельного?
С: *Но́чью.*

Substitute: ве́щь, но́ж, де́нь, о́сень, до́ждь, но́вость, го́сть,
мать, медве́дь, учи́тель, преподава́тель, до́чь, слова́рь

6. Reading Practice. Dialog 1, Dialog Comment 2.

Practice reading this poem until you can read it smoothly. Lines 1 and 3
have two beats, and lines 2 and 4 have three. Translate. (The word слон
means 'elephant'.)

Написа́л я по письму́
Са́ше, Ма́ше, и слону́.
Мне отве́тили письмо́м
Са́ша, Ма́ша,...но не сло́н.

7. Dialog Comment 2.

Substitute for X in the sentence 'I answered X'. Watch the word order:
pronouns normally come *before* the verb.

Я́ отве́тил(а) _____.

your question	her letter
your brother	her sister
his brother	her
him	them
you	their question

Now put the sentence in the future, and substitute мы́ and они́ for я́:

Я́ отве́чу _____.

8.   Plurals: Analysis 1.4.

П: Почему *этот учитель* всегда ругается?
С: Я не знаю. Другие учителя так не делают.

Substitute: Этот врач, этот господин, этот гражданин, этот
медвежонок, твой муж, твоя жена, твоя сестра, профессор,
преподаватель, этот гость, этот студент.

9.   Case review.

Put the word in parentheses in the right form.

1.   Когда я шёл в университет, я увидел ____ и ____.
     (медведь) (медведица)
2.   ____ хорошо жить в этой стране? (кто)
3.   Я разговаривал с твоим ____. (отец)
4.   Мне ____ ваш адрес. (нужно)
5.   У меня нет ____. (сёстры)
6.   Все здесь интересуются ____. (ваши дела)
7.   Мы написали ____. (ваши преподаватели)
8.   Они пошли в ____. (город)
9.   О ____ вы говорите? (кто)
10. Я дал ____ все книги, которые она попросила. (она)

10. Dialog 3, Dialog Comment 10.

Substitute:

     Мне надоел( ) _____.

эти гости   этот гость
эта книга   эти вопросы
это вино   эти упражнения
эта икра   это упражнение

Make the above substitutions, plus the ones below, in the following sentence; note that you use очень (not много) to render the meaning 'a lot,
very much' in this expression.

     Мне очень понравил( )ся/-сь _____.

этот фильм   твой папа
твой концерт   твоя мама
твоя пьеса   твоё письмо
твой профессор   твой письма

11. Family names. Analysis 1.5.

П: Маша, спросите Сашу о *Бородине*.
М: Саша, ты знаешь *Бородина*?
С: Нет, я с *Бородиным* не знаком. Я с *ним* только разговаривал
     по телефону.

Substitute: Иванов, Иванова, Ивановы, Петров, Петрова, Петровы,
Ильин, Ильина, Ильины, братья Карамазовы.

12. Names. Analysis 1.5. Practice in declension of family names.

Fill in the blanks with the correct form of the names, first the
woman, then the man.

(Вера Ивановна Бородина
(Михаил Иванович Бородин) работает у нас в институте. Вы знаете
_____? Нет? А я с _____ часто разговариваю по телефону.
Каждый раз, когда мне плохо, я звоню _____ и говорю 'Мне плохо'.
А _____ мне отвечает 'Это хорошо, что тебе плохо'. Каждый
раз, когда мне хорошо, я тоже звоню _____. Разговаривать с
_____ очень весело. Я не понимаю, как это может быть, что ты
не знаешь _____. Я обязательно познакомлю тебя с _____. Приходи
ко мне в институт, я тебе представлю _____.

13. Conversation. Dialogs 1-3.

(a) Translate.

I met Professor Borodina last night. How did you like her? A lot.
I heard of her, but I don't know what she teaches. Where's she from?
Is she married? What's she interested in? The accusative case. And
other cases too? Yes, all the others ('remaining'). Even the instrumental.
In what language? Russian. How come (откуда) you know so much about
her? I don't know much (='I know little') about her. I'd like to meet
her. I'll introduce you to her. Maybe she'll invite you to dinner.

(b) A and B discuss C, a professor of the Russian language. Then C arrives
on the scene and introductions are make. For variation, C can be a
well-known person or a classmate.

14. Analysis 2.1: consonant alternation с/ш.

Watch out for the word order: pronouns come before the verb (lines 3 and
4). Note: нет еще = 'not yet'. The main stress is on нет.

П: Маша, спросите Сашу, он пригласил Наташу?
М: Саша, ты пригласил *Наташу* на обед?
С: Нет еще. Я *её* завтра приглашу.
М: Не беспокойся, *её* пригласит папа.

Substitute names (masc. and fem.) and plurals: гости, профессора,
студенты, врачи....

15. Dialogs 2, 3; Comment 8.

   П: Са́ша, скажи́те Ма́ше, что вы́ хоти́те *пойти́ в кино́* с Ната́шей.
   С: Ма́ша, я́ бы хоте́л *пойти́ в кино́* с Ната́шей.
   М: А что́ е́сли она́ не хо́чет с тобо́й *идти́ в кино́?*
   С: Тогда́ я́ её приглашу́ *пойти́ в теа́тр.*

   Substitute: the alternative activity in the last speech can either be
      invented or be selected from this list.

   П: ...пойти́ в институ́т с (name of classmate)
     ...занима́ться вини́телным падежо́м с ....
     ...игра́ть на фле́йте с ...
     ...гуля́ть по па́рку с ...
     ...е́сть ка́шу с ...
     ...говори́ть о матема́тике с ...
     ...рисова́ть портре́ты с ...
     ...преподава́ть в шко́ле с ...
     ...смотре́ть фи́льм с ...
     ...говори́ть по-ру́сски с ...
     ...пи́ть вино́ с ...

16. Irregular verb practice. Analysis 2.1

   Я́ да́м Ми́ше я́блоко, и о́н его́ съе́ст.

     Repeat, replacing я́ with ты́, о́н, мы́, вы́, они́.

   Я́ не хочу́ дава́ть Ми́ше я́блоко, о́н его́ съе́ст.

     Repeat, replacing я́ with о́н, мы́, они́.

   Да́й *мне́* я́блоко, я́ его́ съе́м.

     Repeat, replacing мне́ with на́м, е́й, ему́, и́м.

17. More irregular verb practice: Analysis 2.1.

   А: Кто́ е́ст мою́ чёрную икру́?
   Б: *Мы́* еди́м твою́ чёрную икру́.
   А: Почему́ *вы́* еди́те мою́ чёрную икру́?
   Б: Что хоти́м, то́ и де́лаем.

    The last sentence means 'We do whatever we please,' literally, 'What
(we) want, that (we) do'. Replace мы́ with я́, Шу́ра, Шу́ра и Юра,
Генера́л Петро́в, врачи́, учителя́, Зо́рина жена́, ната́шин му́ж. The
pronoun вы́ in line 3 should change accordingly, and the verbs in line four must
be changed.

18. Verb forms. Analysis 2.2 and 2.3.

     Regular verb practice: predictables. Make the following sentences past tense. Mark stress. Translate.

Что они делают?
С кем они разговаривают?
Мы интересуемся вашими делами.
Я работаю в этом институте.
Мы вернёмся к вам.
Профессора у нас всегда ругаются.
Почему вы краснеете?
Мы занимаемся русским языком.
Лена гуляет в парке.

19. Analysis 2.2 and 2.3.

     Regular verb practice: Predictables. Make the following sentences non-past, then translate. Remember that the non-past of perfective verbs translates as future.

Они говорили с нами.
Мы вернулись с севера.
Они часто ходили в парк.
Мы переводили эту книгу.
Мы познакомились с генералом Петровым.
Мы не интересовались вашими делами.
Я вернула все книги в библиотеку.

Занятия кончились.
Мама очень беспокоилась о нас.
Кто позвонил врачу?
Я выучил все эти слова.

20. Dialogs 4 and 5.

     Go around the class as fast as you can, with each student saying the next higher numeral.

П: Скажите, пожалуйста, какое сегодня число?
1: Сегодня первое ноября.
2: А я думал, что сегодня второе ноября.
3: А я думал, что сегодня третье ноября.
4: ...

Now do the same with the following:

(а) П: Скажите, пожалуйста, какой урок нам задали на сегодня?
1: Нам задали первый урок.
2: А я думала, что нам задали второй урок.
3: ...

(б) П: Скажите, пожалуйста, какой сегодня день?
1: Сегодня понедельник.
2: А я думала, что сегодня вторник.
3: ...

(в) П: Скажите, пожалуйста, в каком месяце была октябрьская революция?
1: По-моему, октябрьская революция была в октябре.
2: А по-моему она была в ноябре.
3: А по-моему она была в декабре.
4: ...

21. Non-predictable practice. Analysis 2.4.

> Translate the following sentences, transform to past tense.

> Мы пишем письма нашим родителям.
> Мы пьём вино.
> Я скажу тебе всю правду.
> Я расскажу тебе о мойх родителях.
> Я возьму эту книгу в библиотеке.
> Он кладёт секретные бумаги на стол.
> Он берёт все книги в университетской библиотеке.
> Они откроют дверь.
> Мои сёстры съедят всю икру.
> Мои братья нам дадут словари.
> Когда ему надоест жить в этой стране?
> Как вы живёте?

22. Analysis 2.

> П: Смотри! Они *занимаются русским языком*.
> С: Я тоже хочу *заниматься русским языком*.

> читают советские газеты, играют на флейте, разговаривают с учителем, гуляют по парку, звонят по телефону, едят горячую кашу, открывают дверь, дают урок, пьют вино, смотрят кино, рисуют карандашом, кладут деньги в банк, пишут письма, переводят письма.

23. Analysis 2.

(a) Read aloud and translate.

> Я часто кладу ложки на стол.
> Я часто беру книги в библиотеке.
> Я часто даю сестре яблоки.
> Я часто пишу письма.
> Я часто ем яблоки.

(b) Now change я to он, then они.

(c) Now change to *future* imperfective:

> Я буду писать письма.

(d) Now change to future *perfective*. When you do so, change the object to singular, e.g.,

> Я завтра напишу письмо.

24. Going by vehicle. Dialog 6, Comments 13, 14.

(a) Answer in the affirmative.

    П: Ма́ша, вы́ е́дете на по́чту?
    М: Да́, я _____.
    П: А Са́ша?
    М: О́н то́же е́дет. Мы́ всё е́дем на по́чту.
    П: Ната́ша, кто́ е́дет на по́чту?
    Н: Они́, ка́жется, всё е́дут.

    Similarly:

       Вы́ е́дете на конце́рт?
              в теа́тр?
              на рабо́ту?
              на заво́д?
              в рестора́н?

(b) Repeat, using the verb идти́ иду́т 'on foot'.

(c) Repeat, mixing up е́хать е́дут and идти́ иду́т.

25. More going. Dialog 6.

(a) Say 'They are going to X', making the substitutions below. If X is a
city, country, or part of a country, go by vehicle; otherwise, assume
it's nearby and go on foot.

    Они́ е́дут/иду́т в/на _____.

по́чта	конце́рт
заво́д	рабо́та
теа́тр	Аме́рика
Москва́	фа́брика
за́пад	Сове́тский Сою́з
Ленингра́д	рестора́н

(b) Now change to past tense е́хали/шли́ 'were going'.

26. Conversation.   Dialog 7.

(a) Translate:

> Yesterday it rained. Yesterday morning it was cold. The wind was from the north. Today it is warm. Tomorrow afternoon it will be hot. Tomorrow night it will be cold again. The (= next) it will be hot. Every day it will rain. Even on Saturday. Maybe on Wednesday, too. It will probably be sunny.

(b) You are a TV weatherperson. Announce what day and date it is. Summarize the past weather and prognosticate the future, according to this chart of the thermometer, sky and weathervane:

	вчера́	сего́дня	за́втра
у́тро			
де́нь			
ве́чер			
но́чь			

27. Analysis 2.

(a) The following activities happened yesterday. They weren't finished— note
the imperfective verbs. Translate. Then say them as though you will
get them done tomorrow. Use perfective future. Then translate. Note
that the Perfective verb sometimes translates simply as 'finish'.

> Model: Вчера́ я́ чита́ла кни́гу. →   ...прочита́ю...
>   Вчера́ я́ писа́л письмо́.   *напишу*
>   Вчера́ я́ де́лала упражне́ния.   *сделаю*
>   Вчера́ я́ звони́ла Петру́ Петро́вичу. *позвоню*
>   Вчера́ я́ рисова́ла портре́т бра́та. *нарисую*
>   Вчера́ я́ е́ла ка́шу на обе́д.   *съеду*
>   Вчера́ я́ пи́л вино́.   *выпью*
>   Вчера́ я́ переводи́л письмо́ из Москвы́. *переведу*

(b) Take the same activities as in (a) and rephrase as though they will happen
again tomorrow — but you have no thought of finishing them. Use future
with бу́ду.

> Model: Вчера́ я́ чита́ла кни́гу. → ...бу́ду чита́ть...

28. Analysis 2.
(Perfective verbs).

> П: Я́ хочу́ *написа́ть письмо́ Ивано́ву.*
> С: Хоро́шая иде́я! Мы́ то́же *напи́шем.*

да́ть все́м студе́нтам по я́блоку, да́ть все́м студе́нтам по кни́ге,
верну́ться в Ленингра́д, переда́ть им приве́т, позвони́ть врачу́,
откры́ть две́рь, вы́учить слова́, написа́ть роди́телям, сказа́ть е́й
всю́ пра́вду.

29. Aspect pairs. Analysis 2.2.

(a) (Imperfective → Perfective past)

> П: Я́ *пишу́ письмо́ роди́телям.*
> С: А я́ уже́ *написа́л письмо́ роди́телям.*

звоню́ врачу́ по телефо́ну, рису́ю портре́т бра́та, расска́зываю
ма́ме о на́шем институ́те, пью́ вино́, беру́ кни́гу в библиоте́ке,
перевожу́ кни́гу.

(b) (Imperfective → Perfective future)

> П: Я́ *пишу́ письмо́ роди́телям.*
> С: А я́ за́втра *напишу́.*

     Use the same list as above. When you get proficient at it, substi-
tute other times for tonight, e.g., in the morning, afternoon, at night, etc.

30. More aspect pairs. Analysis 2.2.

П: Máша, спросúте Сáшу, óн *прочитáл всé газéты?*
М: Ты́ *прочитáл всé газéты?*
С: Нéт, я́ ещё *читáю.*
М: Когдá ты́ их *прочитáешь,* мы́ пойдём гуля́ть.

    Read and translate, noting the meaning of the aspects. Then replace the italicized phrase with the following:

откры́л буты́лку, вы́пил всё винó, вы́учил всé словá, кóнчил свóй делá, написáл родúтелям, перевёл всé пúсьма, рассказáл всéм о нáшем инститýте.

31. Analysis 3. Example of preposition usage.

    Read the following tale of Lenin's cap and translate it. Then ask and answer questions based on the drawings: where is Lenin, what's he doing, where's his cap, where did he put his cap, etc. Words marked with an asterisk are translated in the glossary below.

Кудá? Гдé ? Откýда?

   У *Владúмира* Ильичá Лéнина головá*былá большáя и ýмная*. Однáжды* *в гóлову* Лéнина пришлá* идéя* мировóй* революции*. *В головé* Лéнина эта идéя началá растú*. Когдá онá вы́росла*, онá вы́шла*из головы́ Лéнина и завоевáла* вéсь мúр*.

   На головé у Лéнина всегдá былá кéпка*. Когдá Лéнин шёл *в теáтр,* или *на завóд,* или *на собрáние** или *к женé,* óн всегдá надевáл *на гóлову* кéпку. И когдá óн уходúл* *из теáтра,* или *с завóда,* или *с собрáния,* или *от жены́,* óн всегдá надевáл *на гóлову* кéпку. Однáко*, когдá Лéнин бы́л *в теáтре,* или *на завóде,* или *на собрáнии,* или *у жены́,* óн снимáл* кéпку *с головы́.* Лéнин бы́л воспúтанный* человéк.

   Когдá Лéнин приходúл* *на собрáние,* он вставáл* *на стóл* и говорúл рéчь*. Кéпку óн клáл *на стóл* рядом с собóй*. Лéнин стоя́л *на столé* и говорúл рéчь, а кéпка лежáла *на столé* рядом с ним. Пóсле собрáния Лéнин спускáлся* *со столá,* брáл кéпку *со столá* и надевáл её *на гóлову.* Иногдá* Лéнин клáл кéпку *под стóл.* Лéнин стоя́л *на столé* и говорúл рéчь, а кéпка лежáла *под столóм.* Но пóсле собрáния Лéнин по-прéжнему* брáл кéпку *из-под столá* и надевáл её *на гóлову.*

   *На рисýнке** вы́ вúдите Лéнина. Вóт Лéнин стоúт и говорúт рéчь. *Перед Лéниным* большóе бýдущее*. *Позадú Лéнина* слáвное* прóшлое*. *В рукé* Лéнина кéпка, котóрую óн сня́л* *с головы́.* *В головé* Лéнина идéя мировóй революции.

Glossary.

голова́	head
у́мный	smart
одна́жды	once
пришла́ Past of прийти́ (С)	cóme into, arrive
иде́я	idea
мирово́й	world
револю́ция	revolution
расти́ (НС)	grow
вы́росла Past of вы́расти (С)	mature
вы́шла Past of вы́йти (С)	came out
завоева́ть (С)	conquer
ми́р	world
ке́пка	cap
собра́ние	meeting
надева́ть (I)	put on

Note: Translate this past tense, as well as the other Imperfective verbs in this and the next paragraph, with English *would*, e.g., 'he would always put on his cap.'

уходи́ть (I)	leave
одна́ко	however
снима́ть (I)	take off
воспи́танный	well-bred
приходи́ть (I)	come
встава́ть (I)	rise, get up
ре́чь	speech
собо́й Inst. of себя́	self
спуска́ться (I)	get down (off)
иногда́	sometimes
по-пре́жнему	as before
рису́нок	drawing
бу́дущее	future
сла́вный	glorious
про́шлое	past
сня́ть (Р)	take off

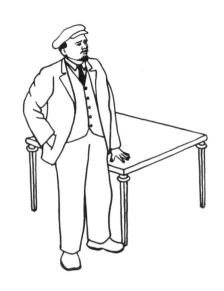

УРОК ДЕВЯТЫЙ

ТЕКСТ: ЧЕТВЕРГ УТРОМ: ЗЮЗЯ ИДЁТ ПОГУЛЯТЬ

(1) На следующее утро Зюзя встала рано. Всё в доме ещё спали. Зюзе не хотелось[1] ходить по квартире и шуметь, но в комнате ей было скучно. Она открыла окно и посмотрела вниз. Внизу на улице никого не было. Зюзя решила пойти погулять. Она уже[2] давно заметила, что ей совсем не трудно ходить по вертикальной стене. Она долго решала[3], куда ей пойти, вниз на улицу или наверх на крышу. Наконец она решила[3], что на улице она уже была, а на крыше ещё нет, и пошла наверх, на крышу.

Наверху, на крыше, было очень интересно. Зюзя увидела вокруг себя[4] много труб и телевизионных антенн, много котов и кошек. Зюзя поздоровалась с[5] котами и кошками и весело пошла вдоль[6] улицы. Она чувствовала себя[7] как дома. Когда она в следующий раз посмотрела вниз, она увидела внизу маленький сад[8]. В саду[8] стояли скамейки, росли деревья и кусты. На одной из скамеек сидела старушка и читала книгу. Рядом с ней маленький мальчик играл сам с собой[4] в мяч.

(2) Прямо под крышей, на которой сидела Зюзя, росло большое высокое дерево. Зюзя вспомнила свои уроки физкультуры в школе, глубоко вздохнула и прыгнула вниз. Она упала на дерево почти бесшумно, но мальчик всё-таки услышал и поднял голову. "Ой, бабушка," - сказал он - "посмотри, какая смешная тётя[9] на дереве сидит."

Старушка посмотрела наверх и уронила книгу.

"Не бойтесь," - быстро сказала Зюзя. - "Меня зовут Зюзя. Обо мне написали в сегодняшней газете."

"В какой газете?" - спросила старушка.

"В Правде," - ответила Зюзя.

"Я сегодняшнюю "Правду" ещё не видела," призналась старушка. - "Мы на "Известия" подписываемся, и на "Вечернюю Москву." А что о вас пишут?"

"Не знаю, я тоже сегодняшнюю газету ещё не читала," - сказала Зюзя, - "Мне директор сказал, что обо мне напишут[10] в газете."

(3) "Тётя, слезай с дерева" - перебил её мальчик. "Прыгай вниз. Давай с тобой вместе в мячик играть."

"Давай," сказала Зюзя, вздохнула, вспомнила свои уроки физкультуры в школе, и спрыгнула с дерева на землю. Прыжок был неудачный. Зюзя почувствовала острую боль в одной из своих правых ног. Она не удержалась на ногах и упала на землю. Старушка и мальчик помогли ей встать, но Зюзя опять почувствовала острую боль. Даже на лице у неё появилась гримаса от боли.

то-есть = id est
_(т.е.)   (i.e.)_

"Что, бо́льно?"[11] - спроси́ла стару́шка. "Мо́жет[12], отвести́[12] тебя́ в
поликли́нику?"

"Не хочу́ в поликли́нику," - сказа́ла Зю́зя. "Всё, что мне ну́жно
- э́то[13] горя́чий компре́сс. То́лько я не по́мню, где я живу́. То-есть, я
по́мню, как попа́сть по кры́шам, а по у́лице - не зна́ю."

"Ах ты, бедня́жка" - сказа́ла стару́шка. "Пойдём к нам, я тебе́ сде́лаю
горя́чий компре́сс. Мы живём здесь, в э́том до́ме." Она́ показа́ла на дом, с
кото́рого Зю́зя так уда́чно спры́гнула на де́рево, с кото́рого она́ так
неуда́чно спры́гнула на зе́млю.

"Спаси́бо, с удово́льствием," - сказа́ла Зю́зя. "Вы не беспоко́йтесь,
горя́чий компре́сс мне сра́зу помо́жет. Я зна́ю, я проходи́ла медици́ну в
университе́те."

Зю́зя, стару́шка и ма́льчик ме́дленно напра́вились к до́му.

Стару́шка и ма́льчик

расти, рос, росла.

Vocabulary

АНТЕ́ННА antenna
БА́БУШКА grandmother
БЕДНЯ́ЖКА poor fellow
БЕСШУ́МНЫЙ noiseless
БОЛЬ pain
БО́ЛЬНО sick, hurt, painful
БОЯ́ТЬСЯ be afraid
БЫ́СТРО rapidly, quickly
ВДОЛЬ along, parallel with
ВЕРТИКА́ЛЬНЫЙ vertical
ВЕЧЕ́РНИЙ evening
ВЗДОХНУ́ТЬ sigh, take a breath
ВНИЗ down
ВНИЗУ́ below
ВОКРУ́Г around, round
ВСЁ-ТАКИ nevertheless
ВСПО́МНИТЬ remember
ВСТА́ТЬ get up, rise
ВЫСО́КИЙ high; tall
ГЛУБО́КИЙ deep
ГОЛОВА́ head
ГОРЯ́ЧИЙ hot
ГРИМА́СА grimace
ДЕ́РЕВО tree
ДО́ЛГО long time
ЗАМЕ́ТИТЬ notice
ИЗВЕ́СТИЕ news, information
КО́МНАТА room
КОМПРЕ́СС compress
КОТ tomcat
КО́ШКА cat
КРЫ́ША roof
КУСТ bush
ЛИЦО́ face
МА́ЛЬЧИК boy
МЕДИЦИ́НА medicine
МЕ́ДЛЕННО slowly
МО́ЖЕТ maybe; perhaps
МЯЧ ball
НАВЕ́РХ up, upward
НАВЕРХУ́ up, above
НАКОНЕ́Ц finally
НАПРА́ВИТЬСЯ make (for); get going
НЕУДА́ЧНЫЙ unsuccessful
НОГА́ foot; leg

О́СТРЫЙ sharp
ПЕРЕБИ́ТЬ interrupt
ПОДНЯ́ТЬ raise, lift
ПОДПИ́СЫВАТЬСЯ sign; subscribe (to)
ПОЗДОРО́ВАТЬСЯ greet
ПОКАЗА́ТЬ show
ПОЛИКЛИ́НИКА clinic
ПОМО́ЧЬ help
ПОПА́СТЬ get to, find oneself (in)
ПОСМОТРЕ́ТЬ look
ПОЧУ́ВСТВОВАТЬ feel
ПОЯВИ́ТЬСЯ appear
ПРИЗНА́ТЬСЯ confess
ПРОХОДИ́ТЬ go (through)
ПРЫ́ГАТЬ jump
ПРЫ́ГНУТЬ jump
ПРЫЖО́К jump
РА́НО early
РЕША́ТЬ decide
РЕШИ́ТЬ decide
РЯ́ДОМ next (to)
САД garden
СЕГО́ДНЯШНИЙ today's
СКАМЕ́ЙКА bench
СЛЕЗТЬ climb
СМЕШНО́Й funny
СПАТЬ sleep
СПРЫ́ГНУТЬ jump down (from)
СРА́ЗУ right away, at once
СТАРУ́ШКА old woman
СТЕНА́ wall
ТЕЛЕВИЗИО́ННЫЙ television
ТЁ́ТЯ aunt
ТО-ЕСТЬ that is to say, namely
ТРУБА́ pipe
УДА́ЧНЫЙ sucessful
УДЕРЖА́ТЬСЯ stand firm, hold one's ground
УРОНИ́ТЬ drop
УСЛЫ́ШАТЬ hear
ФИЗКУЛЬТУ́РА physical training
ХОТЕ́ТЬСЯ want
ЧУ́ВСТВОВАТЬ feel
ШУМЕ́ТЬ make noise, stir

COMMENTS

1. хо́чется + Dative

The difference between я́ хочу́...and мне́ хо́чется ...is roughly, 'I want...' vs. 'I feel like...' The Dative is used with хо́чется/хоте́лось.

Зю́зе не хоте́лось спа́ть.	Zyuzya didn't feel like sleeping.
Мне́ хо́чется погуля́ть.	I feel like taking a walk.
Дава́й погуля́ем.	Let's take a walk.
—Мне́ не хо́чется.	— I don't feel like it.

2. уже́

Do not translate уже́. Russian needs it in sentences of this sort to indicate a preceding past, eg: she *had* long noticed, he *had* already been there.

3. реша́ть/реши́ть

The verbs реша́ть(НС)/реши́ть(С) mean 'decide'. In this case, the Imperfective is best translated into English by adding the words 'try to'.

Она́ до́лго реша́ла.	For a long time she tried to decide.
Наконе́ц она́ реши́ла.	Finally she decided, made up her mind.(The action has an end point, hence the perfective.)

See analysis 2.3

4. себя́

The dictionary meaning of this word is 'self'. However, the English translation frequently will have a simple pronoun 'him, her,' etc. rather than 'himself, herself', etc.

Она́ уви́дела вокру́г себя́ мно́го труб.	She saw a lot of chimneys around *her*.
Он игра́л са́м с собо́й в мя́ч.	He was playing ball by *himself*. (Instrumental.)

5. поздоро́ваться с кем

With this verb don't translate с as 'with'; translate either as 'to greet *somebody*', or 'say hello *to somebody*'.

6. вдо́ль

Вдо́ль means 'along' in the sense 'parallel to'. To express 'along the street' in the sense 'on the street', Russian uses по + Dative. Зю́зя пошла́ по у́лице would be impossible in this case as she is several stories up.

7. чу́вствовать (себя́)

When this verb is used with a noun (i.e., transitively), себя́ does not co-occur with it. When used without a noun (i.e., intransitively), себя́ co-occurs, but don't translate it.

Она́ чу́вствовала бо́ль.	She felt pain.
Ка́к вы себя́ чу́вствуете?	How do you feel?
Я́ чу́вствую себя́ хорошо́.	I feel fine.

8. са́д, в саду́

Russian makes a distinction between ornamental gardens (са́д) and vegetable gardens (огоро́д). The word са́д in the text refers to a small public park; a large park like Central Park in New York City is called a па́рк.

The ending -у in в саду́ is in the Locative case; see 10.2

Са́д also means orchard:

фрукто́вый са́д	orchard (of fruit trees)
Вишнёвый са́д Че́хова	Chekhov's *Cherry Orchard*
де́тский са́д	kindergarten

9. Kinship terms for non-kin.

Тётя means 'aunt' but in this context it simply means 'lady'. To Russian children, unknown women are all тёти and unknown men are дя́ди ('uncles'; sg. дя́дя.) Both children and adults may address older people as ба́бушка ('grandma') or де́душка ('grandpa') without being disrespectful.

10. Future *would*.

Another example of the Russian perfective future corresponding to English *would*; see Lesson 8, text comment 3.

11. Что́, бо́льно? It hurts, huh?

The word что means something like 'Tell me', or 'huh'.

12. Infinitives as sentences.

Translate: 'Should we perhaps take you to the clinic?' You have to supply a subject ('we') in the translation. Also, мо́жет here is short for мо́жет бы́ть 'it may be, maybe, perhaps'.

Further examples of infinitives without subjects:

Накры́ть на сто́л?	(Shall I/we) set the table?
Нали́ть?	(Shall I) pour (some tea, or whatever)?
Увести́ его́?	(Shall I) take him away?

13. Extra э́то.

The word э́то after a dash does not have the usual translation 'this, that, these, those'; supply the verb *is*, *are* in the English translation and leave э́то untranslated: 'All I need is a hot compress.'

Further examples:

Коммуни́зм — э́то сове́тская власть плюс электрифика́ция всей страны́.   (В.И. Ле́нин)

Communism *is* Soviet power plus electrification of the whole country. (V.I. Lenin)

Всё, что я хочу́ — э́то чтобы вы хорошо́ учи́лись.

All I want is for you to do well in your studies.

Giselle at the Bolshoi. Нача́ло means beginning; спекта́кль means performance. Утренний and вечерний are adjectives.

DIALOGS

1. Совершённый вид

    С: Господин профессор, скажите, пожалуйста, как будет[1]
        совершённый вид от глагола переводить?
    П: Разве[2] вы этого не знаете?
        Совершённый вид от глагола переводить будет перевести.

2. Сколько времени?

    С: Сколько сейчас времени?[3]
    М: Сейчас два часа.[4]
    С: А сколько времени будет через три часа?
    М: Через три часа будет пять часов.

3. Надо купить продукты.

    С: Надо пойти в магазин и купить сыру.[5]
    М: Я уже ходила в магазин и купила сыру.
    С: Сколько?
    М: Полкило.
    С: Сколько ты заплатила?[6]
    М: Два рубля.
    С: Это недорого.[8]
    М: А сколько у вас в Америке стоит сыр?
    С: У нас в Америке фунт сыра стоит три-четыре доллара.

Полезные слова:

масло	конфета
мясо	водка
рыба	шоколад
хлеб	фрукты
булка	овощи
молоко	копейка
сметана	цент
колбаса	килограмм[8]
кефир	дешёвый дёшево[8]
	дорогой дорого[8]
	деньги

4. Давай[9] поедем в Крым

    С: Давай поедем в Крым.
    М: Мне надоело ездить в Крым.
        Я туда ездила в прошлом году, два года назад, и пять лет
        назад.
        Ты поезжай один.
    С: Нет, один я не поеду.
        Я не люблю ездить один.

5. Задача[10]

    С: Ты решила задачу?
    М: Нет, я решала её два часа, но не решила. Не смогла.

6. Уберите тарелки - не убирайте рюмки.

     С: Можно убирать со стола?
     М: Да, уберите, пожалуйста, тарелки, вилки и ложки.
        Не убирайте чашки и рюмки: мы ещё будем пить кофе с коньяком.
     С: А, где рюмки?
        Я не вижу на столе рюмок.
     М: Они, наверно, в шкафу.
        Поставьте, пожалуйста, рюмки на стол.
        И всегда после обеда и перед десертом ставьте рюмки на стол.

Полезные выражения:

   — Можно накрыть на стол?
   — Да, накройте, пожалуйста, на стол.
   — Нет, не накрывайте на стол.
   — Они накроют на стол.

Translation

1. Perfective aspect

   S: Professor, sir, tell me, please, what is the perfective aspect of the
      verb переводить?
   T: You really don't know that? The perfective of the verb переводить
      is перевести.

2. What time is it?

   S: What time is it now?
   M: It's now two o'clock.
   S: And what time will it be in three hours?
   M: In three hours it will be five o'clock.

3. We'll have to buy groceries

   S: We'll have to go to the store and buy some cheese.
   M: I already went to the store and bought cheese.
   S: How much?
   M: Half kilo.
   S: How much did you pay?
   M: Two rubles.
   S: That's reasonable.
   M: How much does cheese cost in America?
   S: In America a pound of cheese costs three (or) four dollars.

Useful words:

butter	candy, piece of candy
meat	vodka
fish	chocolate
bread	fruit
loaf of white bread	vegetables
milk	kopeck
sour cream	cent
salami	kilogram
kefir	cheap
	expensive
	money

4. Let's go to the Crimea.

S: Let's go to the Crimea.
M: I'm tired of going to the Crimea. I went there last year, two years
   ago and five years ago. You go by yourself (= alone).
S: No I won't go alone. I don't like to travel alone.

5. The problem

S: Did you solve the problem.
M: No. I worked on it (for) two hours, but I didn't get it solved.
   I just couldn't.

6. Take away the dishes but don't take away the wine glasses.

S: Can (I) clear off the table.
M: Yes, please take away the dishes, forks, and spoons. Don't take away
   the cups and (small) wine glasses: we're still going to drink coffee
   and cognac.
S: But where are the glasses? I don't see any glasses on the table.
M: They are probably in the cupboard. Please put the glasses on the table.
   And always put glasses on the table after dinner before dessert.

Useful expressions:

Can I set the table?
Yes, please set the table.
No, don't set the table.
They will set the table.

ACTIVE WORD LIST

Nouns

бу́лка (о)	white bread
во́дка	vodka
десе́рт	dessert
кефи́р	kefir
колбаса́	salami
конфе́та	candy
конья́к -а́/-у́	cognac
копе́йка (е)	kopeck
ко́фе (ко́фе...) (муж. род)	coffee
ма́сло	butter; oil
молоко́	milk
мя́со	meat
о́вощи -ще́й -ща́м	vegetables
проду́кты -́тов	produce
ру́бль -ля́, -ли́	ruble
ры́ба	fish
смета́на	sour cream
сыр сы́ра/-у	cheese
фру́кты -́тов	fruit
хле́б	bread
це́нт	cent
шокола́д	chocolate
рю́мка (о)	wine glass
ча́шка (е)	cup
Кры́м в -у́	Crimea
магази́н	store
шка́ф на/в -у́	cupboard; closet; wardrobe
ви́д	aspect; view
глаго́л	verb
до́ллар	dollar
зада́ча	problem
килогра́мм, -гра́ммы -гра́мм(ов)	kilogram
полкило́ (-кило́...)	half kilo
фу́нт	pound

verbs

заплати́ть -́тят -чу́ С	pay
купи́ть -́пят -плю́ С	buy
перевести́ -веду́т; -вёл -вела́ -вели́ С	translate
реши́ть -ша́т -шу́ С	decide; solve
пое́хать -е́дут С	go (by vehicle)
смочь -мо́гут; -мо́г -могла́ -могли́ С	be able (to)
накры́ть -кро́ют С	set
убра́ть -беру́т; -брала́ -бра́ли С	take away; clear off
накрыва́ть НС	set
реша́ть -а́ют НС	decide
ста́вить НС	put (in a standing position)
сто́ить -́оят -́ою НС	cost

е́здить е́здят е́зжу НС		go (by vehicle)
убира́ть -а́ют НС		take away; clear off

Adjectives

два́	two
дешёвый	cheap; inexpensive
дорого́й	expensive; dear
недорого́й	reasonable
поле́зный	useful
про́шлый	past
соверше́нный	perfective

Misc.

дёшево	cheaply
до́рого	expensively
наза́д	ago
сейча́с	now
туда́	there
дава́й	let's
мо́жет бы́ть	maybe; perhaps
на́до	must
они́	they
пе́ред	in front of
по́сле	after
пя́ть	five
ра́зве	really
ско́лько	how much
че́рез	through; in

Aspect pairs.

From now on we will list selected new verbs with their aspect partners at the end of each Active Word List. If one of the partners has not occurred in the previous Dialogs, it will be marked with an asterisk.

	Perfective	*Imperfective*
(1)	накры́ть	*накрыва́ть
(2)	реши́ть	реша́ть
	купи́ть	*покупа́ть
(3)	заплати́ть	*плати́ть
	смо́чь	мо́чь
	поста́вить	ста́вить
(4)	перевести́	переводи́ть
(5)	убра́ть	убира́ть
	пое́хать	{ е́хать (ОН) { е́здить

COMMENTS

1. бу́дет 'is'

In questions and answers having to do with problem solving, the future бу́дет corresponds to the English present *is*. Another example:

Ско́лько бу́дет два́ и два́?	How much is 2 + 2 ?
Два́ и два́ бу́дет четы́ре.	Two and two is four.

2. ра́зве: intonation

This word is an expression of surprise, like English *really, can it really be...!?* The high pitch of the question intonation is on the verb, not on ра́зве.

Вы́ ра́зве э́того не зна́ете?

Use ра́зве only in questions.

3. Pronunciation: Ско́лько сейча́с вре́мени?

In fast speech, this commonly used expression is pronounced "Скока щас вре́мни?"

4. два́ часа́

The singular of the word час is stem-stressed, but after numerals it has an irregular shift to the Gen. Sing. ending.
For the use of the Genitive after the numerals, see Analysis 1.3.

5. сы́ру

The ending -у on the word сыр is the Partitive case. The meaning is 'some'. See Analysis 9.1.2. To render the meaning 'some' with the other nouns in this list, use the Genitive.

6. заплати́ть за что́

'To pay for something' requires the preposition за plus the Accusative case.

Я́ заплати́л пя́ть рубле́й за сы́р и два́ рубля́ за вино́.	I paid five rubles for the cheese and two rubles for the wine.

7. килогра́мм

The Gen. Pl. is irregular for some speakers: килогра́мм . For others it is regular: килогра́ммов . As in English, it is often abbreviated to кило́ (indeclinable).

8. до́рого, недо́рого, дёшево

These words mean 'expensive, inexpensive, cheap,' respectively. To say 'That's expensive' you can use the verb 'cost' or no verb at all:

Э́то до́рого сто́ит. } Э́то до́рого.	That's expensive.

9. дава́й(те) *let's*

The Imperfective of the verb дава́ть 'give' is used to mean
let's. If the following verb is Perfective, use the first plural:

Дава́й   встре́тимся...   Let's meet...
Дава́й пое́дем в Кры́м.   Let's go to the Crimea.

In this construction, particularly with verbs of motion, дава́й(те)
can be omitted:

Пое́дем в Кры́м!   Let's go to the Crimea!
Пойдём в кино́!   Let's go to the movies!

If the following verb is Imperfective, use the infinitive, as
in the Dialog in Lesson 8:

Дава́йте изуча́ть вини́тельный   Let's study the Accusative
   паде́ж.   case.

10. зада́ча

This word means 'problem' in the sense of a problem which is
assigned, or a *task*. Do not use it in the sense of 'a worrisome
thing'.

кинотеатр в Москве showing "It Cannot Be"

1. More uses of the Genitive case.

The Genitive case is used in many expressions having to do with quantity. In the following sections we discuss quantity words, the Partitive case, numerals, the notion *some*, and certain time expressions.

1.1 Quantity words

Use the genitive case after these words:

сколько?	how many? how much?
несколько	a few, several
немного	a little bit of, some
много	many, much, a lot of
мало	few, not many, not much, little

Сколько у вас стаканов?	How many glasses do you have?
У меня несколько стаканов.	I have several glasses/a few glasses.
много стаканов.	I have many glasses/a lot of glasses.
мало стаканов.	I have few glasses. I don't have many glasses.

Сколько у вас книг?	How many books do you have?
У меня несколько/много/мало книг.	I have several/many/few books.

Сколько у вас икры?	How much caviar do you have?
У меня немного икры.	I have a little bit of caviar.
много	I have a lot of caviar.
мало	I have little caviar. I don't have much caviar.

Here is an   example from the text of this Lesson; note the Genitive plural forms of антенна 'antenna', кот 'cat (m.)', кошка 'cat (f.)', труба 'chimney'.

Зюзя увидела вокруг себя много труб и телевизионных антенн, много котов и кошек.

Watch out for the word немного — it does *not* mean 'not much'; use мало for that meaning, e.g.,

Сколько он тебе дал?	How much did he give you?
—Мало.	— Not much.

Further examples of мало:

Он мало работает.	He doesn't work much (Lit., 'He works little.')
У него мало денег.	He doesn't have much money.

1.2 The Partitive case.

There are a few masculine nouns which have a special case ending for use in quantity expressions, expressions in which the Genitive is normally used.

The Partitive ending is -у (-ю):

Nominative	*Genitive*	*Partitive*	
ча́й	ча́я	ча́ю	tea
са́хар	са́хара	са́хару	sugar
сы́р	сы́ра	сы́ру	cheese

Ско́лько у него́ ча́ю?   У него́ ма́ло ча́ю.
                са́хару?   са́хару.
                сы́ру?   сы́ру.

Almost all nouns use Genitive in such expressions, e.g.,

Ско́лько у него́ *хле́ба*?   У него́ ма́ло *хле́ба*.

In Genitive expressions where quantity is not involved (and, for some speakers, where the *exact* amount is specified), the Partitive is not used:

цве́т ча́я   the color of tea
э́кспорт сы́ра   cheese export
У на́с не́т сы́ра/сы́ру.   We have no cheese (exactly zero).
фу́нт са́хара/са́хару.   a pound of sugar

Further examples: see below, section 1.4.

```
┌──────────────────────────────────────────────────────────┐
│                      PRACTICE 1                           │
│                                                          │
│     With nouns that denote countable things (like knives,│
│  forks, spoons) use  не́сколько  'a few, several' plus    │
│  Genitive Plural; with nouns that denote noncountable    │
│  things (like caviar, wine, kasha) use  немно́го  'a little│
│  bit of' plus Genitive Singular.                         │
│                                                          │
│     стака́н    кни́га    до́ллар    ча́й                 │
│     ви́лка     молоко́   копе́йка   вино́                │
│     ка́ша      сы́р      хле́б                           │
│     бо́рщ      вода́     са́хар                          │
│     но́ж       ру́бль    ча́с                            │
└──────────────────────────────────────────────────────────┘
```

1.3 Numerals

After the forms два́ (m.,n.), две́ (f.) 'two', три́ 'three' and четы́ре 'four' the following noun is in the Genitive *Singular*. Here are some examples you have met; the Nominative Singular forms are in parentheses with the numeral for 'one':

У на́с два́ со́лнца и две́ луны́.   See Lesson 5, Text.
   (одно́ со́лнце, одна́ луна́)

У Ива́на Ильича́ две́ жены́.   See Lesson 6, Dialog.
   (одна́ жена́)

Три́ медве́дя   See Lesson 5, Dialog.
   (оди́н медве́дь)

The variant два́ is used with masculine and neuter nouns; две́ with feminine.

masc. оди́н стака́н   два́ стака́на
       оди́н ца́рь   два́ царя́

neut. одно́ со́лнце   два́ со́лнца
       одно́ письмо́   два́ письма́

fem.   одна́ фле́йта   две́ фле́йты
       одна́ ды́ня   две́ ды́ни
       одна́ це́рковь   две́ це́ркви

Sometimes the ending doesn't tell you the difference between Genitive Singular and Nominative-Accusative plural, but watch out for stress — it often distinguishes the two:

	Nom. Sing.	Gen. Sing.		Nom. Plur.
	одна́ ру́чка	две́ ру́чки	=	э́ти ру́чки
BUT:	одна́ жена́	две́ жены́	≠	э́ти жёны
	одна́ сестра́	две́ сестры́	≠	э́ти сёстры
	одно́ кольцо́	два́ кольца́	≠	э́ти ко́льца
	одно́ сло́во	два́ слова́	≠	э́ти слова́

The numerals пя́ть and above are followed by a noun in the Genitive *Plural*.

пя́ть стака́нов   два́дцать стака́нов
пя́ть ру́чек   два́дцать ру́чек
пя́ть сло́в   два́дцать сло́в

These rules apply to the last member of a compound numeral (twenty-one, twenty-two, etc.):

два́дцать оди́н стака́н	Nom.-Acc. Sing.	21 glasses
два́дцать одна́ ру́чка	Nom.-Acc. Sing.	21 pens
два́дцать одно́ сло́во	Nom.-Acc. Sing.	21 words
два́дцать два́ стака́на	Gen. Sing.	22 glasses
два́дцать два́ слова	Gen. Sing.	22 words
два́дцать две́ ру́чки	Gen. Sing.	22 pens
два́дцать три́ стака́на	Gen. Sing.	23 glasses
два́дцать три́ слова	Gen. Sing.	23 words
два́дцать три́ ру́чки	Gen. Sing.	23 pens
два́дцать пя́ть стака́нов	Gen. Plur.	25 glasses
два́дцать пя́ть ру́чек	Gen. Plur.	25 pens
два́дцать пя́ть сло́в	Gen. Plur.	25 words

The Nominative case forms of numerals are listed below. (Numerals have all six case forms; avoid, for the time being, situations requiring numerals in case forms other than Nominative, e.g., after prepositions.)

оди́н	шестна́дцать
два́, две́	семна́дцать
три́	восемна́дцать
четы́ре	девятна́дцать
пя́ть	два́дцать
ше́сть	два́дцать оди́н
се́мь	два́дцать два́, две́
во́семь	два́дцать три́
де́вять	два́дцать четы́ре
де́сять	два́дцать пя́ть
оди́ннадцать	два́дцать ше́сть
двена́дцать	два́дцать се́мь
трина́дцать	два́дцать во́семь
четы́рнадцать	два́дцать де́вять
пятна́дцать	три́дцать

When counting, use ра́з instead of оди́н: ра́з, два́, три́, четы́ре, пя́ть, ...

The word ра́з also means 'time' in the sense of *occurrence* (5 times, 10 times, one time = once). The Genitive plural form is irregular; instead of the expected ending -ов, it has zero ending.

ра́з	once	пя́ть ра́з	five times
два́ ра́за	twice	де́сять ра́з	ten times
три́ ра́за	three times	мно́го ра́з	many times

Further examples:

Я́ э́то сде́лал уже́ три́ ра́за.	I've done that 3 times already.
Вы́ зде́сь в пе́рвый ра́з?	Is this your first time here?
Я́ зде́сь во второ́й ра́з.	This is the second time I've been here.

PRACTICE 2

Cover the Russian phrases and look at the arabic numerals. First, practice saying the numerals aloud as fast as you can; then say each numeral aloud with the proper form of the word рубль. Check your answers (column 1). Then repeat, using копе́йка (col. 2) and до́ллар (col. 3).

1	оди́н ру́бль	одна́ копе́йка	оди́н до́ллар
2	два́ рубля́	две́ копе́йки	два́ до́ллара
3	три́ рубля́	три́ копе́йки	три́ до́ллара
4	четы́ре рубля́	четы́ре копе́йки	четы́ре до́ллара
5	пя́ть рубле́й	пя́ть копе́ек	пя́ть до́лларов
6	ше́сть рубле́й	ше́сть копе́ек	ше́сть до́лларов
7	се́мь рубле́й	се́мь копе́ек	се́мь до́лларов
8	во́семь рубле́й	во́семь копе́ек	во́семь до́лларов
9	де́вять рубле́й	де́вять копе́ек	де́вять до́лларов
10	де́сять рубле́й	де́сять копе́ек	де́сять до́лларов
11	оди́ннадцать рубле́й	оди́ннадцать копе́ек	оди́ннадцать до́лларов
12	двена́дцать рубле́й	двена́дцать копе́ек	двена́дцать до́лларов

Arithmetic:

When adding and subtracting, use either the verb бу́дет for English 'is/ are', or a pause. The words плю́с and ми́нус work as in English.

       Ско́лько бу́дет оди́н и два́?
       Оди́н и два́ бу́дет ,три́.
OR: Оди́н и два́ — три́.
OR: Оди́н плю́с два́ бу́дет три́.
       Три́ ми́нус оди́н бу́дет два́.

PRACTICE 3

Cover the Russian; convert from numerals to words.   Check.

2 + 3 = 5   Два́ и три́ бу́дет пя́ть.
4 + 6 = 10 Четы́ре и ше́сть бу́дет де́сять.
7 + 1 = 8   Се́мь и оди́н бу́дет во́семь.
6 + 3 = 9   Ше́сть и три́ бу́дет де́вять.

1.4 Genitive meaning *some*

Lesson 4, Text Comment 5, pointed out that the form вина́ (Genitive of вино́) had the meaning '*some* wine' in this sentence:

Все́ вы́пили вина́.   Everybody drank *some* wine.
                      OR: Everybody drank wine.

If you used the Accusative here the meaning would be slightly different:

Все́ вы́пили вино́.   Everybody drank *their/his/her* wine.

Examine the following pair of sentences, in which this same difference in meaning shows up; the first member of the pair has the Genitive form:

Да́йте мне́ хле́ба, пожа́луйста.   Give me (*some*) bread, please.
Переда́йте, пожа́луйста, хле́б.   Pass *the* bread, please.

If the noun is one of those few masculines that has a Partitive case, this situation is a proper one to use it in:

Да́йте мне́, пожа́луйста, сы́ру.   Give me (*some*) cheese, please.
              ча́ю.   tea
              са́хару.   sugar

versus:
Переда́йте, пожа́луйста, сы́р.   Pass *the* cheese, please.
              ча́й.   tea
              са́хар.   sugar

1.5 The clock: on the hour.

To ask 'What time is it?' you say:

Ско́лько вре́мени?   What time is it?
Ско́лько сейча́с вре́мени?   What time is it now?

Here is a more formal way of expressing these questions; we won't use these expressions in exercises, but you should be familiar with them:

Кото́рый ча́с?
Кото́рый сейча́с ча́с?

The hours are expressed as follows (we'll take up minutes, half hours, etc. later):

Сейча́с ча́с.   It's now one o'clock.
     два́ часа́.   It's now two o'clock.
     три́ часа́.   It's now three o'clock.
     четы́ре часа́.   It's now four o'clock.
     пя́ть часо́в.   It's now five o'clock.
     ше́сть...двена́дцать часо́в.   It's now six...twelve o'clock.

To say '*at a certain time*' use the preposition в:

Когда́ она́ придёт?   When is she going to arrive?
— В ча́с.   At one o'clock.
— В три́ часа́.   At three o'clock.
— В де́сять часо́в.   At ten o'clock.

PRACTICE 4

Answer the question Ско́лько вре́мени? by saying 'one o'clock' through 'twelve o'clock' as fast as you can, using the proper forms of ча́с. Then answer the question Когда́? using the preposition в.

1.6 Dates.

In the expression for *What is the date today* the numeral is Nominative.

Како́е сего́дня число́?   What is the date today?
— Сего́дня два́дцать *пя́тое* ию́ня.   Today is the 25th of June.

For the expression *on* a certain date, use the Genitive, e.g.,

Како́го числа́ (OR: Когда́...) о́н   On what date (When...) did he
   прилете́л?   arrive?
Пе́тя прилете́л два́дцать *пя́того* ию́ня.   He arrived *on* the twenty-fifth of June.
Како́го числа́ ты́ родила́сь?   *On* what date were you born?
— Я́ родила́сь *пе́рвого* ма́рта.   I was born *on* the first of March.

1.7 The word for *year*

The word for year is го́д. After the numerals два́, три́, четы́ре you use the Genitive Singular, according to the rule in 1.3 above: два́ го́да, два́дцать три́ го́да, etc.

However, after the higher numerals, where you would expect Genitive Plural, you use a different word: ле́т, as in пя́ть ле́т, де́сять ле́т, etc. (The form ле́т is the Gen. Plur. of ле́то which is the word for *summer*.)

The other peculiarity of го́д is that after the preposition в it has the ending -у́ where you would expect the Prepositional case, i.e., в про́шлом году́. (This ending is the *Locative* case, to be discussed in more detail in Lesson 10.2.) Similarly, В како́м году́? 'In what year?'

2. Aspect

2.1 The two verbs говори́ть.

The verb говори́ть can be translated 'speak, talk, say, tell'.

Он говори́л по-ру́сски.	He *spoke* Russian.
Он говори́л с сестро́й об икре́.	He was *talking/speaking* to/with his sister about caviar.
Он всегда́ говори́л, что...	He always *said* that...
Он тебе́ мно́го ра́з говори́л, что...	He *told* you many times that...

If you examine the verb government and aspect partners, you will see that there are actually two verbs here:

(1) говори́ть (I), поговори́ть (P) с ке́м о чём   'to be engaged in conversation *with* somebody *about* something; talk, speak.' The Perfective поговори́ть means 'to have a chat with somebody'. *Somebody* is Inst.

(2) говори́ть (I), сказа́ть (P) кому́, что   'to impart something *to* somebody; tell, say'. *Somebody* is Dative.

It is very important to use only с ке́м (*not* кому́) with говори́ть (1). In English you can say either 'I spoke *to* him' or 'I spoke *with* him', but in Russian you can only say Я с ни́м говори́л in meaning (1). If you say Я ему́ говори́л, it will have meaning (2), namely, 'I told him,' which would normally have a direct object or clause with it, e.g.,

Я *ему́* э́то говори́л не́сколько ра́з.	I *told* him that (= I *said* that *to* him) several times.
Я *ему́* говори́л, что на́ша плане́та кру́глая.	I was *telling*(=*saying to* him) him that our planet is round.

Compare:

Я говори́л *с ни́м* о на́шей плане́те.	I was *talking to/with* him about our planet.

Here are some examples of the Perfective partners:

(1) Я хочу́ с ни́м поговори́ть.	I want to have a chat with him.
Я с ни́м поговорю́ об э́том.	I'll have a talk with him about that.
(2) Что́ о́н сказа́л?	What did he say?
Что́ о́н тебе́ сказа́л?	What did he tell you?

```
┌─────────────────────────────────────────────────────────────┐
│                        PRACTICE 5                             │
├─────────────────────────────────────────────────────────────┤
│  Cover the Russian and translate aloud.  Check your answers. │
│ What was she saying?          Что она говорила?              │
│ What was she talking about?   О чём она говорила?            │
│ What did she say?             Что она сказала?               │
│ Who was she talking to?       С кем она говорила?            │
│ She always told the truth.    Она всегда говорила правду.    │
│ She told me that it's now one Она мне сказала, что сейчас    │
│   o'clock.                       час.                        │
│ She said that it's now one    Она сказала, что сейчас        │
│   o'clock.                       час.                        │
│ She spoke Russian.            Она говорила по-русски.        │
│ She had a chat with me.       Она поговорила со мной.        │
│ Who were you talking to?      С кем ты говорил(а)?           │
└─────────────────────────────────────────────────────────────┘
```

2.2 More One-way Verbs: éхать and летéть.

One-way verbs were discussed in Lesson 7.7. These two verbs make the same aspectual distinctions as идти/ходить/пойти. Consult the summary chart at the end of Lesson 7.7.

Imperfective One-Way	Imperfective	Perfective
идти, идут шёл, шла, шли	ходить, ходят, хожу	пойти, пойдут пошёл,-шла,-шли
ехать, едут	ездить, ездят, езжу	поехать, поедут
лететь, летят, лечу	летать, летают	полететь, -ят, -чу

Pronunciation:

Refer back to Lesson 7.8, where the voiced counterpart of ц was discussed. The form езжу has this sound (/yéjju/); it is pronounced as a palatal, not plain.

Examples:

$$я \begin{Bmatrix} ходи́л \\ е́здил \\ лета́л \end{Bmatrix} туда́ вчера́. \qquad I\ went\ there \begin{Bmatrix} on\ foot \\ by\ vehicle \\ by\ plane \end{Bmatrix} yesterday.$$

(Round trip)

$$я\ ча́сто \begin{Bmatrix} ходи́л \\ е́здил \\ лета́л \end{Bmatrix} туда́. \qquad I\ often\ went\ there \begin{Bmatrix} on\ foot \\ by\ vehicle \\ by\ plane \end{Bmatrix}.$$

$$Когда́\ я \begin{Bmatrix} шёл \\ е́хал \\ лете́л \end{Bmatrix} туда́, \qquad On\ my\ way\ there \begin{Bmatrix} on\ foot \\ by\ vehicle \\ by\ plane \end{Bmatrix}, I\ met\ Pete.$$

я́ встре́тил Пе́тю.

$$Где́\ Ва́ня? \qquad\qquad Where's\ Vanya?$$
— Он пошёл в кино́.   — He took off for $\begin{Bmatrix} the\ movies \\ Kiev \\ outer\ space \end{Bmatrix}$.
— Он пое́хал в Ки́ев.
— Он полете́л в ко́смос.

    Recall that this three-way aspectual distinction has to do only with *simple* (i.e. not prefixed) verbs of motion. Prefixed forms have the usual two-way contrast of Perfective vs. Imperfective, e.g.,

	on foot	*by vehicle*	*flying*	
I:	приходи́ть	приезжа́ть	прилета́ть⎫	come, arrive
P:	прийти́	прие́хать	прилете́ть⎭	
I:	уходи́ть	уезжа́ть	улета́ть⎫	go away
P:	уйти́	уе́хать	улете́ть⎭	

...and so forth with other prefixes (to be discussed in detail in Lesson 10).

2.3 Trying and succeeding

    Imperfective verbs can often be translated with the addition of the English verb 'try'.

Три дня́ на́ша а́рмия брала́(I) го́род,   For three days, our army attacked
  и наконе́ц его́ взяла́(P).   (= tried to take) the city,
                        and finally took it.

    In this context, as the English translation shows, the action of taking is interpreted as *trying* (Imperfective) until the point of success is reached (Perfective). A fairly large number of human activities are of this type. Compare the imperfective situations on the left with the perfective ones on the right:

going fishing = trying to catch a fish	catch a fish
working on a problem = trying to solve	solve a problem
arguing a point = trying to prove	prove a point
offering money = trying to bribe	bribe somebody
taking an exam = trying to pass	pass an exam

Here are a few sentences to illustrate the contrast between trying (Imperfective) and succeeding (Perfective):

Я ему́ то́лько что *звони́л*.   Его́   I just phoned (tried to reach him).
нет до́ма.   He isn't home.

Я ему́ уже́ *позвони́л*,   I already phoned him (reached
                                        him).

Я реша́л зада́чу.   I was working on a problem.
Я реши́л зада́чу.   I solved the problem.

Here is an example from the Text of the Lesson:

Зю́зя до́лго *реша́ла*, куда́ ей пойти́, вниз на у́лицу или наве́рх на кры́шу. Наконе́ц она́ *реши́ла*, что на у́лице она́ уже́ была́, а на кры́ше ещё нет, и пошла́ наве́рх, на кры́шу.

Of course, the Imperfective of these verbs can be used in other contexts with the other meanings of Imperfective that we have discussed earlier:

(a) Round trip:

Кто́ брал мою́ кни́гу?   Who took my book (and returned it)?

(b) Repeated action:

Она́ ча́сто брала́ кни́ги в библиоте́ке. She often borrowed books from the
                                        library.

(c) On-going action:

Когда́ она́ брала́ кни́гу, вошёл Пе́тя.   While she was taking the book,
                                        Pete walked in.

2.4 Trying and failing

It is a good rule of thumb that you use Imperfectives with не, e.g.,

Он взял(Р) мою́ кни́гу.   He took my book.
vs. Он не брал(I) мою́ кни́гу.   vs. He didn't take my book.
Кто́ взял(Р) мою́ кни́гу?   Who took my book?
vs. Я не брал(I) .   vs. I didn't take it.

However, if you want to express the meaning 'fail to do something' rather than 'not do something', then use не plus Perfective. By *fail* we mean either trying and failing or not doing something that you were *supposed* to do.

Compare:

Она́ не сдава́ла(I) экза́мен.
: She didn't take the exam. (She didn't even try.)

Она́ не сдала́(P) экза́мен.
: She failed the exam. (She tried, but failed.)

Она́ не реша́ла(I) зада́чу.
: She didn't solve the problem. (She didn't even work on it.)

Она́ не реши́ла(P) зада́чу.
: She failed to solve the problem. (She was supposed to, but she didn't do the assignment; maybe she tried, but in any case, she failed to get it done.)

Я три́ дня *реша́л* э́ту зада́чу, но не *реши́л*. А Ната́ша её *реши́ла* за полчаса́.
: For three days, I worked on (tried to solve) this problem, but I could not solve it. Natasha solved it in a half hour.

Я ему́ вчера́ ве́чером два́ часа́ *дока́зывал*, что земля́ кру́глая, но так и не *доказа́л*.
: Last night, for two hours, I tried to prove to him that the earth is round but I never did succeed in proving it (to him).

Я его́ до́лго *угова́ривал* пое́хать со мно́й в Кры́м, но так и не *уговори́л*. "Поезжа́й," — говори́т, — "са́м."
: For a long time I tried to persuade him to go with me to the Crimea, but I never did persuade him. "Go by yourself," he said.

In the following sentences note the use of the two aspect forms мо́чь(I), смо́чь(P) 'be able to, can, could', with and without negation.

Я два́ часа́ реша́ла зада́чу, но не реши́ла. Не *смогла́*.
: I worked on the problem for two hours, but I didn't solve it. I *couldn't* (tried and failed).

Когда́ Ле́нин бы́л ма́ленький, он не *мо́г* съе́сть пя́ть таре́лок су́па. Он *мо́г* съе́сть то́лько три́ таре́лки. То́лько в октябре́ 1917 го́да он в пе́рвый ра́з *смо́г* съе́сть пя́ть таре́лок су́па.
: When Lenin was little, he *couldn't* eat five bowls of soup. He *could* eat only three. Only in October 1917 did he *manage*, for the first time, to eat five bowls of soup (tried and succeeded).

3. The Imperative of verbs

The imperative form of verbs is used in giving commands or making requests.

3.1 Formation of the Imperative

Listed below are imperative forms you have met in the Dialogs thus far; compare them with the other forms of the verb:

Infinitive	3Pl	1Sg	Imperative	
Group A				
повтори́ть	повторя́т	повторю́	повтори́!	repeat!
попроси́ть	попро́сят	попрошу́	попроси́!	request!
спроси́ть	спро́сят	спрошу́	спроси́!	inquire!
положи́ть	поло́жат	положу́	положи́!	put!
научи́ть	нау́чат	научу́	научи́!	teach!
позвони́ть	позвоня́т	позвоню́	позвони́!	phone!
отвести́	отведу́т	отведу́	отведи́!	take, lead!
разреши́ть	разреша́т	разрешу́	разреши́!	permit!
Group B				
откры́ть	откро́ют	откро́ю	откро́й!	open!
чита́ть	чита́ют	чита́ю	чита́й!	read!
беспоко́иться	беспоко́ятся	беспоко́юсь	беспоко́йся!	worry!
руга́ться	руга́ются	руга́юсь	руга́йся!	swear!
предста́вить	предста́вят	предста́влю	предста́вь!	introduce!

The examples above are all in the informal style; the formal style adds the syllable -те-, e.g.,

A: повтори́те, попроси́те, спроси́те, положи́те, etc.
B: откро́йте, чита́йте, предста́вьте, не беспоко́йтесь, не руга́йтесь

Note that the variant -сь occurs after a vowel (е) in the formal style руга́йтесь, беспоко́йтесь, but the variant -ся is used after a consonant (й) in the informal style руга́йся, беспоко́йся, according to the rule stated in Lesson 4.8.

The difference between Group A and Group B is in their stress patterns: Group A has some of the endings stressed (patterns E or M), while Group B has no endings stressed (pattern S).

For the overwhelming majority of Russian verbs the imperative ending depends on this difference in stress: Group A has the imperative ending -й(те) while Group B has zero ending, with paired consonants palatalized, - hence the мя́гкий знак as in the last example, предста́вь(те).

The imperative is formed on the non-past stem, as illustrated by откры́ть (past stem) откро́ют (non-past stem) откро́й (imperative). Note that the form откро́ют consists of the stem откро́й- plus the ending -ут. (See Lesson 2.2 on the Cyrillic letter Й.)

The major rule for imperatives, in summary, is:

A	any endings stressed (E or M) ⟶	-й́
B	no endings stressed (S) ⟶	-# { й after vowel / ь after consonant

---

PRACTICE 7

Listed below are verbs you have met in Dialogs. All form imperatives according to the major rule. Write the imperatives, say them aloud, and translate.

бра́ть, беру́т
взять, возьму́т
верну́ть, верну́т
верну́ться, верну́тся
сказа́ть, ска́жут, скажу́
говори́ть, говоря́т
де́лать, де́лают
класть, кладу́т
положи́ть, поло́жат, положу́

написа́ть, напи́шут, напишу́
поста́вить, поста́вят, поста́влю
бы́ть, бу́дут
ду́мать, ду́мают
жи́ть, живу́т
занима́ться, занима́ются
игра́ть, игра́ют
идти́, иду́т
отве́тить, отве́тят, отве́чу

Answers: бери́, возьми́, верни́, верни́сь, скажи́, говори́, де́лай, клади́, положи́, напиши́, поста́вь, бу́дь, ду́май, живи́, занима́йся, игра́й, иди́, отве́ть.

There are four minor imperative rules which do not affect many verbs. For now, you'd be better off memorizing the verbs themselves as you meet them, rather than trying to learn the rules as rules.

(1) *Stem-final consonant clusters.*

If a stem stressed (S) verb ends in a cluster of consonants, the imperative ending is unstressed -и rather than the expected zero (- ь).

-мн-	вспо́мнить,	вспо́мнят	⟶ вспо́мни	recall
-нч-	ко́нчить,	ко́нчат	⟶ ко́нчи	finish

(2) *Stem-final /y/ - sound*

If an End-stressed (E) verb ends in the sound /y/, the imperative ending is zero (й) instead of the expected -и́,

сто́ять, стоя́т → сто́й   stand

пи́ть, пью́т (=пи́-ут) → пе́й   drink

(Note the inserted vowel -e-, without which the form пй would be unpronounceable.)

Here are a couple of Russian sayings illustrating this minor rule:

плева́ть, плюю́т → плю́й   spit
Не плю́й в коло́дец.   Don't spit in the well...(you may want to drink the water later).

кова́ть, кую́т → ку́й   forge
Ку́й желе́зо, пока́ (оно́) горячо́.   Strike the iron while it is hot.

(3) *The three -ва- verb-stems.*

These three verbs are peculiar in that they have the syllable -ва- in the infinitive (past) stem, but not in the non-past stem (the first two occur only with prefixes, so we write them with hyphens):

-знава́ть, - *знаю́т*
-става́ть, - *стаю́т*
дава́ть, *даю́т*
               give (Imperfective)

These verbs have peculiar imperatives; the syllable -ва- occurs despite the fact that imperatives are generally formed on the non-past stem.

признава́йся   confess!
оставайся   remain!
дава́й   give! let's!

(4) *Exceptions*

The irregular verb да́ть, даду́т,... (Perfective) 'give' has the imperative form да́йте. You have met the prefixed imperative переда́й 'pass'.

The irregular verb е́сть, едя́т,...'eat' has the imperative form е́шь (те).

The verb е́хать, е́дут,... 'to go' *(by vehicle)* uses an aberrant stem for the imperative and usually occurs with a prefix:

пое́хать, пое́дут → поезжа́й	go
прие́хать, прие́дут → приезжа́й	come, arrive

Practice 8

Write the imperative as you did in the preceding Practice. This list contains examples of minor as well as major rules (the minor ones are marked with an asterisk); it also contains some verbs you haven't met before, but the rules can successfully be applied to them.

нача́ться, начну́тся	передава́ть, передаю́т 'pass' (I)
отве́тить, отве́тят, отве́чу	*стоя́ть, -я́т, -ю́
*пе́ть, пою́т 'sing'	рассказа́ть, -ска́жут, -скажу́
поста́вить, ⸗ят, ⸗влю	пригласи́ть, -я́т, -шу́
рабо́тать, ⸗ают	*пи́ть, пью́т
*вспо́мнить, ⸗ят, ⸗ю	*би́ть, бью́т
чита́ть, -а́ют	смотре́ть, ⸗я́т, -ю́

3.2 Aspect in the imperative

The contrast between Imperfective Aspect and Perfective Aspect in the imperative is not much different from what has already been said about Aspect, i.e., use Perfective when you want to tell somebody to get a specific thing accomplished, and use Imperfective when you want to tell somebody to do something repeatedly or to be engaged in an activity without specifying an end point.

Compare these pairs of sentences; the first of each pair is Perfective:

P: *Откро́йте* окно́!	Open the window!
I: *Открыва́йте* о́кна ка́ждый де́нь!	Open the windows every day!
P: *Прочита́йте* э́тот абза́ц!	Read this paragraph!
I: *Чита́йте!*	Read! Start reading!
P: *Скажи́те* мне́, что́ о́н хо́чет.	Tell me what he wants.
I: Всегда́ *говори́те* пра́вду.	Always tell the truth.
P: *Поговори́те* с ни́м.	Have a talk with him.
I: *Говори́те* с ни́м по-ру́сски.	Talk Russian with him.
P: *Положи́* кни́гу на сто́л.	Put the book on the table.
I: Всегда́ *клади́* ве́щи на свое́ ме́сто.	Always put things in their place.

P: *Напишите* ему́ письмо́.   Write him a letter.
I: *Пиши́те* мне́.   Write me (keep in touch).

P: *Возьми́те* э́ту кни́гу.   Take this book.
I: *Бери́те* кни́ги в библиоте́ке,   Borrow books from the library
    е́сли не хоти́те их покупа́ть.   if you don't want to buy them.

P: *Да́йте* мне́ че́стное сло́во.   Give me your word of honor.
I: *Дава́йте* ча́стные уро́ки, е́сли   Give private lessons if you want
    хоти́те зараба́тывать бо́льше   to earn more money.
    де́нег.

    The rule of thumb about using Imperfective with negation (see Section 2.4 above) works pretty well:

Не открыва́й окно́!   Don't open the window.
Не говори́, что я здесь.   Don't tell (anybody) I'm here.
У меня́ про́сьба: *не говори́те* о   Do me a favor: don't talk about
    фотогра́фиях.   photographs.
Не клади́ сюда́ э́ту ло́жку — она́   Don't put this spoon here – it's
    гря́зная.   dirty.

    One rather specialized aspectual usage has to do with polite requests in host-guest situations; in all of these formal clichés the *Imperfective* is used, despite the fact that a single, specific action is involved. (If you used the Perfective, it would sound more abrupt.)

Сади́тесь!   Do sit down. Have a seat. (Ся́дьте
                                          sounds more abrupt or familiar.)

Входи́те!   Come in! (vs. Войди́те!)
Раздева́йтесь!   Take off your things (coats and
                                          hats)!
Заходи́те!   Stop by (and see us)! (vs. Зайди́те!)
Приходи́те!   Do come! (vs. Прийди́те!)

    If it's not a host-guest situation, then you would more likely use the Perfective of these verbs. If an unknown person knocks on the door, you'd say Войди́те! (P) 'Come in', but if the door is open and somebody appears in the doorway saying:

Мо́жно?
OR: Мо́жно войти́?   May I come in?

you can say either Войди́те! (P) or, more hospitably, Входи́те! (I).

УПРАЖНЕНИЯ

1. Review.

П: Са́ша, спроси́те Ма́шу, что́ она́ хо́чет нарисова́ть.
С: Что́ ты́ хо́чешь нарисова́ть?
М: Я́ хочу́ нарисова́ть *кра́сную* плане́ту.
С: В тако́м слу́чае тебе́ ну́жен *кра́сный* каранда́ш.
М: Я́ не люблю́ рисова́ть *кра́сным* карандашо́м.
С: Тогда́ возьми́ мою́ *кра́сную* ру́чку.
М: Ру́чкой я́ то́же не люблю́ рисова́ть.

Substitute all colors. Variation: start off with a pen instead of a
pencil.

2. Review. Imperfective → Perfective.

As you transform these verbs to Perfective, change plural objects to
singular.

П: Я́ ча́сто пишу́ пи́сьма. → С: Я́ за́втра напишу́ письмо́.

Я́ ча́сто перевожу́ пи́сьма из Сове́тского Сою́за.
Я́ ча́сто пью́ вино́.
Я́ ча́сто е́м икру́.
Я́ ча́сто рису́ю плане́ты.
Я́ ча́сто открыва́ю буты́лки.

Now change the subject to ты́ , then to они́ .

3. Review. Perfective → Imperfective.

П: Ма́ша *прочита́ла* э́ту кни́гу?
С: Ду́маю, что не́т.
П: Спроси́те её.
С: Ма́ша, э́то пра́вда, что ты́ *прочита́ла* э́ту кни́гу?
М: Не́т, я́ её ещё *чита́ю.*

Substitute:

съе́ла всю́ чёрную икру́   перевела́ кни́гу Льва́ Толсто́го
съе́ла всю́ кра́сную икру́   перевела́ э́то письмо́
вы́пила всё бе́лое вино́   перевела́ э́ти пи́сьма
вы́пила всё кра́сное вино́   нарисова́ла жёлтую плане́ту
написа́ла кни́гу   откры́ла буты́лку
написа́ла письмо́   написа́ла все́ упражне́ния

4. Review: verbs with -ся/-сь.

Answer in the affirmative.

Вы́ *вернётесь?* → Да́, я́ *верну́сь.*
Вы́ *интересу́етесь* ру́сским языко́м?
Вы́ с ни́м *познако́митесь?*   — *лю́сь*
Вы́ *занима́етесь* в библиоте́ке?
Вы́ о́чень *беспоко́итесь?*

Repeat, adding Са́ша and мы́. Да́, я́ за́втра верну́сь. Са́ша то́же
вернётся. Мы́ все́ вернёмся.

5.   Aspect pairs: Dialog 1. Review Lesson 8.2.2.

          The word зна́чит means 'means'.

   П: Что́ зна́чит сло́во *есть*?
   С: Сло́во *есть* зна́чит eat.
   П: Ка́к бу́дет совершённый ви́д от э́того глаго́ла?
   С: Не зна́ю. Я спрошу́ Ма́шу.
         Ма́ша, ка́к бу́дет совершённый ви́д от глаго́ла *есть*?
   М: Ра́зве ты́ э́того не зна́ешь? Совершённый ви́д от глаго́ла
         есть бу́дет *съе́сть*.
   С: Интере́сно. Я э́того не зна́л.

   Substitute items from the list of aspect pairs in Lesson 8, Analysis 2.2.

   Then do nouns, e.g. ка́к бу́дет роди́тельный паде́ж от э́того
   существи́тельного?

6.   Mini-conversations.

          Follow the same pattern as above, but talk on different topics.
   Make up suitable answers.

   П: Кака́я бу́дет сего́дня пого́да?
   С: Сего́дня бу́дет хо́лодно.
   П: А кака́я бу́дет за́втра пого́да?
   С: Не зна́ю. Я спрошу́ Ма́шу.
         Ма́ша, кака́я бу́дет за́втра пого́да?
   М: Ра́зве ты́ э́того не зна́ешь? За́втра бу́дет о́блачно.
   С: Интере́сно. Я э́того не зна́л.

   Suggestions:

   Како́е сего́дня число́?   Каки́м падежо́м мы́ бу́дем
   Како́й сего́дня де́нь?   сего́дня занима́ться?
   Отку́да сего́дня ве́тер?   Како́е у на́с зада́ние на
   Что́ бу́дет сего́дня на обе́д?   сего́дня?
   Что́ ест медве́дь?   Что́ бу́дут де́лать сего́дня
   О ко́м пи́шут сего́дня в газе́те?   на́ши студе́нты?
   О чём пи́шут сего́дня в газе́те?
   О како́м падеже́ бу́дет говори́ть
      сего́дня на́ш преподава́тель?

7.   Review: Что́ э́то тако́е?

The phrase что́ тако́е (always neuter) is used in asking for a definition or description of something or in asking for an explanation of an unfamiliar term. Listed below are some things you have met before; give a factually correct answer for the teacher's question Что́ тако́е X? If the thing is a book or play, state the author in a кото́рый clause (Это пье́са, кото́рую написа́л Шекспи́р.); if it's an institution like a museum or university, state the city or country in a кото́рый clause (Это музе́й, кото́рый нахо́дится в Мадри́де.).

П: Что́ тако́е "Сорбо́нна"?
С: "Сорбо́нна"— э́то университе́т кото́рый нахо́дится в Пари́же.
П: Что́ тако́е "Га́рвард"?
                   "Корне́лл"
                   "Колге́йт"
                   "Уотерге́йт"
                   "Кэ́мбридж"
                   "О́ксфорд"
                   "Эрмита́ж"
                   "Пра́до"
                   "Лу́вр"
                   "Метропо́литан"
                   "МГУ"
                   "Большо́й теа́тр"
                   "Бе́лый до́м"

8. Counting.   Dialog 2. Analysis 1.

Practice counting from 1 to 12. Then point to the clock and do Dialog 2 with all different hours.

9. Numbers: cardinals.

Practice counting from 1 to 39. Then answer these questions factually:

Ско́лько студе́нтов у ва́с на заня́тиях сего́дня?
Ско́лько студе́нток у ва́с на заня́тиях сего́дня?
Ско́лько о́кон у ва́с в кла́ссе?
Ско́лько сту́льев?
Ско́лько столо́в?
Ско́лько часо́в вы занима́етесь ка́ждый де́нь?
Ско́лько часо́в в де́нь чита́ете?
Ско́лько часо́в в де́нь вы разгова́риваете с подру́гами?
Ско́лько дне́й в феврале́? В ма́рте?
Ско́лько падеже́й в ру́сском языке́?
Ско́лько дне́й в неде́ле?
Ско́лько неде́ль в семе́стре?

Make up your own questions similar to these.

10. Numbers: cardinals and ordinals. Analysis 1.

Do this exercise with various numerals. The second student always
goes one number higher. Watch out for the sex of your interlocutor:
the masculine verb form in the next to last line is ошибся (without
-л- , like мог, могла).

П: Ма́ша, спроси́те Са́шу, како́й э́то авто́бус, но́мер *оди́н* ?
М: Са́ша, э́то *пе́рвый* авто́бус?
С: Не́т, *второ́й*.
М: А я́ ду́мала, что *пе́рвый*.
С: Ты́ <u>оши́блась</u>.
М: (преподава́телю): Са́ша говори́т, что э́то авто́бус но́мер *два́*.

НС

11. Numbers Game. Analysis 1.

This is an old Italian gambling game called *mola*. Two people
play. They both make a fist, and then, together, open up their
fists with any number of fingers extended. Simultaneously, they
both call out a number from 0 (ну́ль) to 10. The one who calls
out the total number of extended fingers on the two people's
hands wins (я вы́играл! = 'I won'). If neither person calls
the correct number, or if it's a draw, repeat the procedure
until somebody wins.

12. Conversation. Dialog 2. Analysis 1.5.

Make an agreement to go somewhere.

(a) Preparation: translate. Use ты.

What are you doing tonight? Nothing. I'm going to the movies/
to the theater/to a concert (на конце́рт). Let's go to the...
together. I don't want to go (идти́) to X. I want to go (пойти́)
to Y. Let's go to Z. When does the concert/movie/play (спекта́кль)
start? What time is it now? When is it over? I don't want to go today.
I want to study. I want to sit at home and study. I want to read.
I don't want to do anything (ничего́). Tomorrow's better. Ok,
let's go to X tomorrow. Sure ("with pleasure").

(b) Conversation. A and B decide to go somewhere tomorrow
rather than today. They discuss the hours at which the event begins
and ends. The expressions for various sports events are:

на футбо́л	to a soccer game
на хокке́й	to a hockey game
на баскетбо́л	to a basketball game

13. Analysis 1.6.

Answer factually.

П: Ма́ша, спроси́те Са́шу, в како́м ме́сяце о́н роди́лся.
М: Са́ша, в како́м ме́сяце ты́ роди́лся?
С: В ма́е.
М: Како́го числа́?
С: Четвёртого.

14. День рождения 'Birthday'. Analysis 1.6.
    Answer factually.

    П: Cáша, вы не знáете, какóго числá родилáсь Мáша?
    С: Я не знáю. Нáдо её спросить.
       Мáша, какóго числá ты родилáсь?
    М: Я родилáсь 20₀го ноябрá.
    С: Её дéнь рождéния бýдет через мéсяц.

    Instead of **через мéсяц**, you can have up to 12 months or
    через гóд. If it's sooner you can have через однý, двé,
    три недéли or any number of days.

15. Conversation: Where's Vanya?

    (a) Preparation. Translate:

    Where's Vanya? He's not here. Where did he go? He went to the
    libe. What's he doing there? (He's) studying. Working. Reading.
    Reading War and Peace. Writing a book. Doing Russian excercises.
    He often studies in the libe. He often studies Russian in the libe.
    He likes to... Where do you study? At home. In the lab. (It's)
    better to study in the lab. When is Vanya coming back (вернýться)?
    In an hour. In two hours. In five hours. At one o'clock. At five
    o'clock. When he finishes (future perfective: кóнчить) his work/
    excercises/book. My goodness, he works hard (мнóго). Here comes
    Vanya. Vanya, where have you been? I went to the library.

    (b) Scene:

    Students A and B act out a scene in which A asks where C is
    and what he's doing. B says that C is working on various things
    in the lab/libe/at home or wherever. C appears and has to answer
    questions from A and B as to what he's been up to.

16. За столóм. Dialog 3. Analysis 1.2-4.

    П: Cáша, попросите у Мáши *сыр*.
    С: Передáй,   пожáлуйста, *сыр*.
    М: *Сыра* бóльше нéт.
    С: Хорошó, пóсле обéда я пойдý куплю́ *сыру*.

    Note the use of the partitive: сыру = 'some cheese'. The
    phrase пойдý куплю́ without "и" translates the English
    'I'll go and buy'. Substitute for сыр: винó, молокó, óвощи,
    мясо, рыба, конфéты, яблоки, кóфе, чáй, сáхар, мáсло,
    кефир, хлéб, бýлки, коньяк, колбасá, сметáна.

17. Buying things. Dialog 3. Analysis 1.3.

    С: Нáдо купить *сыру*.
    М: Я ужé купила 4 килогрáмма *сыра*.
    С: А нáм нýжно 6 килогрáмм. Нáши гóсти óчень лю́бят
       сыр.

    Replace сыр with: milk, butter, tea, meat, sugar, candy,
    vodka, bread, fish, fruit, chocolate, apples, vegetables.
    For liquids use the word литр or бутылка.

18. В магазине.   Dialog 3.   Analysis 1.1-4.

Да́йте мне́, пожа́луйста, *немно́го сы́ру*.

Substitute the following for сы́р, combining with немно́го or не́сколько as needed:

са́хар, ма́сло, стака́н, но́ж, копе́йка, хле́б, колбаса́, икра́, газе́та, кни́га, ве́щи, фру́кты, о́вощи, бо́рщ, ру́бль, ча́й, ка́ша, вино́.

19. Dialog 3.   Analysis 1.1-4.   Answer factually.

П: Ско́лько в Аме́рике сто́ит полкило́ *сы́ра*?
С: В Аме́рике полкило́ сы́ра сто́ит *четы́ре до́ллара*.

Полкило́ is a little more than a pound.

Substitute: a bottle of milk; a pound of meat; sugar; bread; tea; a bottle of white wine; a pound of apples; candy; vegetables; a bottle of vodka; a pound of coffee; a cup of sour cream; a pound of fish; a cup of coffee.

20. Conversation: На ры́нке 'at the market'.   Dialog 3.

(a) Read and translate.

А: Где́ мо́жно купи́ть сы́р?
Б: Во́т здесь, сле́ва.
А: Да́йте, пожа́луйста, сы́ру.
Б: Ско́лько вы́ хоти́те?
А: Два́ килогра́мма. Ско́лько э́то сто́ит?
Б: Два́ килогра́мма сы́ра сто́ят три́ рубля́.
А: Во́т ва́м пя́ть рубле́й.

(b) Translate.

Tell me, please, how much does the meat cost here? A kilo costs four rubles. Tell me, please, how much did you pay? I paid three rubles. That's expensive. That's not expensive. Give me some sausage please. How much? Two kilograms. How much does it cost? Where can I buy sour cream? Here on the left. Where can I buy vegetables? Here on the right. Do you have milk? We don't have any more milk. Do you have any melons? We don't have any more melons. Do you have bread. No. You can buy bread in the store. Let's buy bread in the store.

(c) Pretend you are in a Russian farmers' market (ры́нок). Hold conversations like the one above. You may want to haggle over prices (Э́то до́рого! Э́то мно́го! Не́т, э́то не до́рого! Э́то дёшево!) You might want to print out money but hold the change because you only know numbers from one to thirty. You might assign students different posts and write out shopping lists for the buyers.

21. Translate. Analysis 2.1

    1. I have to have a talk with Kuznetsov. I'll tell him the
       whole truth about us.
    2. I talked to him. (Use Perfective: "had a talk")
    3. She said her brother was born on April 1.
    4. I'll go (and) have a talk with your professor. I'll tell him
       that you're a good student.

22. Dialog 4, Analysis 2.2.

   П: Са́ша, вы́ *е́дете* в Кры́м?
   С: Да́, я́ *е́ду* в Кры́м. Ва́ся то́же *е́дет* в Кры́м. Мы́ все́ *е́дем*
      в Кры́м.
   П: Ма́ша, кто́ *е́дет* в Кры́м?
   М: Они́ все́ *е́дут* в Кры́м.

Do the same with the following sentences:

      Вы́ за́втра пое́дете в Кры́м?
      Вы́ ча́сто е́здите в Кры́м?
      Вы́ лети́те в Кры́м?
      Вы́ за́втра полети́те в Кры́м?
      Вы́ ча́сто лета́ете в Кры́м?

23. Dialog 4. Analysis 2.2.

The teacher asks Sasha a question. Masha then asks the question with
ча́сто.

   П: Где́ тво́й бра́т? В Москве́?
   С: Да, о́н *пое́хал в Москву́.*
   М: О́н ча́сто *е́здит в Москву́?*
   С: О́чень ча́сто. О́н вернётся *в пя́тницу и в понеде́льник*
      опя́ть *пое́дет.*

    Replace пое́хал в Москву́ with:

    went to Kiev, the movies, Vanya's, (his) parents, Leningrad,
the doctor's, south, north, east, west, America, the institute, and
so on.

    Change the last sentence at will, but be sure to keep it logical.
If the trip is short, replace days of the week with hours or times of
the day. Use any hour and any day of the week, but the second time
must be three units later than the first.

    Also, use пойти́/ходи́ть for trips to places reachable on
foot. Then do it again with полете́ть in place of пое́хать .

24. Analysis 2.2.

Где Со́ня? Почему́ её нет на заня́тиях?
Где Ва́ня? Почему́ его́ нет на заня́тиях?

Он/она́ ――――――――――――― в кино́ (on foot)
        е́хала ――――― в Москву́ (by car)
        ――――――――――――― в Ленингра́д (by plane)
        ――――――――――――― в теа́тр (on foot)
        ――――――――――――― в па́рк (on foot)
        полете́ла ―― в Аме́рику (by plane)
        ――――――――――――― на се́вер (by plane)
        ――――――――――――― на юг (by plane)

25. Analysis 2.

П: Где Со́ня? Почему́ её нет на заня́тиях?
С: Она́ пое́хала в Москву́.
П: Когда́ она́ вернётся?
С: 10 ноября́.
П: Зна́чит, через неде́лю.

     Зна́чит means 'that means'. Sasha can choose any time for
Sonya's return, but Masha's response must be based on today's
date.

26. Conversation: a trip. Dialog 4.

     (a) Translate.

     Let's go to the Crimea. Let's go to Moscow. Let's go to
Leningrad. When? Now. When? In two hours. In three hours. In
a day. In two days. In five days. Let's go to Kiev on Monday.
Let's go to America on Tuesday. No, on Wednesday. No, on Thursday.
No, on Friday. No, on Saturday. No, on Sunday. Let's go to Moscow
in a week. Let's go to the Crimea in a month. Let's go to Odessa
in February. Let's go tomorrow. Let's go to Tashkent in March.
No, in April. Let's go to the Crimea. I'm tired of going to the
Crimea. Let's read a book. I'm tired of reading books. Let's go
to Masha's. I'm tired of going to Masha's. Let's go to the
movies (on foot). I'm tired of going to the movies.

     (b) A suggests 3 places to fly to, and B finally agrees to the
third. A suggests 3 times (dates or days or seasons), and B finally
agrees to the third. Then the same with places on foot, using times
of the day. Watch out for aspect: A uses Perfective and B uses
Imperfective (with надое́ло or не люблю́ , as in Dialog 4).

27. Analysis 2.2.

In Sasha's first speech he uses a verb meaning 'round trip'; in his second speech, the verb means 'one-way; while I was on my way'. (The verb встре́тить means 'meet, bump into'.)

П: Са́ша, скажи́те пожа́луйста, вы́ бы́ли в *институ́те?*
С: Да́, я *ходи́л* в институ́т неде́лю наза́д.
П: Вы́ ви́дели профе́ссора Бороди́на?
С: Да́, я его́ встре́тил, когда́ я шё́л в институ́т.

Make substitutions for институ́т. If the substitute is a country, use лета́ть/лете́ть ; if it's a city, use е́здить/е́хать ; otherwise, use ходи́ть/идти́   for places reachable on foot.

библиоте́ка	Москва́	Аме́рика
шко́ла	Ленингра́д	Ита́лия
фа́брика	Босто́н	Сове́тский Сою́з

28. Aspect pairs, past and imperative forms. Dialog 6, Analysis 3.

(a) Here are some Perfective past tense forms; change them to Imperfective and insert the negative particle as you do so.

Model: The first speaker (teacher) says something has to be done, and the second speaker gently suggest that maybe (может = Мо́жет бы́ть) we don't really have to.

П: На́до убра́ть.
С: А мо́жет не убира́ть?

реши́ть	поста́вить	нарисова́ть
купи́ть	положи́ть класти	переда́ть
заплати́ть	накры́ть	вы́пить
перевести́	убра́ть	съе́сть

(b) Now make the same change (P → I) in the Imperative.

Model: Убери́! → Не убира́й!

Watch out for переведи́ (перевести́ переведу́т)vs. не переводи́ (переводи́ть перево́дят): the only difference in pronunciation is in the unstressed third syllable (/ui/ vs. /va/).

29. Analysis 3. Imperatives: positive commands.

Go through all the verbs below and change to imperative (уберёт → убери).
Then translate. Then perform the conversation with each sentence. Note
that all the verbs in this exercise are Perfective.

П: Кто́ *уберёт* э́ти ве́щи со стола́?
С: Ма́ша, *убери́* пожа́луйста, э́ти ве́щи со стола́.
М: Я не смогу́. У меня́ вре́мени нет. Ди́ма их *уберёт*.

Кто́ вернёт его́ кни́ги в библиоте́ку?
Кто́ реши́т э́ту зада́чу?
Кто́ переведёт э́тот глаго́л?
Кто́ поста́вит рю́мки на сто́л?
Кто́ запла́тит за вино́?
Кто́ ска́жет, ско́лько вре́мени?
Кто́ поло́жит его́ бума́ги на сто́л?
Кто́ начнёт чита́ть?
Кто́ позвони́т врачу́?
Кто́ спро́сит преподава́теля, когда́ бу́дет экза́мен?
Кто́ напи́шет письмо́ в газе́ту?
Кто́ да́ст на́м ча́ю?
Кто́ нарису́ет портре́т генера́ла?
Кто́ переда́ст ему́ от на́с приве́т?
Кто́ вы́пьет э́то молоко́?
Кто́ съе́ст э́ту   ка́шу?
Кто́ накро́ет на сто́л?

Now change the last sentence to:

    Ди́ма и Пе́тя их уберу́т.

30. Analysis 3. Imperatives: negative commands.

Do as you did the preceding exercise. Note that all the verbs in this
exercise are Imperfective.

П: Ма́ша, что́ вы́ де́лаете сейча́с? Вы́ чита́ете?
М: Да́, я чита́ю.
П: Са́ша, по-мо́ему, на́м на́до идти́.
С: Да́. Ма́ша, не чита́й сейча́с, на́м на́до идти́.

    Replace чита́ть with:

лежа́ть на дива́не   накрыва́ть на сто́л
де́лать уро́ки   рисова́ть автопортре́т
писа́ть письмо́   пи́ть молоко́
игра́ть на фле́йте   е́сть конфе́ту
переводи́ть дома́шнее зада́ние
игра́ть на гобо́е

31. Поста́вить vs. положи́ть.   Analysis 2.4.

Use поста́вить or положи́ть as appropriate. The verb поста́вить is used in several contexts where English would *lay* instead of *stand*, e.g., plates, breadbaskets, butter dishes, etc.

(a)Perfective with negation. Go around the class. Each student tells what (s)he failed to put on the table.

П: Вы́ ко́нчили накрыва́ть на сто́л?
С₁: Не́т, я ещё не поста́вила стака́ны.
С₂: Не́т, я ещё не положи́л ло́жки.

Substitute: glasses, forks, knives, plates, cups, napkins, bread, wine, dessert, sausage, candy, coffee, butter, sour cream, cheese.

(b) Imperfective with negation. Go around the class, as in (a); each student tells what action (s)he did not engage in. Substitute the same nouns as in (a).

П: Кто́ положи́л ма́сло в шка́ф?
С: Я не зна́ю. Я не кла́л.

32. Conversation.   Dialog 6.

Setting the table.

(a)Preparation: read aloud and translate.

А: Накро́йте, пожа́луйста, на сто́л: поста́вьте таре́лки, стака́ны, положи́те ви́лки, ло́жки, ножи́.
Б: Таре́лки уже́ стоя́т на столе́. А заче́м на́м стака́ны?
А: Мы́ бу́дем пи́ть вино́. Почему́ ви́лки лежа́т спра́ва от таре́лок? Ви́лки всегда́ кладу́т сле́ва от таре́лок.
Б: Прости́те, я оши́бся.

(b)Two people set the table for the Sunday brunch. A orders B around. B objects to everything (заче́м на́м X?).

(c)Two people clear off the table after the Sunday brunch. A orders B around. Every time A wants B to do something, B says (s)he wants to eat some more.

УРÓК ДЕСЯ́ТЫЙ
КВАРТИ́РА

Стару́шка, ма́льчик и Зю́зя подняли́сь по ле́стнице на четвёртый эта́ж. Стару́шка доста́ла из карма́на ключ и откры́ла дверь в кварти́ру. Они́ вошли́ в ма́ленькую пере́днюю, где бы́ло соверше́нно темно́. Зю́зя, одна́ко, прекра́сно ви́дела в темноте́, и да́же до того́, как[1] стару́шка включи́ла свет, она́ успе́ла уви́деть пе́ред собо́й дли́нный коридо́р. В коридо́ре бы́ло пять двере́й: две две́ри спра́ва и три две́ри сле́ва. Пе́ред ка́ждой две́рью лежа́л ма́ленький ко́врик[2]. Ря́дом с ка́ждой две́рью на стене́ была́ ве́шалка. На ве́шалках висе́ли пальто́[3] и ша́пки. Стару́шка подошла́ к тре́тьей две́ри сле́ва, доста́ла из карма́на друго́й ключ и откры́ла дверь.

На́ши геро́и вошли́ в просто́рную све́тлую ко́мнату. Напро́тив две́ри бы́ли два окна́. Они́ выходи́ли[4] на восто́к, и че́рез них уже́ я́рко свети́ло у́треннее со́лнце. Ме́жду о́кнами стоя́л шкаф[5] с посу́дой; у пра́вой стены́, бли́же к две́ри, стоя́л кру́глый обе́денный стол и пять сту́льев. Спра́ва от две́ри, в углу́, стоя́л холоди́льник. Вдоль ле́вой стены́ стоя́ли дива́н и де́тская крова́тка, ме́жду ни́ми стоя́л ещё оди́н шкаф[5], очеви́дно с бельём и игру́шками. Большинство́ игру́шек, одна́ко, лежа́ли не в шкафу́, а на полу́, на ковре́, кото́рый покрыва́л всю середи́ну ко́мнаты.

"Сядь, ми́лая, посиди́"[6] - сказа́ла стару́шка Зю́зе. "Ко́стя" - обрати́лась она́ к ма́льчику - "разде́нься и покажи́ тёте свои́ игру́шки. Я пойду́ сде́лаю[7] компре́сс."

"Мо́жет быть, я пойду́ с ва́ми в ва́нную и там подержу́ но́гу в горя́чей воде́?" предложи́ла Зю́зя.

"У нас нет ва́нной[8]." - сказа́ла стару́шка, "у нас на ку́хне горя́чая вода́ есть. Я принесу́ воды́ в та́зике."

Действи́тельно, стару́шка че́рез мину́ту верну́лась с та́зиком горя́чей воды́. Зю́зя опусти́ла но́гу в во́ду, и ей сра́зу ста́ло[9] лу́чше.

"Ко́стя, пора́ за́втракать" - сказа́ла стару́шка. –"Я уже́ ча́йник поста́вила[10] и ма́ме в дверь[11] постуча́ла. Ты мне помоги́ накры́ть на стол. Я тебе́ бу́ду дава́ть ви́лки, ло́жки и ножи́, а ты их клади́ на стол. Хорошо́?"

"Хорошо́" - отве́тил ма́льчик. "Сего́дня нам ну́жно четы́ре ло́жки, потому́ что у нас тётя в гостя́х."

"А для кого́ четвёртая ло́жка? - спроси́ла Зю́зя.

"Для мамы." - ответил мальчик. -"Она в другой комнате спит."

"У нас две комнаты" -объяснила Зюзе старушка. -"В комнате напротив раньше семья жила, муж с женой, он в магазине работал продавцом, а она в столовой[12] поваром. Потом им дали однокомнатную квартиру в новом районе, а мы подали в райжилотдел[13] заявление на их комнатку, и нам её дали, потому что у Наташи Костя тогда родился. Мы очень рады были и что комнату получили, и что эти соседи от нас уехали[14]. Он очень[15] выпивать любил, и когда пьяный, всегда скандалил и за женой по квартире бегал. Она очень плакала, не хотела с ним в отдельную квартиру ехать[14]. Здесь, говорит[16], хоть соседи меня защищали, а там что я с ним одна буду делать. И телефона нет. Но, говорят[16], он, когда на новую квартиру переехал[14], пить меньше стал[9], полочки на кухне построил, пол лаком покрыл. Она приезжала поболтать, говорит, что район у них хороший, магазин близко и автобусная остановка прямо перед домом, так что на работу и с работы ездить удобно. А моя Наташа встаёт в шесть утра и целый час едет на работу. Хорошо, что она работает не каждый день. Сегодня она не работает, будет с нами завтракать.

Открылась дверь и в комнату вошла молодая высокая женщина. Это была Наташа. Она познакомилась с Зюзей, и все сели за стол завтракать.

a Georgian wine, vinegar, bay leaves topped by tomatoes

Vocabulary

АВТО́БУСНЫЙ bus (adj.)	ПО́ВАР cook
БЕ́ГАТЬ run	ПОДА́ТЬ give, offer; serve
БЕЛЬЁ linens; (under)clothing	ПОДЕРЖА́ТЬ keep for some time
БЛИ́ЖЕ closer	ПОДНЯ́ТЬСЯ go up
БЛИ́ЗКИЙ close	ПОДОЙТИ́ approach
БОЛЬШИНСТВО́ majority	ПОКРЫВА́ТЬ cover
ВА́ННАЯ bathroom	ПОКРЫ́ТЬ cover
ВЕ́ШАЛКА rack	ПОЛ floor
ВИСЕ́ТЬ hang	ПОЛО́ЧКА shelf
ВКЛЮЧИ́ТЬ turn on	ПОЛУЧИ́ТЬ receive
ВОДА́ water	ПОРА́, it is time (for)
ВОЙТИ́ enter	ПОСИДЕ́ТЬ sit
ВЫПИВА́ТЬ drink; get drunk	ПОСТРО́ИТЬ build
ВЫХОДИ́ТЬ look out on, face; go out	ПОСТУЧА́ТЬ knock
ГЕРО́Й hero	ПОСУ́ДА, set of dishes
ДВЕ́РЬ door	ПРЕДЛОЖИ́ТЬ suggest
ДЕ́ТСКИЙ children's	ПРЕКРА́СНЫЙ beautiful
ДИВА́Н sofa	ПРИЕЗЖА́ТЬ arrive, come
ДЛИ́ННЫЙ long	ПРОДАВЕ́Ц salesman
ДЛЯ, for	ПРОСТО́РНЫЙ spacious
ДОСТА́ТЬ take out	ПЬЯ́НЫЙ drunken
ЗА́ВТРАКАТЬ eat breakfast	РАЗДЕ́ТЬСЯ, take off one's coat; **undress**
ЗАЩИЩА́ТЬ defend	РАЙЖИЛОТДЕ́Л district housing office
ЗАЯВЛЕ́НИЕ statement	РА́НЬШЕ earlier
ИГРУ́ШКА toy	СВЕТ light
КАК РА́З just	СВЕТИ́ТЬ shine
КЛЮЧ key	СВЕ́ТЛЫЙ bright
КОВЁР rug	СЕМЬЯ́, family
КО́ВРИК little rug	СЕРЕДИ́НА middle
КО́МНАТКА little room	СКАНДА́ЛИТЬ brawl; start a row
КОРИДО́Р corridor, hall	СОВЕРШЕ́ННО completely
КРОВА́ТКА little bed	СОСЕ́Д neighbor
КУ́ХНЯ kitchen	СТА́ТЬ begin; become
ЛАК varnish	СТОЛО́ВАЯ dining room; **restaurant**
ЛЕ́СТНИЦА stairs	ТА́ЗИК little basin
МЕ́НЬШЕ less, smaller	ТЕМНОТА́ dark, darkness
МИ́ЛЫЙ, dear	У́ГОЛ corner
МОЛОДО́Й young	УДО́БНЫЙ comfortable
ОБЕ́ДЕННЫЙ dinner	УЕ́ХАТЬ leave, go away
ОБРАТИ́ТЬСЯ turn	УСПЕ́ТЬ manage, have time
ОБЪЯСНИ́ТЬ explain	У́ТРЕННИЙ morning
ОДНОКО́МНАТНЫЙ one-roomed	ХОЛОДИ́ЛЬНИК refrigerator
ОПУСТИ́ТЬ lower	ХОТЬ at least
ОСТАНО́ВКА stop	ЦЕ́ЛЫЙ whole
ОТДЕ́ЛЬНЫЙ separate, individual	ЧА́ЙНИК tea kettle
ОТКРЫ́ТЬСЯ open	
ОЧЕВИ́ДНО obviously	ША́ПКА hat, cap
ПАЛЬТО́ coat	
ПЕРЕ́ДНЯЯ foyer	ЭТА́Ж floor
ПЕРЕЕ́ХАТЬ move	Я́РКИЙ clear; bright
ПЛА́КАТЬ cry	
ПОБОЛТА́ТЬ chatter	

COMMENTS

1. до того́, как

   Translate this three-word phrase with the English word 'before'.

2. Коммуна́льная кварти́ра.

   This is clearly a communal (shared) apartment: an apartment shared by many families, each of which lives in one room. The kitchen and bathroom are used by all. Communal apartments are still common in the old houses in the centers of cities. Many people who used to live in them have since been moved to the vast housing developments on the outskirts of town. Apartment rental in the Soviet Union is a subject in itself. If you want to move to a new apartment, you apply for it (пода́ть заявле́ние). If the living space of your present quarters is judged too small (less than 9 square meters, approximately 10 x 10 per person) you are considered eligible, and all you have to do is wait (anywhere between a few months, if you know the right people, to ten years.) Another way of finding a new place to live is to exchange apartments with someone else. A couple who is divorcing is often happy to exchange their single apartment for two rooms in communals in widely separated parts of town.

3. пальто́.

   Пальто́, like кино́, is indeclinable. You can tell it's plural by the verb, висе́ли.

4. выходи́ть

   The literal meaning is 'go out, exit'. Said of windows, it should be translated here as 'They *faced* east.'

5. шка́ф

   This word means 'a piece of furniture in which things are stored (dishes, clothing, books, toys). Depending on what is stored in it the translation will be either 'cupboard', 'wardrobe', or 'dresser'. Thus, шка́ф с посу́дой = 'cupboard' and шка́ф с бельём = 'dresser'.

6. се́сть ся́дут vs. посиде́ть посидя́т

   Russian has different verbs for 'get into a sitting position' and 'be in a sitting position'. The common expression 'ся́дь, посиди́' combines both of them: literally 'sit down and stay (sit) for a while'. For verbs meaning 'sit', see Analysis 4.

7. пойду́ сде́лаю

   Lit. 'I will go I will make'; translate as 'I will go *and* make'.

8. ва́нная vs. убо́рная

   These are two separate rooms, as is the convention in Europe. The ва́нная has a bath tub, the убо́рная has a toilet.

9. стать   станут

When followed by an infinitive this verbs is translated 'start, begin'.
Elsewhere it is translated 'become'.

Пить меньше стал.	He started to drink less.
Он стал врачом.	He became a doctor.
Ей стало лучше.	She became better. (= She felt better.)

10. чайник поставила

Supply the word 'on (the stove)' in your translation: 'I've already put the teakettle on'.

11. Я маме в дверь постучала.

'Knocked on mama's door'; literally a combination of стучать маме (to whom — Dative) and стучать в дверь (where — Accusative).

12. столовая

This word can refer both to a room in a house (dining room) or an eating establishment (dining hall; cafeteria).

13. райжилотдел

Райжилотдел is an acronym for *regional housing department*, the office you go to to see about a change in living quarters. The combination подать заявление means 'apply'; подать заявление на + Acc. means 'apply for', 'make an application for'.

14. ехать, переехать, уехать

This verb ordinarily means 'go' by some means of transportation (Lesson 8, Dialog Comment 14). It is also used to mean 'move (one's household).'

Они от нас уехали.	They moved away.
Они переехали в новую квартиру.	They moved to a new apartment.

15. очень

The usual translation is 'very', but in some contexts 'a lot' or 'very much' is more appropriate:

Мы были очень рады.	We were *very* glad.
Я очень люблю борщ.	I like borsch *very much*.
Он очень выпивать любил.	He *really* liked to get drunk.
Она очень плакала.	She cried *a lot*.

16. говорит, говорят

The old woman's speech is very colloquial in style. She inserts phrases like 'she sez', 'they say', etc., and she runs sentences together.

DIALOGS FOR MEMORIZATION

①. Давай пойдём в кино!

     М: Давай встретимся в полпятого[1]   и пойдём в кино.
     С: В полпятого я не могу. Я иду искать комнату.
          Мне было бы[2] удобнее встретиться около[3] восьми.
     М: Хорошо, давай встретимся без[3] пятнадцати восемь.

②. Отнесите лампу в другую комнату.

     С: Где лампа?
     М: Она стоит на шкафу[4] в столовой.[5]
     С: Нет, я не хочу, чтобы она стояла в столовой.
          Отнесите её в мою комнату.
     М: Поставить её на ваш стол?
     С: Нет, не ставьте её на стол. Поставьте её на книжную полку.

Полезные слова:[4]

       в саду, (сад)   *garden*
       в углу, (угол)   *corner*
       на полу (пол)   *floor*
       в, на шкафу (шкаф)

Комнаты:

       кабинет
       кухня
       ванная[5]
       уборная[5]
       коридор
       столовая[5]
       спальня

③. Почему ты ещё в кровати?

     С: Почему ты ещё в кровати?
          Когда ты обычно встаёшь?
     М: Обычно я встаю без четверти восемь,
          но сегодня я встану в десять.
     С: Почему?
     М: Потому что обычно я ложусь в час ночи[6], а вчера я
          легла в десять минут четвёртого.

4. Вы́ сдаёте ко́мнату?

    С: Вы́ сдаёте ко́мнату?
    М: Да́, сдаю́. Ко́мната больша́я, све́тлая, три́дцать пя́ть рубле́й в ме́сяц.
    С: А кни́жная по́лка е́сть в ко́мнате?
       Я, зна́ете, студе́нт, у меня́ мно́го кни́г.
    М: Вы́ студе́нт? Извини́те, я студе́нтам не сдаю́.
    С: Почему́?
    М: Студе́нты мно́го пью́т, ку́рят и игра́ют гро́мкую му́зыку.
    С: Ка́к хоти́те.

5. Поздра́вь меня́!

    С: Мо́жно войти́?
    М: Коне́чно, входи́! Ка́к дела́?
    С: Поздра́вь меня́: я сня́л [7] себе́ [8] ко́мнату.
    М: Поздравля́ю. Больша́я ко́мната?
    С: Два́дцать ме́тров. У меня́ та́м стои́т пи́сьменный сто́л, кре́сло, дива́н и холоди́льник.
       Всё, что мне́ ну́жно.
    М: А крова́ть е́сть?
    С: Не́т, крова́ти не́т. Я могу́ спа́ть на дива́не.

Поле́зные слова́:

    Каки́е е́сть кварти́ры? [9]
        одноко́мнатная кварти́ра
        двухко́мнатная
        трёхко́мнатная
        отде́льная
        коммуна́льная

Translation

1. Let's go to the movies.

    M: Let's meet at half past four and go to the movies.
    S: I can't at half past four. I'm going to look for a room. It would be more convenient for me to meet around eight.
    M: Good, let's meet at 7:45 (15 before eight).

2. Take the lamp to the other room.

    S: Where's the lamp?
    M: It's (standing) on the cupboard in the dining room.
    S: No, I don't want it (to stand) in the dining room. Take it to my room.
    M: Shall I put it on your table?
    S: No, don't put it on the table. Put it on the bookshelf.

3. Why are you still in bed?

   S: Why are you still in bed?
      When do you get up?
   M: I usually get up at quarter of eight, but today I'm going to get up
      at ten.
   S: Why?
   M: Because I usually go to bed at one, but yesterday I went to bed at ten
      after three (Lit., 'ten of the fourth (hour)').

4. Do you have a room for rent (Lit., 'are you renting?').

   S: Do you have a room for rent?
   M: Yes, I do. It's a big well-lit room, — thirty five roubles a month.
   S: Is there a bookshelf in the room?
      I'm a student, you know, and I have a lot of books.
   M: You're a student? Sorry, I don't rent to students.
   S: Why (not)?
   M: Students drink a lot, smoke, and play loud music.
   S: As you wish.

5. Congratulate me!

   S: May I come in?
   M: Sure, come in!   How are things?
   S: Congratulate me; I've rented myself a room.
   M: Congratulations. Is it a big room?
   S: Twenty (square) meters. I've got a writing table, an armchair, a sofa,
      and a refrigerator.
   M: Is there a bed?
   S: No, no bed. I can sleep on the sofa.

ACTIVE WORD LIST

Nouns

ла́мпа	lamp
дива́н	sofa
кре́сло (e)	arm chair
крова́ть	bed
холоди́льник	refrigerator
кабине́т	study
кварти́ра	apartment
ко́мната	room
коридо́р	corridor
ку́хня	kitchen
музе́й	museum
по́л на -у́; -ы́	floor
поликли́ника	polyclinic
по́лка	shelf
са́д в -у́; -ы́	garden
спа́льня; спа́льни спа́лен	bedroom
у́гол (о) угла́ в -у́; -ы́	corner

бабушка (е)	grandmother
восемь (е) (ж)	eight
десять -ти (ж)	ten
метр	meter
музыка	music
пятнадцать (ж)	fifteen
четверть (ж)	quarter

Verbs

лечь лягут; лёг легла легли С	lie down
отнести -несут; -нёс -несла -несли С	carry away, off
поздравить -вят -влю С	congratulate
снять снимут сниму; сняла сняли С	rent, take
войти войдут; вошёл -шла -шли С	enter
встать встанут; встала С	get up
встретиться -тятся -чусь С	meet (with)
вставать встают НС	get up
ложиться -жатся -жусь НС	lie down
искать ищут ищу НС	look for
сдавать сдают НС	rent out
входить -дят -жу НС	enter
спать спят сплю НС	sleep
курить -рят -рю НС	smoke
поздравлять -ляют НС	congratulate

Adjectives

ванная	bathroom
громкий	loud
двухкомнатный	two-room
книжный	book (adj.)
коммунальный	communal
однокомнатный	one-room
отдельный	separate; individual
письменный	writing (adj.)
светлый	light; bright
столовая	dining room; restaurant
трёхкомнатный	three-room
уборная	lavatory
удобный	comfortable

Misc.

обычно	usually
без	without
ж	*emphatic particle*
ну	well
около	near
пол-	half
потому что	because
себя	oneself; myself, yourself, himself, etc.

Aspect pairs

Perfective	*Imperfective*
лечь	ложи́ться
*сесть ся́дут; се́ла	сади́ться
встать	встава́ть
снять	*снима́ть -а́ют
*сдать (=да́ть)	сдава́ть
отнести́	*относи́ть ⸌сят -шу́
войти́	входи́ть
поздра́вить	поздравля́ть

COMMENTS

1. в по́лпя́того

Literally, 'half of the fifth (hour)'. See Analysis 1.3 for telling time.

2. бы́ло бы

The word бы plus the —л— form means 'would'. See хоте́ла бы in Lesson 8, Dialog 3a, Comment 8.

3. о́коло, без

These two prepositions are invariably followed by the Genitive case. For the Genitive forms of numerals and the uses of prepositions in time expressions, see Analysis 1.

4. Locative case.

You've met this form in Lesson 9 (Text Comment 8: в саду́, and Dialog 6: в шкафу́). It is discussed below in Analysis 2.

5. Adjectives used as nouns.

Some words have noun-like meanings but have adjectival endings. Certain proper names are like that, e.g., Толсто́й, Достое́вский. The word for 'noun' itself is an adjective: существи́тельное (see Lesson 8, Dialog Comment 2.) Words marked with this footnote number in this lesson are all adjectival nouns. They are all feminine, because they are abbreviations of adjectives plus ко́мната (столо́вая ко́мната, Lit., 'table room').

6. в ча́с но́чи

To say *at night* use Instrumental: но́чью (у́тром, ве́чером, днём) — see Lesson 7.4; however, if you state the hour, use the Genitive: в ча́с *но́чи* (в де́вять часо́в *утра́, ве́чера*).

7. снять комнату

English uses the same verb *rent* in two different situations: 'to rent *out to* somebody' vs. 'to rent *from* somebody'. Russian uses different verbs:

Я снял комнату.
Я сдал комнату.

I rented a room ('took').
I rented a room ('gave').

8. Dative 'for': себе

Note this use of the dative, corresponding to certain uses of the English preposition *for*.

Я снял себе комнату.
Я купил себе книгу.
Я купил тебе книгу.

I rented me a room (for myself).
I bought me a book (for myself).
I bought you a book (for you).

9. Квартиры

Однокомнатная кв. can be translated either as 'one-room' or, better, 'studio apartment'. Двухкомнатная кв. = 'two room' or 'one-bedroom apartment'. Отдельная literally means 'separate', but in this context either 'private apartment' or simply 'apartment' is best. Коммунальная кв. = 'shared apartment'.

ANALYSIS

1. More Genitive usages

1.1 Objects of negated verbs

You have learned that the Genitive case is obligatory with нéт.

Гдé икрá?   —Икры́ нéт.

When a verb is negated with не, the object *may* be in the Genitive case, but, unlike the нет-construction, it isn't always obligatory.

Я́ не хочу́ икры́.   I don't want any caviar.

Notice the word *any* in the above translation; it means something like "zero quantity", as contrasted with the more specific meaning of *the*, e.g.,

Я́ не ви́дел икры́. (Gen.)   I didn't see *any* caviar.
Я́ не ви́дел икру́. (Acc.)   I didn't see *the* caviar.

If the noun is a highly specific one, like a proper name, then use the Accusative, not the Genitive:

Я́ не зна́ю Áнну Петро́вну.   I don't know Anna Petrovna.

If the noun is animate plural or masculine, you don't have to worry about Acc. vs. Gen. because there's no distinction:

Я́ не ви́дел твоего́ бра́та. (Acc. = Gen.)
        твои́х сестёр. (Acc. = Gen.)

It is very difficult to make a hard and fast rule about Acc. *vs.* Gen. direct objects. The most important thing to remember is that the more indefinite the noun is, the more likely is Russian Genitive (or English *any*); the more definite and specific the noun, the more likely Accusative (or English *the*). Sometimes an adjective will make the phrase very specific, in which case use Accusative, e.g.,

Я́ не чита́л сего́дняшнюю газе́ту.   I didn't read *today's* newspaper.

1.2 Genitive case forms of numerals

Numerals, like nouns, have case forms. In this lesson we will present only the genitive case forms, because they are the ones needed in telling time.

Nom.	Gen.
двá } двé }	дву́х
три́	трёх
четы́ре	четырёх

The Genitive Singular rule for nouns after двá, двé, три́, четы́ре (однá минýта/двé *минýты*/пя́ть минýт) applies *only* to the specific forms двá, двé, три́, четы́ре, not to their other case forms. Thus, nouns after двýх/трёх/ четырёх are *plural* (бéз двýх минýт - Gen. *Plur.*).

Numerals ending in -ь (пять, шесть, ...) have the same ending as ~~a~~
feminine nouns ending in -ь (see Lesson 7.1); we list them all through *thirty*
— watch out for shifting stress:

пя́ть	пяти́
ше́сть	шести́
се́мь	семи́
во́семь	восьми́
де́вять	девяти́
де́сять	десяти́
оди́ннадцать	оди́ннадцати
двена́дцать	двена́дцати
трина́дцать	трина́дцати
четы́рнадцать	четы́рнадцати
пятна́дцать	пятна́дцати
шестна́дцать	шестна́дцати
семна́дцать	семна́дцати
восемна́дцать	восемна́дцати
девятна́дцать	девятна́дцати
два́дцать	двадцати́
два́дцать оди́н	двадцати́ одного́
два́дцать два́	двадцати́ двух́
два́дцать три́	двадцати́ трёх
два́дцать четы́ре	двадцати́ четырёх
два́дцать пя́ть	двадцати́ пяти́
два́дцать ше́сть	двадцати́ шести́
два́дцать се́мь	двадцати́ семи́
два́дцать во́семь	двадцати́ восьми́
два́дцать де́вять	двадцати́ девяти́
три́дцать	тридцати́

1.3 Telling Time

Just as English uses *of* for the minutes on the left of the clock face but
after for minutes on the right, so Russian has two sets of expressions for the
two sides of the clock.

On the left side of the clock, use the preposition без 'without' plus the
Genitive case of the numeral (section 1.2 above) when referring to the minutes.
The hour comes next in the nominative:

Сейча́с без пяти́ мину́т три́.	It's now five minutes to three.
(Gen) (GPl) (Nom)	(Literally, without five minutes three)
Сейча́с без десяти́ мину́т четы́ре.	It's now ten minutes to four.
Сейча́с без пятна́дцати мину́т пя́ть.	It's now ˍ 15 minutes to five.

You can drop the word мину́т if the numeral is rounded off to something
ending in 5 or 0:

Ско́лько вре́мени? Бе́з двадцати́ два́.	What time is it? Twenty of two.

BUT:

Без дву́х мину́т два́.	Two minutes of two.

Note that each element of a compound numeral is declined:

Ско́лько вре́мени?	What time is it?
— Без двадцати́ пяти́ де́вять.	Twenty-five of nine.

For the quarter hour, the word че́тверть may be used.

Ско́лько сейча́с вре́мени?	What time is it now?
— Сейча́с без че́тверти во́семь.	It's now a quarter to eight.

PRACTICE 1

Say the numerals aloud in this sentence meaning 'It is now x of ten'. The word мину́т (Gen. Pl.) is optional with round figures.

Сейча́с без _____ де́сять.

20	12	20	27	26
5	13	21	28	
25	14	22	29	
2	15 = ¼	23	10	
3	17	24	11	
4	18	25	19	

The right side of the clock — from the hour to the half hour — works differently from English. English looks back to the hour just past, Russian looks forward to the hour that will be. The clock time 6:10 is ten after six in English, but "ten of (into) the seventh" in Russian. Here are some examples:

де́сять мину́т пе́рвого	12:10 (ten minutes into the first)
пя́ть мину́т второ́го	1:05 (five minutes into the second)
пятна́дцать мину́т тре́тьего	2:15 (fifteen minutes into the third)

Note that it is the ordinal number (пе́рвого) that refers to the hour. It comes in last place and goes in the Genitive case. The word мину́т in all of the above examples is the Genitive Plural of мину́та, because we chose a number of minutes other than 1, 2, 3, or 4. For 1, say одна́ мину́та; for 2, 3, 4, use the Genitive Singular мину́ты, according to the rule for nouns after numerals (Lesson 9.1.5).

Сейча́с одна́ мину́та шесто́го.	It is now one minute after five.
Сейча́с две́ мину́ты шесто́го.	It is now two minutes after five.
Сейча́с три́ мину́ты шесто́го.	It is now three minutes after five.
Сейча́с четы́ре мину́ты шесто́го.	It is now four minutes after five.

PRACTICE 2

Follow the pattern by using the Genitive ·of the ordinal numerals.

Сейча́с де́сять мину́т пе́рвого.	12:10
второ́го.	1:10
	2:10
	3:10
	⋮
	11:10

The word 'half' is половѝна, often abbreviated по́л:

Сейча́с половѝна пе́рвого.   It is now half past twelve (Lit.,
(= Сейча́с по́л-пе́рвого.)   half of the first).

Сейча́с че́тверть пе́рвого.   It is now quarter after twelve.

PRACTICE 3

All of these sentences mean 'x minutes after 8', (Lit., 'of the ninth'). Say the correct Russian word for the arabic numeral and use the correct form of мину́та. (Don't use мину́та with quarter and half hour.)

Сейча́с пять мину́т девя́того. (8:05)

10	25	2	7
15	30	6	3
¼	½	8	23
20	1	4	27

To say *at* a certain time, use the preposition в plus Accusative.

Когда́ о́н придёт?   When will he arrive?
— В пять мину́т шесто́го.   — At five after five.
— В че́тверть шесто́го.   — At 5:15.

The preposition в is omitted before без:

О́н придёт без пя́ти (мину́т) ше́сть.   He will arrive at 5:55.

With the word for *half* use Prepositional rather than Accusative, or avoid using a case form by saying пол-:

О́н придёт в половѝне шесто́го.}   He will arrive at 5:30.
Or: О́н придёт в по́л-шесто́го. }

(2.) Locations and spatial relationships

2.1 Locative case

You have learned that the Prepositional Case is used after в and на (location) to mean 'in, at, on'. There are a few dozen nouns that have a special ending, called the Locative, to express this meaning.

Compare:

Он говорил о *шкафе*. He was talking about the cupboard.
Чашки наверно стоят в *шкафу*. The cups are probably in the cupboard.

The Locative ending is -ý- . It is always stressed, no matter what the stress pattern of the noun.

The Locative case is different from other cases in that only a small group of nouns has it. All other nouns, and all adjectives, make do with the Prepositional. Therefore, when you learn a noun like шкаф, you must learn that it has a Locative case. Here is a representative list of such nouns:

шкаф	в/на -ý	в шкафý, на шкафý	cupboard; closet
ýгол (о)	в -ý	в углý	corner
пол	на -ý	на полý	floor
Крым	в -ý	в Крымý	Crimea
снег	в -ý	в снегý	snow

The word час also has a Locative : В котóром часý. (See Lesson 9.1.5)

2.2 Adverbial phrases with Locative endings

Recall that Accusative is used with в and на to indicate motion, and Prepositional (or Locative) to indicate location.

Он постáвил чáшки в шкáф. He put the cup in the cupboard.
Чáшки стоят в шкафý. The cups are in the cupboard.

Now observe the same phenomenon in these adverbial phrases:

Он пошёл внúз. He went down(stairs).
Он внизý. He's down below (downstairs).

Он пошёл навéрх. He went up(stairs).
Он наверхý. He's up above (upstairs).

The forms внúз/внизý and навéрх/наверхý are spelled as single words, but they obviously consist of prepositions plus objects with the expected case endings: zero Accusative and -ý Locative.

2.3 До́ма/домо́й

The distinction between motion and location is maintained in the adverbial pair expressing the ideas 'be home' and 'go home'. When location is indicated, Russian uses до́ма ; when motion is indicated it uses домо́й:

О́н пошёл домо́й.   He went home. (homeward)
О́н до́ма.   He's at home.

The difference between до́ма and домо́й is analogous to вни́з/внизу́ , наве́рх/ наверху́ and где́/куда́. The words for *here* and *there* follow the same pattern.

Location (Prepositional)	Motion (Accusative)	
где́	куда́	where
внизу́	вни́з	down
наверху́	наве́рх	up
до́ма зд́есь та́м	домо́й сюда́ туда́	home here there

3. Reported imperatives: чтобы + -л-

In the following dialog sentence (1) contains an imperative (положи́те) and sentence (3) contains somebody else's *report* of what the first speaker said:

(1) Положи́те ло́жки на сто́л.
(2) Что́ он сказа́л?
(3) Он сказа́л, чтобы вы́ положи́ли ло́жки на сто́л.

'He said that you are to put...'
OR: 'He told you to put...'

Reported imperatives are formed by introducing the clause with чтобы and using the -л- form of the verb. The -л- form usually means 'past tense', but in this construction there is no connotation of tense.

(You have already met чтобы in a different construction with the meaning 'in order to', e.g., Заче́м тебе́ стака́н? — Чтобы пи́ть.)

PRACTICE 4

In the second of each pair of sentences put the verb in the -л- form. Check your answers below.

(a) Говори́те по-ру́сски!
(b) Он мне́ сказа́л, чтобы я́ _____ по-ру́сски.
(a) Чита́йте Толсто́го.
(b) Он мне́ сказа́л, чтобы я́ _____ Толсто́го.
(a) Поста́вьте стака́н на сто́л.
(b) Он мне́ сказа́л, чтобы я́ _____ стака́н на сто́л.
(a) Помоги́те мне́ накры́ть на сто́л.
(b) Он мне́ сказа́л, чтобы я́ _____ на сто́л.
(a) Не руга́йтесь.
(b) Он мне́ сказа́л, чтобы я́ _____ .
(a) Не ду́майте так мно́го.
(b) Он мне́ сказа́л, чтобы я́ _____ так мно́го.
(a) Возьми́те каранда́ш!
(b) Он мне́ сказа́л, чтобы я́ _____ каранда́ш.

Answers: говори́л(а)   не руга́лся/руга́лась
          чита́л(а)   не ду́мал(а)
          поста́вил(а)   взя́л(а́)
          накры́л(а)

Warning: Don't use a Russian infinitive in such sentences. It is tempting to do so, because English uses infinitives in reporting imperatives (e.g., He told me *to speak* Russian); avoid the temptation. Use чтобы + -л- .

```
┌─────────────────────────────────────────────────────────┐
│                      PRACTICE 5                          │
├─────────────────────────────────────────────────────────┤
│   Translate.                                             │
│                                                          │
│   1. He told me to read this book.                       │
│   2. He told her to write Sasha.                         │
│   3. They told us to drink vodka.                        │
│   4. I told you to drink the tea.                        │
│   5. She told me to clear the table.                     │
│   6. I told her to clear the table.                      │
│   7. I told her to set the table.                        │
│                                                          │
└─────────────────────────────────────────────────────────┘
```

The чтобы + -л- construction is also used after the verb хотеть:

Она хочет, чтобы я положил ложки   She wants me to put the spoons on
на стол.   the table.

Она хотела, чтобы я положил   She wanted me to put the spoons
ложки на стол.   on the table.

With the verb просить/попросить you have a choice: use either an infinitive or a чтобы + -л- clause:

Я её попросила уйти.   ⎫
Я попросила, чтобы она ушла. ⎬   I asked her to leave.

In sum, in order to know when to use the чтобы + -л- construction, you must know which verbs require it (сказать, хотеть) and which verbs allow it optionally (просить).

4. Standing, lying, sitting.

In this section we bring together all the verbs having to do with *being* in a position, *getting into* a position and *putting something* somewhere. You have met a number of these verbs already; we add here their aspect partners.

4.1 Be verbs: standing, lying, sitting.

The Russian verbs that cover these positions are стоять, лежать, сидеть, resp.

Be verbs		
standing	*lying*	*sitting*
Impf. стоять -оят -ою	лежать -жат -жу	сидеть -дят -жу

Note that all three verbs are conjugation II and all three are imperfectives, because they denote a continuous state.

The verbs стоять and лежать (not сидеть) are used in Russian to indicate the position of objects in contexts where English is much more likely to use 'be':

Стакан стоит на столе.   The glass is on the table. (Lit.,
                                         The glass is standing on the table.)

Ручка лежит на столе.   The pen is on the table. (Lit.,
                                         The pen is lying on the table.)

4.2 Getting into a position.

Each of the "be" verbs has a corresponding verb or verbs that denotes getting into a position: *get up, lie down, sit down.*

be (I)	стоя́ть	лежа́ть	сиде́ть
get (I)	встава́ть встаю́т	ложи́ться -жа́тся -жу́сь	сади́ться -дя́тся -жу́сь
get (P)	вста́ть вста́нут	ле́чь ля́гут лёг, легла́, легли́	се́сть ся́дут се́л, се́ла

The pair встава́ть/вста́ть means 'to get up from a sitting or lying position' and is also used to mean 'get out of bed, rise', e.g.,

Я ка́ждый де́нь встаю́ в по́л-седьмо́го,   Every day I get up at 6:30, but
но сего́дня я вста́л в се́мь.   today I got up at 7:00.

The pair ложи́ться/ле́чь is also used to mean 'go to bed, lie down', e.g.,

Я обы́чно ложу́сь в по́л-двена́дцатого,   Usually I go to bed at 11:30, but
но вчера́ я лёг в двена́дцать.   yesterday I went to bed at 12:00.

These verbs are all non-predictable, except for ложи́ться and сади́ться, and therefore require a fair amount of study and practice to learn. It may be useful to note the similarities between ле́чь and се́сть : both have a very unusual vowel change from -е- (past stem) to -я- (non-past stem). Also note that the roots of these verbs are very like English: the root сто-/ста- is the same root as that of *stand, stood*; the root леж-/лож-/лег- is the same as that of *lie, lay*; the root сид-/сад-/сяд- is the same as that of *sit, set, sat, seat.*

PRACTICE 6

Getting into position: Imperfective

Ва́ня всегда́ *встаёт* в 10 мину́т восьмо́го.
(replace: я́, мы́, Шу́ра и Ю́ра, Ива́н Петро́вич)

Мы́ всегда́ *ложи́мся* в по́л-двена́дцатого.
(replace: я́, Ни́на Серге́евна и Ива́н Петро́вич, Дире́ктор институ́та)

Президе́нт всегда́ *сади́тся* рабо́тать без пяти́ во́семь.
(replace: Дире́ктор ЦРУ, Ива́н Петро́вич, я́, мы́)

Getting into position: Perfective

Профе́ссор Бороди́н встал в 15 мину́т восьмо́го.
(replace: я́, па́па, роди́тели, оте́ц, ба́бушка)

Роди́тели вы́пили молоко́ и *легли́.*
(replace : мои́ се́стры, о́н, она́, Са́ша, Пе́тя, Наде́жда Петро́вна)

Учителя́ се́ли рабо́тать.
(replace: профессора́, я́, ба́бушка, мо́й бра́т)

The distinction between location and motion (где vs. куда or prep./loc. vs. acc.) shows up in *be* verbs vs. *get* verbs.

Пётр Петрович сел на стул.	P. P. sat down in the chair.
Пётр Петрович сидит на стуле.	P. P. is sitting in the chair.
Нина Сергеевна легла на пол.	N. S. lay down on the floor.
Нина Сергеевна лежит на полу.	N. S. is lying on the floor.
Нина Сергеевна легла на пол, потому что был только один стул, и на нём сидел Пётр Петрович.	N. S. lay down on the floor because there was only one chair and P. P. was sitting in it.

4.3 *Put* verbs.

Each of the *be* and *get* verbs has a corresponding *put* verb: *stand* (something), *lay* (something), *seat* (somebody).

be (I)	стоять	лежать	сидеть
get (I) (P)	вставать встать	ложиться лечь	садиться сесть
put (I)	ставить ´-вят ´-влю	класть кладут клал клала	сажать, -ают
(P)	поставить ´-вят ´-влю	положить ´-жат -жу	посадить ´-ят -жу

You have already met all of these *put* verbs, except the last one, *to seat* (someone). We add it here for the sake of completeness,—it isn't used as much as the other ones because the situation of seating people doesn't crop up as often in real life. We won't use it in subsequent exercises.

Examples:

Где мясо? Мы положили его на стол.	Where's the meat? We put it on the table.
Почему вы кладёте мясо на стол?	Why are you putting the meat on the table?
Где сметана? Я поставила её на стол.	Where's the sour cream? I put it on the table.
Почему ты ставишь сметану на стол?	Why are you putting sour cream on the table?

The distinction between motion and location is observed here too.

Книга стоит на столе.	The book is standing on the table.
Я поставил книгу на полку.	I stood the book on the shelf.

```
┌─────────────────────────────────────────────────────────────────┐
│                        PRACTICE 7                                 │
├─────────────────────────────────────────────────────────────────┤
│                                                                   │
│  Show how the items in column A got into their positions (you will│
│  want a perfective verb).                                         │
│                                                                   │
│  Книга стоит на полке.          Мы поставили книгу на полку.      │
│  Коньяк стоит на столе.                                           │
│  Вино стоит в шкафу.                                              │
│  Нож лежит на столе.                                             │
│  Масло лежит на столе.                                           │
│  Яйца лежат в шкафу.                                             │
│                                                                   │
└─────────────────────────────────────────────────────────────────┘
```

5. More on motion verbs

5.1 The special prefix *c* : quick round trip

The imperfective forms ходить, ездить, летать have the meaning 'round trip'. But if you want to specify 'quick round trip' — the kind of round trip where you're thinking about returning before you even set out — you add the special prefix с- to the imperfective forms. The results are the perfective verbs сходить, съездить, слетать. The verbs сходить and съездить are very common, especially to indicate a trip that's just about to take place. The verb слетать doesn't come up very often, although it is certainly possible:

Я слетаю в Москву, вернусь завтра.   I'm going to fly to Moscow, I'll be back tomorrow.

Я съезжу в магазин.   I'll make a quick trip to the store.
Откуда у нас вино?   Where'd we get the wine? (Lit., from
-Маша сходила в магазин.   where do we have the wine) Masha went to the store.

Thus, the chart presented in Lesson 9.2.2 can be expanded as follows:

Impf.	Quick round trip perfective	One Way Impf.	'Set out' Perf.
ходить	сходить	идти	пойти
ездить	съездить	ехать	поехать
летать	слетать	лететь	полететь

5.2 Carrying and leading

Two more very common verbs of motion are those meaning 'carry' and 'lead by the hand'. In both cases, the most idiomatic English translation is usually 'take': (English 'take' is highly ambiguous: it covers not only these two verbs, but also взять/брать). As might be expected, the verbs for carrying and leading work analogously to ходить, ездить, летать. The special 'quick trip' prefix *c*- works only with водить, however.

	Imperfective	One Way Impf.	'Set out' Perf.
carry	носить, носят, ношу	нести, несут нёс, несли	понести, -несут понёс, -несли
lead	водить, водят, вожу	вести, ведут вёл, вели	повести, -ведут повёл, -вели

It will be easier to memorize these verbs if you note the similarities between them. Носить and водить are both predictable second conjugation verbs with shifting stress in the non-past. Нести and вести are both non-predictable first conjugation verbs with end stress in both past and non-past.

Unlike the verbs for walking, riding, and flying, these verbs are transitive. Here are some examples:

Что вы несёте, Борис Михайлович?
-Бутылку коньяка.

What are you carrying, Boris Mikhailovich? -A bottle of cognac.

Когда я видела Бориса Михайловича, он нёс бутылку коньяка.

When I saw B. M., he was carrying a bottle of cognac.

Борис Михайлович всегда носит с собой бутылку коньяка. Он любит пить.

B. M. always carries a bottle of cognac on him. He likes to drink.

Куда ты идёшь, Маша?
-В школу. Я веду Илюшу в школу.

Where are you going, Masha? To school. I'm taking Ilyusha to school.

Когда я видела Машу, она вела Илюшу в школу. Она всё время водит его куда-то: то в школу, то к бабушке, то в парк.

When I saw Masha she was taking Ilyusha to school. She's always (lit., all the time) taking him somewhere: to school, to his grandmother's, to the park.

PRACTICE 8

Translate; specify the use of aspect (Impf., OW, 'Set out' Perf., 'quick round trip' Perf.). Then change to past tense without changing the aspect.

1. Я схожу́ в университе́т.
2. Дире́ктор ЦРУ слета́ет в Нью-Йо́рк.
3. Дире́ктор КГБ слета́ет в Ленингра́д.
4. Ба́бушка пойдёт к врачу́.
5. Мы пое́дем в па́рк.
6. Мы е́дем в па́рк.
7. Роди́тели летя́т в Ленингра́д.
8. Па́па е́дет на рабо́ту.
9. Пе́тя ведёт бра́та в шко́лу.
10. Бра́т несёт кни́ги.

Answers.

1. сходи́л(а)	6. е́хали
2. слета́л	7. лете́ли
3. слета́л	8. е́хал
4. пошла́	9. вёл
5. пое́хали	10. нёс

метро (subway station)

УПРАЖНЕНИЯ

1. Review: "take"

    If you have associated in your mind a number of specific Russian verbs with this very common English verb, you may have trouble sorting them out. Recall that all of these verbs may *translate* as 'take', but they *mean* different things:

отвести́/отводи́ть	conduct, lead off to some place (on foot)
убра́ть/убира́ть	take off, clear off, clean up
взять/бра́ть	take in hand, grasp; borrow (a book in the library — Prepositional)

    Fill in the blanks with the imperative form of the verb that fits the context. If не occurs before the blank, use Imperfective aspect (не отводи́); otherwise, use Perfective aspect (отведи́).

_____ Са́шу в шко́лу.

_____ стака́н из шка́фа.

_____ стака́ны со стола́.

Не _____ стака́ны со стола́.

Не _____ стака́н в ру́ку.

_____ ло́жку и переда́йте её Ната́ше.

Не _____ Са́шу в шко́лу.

_____ э́тих студе́нтов в библиоте́ку.

_____ э́ту кни́гу в библиоте́ке.

2. Dialog 6. Analysis 2 and 3.

   Translate these pairs of sentences. One sentence in each
pair takes a Perfective verb, the other and Imperfective.

1. Take the glasses off the table.
   Don't take away the cups.
2. Open the window!
   Open the windows every day!
3. Have you solved the problem?
   No, I'm still working on it (solving it).
4. Don't eat soup with a fork. It's not nice (некрасиво).
   Eat soup with a spoon, like everybody.
5. What are you doing? I'm reading the newspaper.
   I'll read the newspaper this evening.
6. I'll go have a talk with your teacher.
   I talk to him about you every day.
7. I'll tell him that he doesn't understand you.
   I tell him this every day.
8. Always put the dictionary on my table.
   Put the dictionary on the table.
9. Don't take apples from the table.
   Take this apple.
10. Yesterday for the first time I managed to understand him.
    Before that (раньше) I couldn't understand him.
11. Yesterday for the first time (в пе́рвый ра́з) I managed to
    speak Russian.
    Before that, I couldn't speak Russian.
12. Yesterday for the second time (во второ́й ра́з), I managed
    to speak Russian.
    I have been studying Russian (for) three months, but I couldn't
    speak.

3. Dialog 5. Analysis 2.4.

   (a) Perfective with negation.

C: Почему́ ты́ не съе́ла *мя́со*? (Why didn't you finish up the
                                meat?)
M: Я́ не смогла́. Та́м бы́ло о́чень мно́го *мя́са*.

   Substitute: ры́ба, хле́б, бу́лка, молоко́, смета́на,
колбаса́, кефи́р, конфе́ты, во́дка, шокола́д, фру́кты,
о́вощи.

   Use вы́пить instead of съе́сть where appropriate.

   (b) Imperfective with negation.

C: Почему́ ты́ не е́ла *мя́со*? (Why didn't you touch the meat?)
M: Я́ никогда́ не е́м мя́со. Не говори́ со мно́й о *мя́се*.

   Substitute as above.

4. Conversation. Dialog 6.

    Sunday breakfast (за́втрак).

    (a)Preparation. Read aloud, translate.

A: Когда́ мы́ бу́дем е́сть?
Б: Че́рез ча́с.
A: Кто́ бу́дут на́ши го́сти?
Б: Два́ врача́ из институ́та.
A: Что́ мы́ им дади́м?
Б: Сы́ру, хле́ба, ко́фе с молоко́м.
A: У на́с не́т молока́.
Б: На́до купи́ть молока́.

    (b)Preparation. Translate.

When will we eat? At 11:00, at 10:00, at 12:00. In two hours, in three hours. Who will our guests be? The general and his wife. Three students (male). Five students (female). What will we give them to eat? Bread and cheese and wine. But we have no bread. We'll have to buy some bread. But we have no butter. We'll have to buy butter. We'll have to buy eggs and coffee.

    But we have no money. I don't have much money (="I have little money."). I have a lot of money. I have a few rubles. I have ten rubles. I have four rubles. How much does coffee cost? Four rubles. How much do eggs cost? Ten eggs cost one ruble. Go to the store and buy bread, cheese, and eggs. Give me ten rubles.

    (c)Enact the situation you have been working on above. You are expecting guests. What will you serve them? You are short of practically everything. You have to go to the store. How much money do you have? How much do things cost?

(5) Dialog 1 Analysis 1.

    Do Dialog 1 substituting different times; write 3 different times on the board and perform the dialog.

(6) Dialog 1 Analysis 1.

    Make the substitutions indicated below; or use a clock or blackboard.

П: Спроси́те Ма́шу, ско́лько сейча́с вре́мени?
C: Скажи́, пожа́луйста, ско́лько сейча́с вре́мени.
M: Сейча́с _____ .

    Substitute: 10:30, 11:30, 1:30, 4:45, 5:50, 7:40, 9:10, 7:15, 12:20, 8:55.

(7.) Dialog 1.

Do the following variation on Dialog 1 and make substitutions as above. In the next to last speech the time is always a half hour later than the time suggested in the first speech.

M: Давай встретимся в *полпятого* и пойдём в кино.
C: В *полпятого* я не могу.
M: А когда ты сможешь?
C: В *пять*.
M: Хорошо, давай встретимся в *пять*.

Substitute for полпятого: 4:15, 4:45, 3:45, 5:30, 6:45, 6:30, 6:15. Invariably, C can only meet one half hour later.

(8.) Conversation.

(a) What did you do last night? Who were you with last night? Where did you meet Sasha yesterday? We met at the theater. We went to the theater. When did you go to (set out for) the theater? When did you meet? When did you return home?

(b) A makes a date with B. A day passes. C comes up to A and asks questions as in (a) above.

(9.) Dialog 2. Analysis 2 and 3.

Perform Dialog 2 substituting different things for лампа, шкаф, and different rooms.

10. Analysis 2: Locative case.

A: О чём вы думаете?
Б: Мы думаем о *саде*. Мы думаем о том, как приятно сидеть в *саду*.

Substitute for сад: ваша кухня, ваш кабинет, угол, пол, ванная, шкаф, ваш дом, снег, ваша комната,

Note: the word том in the last sentence has no English equivalent; it is the Prepositional case of тот, as required by the preposition о 'about'. The phrase о том, как приятно means 'about how pleasant [it is]'.

11. Analysis 3.   Чтобы practice.

   Change each verb to its past form. Then transform the sentences
   according to the model. Translate.

   А: Решите эту задачу!
   Б: Он мне сказал, чтобы я решил эту задачу.
   А: Накройте на стол!
        Расскажите о Советском союзе!   Помогите мне решить эту задачу!
        Принесите мне масло!   Помогите родителям во всём!
        Поставьте мясо на стол!   Нарисуйте портрет Президента!
        Занимайся хорошо!   Купите мне кефир!
        Возьмите эту книгу!   Позвоните врачу в поликлинику!
        Заплатите за книги!
        Скажите мне, сколько сейчас времени!

12. Translate.

   1. The professor told me to speak Russian.
   2. The professor told him to speak Russian.
   3. We told the students to study hard.
   4. He told me to solve the problem.
   5. You told me to help you.

13. Review

        (a) Translate

   А.   Я хочу купить три карандаша. Сколько стоят   карандаши?
   Б.   Один карандаш стоит двадцать одну копейку.
   А.   У меня только двадцать копеек.
   Б.   Возьмите один карандаш. Мне ваша копейка не нужна.
   А.   Я хочу купить и ручки.
   Б.   У меня сегодня нет ручек. Идите к Маше, по-моему у неё есть.

        (b) Translate

        I want to buy three pencils. I want to buy five pencils. How much
   do   pencils cost? How much do   apples cost? How much does a
   newspaper cost? A newspaper costs five kopecks. A book costs 20 kopecks.
   I only have 19 kopecks. I only have 15 kopecks. We don't have any apples
   today. We don't have any more newspapers. Go to Masha, I think she has
   newspapers. Go to Petya, I think he has rolls. Go to Yura, I think he
   has knives.

        (c) A buys from B, but has one kopeck (or ruble) less than the
   asking price. A asks B for a second item and is sent to C, who then
   plays the role that B did.

14. Dialog 2. Analysis 3.

The teacher and 3 students do this conversation. Masha has to know the Imperative form, Vanya has only to remember what the teacher said, and Sasha has to know the Imperfective partner of the verb.

Before you do the conversation, practice the Imperatives and the Imperfective partners alone, e.g.,

поста́вить → поста́вь!   →   (ста́вить) ста́влю
положи́ть → положи́!   →   (класть) кладу́

etc.

П: Ма́ша, скажи́те Са́ше, чтобы о́н поста́вил таре́лку на сто́л.
М: Са́ша, поста́вь таре́лку на сто́л.
П: Ва́ня, что́ она́ хо́чет?
В: Она́ хо́чет, чтобы Са́ша поста́вил таре́лку на сто́л.
П: (While Sasha is doing it) Са́ша, что́ вы́ де́лаете?
С: Я ста́влю таре́лку на сто́л.
П: (After Sasha has done it) Ма́ша, что́ о́н сде́лал?
М: О́н поста́вил таре́лку на сто́л.

Substitute other items for таре́лка , then do the following:

положи́ть ру́чку на сто́л
взя́ть колбасу́
написа́ть сло́во "кефи́р"
нарисова́ть портре́т преподава́теля
перевести́ сло́во "холоди́льник"
отвести́ э́того студе́нта в коридо́р
откры́ть буты́лку
накры́ть на сто́л
убра́ть со стола́
съе́сть э́то я́блоко

15. Dialog 3. Analysis 1.

Answer truthfully. Do not bring in days of the week.

П: Спроси́те Ма́шу, *когда́ начина́ется* её пе́рвое заня́тие.
С: Когда́ начина́ется твоё пе́рвое заня́тие?
М: Моё пе́рвое заня́тие начина́ется в *де́сять мину́т одиннадцатого.*

Other questions:

Когда́ она́ встаёт ?
Когда́ она́ идёт в университе́т?
Когда́ начина́ется её пе́рвое заня́тие?
Когда́ конча́ется её пе́рвое заня́тие?
Когда́ начина́ется её второ́е заня́тие?

16. Dialog 3.   Analysis 4.

      Transform these verbs from '*be* somewhere' (Imperfective) to '*get* somewhere' (Perfective past). E.g.,

     Óн сиди́т (сиде́ть) → Óн сéл (сéсть)
     Óн лежи́т (лежа́ть) → Óн лёг (лéчь)

Don't forget to change the case form (location → direction).

Ва́ня сиди́т на сту́ле.
Ма́ша сиди́т на сту́ле.
Ва́ня лежи́т на дива́не.
Ма́ша лежи́т на дива́не.
Они́ лежа́т на дива́не.
Она́ сиди́т на моём ме́сте.
Они́ сидя́т на полу́.
Óн сиди́т в удо́бном кре́сле.
Ва́ня лежи́т в крова́ти.
На́ш го́сть сиди́т за столо́м.

17. Dialog 3.   Analysis 4.

      Translate. Then substitute я́, мы́, and они́.

Она́ обы́чно *встаёт* в се́мь часо́в утра́.
Она́ обы́чно *ло́жится* спа́ть в два́ часа́ но́чи.
Она́ за́втра *вста́нет* в се́мь часо́в утра́.
Она́ за́втра *ля́жет* спа́ть в два́ часа́ но́чи.
Она́ вчера́ *встала*в се́мь часо́в утра́.
Она́ вчера́ *легла́* спа́ть в два́ часа́ но́чи.
В про́шлом году́ она́ *встава́ла* в ше́сть, а в э́том году́ она́ *встаёт* в се́мь.
В про́шлом году́ она́ *ложи́лась* в ча́с, а в э́том году́ она́ *ло́жится* в два́ часа́.
В э́том году́ она́ *спи́т* то́лько ше́сть часо́в.
Она́ *спала́* то́лько ше́сть часо́в и в про́шлом году́.

18. Dialog 3.   Analysis 4.

(a) Change from present Imperfective (встава́ть) to future Perfective (вста́ть).   Add 10 minutes to whatever time the first speaker says.

П: Почему́ ты́ ещё в крова́ти? Ты́ обы́чно *встаёшь* в се́мь часо́в.
С: Да́, я́ обы́чно *встаю́* в се́мь часо́в, но сего́дня я́ *вста́ну* в де́сять мину́т восьмо́го.

Substitute: 7:15, 7:30, 7:45, 8:00, etc.

(b) As above, but with ложи́ться НС/ле́чь С.

П: Когда́ ты́ обы́чно ло́жишься спа́ть? В де́сять часо́в?
С: Да́, я́ обы́чно ложу́сь спа́ть в де́сять часо́в, но сего́дня я́ ля́гу в де́сять мину́т оди́ннадцатого.

Substitute: 10:15, 10:30, 10:45, 11:00, etc.

(c) As in (a) and (b), but substitute *Ма́ша* for *ты́*.

П: Почему́ Ма́ша ещё в крова́ти?....

19. Conversation: Dialog 3.   Analysis 4.

(a) Translate.

When do you usually go to bed? When did you go to bed yesterday?
I used to go to bed at 10:30. I used to get up at 8:30. Yesterday I
got up at 9:30. Tomorrow I'll go to bed at 11:30. I will always (Imperfective future!) go to bed at 11:30. I like to get up early (páно). I
like to go to bed late (поздно).

(b) Two students talk about when they retire and rise.

20. Dialogs 4 and 5.

П: У вас в квартире есть кровать?
С: Нет, у нас в квартире кровати нет.

Substitute: стол, письменный стол, диван, удобный диван, телефон,
   кресло, большое кресло, шкаф, книжный шкаф, лампа, хорошая
   лампа, посуда, ванная, уборная, столовая, кабинет, спальня,
   кухня.

21. Dialog 5.

A asks B what kind of apartment he has; B answers with an adjective
(big, well-lit, shared, expensive...) and then asks C. Go around the
class until you run out of adjectives.

П: Какая у вас квартира?
А: У меня двухкомнатная квартира.
    А у тебя какая?
Б: У меня дешёвая квартира.
    А у тебя какая?
В: У меня плохая квартира.
    А у тебя какая?...

22. Dialog 5.

Answer factually. If you don't have an apartment say so, and say you
have a room somewhere. If you live in a dormitory, say: У меня
комната в общежитии (общежитие = 'dormitory') or Я живу в ...

П: Какая у вас квартира?

23. Conversation.   Dialogs 4 and 5.

(a) Translate.

I'm looking for an apartment. Do you have an apartment for rent?
Yes, I do. Good, I want to rent an apartment. What kind? A studio
apartment. I don't have a three-room apartment. Is there a refrigerator
in the apartment? How much is it a month? Twenty three rubles. Good,
here's twenty five rubles. Thanks. Here's two rubles. You can move
in (переехать) tomorrow.

(b) A rents an apartment from B.

24. Another "take". Analysis 5.2.

Recall the three verbs from Exercise 1. This exercise is similar, but with the addition of the verb отнести/относить = carry, carry off to someplace (on foot).

Fill in the blanks with the infinitive of the correct one of the four verbs that fits the context. First do the exercise with Perfective verbs; then negate the sentence (Она́ не хо́чет...) and use Imperfective verbs. Translate.

Она́ хо́чет _____ Са́шу в шко́лу.

Она́ хо́чет _____ ла́мпу в другу́ю ко́мнату.

Она́ хо́чет _____ стака́ны со стола́.

Она́ хо́чет _____ кни́ги в библиоте́ке.

Она́ хо́чет _____ кни́ги в библиоте́ку.

Она́ хо́чет _____ студе́нтов в библиоте́ку.

Она́ хо́чет _____ со стола́.

25. Analysis 5.2.

Choose between отнести́ 'take, carry' and отвести́ 'take, lead'.

П: Я не хочу́, чтобы ла́мпа здесь стоя́ла.
С: Хорошо́, я *её отнесу́* в другу́ю ко́мнату.

Substitute: чтобы Ва́ся здесь сиде́л
                     Ма́ша здесь сиде́ла
                     карандаши́ здесь лежа́ли
                     го́сти сиде́ли на полу́
                     кре́сло здесь стоя́ло
                     крова́ть здесь стоя́ла
                     медвежо́нок здесь стоя́л

Now change the response to:

        С: Хорошо́, Ма́ша её отнесёт в другу́ю ко́мнату.

Then change it to past:

С: А я ду́мал, что Ма́ша её отнесла́ в другу́ю ко́мнату.

26. Analysis 5.

    Choose the correct form in parentheses. Note the aspectual meaning.

1. Ива́н Петро́вич (пошёл, ходи́л) в лес. Когда́ он (ходи́л, шёл) в лес, он уви́дел медве́дя. Медве́дь лежа́л в снегу́ и пил конья́к. Ива́н Петро́вич не хоте́л (идти́, пойти́) да́льше. В э́том лесу́ (иду́т, хо́дят) медве́ди, сказа́л он.

2. Сего́дня у́тром, когда́ я (е́здила, е́хала) в институ́т, я ви́дела Ма́шу. "Зна́чит, ты ка́ждый день (е́здишь, е́дешь) на рабо́ту," сказа́ла Ма́ша. "Я не зна́ла. Мы все ду́мали, что ты (идёшь, хо́дишь) на рабо́ту."

3. Когда́ я (пое́ду, е́ду) в Москву́, я возьму́ тебя́ с собо́й. Москва́ о́чень интере́сный го́род. Ты смо́жешь мно́го часо́в (идти́, ходи́ть) по го́роду.

27. Analysis 5.

    Translate.   Note the use of aspect (Impf., OW, 'set out' Perf., 'quick round trip' Perf.).   Then change to past tense without changing the aspect.

Я схожу́ в университе́т.   Мы е́дем в парк.
Дире́ктор ЦРУ слета́ет в Нью-Йо́рк.   Роди́тели летя́т в Ленингра́д.
Дире́ктор КГБ слета́ет в Ленин-   Пе́тя ведёт бра́та в шко́лу.
   гра́д.   Брат несёт кни́ги.
Ба́бушка пойдёт к врачу́.   Па́па е́дет на рабо́ту.
Мы пое́дем в парк.   Он съе́здит в магази́н.

28. Analysis 5. Verb forms.

   (a) Read aloud and translate.
   (b) Change all the verb vorms from они́ to он ; then to я .
   (c) Transform the sentences, substituting он and я for они́.

1. Они́ ку́рят.
2. Они́ спят.
3. Они́ вхо́дят в ко́мнату.
4. Они́ войду́т в ко́мнату.
5. Они́ и́щут двухко́мнатную кварти́ру.
6. Они́ встре́тятся с ней в полчетвёртого.
7. Они́ сни́мут отде́льную кварти́ру.
8. Они́ сдаду́т отде́льную кварти́ру.
9. Они́ сдаю́т ко́мнату в коммуна́льной кварти́ре.
10. Они́ ча́сто лета́ют в Москву́.
11. Они́ схо́дят в магази́н.
12. Они́ съе́здят в магази́н.
13. Они́ иду́т в поликли́нику.
14. Они́ е́дут в поликли́нику.
15. Они́ летя́т в Москву́.

29. Analysis 5. Quick round trips.

А: Дава́й пойдём в музе́й.
Б: Хорошо́, то́лько снача́ла я *схожу́ в магази́н.*

 Places to make quick trips to (on foot): the toilet, the institute, the store, the university, the library, home, Masha's, Nina's, Petya's, Ivan's.

 Places to make quick trips to (in a car): the institute, the university, the library, Petya's grandmother's, Borya's.

 Places to make quick trips to (in a plane): Moscow, Kiev, Leningrad, New York, Washington.

30. Conversation.

(a) Translate.

Ты́ не хо́чешь пойти́ со мно́й в кино́?
Бы́ло бы лу́чше пойти́ в теа́тр.
Бы́ло бы хорошо́ сиде́ть до́ма.
Дава́й встре́тимся в во́семь.
Встре́титься в во́сем бы́ло бы тру́дно.

(b) Translate.

It would be pleasant to go to the museum.
I don't like museums.
It would be boring.
It would be easy to sit at home and read.
It would be difficult to just sit at home.
I have to study.
I have to go to the post office; then we can meet here.

(c) One student invites the other someplace. Arrange a time. It's possible that the second student can't go because he has things to do. Or he may just have to make a *quick* trip somewhere.

This appendix summarizes the forms of Russian words and lists irregularities. It contains the following sections:

1. Nouns

2. Pronouns

3. Adjectives

4. Verbs

5. Prepositions

6. Numerals

The lists in the appendix include all the relevant words from the Active Word Lists; they exclude words that occur only in the passive Text Vocabularies.

1. Nouns.

The regular endings are listed and illustrated in Lesson 7.9.

1.1 Spelling peculiarities.

See Lessons 1.4, 2.2, and 3.1 for spelling rules.

Prepositional Singular.

This ending is spelled -и rather than -e in nouns that end in -ий, -ие or -ия:

ге́ний	о ге́нии
упражне́ние	об упражне́нии
лаборато́рия	о лаборато́рии

Zero endings.

The sound /y/ is spelled й at the end of a word (Nom. Sg. музе́й —zero ending) but with a palatal indicator vowel letter when a vowel ending follows (музе́я, музе́е, etc.). This spelling rule applies to the zero ending of the Gen. Plur. (fem., neut.) as well as to the Nom. Sg. (masc.), e.g.,

лаборато́рия	→ лаборато́рий	(Gen. Pl. zero ending)
упражне́ние	→ упражне́ний	(Gen. Pl. zero ending)
статья́(e)	→ стате́й	(Gen. Pl. zero ending with inserted vowel)

Here are sample paradigms of nouns whose stem end in the sound /y/:

	masc.		*fem.*	
	Sg.	*Pl.*	*Sg.*	*Pl.*
N	ге́ний	ге́нии	статья́	статьи́
G	ге́ния	ге́ниев	статьи́	стате́й
D	ге́нию	ге́ниям	статье́	статья́м
A	ге́ния	ге́ниев	статью́	статьи́
I	ге́нием	ге́ниями	статье́й	статья́ми
P	ге́нии	ге́ниях	статье́	статья́х

If the stem of a noun ends in a palatalized consonant, the мягкий знак is written when the ending is zero (Nom. Sg. masc. of Gen Pl. fem.):

	masc. Sg.	Pl.	*fem.* Sg.	Pl.
N	*словарь*	словари́	ды́ня	ды́ни
G	словаря́	словаре́й	ды́ни	*ды́нь*
D	словарю́	словаря́м	ды́не	ды́ням
A	*словарь*	словари́	ды́ню	ды́ни
I	словарём	словаря́ми	ды́ней	ды́нями
P	словаре́	словаря́х	ды́не	ды́нях

1.2 Masculine Genitive Plural endings: -ов vs. -ей.

The choice between these two endings depends on the stem final consonant of the noun:

(a) -ов after paired plain consonants, ц, and the sound /y/.
(b) -ей after all others (paired palatalized consonants and non-paired ч щ ш ж). Note the spelling -ев (unstressed after ц and the /y/-sound) and the spelling -ёв (stressed, indicating the /y/-sound).

Examples of (a):

Nom. Sg.	*Nom. Pl.*	*Gen. Pl.*
сто́л	столы́	*столо́в*
стака́н	стака́ны	*стака́нов*
оте́ц(е)	отцы́	*отцо́в*
америка́нец(е)	америка́нцы	*америка́нцев*
музе́й	музе́и	*музе́ев*
сло́й	слои́	*слоёв*
бра́т	бра́тья (Irregular stem final /y/-sound in the plural.)	*бра́тьев*

Examples of (b):

слова́рь	словари́	*словаре́й*
мя́ч	мячи́	*мяче́й*
това́рищ	това́рищи	*това́рищей*
каранда́ш	карандаши́	*карандаше́й*
но́ж	ножи́	*ноже́й*

1.3 Minor declension types.

вре́мя

See Lesson 8.2 for sample paradigm.
There are about a dozen such nouns; of them you have met вре́мя 'time' and и́мя 'name'.
They have 3 peculiarities:

(a) they are neuter (though they don't end in -о or -е);
(b) their other case forms have the syllable -ен- (вре́мени);
(c) three singular case forms have endings like F II nouns: Gen./Dat./Prep. вре́мени

ма́ть, до́чь

The paradigms of these two Fem. II nouns are displayed in Lesson 7.1. They have two peculiarities:

(a) their other case forms have the syllable -ер- (ма́тери); no other nouns in the language have this peculiarity;

(b) the Inst. Plur. of до́чь is irregular: дочерьми́.

-анин

See Lesson 8, Text Comment 2.

Nouns of this rather rare type drop the syllable -ин- in the plural forms, have the irregular Nom. Plur. ending -е , and have zero instead of -ов in the Gen. Plur., e.g.,

гражданйн, *гра́ждане гра́ждан*

The noun господи́н works like this too, except that it has Nom. Plur. -а :

господи́н, *господа́, госпо́д*

1.4 Minor case forms.

Partitive case

About a half dozen masculine nouns have an ending -y which is used instead of the Genitive to render the meaning 'some'. See Lesson 9.1.2 for details.

Nom.	*Gen.*	*Part.*
сы́р	сы́ра	сы́ру
са́хар	са́хара	са́хару
ча́й	ча́я	ча́ю

Locative case

Several score masculine nouns have an ending -y (always stressed) which is used instead of the Prepositional to render the meaning *location* after the prepositions в and на . See Lesson 10.2.1 for details.

Nouns of this type that you have met in Lessons 1-10 are listed below.

Nom.	*Prep.*	*Loc.*
шка́ф	о шка́фе	в/на шкафу́
са́д	о са́де	в саду́
у́гол	об угле́	в/на углу́
по́л	о по́ле	на полу́
Кры́м	о Кры́ме	в Крыму́
го́д	о го́де	в году́
ча́с	о ча́се	в часу́

1.5 Suppletion

There are a few nouns that use a completely different stem in the plural forms.

человек 'man, person' → *люди* людей людьми 'people'

BUT: after numerals the irregular genitive plural человек (zero ending) is used, e.g., пять человек vs. много людей

ребёнок(о) 'child' → *дети* детей детьми 'children'

год 'year' is supplanted by лет after quantity words and numerals where the Gen. Plur. is expected, e.g.,

один год   пять *лет*
два года   много *лет*

1.6 Plural only

Some nouns do not have singular forms (cf. English *scissors, trousers,* etc.). Therefore they have no gender and, consequently, their Gen. Plur. forms are not predictable. Examples:

Nom.	*Gen.*
о́вощи	овоще́й
проду́кты	проду́ктов
де́ти	дете́й
лю́ди	люде́й
де́ньги	де́нег

1.7 Gender: declension, indeclinables, and variables

The general rule for determining the gender of a noun is:

\# -decl.   = masc.

о -decl.
indeclinables } = neut.

а -decl.
Fem. II } = fem.

If a noun ends in -ь you can't tell if it's masc. or Fem. II, but see Lesson 7.1 for helpful hints.

The main departures from the general rule are:

(a) a -decl. nouns referring to males are masculine.

Мо́й *па́па* пришёл.
Мо́й *колле́га* пришёл.
vs. Моя́ *колле́га* пришла́.

(b) \# -decl. nouns referring to females are feminine with respect to verb agreement and pronoun substitution, but not with respect to adjective agreement. If a doctor is a woman, for example, you say:

На́ш (masc.) *вра́ч* пришла́ (fem.). Она́ (fem.) здесь.

(c) One indeclinable noun is masculine: чёрный (masc.) *ко́фе.*

(d) *Вре́мя*-type nouns are neuter. (See 1.3 above.)

There are a few other departures from the general rule, but they haven't appeared in this book.

1.8 на nouns.

Some nouns use the preposition series на/на/с where you would expect в/в/из (see Lesson 8.1.3). There are a fair number of such nouns, many of which refer to events or places of work (like заво́д 'plant', конце́рт 'concert'). Those you have met in Lessons 1-10 are listed below.

восто́к	неде́ля	уро́к
заво́д	по́чта	фа́брика
заня́тие	рабо́та	юг
за́пад	се́вер	

1.9 Irregular nouns.

Types of irregularities in nouns are described in Lesson 8.1.

Here is a list of all of the irregular nouns in Lessons 1-10; it does not include nouns whose only irregularity is the inserted vowel or being a на-noun or being a Fem. II noun.

```
а́дрес, адреса́
брат, бра́тья
весна́ (е), вёсны
ве́чер, вечера́
вещь, ве́щи веще́й -а́м (ж)
вино́, ви́на
во́семь (е) (ж)
врач врача́, -и́
вре́мя вре́мени вре́менем, времена́ времён -а́м (сред. род)
год го́да в -у́, го́ды -о́в -а́м
го́род, города́
господи́н, господа́ госпо́д -а́м
гость, го́сти -е́й -я́м
граждани́н, гра́ждане гра́ждан
дека́брь декабря́
де́ло, дела́
деся́ть -ти́ (ж)
дождь дождя́, -и́
дом, дома́
жена́, жёны
зима́ зи́му, зи́мы
и́мя и́мени и́менем, имена́ имён -а́м (сред. род)
ка́мень (е), ка́мни камне́й -я́м
каранда́ш -а́, -и́
килогра́мм, -гра́ммы -гра́мм
кольцо́ (е), ко́льца
коне́ц (е) конца́, -ы́
коньяк -а́
ко́фе (ко́фе...) (муж. род)
Крым в -у́

медвежо́нок (о), медвежа́та медвежа́т
ме́сто, места́
муж, мужья́ муже́й
нож ножа́, -и́
ночь, но́чи ноче́й -а́м
ноя́брь ноября́
```

овощи -щей -щам
окно (о), окна
октябрь октября
падеж падежа, -и
письмо (е), письма
пол на -у, -ы
продукты -тов
профессор, профессора
раз, разы раз -ам
рубль -ля, -ли
рука руку, руки рук -ам
сад в -у, -ы
сентябрь сентября
сестра (ё), сёстры сестёр сёстрам
словарь словаря, -и
слово, слова
слон слона, -ы

снег снега в -у, снега
спальня, спальни спален
среда среду, среды
стол стола, -ы
сторона сторону, стороны сторон -ам
страна, страны
стул, стулья
сыр сыра/-у
тридцать тридцати (ж)
угол (о) угла в -у, -ы
учитель, учителя
февраль февраля
фрукты -тов

цвет цвета, цвета
час часа, часы
чёрт, черти -ей -ям
четверг четверга, -и
число (е), числа
шкаф на/в -у
яблоко, яблоки
язык языка, языки
яйцо, яйца яиц яйцам
январь января

2. Pronouns.

The forms of the personal pronouns and the question-words чтó and ктó
are displayed in Lesson 6.7.
The reflexive pronoun себя́ 'self' is identical to ты́, тебя́, etc.,
except that it has no Nominative form:

Gen.	себя́
Dat.	себе́
Acc.	себя́
Inst.	собо́й
Prep.	себе́

3. Adjectives.

There are two types of adjectives, *ordinary* adjectives and *special* adjectives.

3.1 Ordinary adjectives

The endings of ordinary adjectives are displayed in Lesson 7.9.
Variants of the basic endings are listed below.

Nom. Sg. masc.: -ой

Adjectives with end-stress have this variant.

молодо́й, большо́й (vs. бе́лый, хоро́ший)

Spelling rules

(a) After к г х ч ж ш щ use -и- (not ы).

NSg. m.	*хоро́ший*	ру́сский	vs.	бе́лый
ISg. m.n.	хоро́шим	ру́сским	vs.	бе́лым
Plur.	хоро́шие	ру́сские		бе́лые
	хоро́ших	ру́сских		бе́лых
	хоро́шим	ру́сским	vs.	бе́лым
	хоро́шими	ру́сскими		бе́лыми
	хоро́ших	ру́сских		бе́лых

(b) After ч ж ш щ use -е- unstressed (not о).

NSg. n.	хоро́шее			большо́е
Gen.	хоро́шего	хоро́шей		большо́го	большо́й
Dat.	хоро́шему	хоро́шей	vs.	большо́му	большо́й
Inst.		хоро́шей			большо́й
Prep.	хоро́шем	хоро́шей		большо́м	большо́й

Palatalized stem final consonant

A small group of ordinary adjectives have stems that end in palatalized /ņ/; consequently, *all* of the endings begin with a palatal indicator (и, е, я, ю). Most of them refer to spacial or temporal things, e.g., послéдний 'last', здéшний 'local', сегóдняшний 'today's', etc. The word сúний 'dark blue' is exceptional in this respect.

	masc.	*neut.*	*fem.*	*plur.*
N	сúний	сúнее	сúняя	сúние
G	сúнего		сúней	сúних
D	сúнему		сúней	сúним
A	N/G		сúнюю	N/G
I	сúним		сúней	сúними
P	сúнем		сúней	сúних

3.2 Special adjectives.

Special adjectives differ from ordinary adjectives in the following respects:

(a) Five forms have noun-like endings: all four nominative forms and the Acc. Sg. fem.

Nom. Sg. m.	вáш		бéлый	
Sg. f.	вáша		бéлая	
Sg. n.	вáше	vs.	бéлое	
Pl.	вáши		бéлые	
Acc. Sg. f.	вáшу		бéлую	

(b) No endings begin with -ы- ; most have -и- instead even when the spelling rules don't require it; two have -e- .

Inst. Sg. m.n.	э́тим	всéм	бéлым	
All Plur.	э́ти	всé	бéлые	
	э́тих	всéх	бéлых	
	э́тим	всéм	vs	бéлым
	э́тими	всéми		бéлыми
	э́тих	всéх		бéлых

(c) Some special adjectives have éй where you might expect óй or ёй : моéй, твоéй, своéй, всéй (vs. бéлой, большóй).

(d) Some special adjectives have a peculiar stem in the Nom. Sg. masc.: одúн, э́тот, тóт, трéтий, and вéсь.

(e) The word сáм, самá 'he himself, she herself', etc. is a special adjective; the Acc. fem. sing. has three variant forms: самý, самоё, and самую; the latter two are archaic. Сáм is the only adjective that has stress shift (Nom. Pl. сáми).

These peculiarities are highlighted by italics in the following paradigms. Neuter forms are listed only in the Nom. Sg. because they are otherwise identical to masculines.

Singular m., n.

N	*э́тот,*	*ва́ш,*	*мо́й,*	*то́т,*	*ве́сь,*	*тре́тий,*	*са́м,*
	э́то	*ва́ше*	*мое́*	*то́*	*все́*	*тре́тье*	*само́*
G	э́того	ва́шего	моего́	того́	всего́	тре́тьего	самого́
D	э́тому	ва́шему	моему́	тому́	всему́	тре́тьему	самому́
A	N/G	N/G	N/G	N/G	N/G	N/G	N/G
I	*э́тим*	ва́шим	мои́м	*те́м*	*все́м*	тре́тьем	*сами́м*
P	э́том	ва́шем	мое́м	то́м	всё́м	тре́тьем	само́м

Singular f.

N	*э́та*	*ва́ша*	*моя́*	*та́*	*вся́*	*тре́тья*	*сама́*
G	э́той	ва́шей	*мое́й*	*то́й*	*все́й*	*тре́тьей*	само́й
D	э́той	ва́шей	*мое́й*	*то́й*	*все́й*	*тре́тьей*	само́й
A	*э́ту*	*ва́шу*	*мою́*	*ту́*	*всю́*	*тре́тью*	саму́
I	э́той	ва́шей	*мое́й*	*то́й*	*все́й*	*тре́тьей*	само́й
P	э́той	ва́шей	*мое́й*	*то́й*	*все́й*	*тре́тьей*	само́й

Plural

N	*э́ти*	*ва́ши*	*мои́*	*те́*	*все́*	*тре́тьи*	*са́ми*
G	*э́тих*	ва́ших	мои́х	*те́х*	*все́х*	тре́тьих	*сами́х*
D	*э́тим*	ва́шим	мои́м	*те́м*	*все́м*	тре́тьим	*сами́м*
A	N/G	N/G	N/G	N/G	N/G	N/G	N/G
I	*э́тими*	ва́шими	мои́ми	*те́ми*	*все́ми*	тре́тьими	*сами́ми*
P	*э́тих*	ва́ших	мои́х	*те́х*	*все́х*	тре́тьих	*сами́х*

Similarly:

оди́н,	на́ш,	тво́й,
одно́	на́ше	твое́
		сво́й,
		свое́

In addition to the above list there are two fairly large groups of words that have forms like special adjectives:

Possessive adjectives from a-declension animate nouns.

These have no peculiarities except those listed in (a) above.

Example: се́стрин се́стрино 'sister's' (from сестра́)

Adjectival derivatives, mostly from names of animals.

Example: во́лчий во́лчье 'wolf, lupine' (from во́лк 'wolf')

The word тре́тий, тре́тье 'third' is exceptional in that it has the same endings as this class but it doesn't refer to an animal.

This class has the peculiarities listed in (a) and (d) above.

	sister's	*third*
Singular, m., n.		
N	*сёстрин, сёстрино*	*трётий, трётье*
G	сёстриного	трётьего
D	сёстриному	трётьему
A	N/G	N/G
I	сёстриным	трётьем
P	сёстрином	трётьем
Singular, f.		
N	*сёстрина*	*трётья*
G	сёстриной	трётьей
D	сёстриной	трётьей
A	*сёстрину*	*трётью*
I	сёстриной	трётьей
P	сёстриной	трётьей
Plural		
N	*сёстрины*	*трётьи*
G	сёстриных	трётьих
D	сёстриным	трётьим
A	N/G	N/G
I	сёстриными	трётьими
P	сёстриных	трётьих

3.3 Mixed declension: proper names in -ин and -ов.

The endings of people's last names in -ин and -ов (Ильйн, Иванóв) are a mixture of noun and adjective endings. See Lesson 8.1.5 for a complete paradigm.

3.4 Short adjectives.

Some adjectives have a set of only four gender endings and this set is used only as predicates ('is, am, are'), not as noun modifiers.

Example: рáд, рáда, рáдо, рáды 'glad'

Я рáд.	I *am* glad.
Онá рáда.	She *is* glad.

Similarly:

Óн женáт.	He *is* married.
Óни женáты.	They *are* married.

Four such adjectives occurred in Lessons 1-10:

рáд
женáт
знакóм
нýжен, нужнá, нýжно, нужнú

Listed below are short adjectives you have met only in the neuter form.
The neuter form has two functions: the predicative function ('it *is*' — as
described above) and the adverbial function (like English -*ly*).

Example: ясно 'clear; clearly'
Predicate: Ясно.'It *is* clear.'
Adverb: Он говорит очень ясно.   He speaks very *clearly*.

The Dative case may be used with these forms to indicate the person involved:

Мне холодно.   I'm cold (Lit., For me it *is* cold.).

трудно	весело	холодно
легко	скучно	тепло
просто	приятно	жарко
хорошо		
лучше		

4. Verbs.

The forms of a verb are:

Non-past tense: see Lesson 8.2 for paradigms, stress patterns, and consonant
   alternations.

Imperative: -й or zero (-ь, -й); see Lesson 9.3 for rules.

Infinitive: suffix -ть (-ти if stressed; a few with -чь, e.g. лечь).

Past tense: suffix -л- plus four gender endings.

Conditional/Subjunctive: бы plus past tense.

Most verbs are matched with an aspect partner, e.g. писать Imperfective
with написать Perfective. Unprefixed verbs of motion have an additional
partner to denote one-way motion, e.g. ходить (Imperfective) with идти
(One-Way Imperfective).

	Imperfective	*Perfective*
Present meaning	читают	- - - -
Imperative	читай	прочитай
Future meaning	будут читать	прочитают
Infinitive	читать	прочитать
Past	читала	прочитала
Conditional/Subjunctive	читала бы	прочитала бы

4.1 Verb stems: predictable and non-predictable.

Verbs have two stems, a past stem (писа-: писать, писала) and a
non-past stem (пиш- : пишут, пиши). Most verbs are predictable: given
one stem you can predict what the other is (рисовать↔рисуют). The six
prediction rules are given in Lesson 8.2.3. All non-predictable verbs occurring
in Lessons 1-10 are listed here.

брать
  убрать
быть
вести
  отвести
  перевести
взять
видеть
  увидеть
вставать
встать
давать
  задавать
  передавать
  сдавать
дать
  задать
  передать
  сдать
есть
  надоесть
  съесть
ехать
  поехать
жить
звать
  назвать
идти
  войти
  пойти

искать
казаться
класть
лежать
лететь
  полететь
лечь
мочь
  смочь
накрыть
  открыть
начать
  начаться
нести
  отнести
писать
  написать
пить
  выпить
родиться
сидеть
сказать
  рассказать
слышать
смотреть
снять
спать
стоять
хотеть

4.2 Aspect pairs.

All verbs whose aspect partners have been listed or discussed in Lessons 1-10 are listed here.

Imperfective	Perfective	Imperfective	Perfective
бра́ть	взя́ть	отвеча́ть	отве́тить
ви́деть	уви́деть	отводи́ть	отвести́
встава́ть	вста́ть	открыва́ть	откры́ть
входи́ть	войти́	ошиба́ться	ошиби́ться
говори́ть	сказа́ть	переводи́ть	перевести́
говори́ть	поговори́ть	писа́ть	написа́ть
дава́ть	да́ть	пи́ть	вы́пить
де́лать	сде́лать	повторя́ть	повтори́ть
е́здить	пое́хать	поздравля́ть	поздра́вить
е́сть	съе́сть	приглаша́ть	пригласи́ть
е́хать	пое́хать	проси́ть	попроси́ть
задава́ть	зада́ть	разреша́ть	разреши́ть
звони́ть	позвони́ть	расска́зывать	рассказа́ть
идти́	пойти́	реша́ть	реши́ть
изуча́ть	изучи́ть	рисова́ть	нарисова́ть
кла́сть	положи́ть	сдава́ть	сда́ть
конча́ть	ко́нчить	слы́шать	услы́шать
конча́ться	ко́нчиться	спра́шивать	спроси́ть
лета́ть	полете́ть	ста́вить	поста́вить
лете́ть	полете́ть	убира́ть	убра́ть
ложи́ться	ле́чь	ходи́ть	пойти́
мо́чь	смо́чь	чита́ть	прочита́ть
называ́ть	назва́ть		
накрыва́ть	накры́ть		
начина́ть	нача́ть		
начина́ться	нача́ться		
нра́виться	понра́виться		

5. Prepositions.

This list of prepostions contains only the meanings and uses discussed in Lessons 1-10. A few of these prepositions góvern cases in addition to those listed here (по, о, and с).

Variant forms with the added vowel -о (like с/со, к/ко, в/во) occur before мне, мной, forms of весь that begin with вс- (всём, всём...), and certain consonant clusters, e.g., со стола, во втором уроке. The variant об occurs before words spelled with initial и, э, а, о, у ; the variant обо before мне, всём, всех; and the variant о elsewhere.

Genitive

у	at, by
от	from, away from
из	from, out of
до	up to, until, before
после	after
около	around, near
без	without
посередине	in the middle of
из-под	out from under
позади	behind, in back of

Dative

по	apiece; along
к	to, up to, toward

Accusative

через	through, in (in time expressions)

Instrumental

между	between
перед	in front of, before
рядом с	alongside of

Instrumental/Genitive

с + Inst.	with
с + Gen.	from, off of

Instrumental/Accusative

под + Inst.	under (location)
под + Acc.	under (motion)
за + Inst.	for (to fetch); beyond (location)
за + Inst.	for (in return for); beyond (motion)

Prepositional

о	about

Prepositional/Accusative

в + Prep.	in, at (location)
в + Acc.	in, to (motion)
на + Prep.	on; in, at (location)
на + Acc.	on; to (motion)

6. Numerals.

Ordinal numerals (like *first, second*, etc.) are all ordinary adjectives except тре́тий, тре́тья, тре́тье, which is a special adjective. In compound ordinal numerals, only the last member is declined, e.g. в два́дцать *пя́том* уро́ке.

пе́рвый	восьмо́й	пятна́дцатый
второ́й	девя́тый	шестна́дцатый
тре́тий	деся́тый	семна́дцатый
четвёртый	оди́ннадцатый	восемна́дцатый
пя́тый	двена́дцатый	девятна́дцатый
шесто́й	трина́дцатый	двадца́тый
седьмо́й	четы́рнадцатый	тридца́тый

Cardinal numerals (like *one, two, three*, etc.) are listed below in their Nominative and Genitive case forms. The numeral оди́н is a special adjective; the numerals два́/две́, три́, четы́ре have irregular adjective-like endings; the other numerals you have had so far have the forms of Fem. II nouns.

Два́ is used with masc. and neut. nouns; две́ with fem.

In compound cardinal numerals all elements are declined, e.g., без *двадцати́ пяти́* мину́т.

	Nominative	*Genitive*
1	оди́н (special adjective)	
2	два́, две́	дву́х
3	три́	трёх
4	четы́ре	четырёх
5	пя́ть	пяти́
6	ше́сть	шести́
7	се́мь	семи́
8	во́семь	восьми́
9	де́вять	девяти́
10	де́сять	десяти́
11	оди́ннадцать	оди́ннадцати
12	двена́дцать	двена́дцати
13	трина́дцать	трина́дцати
14	четы́рнадцать	четы́рнадцати
15	пятна́дцать	пятна́дцати
16	шестна́дцать	шестна́дцати
17	семна́дцать	семна́дцати
18	восемна́дцать	восемна́дцати
19	девятна́дцать	девятна́дцати
20	два́дцать	двадцати́
30	три́дцать	тридцати́

PASSIVE VOCABULARY GLOSSARY

BEGINNING RUSSIAN, VOL. I

This glossary contains all of the words other than personal names that occur in the Texts of Lessons 1-10, with this exception: if a word occurs in a Dialog (Active Word List) prior to its first occurrence in a Text, the student is assumed to have memorized it and it is therefore not listed in this Glossary.

Numbers in parentheses indicate the total number of times the word occurs in all of the Texts of volumes 1 and 2 (Lessons 1-24).

The abbreviations C and HC stand for perfective and imperfective aspect, respectively.

а (58)   and, but
автобусный (1)   bus
аге́нт (16)   agent
аге́нтство (1)   agency
Азия (9)   Asia
акце́нт (2)   accent
алба́нский (3)   Albanian
америка́нец (5)   American
америка́нский (11)   American
англи́йский (5)   English
анте́нна (1)   antenna
апельси́н (5)   orange
аплодисме́нты (1)   applause
атеи́ст (4)   atheist
атмосфе́ра (1)   atmosphere
аудито́рия   (2)   auditorium, class-
                          room
аэропо́рт (2)   airport
ба́бушка (4)   grandmother
бе́гать (1)   HC   run
бедня́жка (1)   poor fellow/girl
без (7)   without
бе́лый (11)   white
бельё (1)   linen; underwear
бесшу́мный (1)   noiseless
биле́т (5)   ticket
бли́же (1)   closer
бли́зкий (2)   close
блоки́ровать (1)   HC   block

бо́г (7)   god
бога́тый (2)   rich
болга́рский (2)   Bulgarian
бо́ль (3)   pain
бо́льно (1)   hurt; painful
большинство́ (1)   majority
большо́й (27)   large
борьба́ (1)   struggle
боя́ться (2)   HC   be afraid
бро́сить (2)   C   throw; quit

буты́лка (2)   bottle
бы́стро (7)   rapidly, quickly
бы́ть (84)   C   be
в (137)   in
ва́жный (5)   important
ва́нная (3)   bathroom
ваш (15)   your
вдо́ль (2)   along, parallel with
ве́рить (6)   HC   believe, have
                          faith in
верне́е (1)   rather
вертика́льный (2)   vertical
ве́сь (45)   all
ве́чер (14)   evening
вече́рний (1)   evening
ве́шалка (2)   coat rack
вздохну́ть   (5)   C   sigh, take
                          a breath

ви́лка (8) fork
висе́ть (4) НС hang
включи́ть (3) С include, turn on

влете́ть (1) С fly into
вме́сте (8) together
внача́ле (1) at first, in the beginning
вни́з (7) down
внизу́ (3) below
вода́ (7) water
вое́нный (4) military
войти́ (13) С enter
вокру́г (1) around
во́т (15) here, there
вра́ч (8) doctor
вре́мя (15) time
всё (2) everyone
всё-таки (4) nevertheless, all the same
всегда́ (12) always
вспо́мнить (3) С remember, recall
встава́ть (4) НС get up, rise
вста́ть (5) С get up, rise
встре́ча (4) meeting, encounter
второ́й (13) second
вчера́шний (1) yesterday's
вы́ (48) you
вы́глядеть (4) НС look (like)
вы́йти (19) С go out, come out, exit
выпива́ть (1) НС drink
вы́пить (5) С drink, have a drink
высо́кий (5) tall, high
выходи́ть (5) НС look out on, face, go out
газе́та (16) newspaper
где́ (32) where
геро́й (6) hero
гипо́теза (1) hypothesis
гла́вный (2) main, chief, principal
глубо́кий (1) deep
говори́ть (38) НС speak
голова́ (5) head
горя́чий (11) hot
господи́н (19) sir, master
го́сть (7) guest, visitor
госуда́рство (2) state
Гре́ция (1) Greece
грима́са (1) grimace
гуля́ть (4) НС take a walk, take a stroll

да́ (10) yes
дава́й (9) let's
дава́ть (4) НС five
давно́ (7) for a long time; long ago
далеко́ (1) far, far off
да́ма (2) lady
два́ (13) two
две́ (7) two
две́рь (24) door
действи́тельно (6) really, indeed
де́лать (29) НС make, do
де́нь (13) day
де́рево (8) tree
де́тский (14) child's, children's
дива́н (3) sofa
дире́ктор (47) director
дли́нный (4) long
для́ (9) for
до́ждь (10) rain
докла́д (5) report, announcement
до́лго (4) a long time
до́лжен (10) should, ought to, have to
до́м (27) home, house, building
до́ма (7) at home
дорого́й (11) dear, expensive
доста́ть (4) С get, obtain
до́чка (4) daughter
до́чь (2) daughter
дру́г (9) friend
друго́й (30) different, other
ду́мать (22) НС think
жда́ть (5) НС wait (for), await, expect
же (17) emphatic particle
же́нщина (11) woman
живо́тное (5) animal
жи́знь (6) life
жи́ть (16) НС live
журнали́ст (12) journalist
за́втрак (6) breakfast
за́втракать (5) НС eat breakfast
зага́дочный (2) mysterious
задава́ть (3) НС ask (question), assign
заме́тить (4) С notice
занима́ться (8) НС study, do
захоте́ть (2) С want
защища́ть (1) НС defend
заявле́ние (1) statement, aplication
зва́ть (33) НС call

здесь (11) here
здороваться (1) НС greet
здоровье (6) health
здравствуйте (6) hello
земля (10) earth
зима (7) winter
знать (52) НС know
зонтик (6) umbrella
и (25) and
игрушка (5) toy
идти (33) НС go
известие (1) news, information
издалека (1) from afar
изобрести (1) С devise, contrive,
икра (16) caviar   [invent
институт (20) institute
интересный (11) interesting
инфляция (1) inflation
испугаться (2) С be frightened
                of, scared of
исторический (1) historical, historic
история (1) incident, event; history
к (46) to; by (in time expressions)
кабинет (18) study, office
казаться (9) НС seem
как (32) how; as
какой-то (8) some kind of, some
капитализм (1) capitalism
карман (6) pocket
картина (4) picture
картинка (4) picture
квадратный (3) square
квартира (13) apartment
климат (2) climate
ключ (2) key
ковёр (1) rug
коврик (1) rug
когда (30) when
коллега (5) colleague
комитет (3) committee
коммунистический (1) communist
комната (24) room
комнатка (1) room
компресс (4) compress
компромисс (2) compromise
конечно (11) of course
контакт (2) contact
кончить (2) С end, finish
коридор (5) corridor, hall
космонавт (2) cosmonaut
космос (7) cosmos
кот (2) tomcat
который (49) which
кошка (2) cat, tabby

красивый (2) beautiful
красный (14) red
кроватка (1) bed
круглый (7) round
крыша (6) roof
кто (33) who
купить (17) С buy
куст (1) bush
кухня (3) kitchen
лаборатория (2) laboratory
лазер (1) laser
лак (1) varnish, lacquer
лестница (5) stairs
летать (3) НС fly
лимон (5) lemon
лицо (3) face
ложка (9) spoon
луна (10) moon
люди (7) people
маленький (12) small, little
мало (5) few, not many, not much,
                little
мальчик (14) little boy
мама (3) mama, mother
марксистско-ленинский (1) marx-
                ist-leninist
математик (1) mathematician
математика (5) mathematics
медицина (1) medicine
медленно (1) slowly
между (8) between
меньше (2) less, smaller
мечеть (3) mosque
мечтать (2) НС dream, day dream
микрофон (1) microphone
милый (1) dear
министр (26) government min-
                ister
мир (14) world; peace
много (15) many, much, a lot of
может (3) maybe, perhaps
может быть (8) perhaps, maybe
мой (26) my
молодец (7) good fellow! nice
молодой (7) young   [going!

момент (6) moment
Москва (6) Moscow
мочь (16) НС be able
мы (51) we
мяч (1) ball
мячик (1) ball
на (107) on, in; at
наверно (7) probably

наве́рх (5) up, upward
наверху́ (2) up, above
на́до (16) must, (one) has to

надое́сть (3)   C be sick and
                    tired of, fed up
наи́вный (3) naive
наконе́ц (2) finally
напра́виться (3) C make (for),
                      get going
напро́тив (6) opposite, across the way
наро́д (5) people
наступи́ть (2) C come, set in
научи́ться (3) C learn
нача́ть (16) C begin
на́ш (30) our
не (73) not
не́бо (1) sky
небольшо́й (3) small
незначи́тельный (1) insignificant,
                          negligible
неизве́стный (3) unknown
не́который (2) some, certain
неме́дленно (7) immediately
ненадо́лго (2) for a short while,
                    not for long

непреме́нно (1) without fail, cer-
                      tainly
непреры́вно (2) continuously, un-
                      interruptedly
нетру́дный (1) rather easy
неуда́чный (2) unsuccessful
никогда́ (12) never
никто́ (5) no one
ничто́ (17) nothing
но́ (25) but
но́вость (10) news
но́вый (6) new
нога́ (6) foot, leg
но́ж (7) knife
но́чь (5) night
ну́ (6) well! well then!
ну́жен (16) is necessary, needed
о (46) about
обе́денный (1) dinner
обма́нывать (1) HC deceive
о́браз (1) way of, mode of
образова́ние (1) education
обрати́ться (7)   C   turn to,
                          address
обра́тно (4) back
объяви́ть (6) C announce

объясни́ть (8) C explain
оде́жда (5) clothing
оди́н (33) alone; one
однако (8) however
однокомнатный (2) one-room
оказа́ться (3) C turn out to be,
                     prove to be
око́нчить (1) C finish, end
о́н (87) he
она́ (104) she
они́ (32) they
оно́ (2) it
опусти́ть (1) C lower
остано́вка (2) stop
оста́ться (5) C remain, stay
                     behind
о́стров (3) island
о́стрый (3) sharp
от (21) from
отве́т (3) answer
отве́тить (15) C answer
отде́льный (2) separate, in-
                    dividual
отдыха́ть (1) HC rest, relax
откры́ться (3) C open
отку́да (5) from where
очеви́дно (1) obviously
о́чень (30) very
пальто́ (6) coat
па́ртия (1) party; match (in a game)
па́спорт (15) passport
пассажи́р (3) passenger
па́уза (2) pause
пенсионе́р (3) pensioner, retired
пе́рвый (24) first   [person
переби́ть (6) C interrupt
пе́ред (14) in front of, before
передава́ть (6)   HC pass;
       tell, communicate; broadcast
переда́ть (17) C pass
пере́дняя (1) foyer
перее́хать (1) C move; cross
писа́ть (8) HC write
письмо́ (8) letter
пла́кать (5) HC cry
пла́н (4) plan
плане́та (37) planet
по (45) each; on; around; along

по-пре́жнему (2) as before, as
                     usual
по-ру́сски (12) (in) Russian
поболта́ть (1) C chatter
по́вар (1) cook

повторить (6) C repeat
погулять (9) C take a walk, take a stroll
под (12) under
подарить (1) C give, make a present
подать (3) C give, offer, serve
подержать (1) C keep for some time
поднять (3) C raise, lift
подняться (4) C go up, rise
подойти (3) C approach
подписываться (1) HC sign; subscribe (to)
подходить (2) HC approach, go up to
поехать (12) C go (by vehicle)
позвать (1) C call
позвонить (8) C phone
поздороваться (2) C greet
познакомиться (9) C meet, get acquainted
показать (5) C show, point[quainted
показывать (3) HC show, point
покраснеть (2) C turn red, blush
покрывать (1) HC cover
покрыть (2) C cover
пол (5) floor
полететь (3) C fly
поликлиника (3) clinic
половина (3) half
полочка (1) shelf
получить (4) C receive
полчаса (1) a half hour
помнить (6) HC remember
помочь (10) C help
понимать (11) HC understand
попасть (3) C get to, find oneself (in)
пора (1) it is time
порядок (2) order
посидеть (1) C sit a while
посмотреть (9) C look
построить (1) C build
постучать (2) C knock
посуда (3) crockery, plates and dishes
потенциал (3) potential
потом (18) then
потому что (15) because
похожий (4) resembling, similar
почётный (1) respected, honored

почти (6) almost
почувствовать (5) C feel
поэтому (3) therefore
появиться (3) C appear
правда (11) truth
предлагать (1) HC suggest, offer
предложить (3) C suggest
предмет (2) subject, object, thing
представитель (1) representative
представлять (1) HC represent,
президент (42) president [present
прекрасный (3) beautiful, fine
пресс-конференция (4) press conference
пригласить (3) C invite
приезжать (3) HC arrive, come
приземлиться (3) C land
признаться (1) C confess
прийти (15) C arrive, come (by foot)
прилететь (18) C arrive, come, (by plane)
принести (5) C bring
приходить (6) HC come (on foot), arrive
приятно (10) pleasant
прогрессивный (1) progressive
прогулка (1) walk, stroll
продавец (1) salesman, store clerk
просторный (3) spacious
просьба (1) request
проходить (3) HC go through, go past
прочитать (4) HC read
прыгать (1) HC jump
прыгнуть (1) C jump
прыжок (1) jump
пусть (7) let
пьяный (3) drunken, a drunk
работа (18) work
работать (19) HC work
равно (3) alike, in like manner
рад (5) happy, glad, pleased
радио (3) radio
раз (13) time
разговаривать (7) HC talk, speak, converse
разговор (5) conversation
раздеться (2) C take off one's things; get undressed

ра́зный (1) different, various
райжилотде́л (2) district housing
                 office
райо́н (4) region
раке́та (24) rocket
ра́но (3) early
ра́ньше (5) earlier; formerly
расска́з (4) account, narrative,
              story
расска́зывать (6) НС tell
расти́ (5) НС grow
респу́блика (1) republic
реша́ть (2) НС decide
реши́ть (8) С decide
роди́тель (4) parent
ру́сский (6) Russian
ру́чка (20) pen
ря́дом (9) next (to)
с (44) with; from
са́д (5) garden
сади́ться (5) НС sit down, take
                  a seat
са́м (14) myself, yourself, himself,
           etc.
самолёт (8) plane
са́мый (16) most (superlative); the
све́т (2) light   [very
све́тить (2) НС shine
све́тлый (4) bright
свобо́дный (2) free
сде́лать (13) С make, do
себя́ (23) oneself, myself, your-
            self, etc.
сего́дня (29) today
сего́дняшний (4) today's
секре́т (2) secret
секрета́рь (5) secretary
секре́тный (9) secret
семья́ (4) family
середи́на (4) middle
се́сть (9) С land, sit down, sit
синаго́га (3) synagogue
скаме́йка (10) bench
сканда́лить (1) НС brawl, make a
ско́ро (4) soon   [ruckus
скры́ть (1) С conceal, hide
ску́чно (10) bored
ску́чный (1) boring
сле́ва (6) to the left
сле́дующий (7) following, next
сле́зть (1) С come down (from)
случа́йно (1) by chance, by ac-
               cident
смешно́й (1) funny

смея́ться (1) НС laugh
собра́ться (1) С gather, assem-
совершённо (3) completely [ble
согласи́ться (3) С agree
соединённый (3) united
со́лнце (5) sun
со́н (1) dream
сосе́д (4) neighbor
состоя́ться (1) С take place
социалисти́ческий (2) socialist
спаси́бо (9) thank you
спа́ть (4) НС sleep
спи́кер (1) speaker
спра́ва (5) on the right
спра́шивать (6) НС ask
спроси́ть (16) С ask
спры́гнуть (3) С jump down (from)
спу́тник (3) satellite
сра́зу (6) right away, at once
среда́ (3) Wednesday
стака́н (17) glass
стару́шка (21) old lady
ста́ть (5) С begin; become
статья́ (1) article
стена́ (8) wall
сто́л (35) table
столи́ца (1) capital
столо́вая (4) dining room, dining
стоя́ть (23) НС stand   [hall
стра́нный (3) strange
сухо́й (1) dry
сфотографи́ровать (2) С photo-
счастли́вый (1) happy   [graph
та́зик (2) basin
тако́й (17) such
та́м (18) there
та́сс (1) телеграфное агентство
          советского союза
тво́й (6) your
те́кст (12) text
телевизио́нный (1) television, TV
телеви́зор (1) television
телегра́фный (1) telegraph
темнота́ (1) dark, darkness
тёмный (8) dark
тепе́рь (8) now
тепло́ (6) warm
тёплый (4) warm
тётя (7) aunt; lady
то́-есть (1) that is to say,
             namely
това́рищ (22) friend, comrade
то́же (18) also
толпа́ (4) crowd

только (26) only; только что just

тот (18) that, those; the latter

тот же same

третий (11) third

труба (1) pipe

туда (4) there

турист (9) tourist

ты (53) you

тюрьма (2) jail, prison

уверенный (4) sure

увидеть (11) С see, catch sight of

угол (7) corner

удачный (2) successful

удержаться (1) С stand firm, hold one's ground

удивиться (2) С be surprised, amazed

удобный (4) comfortable

удовольствие (6) pleasure

уехать (1) С leave, go away

уже (35) already

узнать (10) С recognize, find out

улететь (3) С fly away, leave (by plane)

улица (24) street

уметь (7) НС be able to, know how to

упасть (7) С fall

упражнение (2) exercise

урок (9) lesson

уронить (1) С drop

услышать (5) С hear

успеть (4) С manage, have time

установить (2) С establish

утренний (2) morning

утро (20) morning

учить (9) НС teach

учиться (4) НС study

физкультура (2) physical education

философ (2) philosopher

философия (3) philosophy

флаг (10) flag

фотографировать (2) НС photograph

фотография (8) photograph [graph

холодильник (2) refrigerator

хор (9) chorus

хороший (6) good, fine

хорошо (22) good, well, fine

хотеть (40) НС want

хотеться (2) НС want

хоть (1) although; even if; at least

царь (2) czar

целый (2) whole, entire

центральный (2) central

церковь (4) church

цивилизация (3) civilization

цру (7) CIA

чайник (1) tea kettle

час (15) hour, o'clock

часто (5) often

человек (9) man, human being, person

человечество (2) humanity, mankind

через (8) through, in

четверг (8) Thursday

четвёртый (5) fourth

четыре (3) four

читать (16) НС read

чувствовать (1) НС feel

шапка (7) hat

Швейцария (1) Switzerland

шесть (2) six

школа (7) school

штат (3) state

шуметь (1) НС make noise, stir

этаж (6) floor

это (68) this is, these are; that is, those are

этот (44) this, that

я (148) I

яркий (2) bright

Active Word Index

This index contains all *Russian words* (other than personal names) that occur in the Dialogs (Active Word Lists) or are introduced in Analyses. Each word is accompanied by *grammatical information* about its forms (verb stems, stress, irregularities). The first number after each word indicates the Lesson number of its *first occurrence*. Subsequent numbers, if any, indicate *where it was discussed* in the Comments or Analyses.

If you want to find an *English equivalent* to a Russian word, take note of the lesson number of its first occurrence and you will find the English equivalent in the Active Word List of that lesson. A few words, however, are introduced in Analyses.

The grammatical information is supplied according to the system described in Analysis 8; the symbols and abbreviations presented there are summarized below:

Symbol		*Example*
( )	= inserted vowel	коне́ц(е) конца́; концы́
(...)	= indeclinable	кино́ (кино́...)
(на)	= на noun	заво́д (на)
,	= plural forms follow (nouns)	коне́ц(е) конца́; концы́
	OR: past forms follow (verbs)	класть кладу́т; кла́ла
/	= Partitive case	ча́й ча́я/-ю
-у́	= Locative case	ле́с ле́са в -у́; леса́
(ж)	= Fem. II Declension	любо́вь(о) любви́ любо́вью (ж)
(ср. род)	= neuter	и́мя и́мени и́менем; имена́ имён имена́м (ср. род)
!	= Imperative (irreg.)	дава́ть даю́т дава́й!
ТК	= Text Comment	ТК 8:2 Lesson 8, Text Comment 2
ДК	= Dialog Comment	ДК 8:2 Lesson 8, Dialog Comment 2
АН	= Analysis	АН 8:2.5 Lesson 8, Analysis section 2.5.
С	= соверше́нный вид "Perfective aspect"	
НС	= несоверше́нный вид "Imperfective aspect"	
НС/ОН	= " однонапра́вленный "One Way"	

ACTIVE WORD INDEX   NOUNS

ACTIVE WORD INDEX

414

ACTIVE WORD INDEX

VERBS

ACTIVE WORD INDEX

ACTIVE WORD INDEX

ACTIVE WORD INDEX

ADJECTIVES

ACTIVE WORD INDEX

ACTIVE WORD INDEX

OTHERS

ACTIVE WORD INDEX

ACTIVE WORD INDEX

чтобы		3	ДК 6:1. АН 10:3
это	1		
я	1		
ясно	8		

INDEX

Locations of discussions are abbreviated as follows: the Lesson number precedes the colon, and the section of the Analysis follows the colon. Thus, 2:3.4 means "Lesson 2, Analysis section 3.4." The abbreviations for other locations are:

TC = Text Comments
DC = Dialog Comments

If you want to find the location of discussions of specific Russian words, consult the Active Word Index.